The History and Theory of Children's Citizenship in Contemporary Societies

Brian Milne

The History and Theory of Children's Citizenship in Contemporary Societies

Springer

Brian Milne
Independent Consultant
Calès, France

ISBN 978-94-007-6520-7 ISBN 978-94-007-6521-4 (eBook)
DOI 10.1007/978-94-007-6521-4
Springer Dordrecht Heidelberg New York London

Library of Congress Control Number: 2013934953

Printed on acid-free paper

Springer is part of Springer Science+Business Media (www.springer.com)

This book is dedicated to the memory of people who have campaigned for or studied children but are no longer with us. They include Professor Samir Ghosh, Joan Lestor, Martin Ennals, Tara Ali Baig, Professor Adam Lapotka, Alan Grounds and Mike Jupp. I was lucky enough to have met each of them, spoken a little, at length or got to know them well. They may be forgotten by most, but I remember how much they cared. I also remember that what I learned from any of them is to be passed on to others; in this work I also attempt to do that with them in mind.

Preface

This research that gave life to this book was carried out on the basis of a quite short and quite simple question: *Is the notion of children's citizenship a reality or romanticism?* It looked at the status and extent of our knowledge of the position of children over a period of about 2,500 years in the past and toward an as yet unpredictable time in the future. In so doing, it looks at not only 'ourselves' (Western European societies) but other cultures, traditions and beliefs that broaden the question's base. It considers branches of knowledge such as the social sciences, theology and philosophy. Those are disciplines that have examined humanity with varying amounts of reference to children or childhood for at least as long as any of them has existed.

The choice of methods included analytic induction, morphological analysis and content analysis cum symptomatic reading. Those choices are governed by the fact that most parts of all data are printed texts. Some of the content is also my own work, partially field based and other parts published texts. Some of my more recent, undocumented field-based work has also raised questions that require answers that a work of this nature might provide.

This work moves on and away from *child participation using a children's rights-based argument* toward examination of the *relationship of the child with the state*, thus as a potential full member citizen, including *children's rights as part of the broader human rights agenda*. In so doing, the conclusions complete research that has taken a course in which the intent before examining evidence was to reach a position that was partly advocacy for full citizenship. The conclusions bearing the weight of historically and geographically widespread data now look at a better informed reality of the possibility of that being realised.

Independent Consultant, Calès, France Brian Milne

Acknowledgements

Many people have contributed to this work, usually unknowingly. Among the principal ones I would like to thank for their contribution are Antonella Invernizzi, Judith Ennew, Nigel Cantwell, Manfred Liebel, Jens Qvortrup, Michael Freeman, Henk van Beers and Priscilla Alderson. Each of them has said or written something that struck a particular note or had a very direct influence on how this work developed. Something written, said or inspired by each of them has consequently been included somewhere.

Over the years a number of people including Alejandro Cussianovich, Nandana Reddy, Kavita Ratna and Fabrizio Terenzio have been part of relevant and very durable projects or have said something that has taught me a few extremely useful points that are borne in mind in my research. The many others are no less influential but will surely know they are meant if they ever read this work.

Many thanks to my doctoral research external examiner Bob Franklin whose work I admire immensely and whose comments I very much appreciate since they helped me take this project forward. Most grateful thanks to my supervisor Peter Raynor. His knowledge of classical philosophy and history were particularly helpful since I began this work with a basic knowledge but almost blind. He often knew where to look. As fortune would have it, he particularly liked parts of this work I enjoyed, but often felt uncertain about. With his support I feel I have a far more rounded knowledge of philosophy, theology and history – at least where any question regarding children and childhood is concerned.

Over the last two decades or so, I have met many people in a large number of very diverse countries. I would particularly wish to extend thanks to the many people in different parts of Viet Nam, often the poorest and yet amongst the happiest people I have ever met. I have met people and seen things in South America, Central and Southeast Asia and parts of Africa that have allowed me to see the world in a very different way to that which many other individuals are ever able to see. It gave me the ability to appreciate the importance of diversity that I have at least attempted to include in this work.

My family too deserves thanks, especially my wife who is also the first person mentioned on the previous page and with whom I sometimes work and am forever exchanging ideas. There are also our children, Ceri and Daryl, our dogs, Alex I (since deceased and much missed), now replaced by Alex II and Placido, and two cats, Chocolat and Molly, who are always there and provide necessary diversions that give me space to think in.

Contents

Chapter 1
Introduction: The Children's Citizenship Paradigm

This book is a continuation of a doctoral research that set out to examine the question of whether the notion of children's citizenship is *realism* or *romanticism*. The nature of citizenship itself is a question that is often debated rather than resolved and there is no general agreement on a single definition. This book does not set out to conclude with an unreserved or definitive solution. That is something that, like examination of many other social phenomena, requires time but also depends on substantial evidence for change to be facilitated and then further substantiation accrued to prove that what may be shown in theory can also be proven by practice.

I also wish to avoid hubris. I am acutely aware of comparable arguments against women ever acquiring rights that make them full citizens. Indeed, in some parts of our world that mindset is still the everyday reality for many women. Whilst change itself is a relatively short history, the fact is that progress from virtually being a 'chattel' of the most closely related or, in the absence of family, appointed male has been excruciatingly slow and in substantial parts of the world is still a process that has not yet begun and may never begin. Thus it might be possible to say that the birth of a girl is the beginning of a whole life without full citizenship, whereas for a boy his childhood is the period before he achieves that. Bearing that in mind, the task of arguing for full citizenship becomes all the more complicated. Nonetheless I shall set out to look at the possibility of full membership of civil society equal to that of adults is feasible for both sexes.

What Is a Child?

Throughout this work the definition of a *child* is that used by the United Nations Convention on the Rights of the Child (CRC) (see also Appendix I):

Who is the citizen, and what is the meaning of the term? For here again there may be a difference of opinion. (Aristotle 1999b:52)

B. Milne, *The History and Theory of Children's Citizenship in Contemporary Societies*, DOI 10.1007/978-94-007-6521-4_1,

Part I
Article 1
For the purposes of the present Convention, a child means every human being below the age of 18 years unless, under the law applicable to the child, majority is attained earlier.

There are many exceptions. Historically there was no exact point in time at which childhood ended. It begins at birth in most cases, although some kind of blessing, acceptance ceremony, baptism, circumcision or other ritual have marked the beginning of life in some societies. Thus, for instance, children who are stillborn or die soon after birth are likely never to have been 'people', whereas those who are 'initiated' are given a name and status in their society. Whilst there are several divisions within the CRC definition, often the best way of looking at this question is when a person becomes an adult. Adulthood has been primarily determined by the start of puberty (the *menarche* for women, ability to ejaculate for men and the appearance of pubic hair for both sexes). Thus, in the modern medical world *biological childhood* is the period from birth to puberty.

Since the social construction of a notion of *adolescence*, adulthood has been separated into two forms: *biological* and *social adulthood.* Thus, biological adults are those who have reached and passed puberty and social adults are recognised by cultural and legal standards. Historically people normally moved from being a child directly to becoming an adult. In many societies that transition was marked by some type of ritual, ceremony, *rite de passage* (for instance, see van Gennep 1960:21pp) or coming-of-age test.

The CRC definition is not always universally accepted and practiced. There are many different ages at which people attain various markers that describe social adulthood. Some traditional ideas conflict with civil legal standards in nations where the CRC should be the standard. However, on the basis of the CRC having been ratified and adopted into law by all nations but two at the time of writing, age 18 years in the contemporary world is the preferred definition. Where exceptions occur and are of relevance to this study they will be explained contextually.

Structure

This book is set out in 12 chapters.

- Chapter 1 introduces and describes the task of the research and particularly the arguments and ideas behind it. The other 11 chapters are set out thus:
- Chapter 2 was originally the research design. It described the methodology and methods chosen for analysis of Chaps. 4, 5, 6, 7, 8, 9, 10 and 11. In this version some of this has been reworked to explain what the objective of this work is in a far more readable manner.
- Citizenship is examined in Chap. 3. It was set out to be a discerning examination of what is often a contested notion that examines citizenship specifically in the context of children and youth. Thus, debates about what citizenship is and more recent interest in concepts such as 'global citizenship' with implications for a

notion of a 'global childhood' are not examined. They would be a divergence from the core question as to whether children have ever been, are today or at some point in the future will be full citizens. There are many aspects of citizenship that even some of the best texts on the topic omit or avoid. This version also includes *inclusion* and *exclusion* whereby the original gave the latter only the briefest consideration to an area that has proven to be at the very least enigmatic if not sometimes simply prevaricated in other works. It also provides the context for this book. It is consequently one of the keys to identifying children's citizenship in concluding chapters.

- Examination then turns to the emergence of childhood with Chap. 4 looking at accounts of the position of children in the ancient and medieval world up to the sixteenth century. It is in practice almost impossible to divide the world into perfect 'halves'. Thus this chapter looks at the longer of two divisions of history up to the early modern period. As with the work of the most thorough historians there are very large temporal 'holes'. These lacunae do not suggest an absolute absence of children from history but are disposed more toward reflection of the historian's manner which is to place greater emphasis on particular periods and events. Chapter 4 thus leads not only into Chap. 5 but also begins to introduce some of the elements of Chap. 6.
- Chapter 5 then examines the world from the Enlightenment to the present. As with the preceding chapter there are lacunae. Emphasis is necessarily placed on key names, places, events and so on throughout a very busy period. It begins to prepare the ground for some of the material and contexts used for Chap. 7.
- Both chapters incorporate several types of historical data that include elements of demographic, economic, epidemiological and social history. They also use some of the bases of philosophical thought that draw on childhoods contemporaneous to work of a number of great thinkers. Some names (for instance, Plato or Rousseau) and events appear and reappear in Chaps. 4 and 6 or 5 and 7 respectively. They are used for historical data in the former instance and develop on examination of ideas in the latter. Repetition is kept to the absolute minimum possible and where it is used, is done to place emphasis on the two different contextual uses. The emphasis over those chapters is naturally on where children belong in history rather than presenting an accurate timeline and portrayal of events over roughly 2,500 years. The division of a long history into two chapters is only partially because of the length a single chapter would be. The main reason is that during the longer period from antiquity to the Enlightenment relatively little is known about children but thereafter.

After the Wars of Religion during the sixteenth and seventeenth centuries, European societies were ready to try secular alternatives. The humanistic philosophies of Rationalism and Empiricism that were reinforced by the scientific revolutions, led a number of philosophers in the direction of a progressive view of history established in classical philanthropy. Some of them proposed that philanthropy was the key to human happiness. That was considered a kind of 'healthy state' in which humanity lived in harmony with nature and their circumstances. The self-development of the individual manifested itself in good deeds toward others, thus attention turned toward children who were considered still innocent and thus most easily lead down this path. In so doing, interest in children and knowledge of children began to develop. This began to increase as the post Wars of Religion period developed into the Enlightenment.

Ariès (1962) argued that childhood is not a natural phenomenon but a creation of society, a point that Cunningham (2006) developed further. In their view, it is Rousseau who should be accredited with giving us the modern notion of childhood, which he saw as a short period of sanctuary before people were confronted with the pitfalls and privations of adulthood. Documentation of childhood is far greater from this point on than ever before, providing a clear line between pre-Enlightment and Enlightenment onward knowledge.

- Chapters 6 and 7 follow the history through an examination of relevant elements of intellectual discourse, beliefs, moral and ideological positions on children from antiquity until the present day.
- Chapter 6 covers areas that are inclusive of children from antiquity to the high Middle Ages. In common with Chap. 4 it also makes large 'leaps' in time. These particularly reflect the fact that children whilst appearing very significantly in the works examined did not appear especially frequently. This chapter also leads into the next and shorter period.
- Chapter 7 then moves on from the Early Modern period to the present. To a greater extent this is the chapter that sets the context for Chap. 8 and has been to some extent influential in the development of the New Sociology of Childhood.
- Philosophy and theology are two main sources of data for Chaps. 6 and 7. There is, as already said, in particular reuse of some of the great thinkers included in the immediately preceding chapters. Here the emphasis is on the intellectual content of their work, where and when it relates to children rather than describing significant aspects of the world those people lived in.

As has already been said of Chap. 5, we also know more about the period covered by Chap. 7 because of children's inclusion in written works. The Early Modern period starts with the Reformation in the early fifteen hundreds and last until, thus overlaps with the Enlightenment and the eighteenth century period of revolutions. The new philosophy began as thinkers from the time of Niccolò Machiavelli (1532) to René Descartes (see 185) in the mid-seventeenth century, who is known as the father of modern philosophy, began to move on from the Aristotelian tradition. It was Descartes and other philosophers such as Thomas Hobbes (1642, 1650) whose work contributed to the birth of Rationalism.

European theology had a single central concern with children, one that was shared by Catholics and early Protestants that they were born out of 'original sin'. It was their rebirth through baptism that put them on the road the righteousness although driven by lust and carnality to repeat Adamic sin. On the other hand, the doctrine of the Protestant denominations was resolute about an obligation of children to respect, obey, and assist parents. Their parents had a corresponding duty to care for and discipline their children, both for the protection of children and importance of creating stable community. This responsibility was also extended to illegitimate children, contrasting with their treatment under Catholicism. Reformers' beliefs about child care became popular through many books on child rearing (see Marshall 1991; Ozment 1983; Pollock 2001) that give us early information on where children belonged in society.

- Chapter 8 then looks at the relatively recent phenomena of child sciences, childhood studies and the social sciences. Historically the child sciences are very recent, generally beginning a little over a century ago. The study of childhood as a specialist topic area is far more recent and the consolidation of the position of children in the social sciences an ongoing process at present.
- Chapter 9 examines children's rights and the contemporary interest in child participation. This is one of the key areas when looking at the present and toward the future. Children's participation has frequently been construed to be the *same* as citizenship and is therefore given particularly close scrutiny. During the time the original research was carried out, a new trend was to look at participation critically. However, at the time of completion publications are for the greater part still 'forthcoming'. Thus the critical examination of participation in this chapter is also intended as a contribution to developing and even 'embryonic' arguments.
- Chapter 10 thus turns to legal and welfare views of children that are broadly speaking contemporary to this work. This is one of the key areas when looking at the present and toward the future. It also looks at children's inclusion and their position in policy making and governance. This is an important element. If full citizenship for children is a viable option which the world must accept and prepare for, then it must be one of the starting points for law makers who will bear ultimate responsibility for opening that door.
- Chapter 11 takes in a number of additional issues that are significant in terms of a global notion of children's citizenship and may bear some influence on how it develops.
- Chapter 12 draws Chaps. 4, 5, 6, 7, 8, 9, 10 and 11 together for analysis of the content the eight chapters describe. It subsequently develops beyond analysis to reach conclusions that relate back to the original question, asking whether the notion of children's citizenship is *realism* or *romanticism*. It also attempts to search for elements of citizenship described in Chap. 3 to that end. If they are at all present. The conclusion furthermore projects toward a possible future in which children may be citizens. It also attempts to stimulate discourse that may offer a significant contribution to the more vexing question of definitive resolution to such questions as 'how', 'why', 'when' and 'where' that might begin.

Arguments and Ideas Supporting Examination of This Topic

This book sets out to look at contexts, aims and objectives toward concluding the question of *realism* or *romanticism*. It also looks at *citizenship* in the context of this work, thus as it relates to children specifically. This is done so in the light of far more complex questions that would arise if this was solely about citizenship.

The romantic view has been most commonly addressed in discussion and debate at conferences, seminars and such meetings where opinion is often tested. It has been less frequently written, published and subjected to the scrutiny of peer review. Realism has often been somewhat obscured by the assumption that children's full citizenship is something that will evolve as an outcome of the advancement of children's rights during the twentieth and into the twenty-first century. Thus two particular lines of argument have been pursued. The first is one that compares with the changing position of women over just over a century. The second is use of extraordinary children whose names are used as exemplars of what all children might be.

Despite increased effort by women and their supporters from the early twentieth century on, and especially more recent feminist contributions, sizeable vestiges of absolute male domination tend to survive in even the most 'liberal' European regimes. It is inadvisable for any researcher to draw assumptions out of the experience of women as a standard for reaching a conclusion about children. There are nonetheless always commonalities and parallels that cannot be ignored. Thus, when drawing on philosophical and early social scientific texts it is possible to find both women and children viewed as '*property*' *of* or *of inferior status to* men. I have, however, not been tempted to settle for those texts as my starting point but have usually borne them in mind whilst further exploring places where children are directly referred to. Occasionally this locates them directly under the authority of adults, including women who are frequently still ranked socially and economically below men.

The positions occupied by women and children are fundamentally different despite the issues that may be compared. Where no separation is evident, then those become starting points for looking toward contemporary views and where dichotomisation began. There are notably exceptional women: one might turn to such as Queen Elizabeth I of England (1533–1603) or Cleopatra VII Philopator (69–30 BC), the last pharaoh of Ancient Egypt whose rule dominated and rivalled male contemporaries. There have been boy and girl monarchs, but they do not have the reputation of those monarchs and several other historically strong women. There are also women whose standing came with social status, wealth, powerful position in a religious order or as a writer, artist of political activist. Most of them have a particularly privileged background. For example, one might take Mary Wollstonecraft (1759–1797) who is known as a (if not *the*) founder of feminism. Whilst her childhood may have been difficult with a father who speculated away relative economic comfort, it was still privileged compared to most other girls and women with the benefits of education and an intellectual social environment.

Children are sometimes exceptional, as was Wollstonecraft's contemporary Wolfgang Amadeus Mozart (1756–1791). His father, Leopold Mozart (1719–1787), was assistant *Kapellmeister* to the court orchestra of the Archbishop of Salzburg, a minor composer and also experienced teacher who taught his children languages and academic subjects besides music. It is possible that with another father Wolfgang Amadeus would not have learned his skills. However, Mozart is nonetheless exceptional, as are so-called *geniuses* in the modern world. Beyond his contribution to music little is made of his early life other than that he was a prodigy. He, as too comparable children, does not really tend to contribute to changing the status of children as extraordinary women most clearly have through political actions and words.

Where children appear alone, they may well be foundlings, orphans, vagabonds or more recently homeless or street children and youth. This places them on the fringes of society, more unwanted than wanted, thus less likely to have been fully and objectively documented as individuals. As a useful counterbalance here, one has fiction where well rounded portrayals of children can be found, consequently authors like Charles Dickens and Mark Twain play almost as important a role as more 'serious' authors. When we closely examine the Artful Dodger or Huckleberry Finn their activities can be understood as 'genial'. Yet both boys remain outside of mainstream society, perhaps more devious outlaws than geniuses.

Since 1989 the United Nations Convention on the Rights of the Child (CRC) has brought this topic forward a little. Particular emphasis on the participation of children in civil society has been driven by the CRC recently although, despite some widespread misunderstanding, it is not the same thing as citizenship. Furthermore, children's participation has been so thoroughly possessed by activists, campaigners and researchers that it is gradually becoming bogged down by a plethora of definitions, tools for measuring and modelling modes of operation. All of that overlooks one simple fact: in one sense or another, children are already participants in civil society. That is a key part of the motivation behind this research.

There is also personal frustration with what appears to be a temptation by people who one might expect to not be so easily seduced by a 'romantic' view of a past in which children and adults were somehow 'indistinguishable'. It is important that we look in greater depth to see what one might extrapolate from the past. Likewise, we also need to look at a wider geographical perspective to understand what a society into which a child is born actually is. Although that is a simple enquiry that is probably all too obvious, it would appear that nobody has attempted to address it. Many people have sought knowledge, have most frequently looked principally at Western European society and have arrived at unconvincing starting points. They include overenthusiastic interpretation of the work of Jean-Jacques Rousseau or the version of history Philippe Ariès extrapolated from mainly France and to a limited extent the rest of Europe. Children existed before the periods they inform us about. Moreover such 'samples' are generally very limited.

Neither projects a world view, but summon up rather selective French history, albeit some ideas Rousseau expounded have universal appeal. Histories have particularly looked at a single cultural environment and many of them have done so within a relatively short window in time.

On the other hand some people have examined the 'other', often using ethnographies of societies in which children share much of every aspect of life with adults. In some of these studies children are often barely, if at all, discernible. This book nonetheless examines those narrow perspectives to contribute to answering the broader question which is necessary given the sparse resources available. There are also pseudo-ethnographies that rely on romantic notions supplemented with fact. In an attempt to use romantic arguments as part of the means to reaching conclusions on reality, it has been necessary to revisit some of the literature that inspires to understand the attraction of notions of Golden Age and utopian thought.

Sir Thomas More's *Utopia* (1516) does not in fact describe a perfectly egalitarian world. There are those who wish it to do so. *Utopia* appears to be for a large part a cleverly modified version of Plato's *Republic*. In it the graces of a seemingly egalitarian, pacifist society hold sway over the inhabitants of a fictional island. Society's normal tribulations such as poverty and misery are all gone. It has few laws, thus no lawyers are necessary. It rarely sends citizens to war although they are all ready to fight if necessary. Instead they hire mercenaries from more bellicose neighbours. They are sent into perilous situations in the hope that more confrontational populations in adjacent countries will be removed, leaving only peaceful people.

Utopian society encourages tolerance of all religions except atheism. In Utopia there is no private property. Goods are stored in communal warehouses and people simply request what they need. There are also no locks on doors however residence at any house is rotated between citizens each 10 years. Agriculture is the most essential area of occupation on the island. Everybody is taught agricultural work and must live in the countryside to work in farming for 2 years at a time. Women do exactly the same work as men. Every citizen must also train in at least one of a number of other important occupations whereby weaving is mainly done by women and carpentry, masonry and such trades by men. There is methodical minimalism within these trades so that all people wear the same types of simple clothes and have no real need for fine attire to display rank or privilege. The products of trades are also simple and plain.

All fit citizens must work, thus unemployment is eliminated. The working day is minimised so that people only need to work 6 hours, although many happily work longer. Slavery is normal in Utopian life. Every household has two slaves who are either from other countries or Utopian criminals. Some people are selected for their ability to learn during compulsory primary education and set on course to become governing officials or priests. However all citizens are encouraged to apply themselves to learning in their generous leisure time.

However, no matter how well we scrutinise Utopia it is hard to see where children fit in since it is described through the adults. That includes More's descriptions of the medium of education. Since it is rather more ideal than a real world, the tendency of humanity to produce less than perfect *other* human beings is almost entirely overlooked. The exception is only the criminals who become slaves. More rarely mentioned children, so their absence means one must make assumptions about them. Those suppositions will nearly always be biased because Utopia is presumed to be egalitarian. There is also nothing to conclusively prove otherwise.

The central message of *Utopia* is to emphasise the need for order and discipline instead of liberty. It describes an almost totalitarian society that is a long way away from contemporary ideals of freedom. It is a world in which any endeavour to discuss public policy outside of officially sanctioned forums is punishable by death. One paradox is that if children are included on an absolutely equal basis then some of the values extolled by supporters of Articles 12, 13, 14 and 15 CRC particularly and Articles 16, 35, 36 and 37 (see Appendix I) could almost undoubtedly never be applied in Utopia. Notably, those first four articles have, in their turn, particularly been considered utopian by CRC critics.

Utopia takes Plato's *Republic* a few steps toward a carefully reconstructed, but equally totalitarian paradise, perhaps even some elements of a *Garden of Eden*. In Utopia even the tree of knowledge of good and evil is metaphorically ever present and occasionally visited. That also seems to take in more modest aspects of the Germanic *Schlaraffenland* (*Cockaygne* in English). That is a land of extravagance and excess rather than simplicity and godliness. Everybody is liberated from any kind of work and everything essential is free and readily available. In Schlaraffenland there is a fountain of eternal youth which keeps everybody young. Because people are eternally young, childhood is indistinguishable from adulthood thus only the eternal youthful adult is ever described. All in all, it gives an impression that there is a more common wish to have at least some element of a golden age in mind when attempting to develop a thesis of what might be in the future.

What separates the real and the 'wished for' is that history is recorded and selective use of that knowledge fills in spaces in a projection of an unforeseeable future. Utopia, *Schlaraffenland* and such *wished for* places are mainly constructed out of a history that is mainly myth. It recognises a golden age where all human imperfections such as inequalities are either absent or carry a punishment of banishment, chastisement or death. There is no distinction between adult and child because there is no difference. Children are citizens, because without it being explicitly stated everybody is assumed to be a citizen. Golden age thought idealises the differences between adulthood and childhood out of existence along with all other distinctions.

Utopia and other imagined 'perfect' places, selective histories, imagined anthropologies and even fiction contribute little to guiding us toward a hypothesis about what the future *may* bring. The recorded past has a great deal more to tell us. However, it must be accepted that some of each romantic idea has some value. Indeed some philosophy and theology is little more. Thus, my argument is that the greater balance is provided by what has occurred in the lives of real and living people but romantic views have fuelled imagination and innovation.

Historians of childhood have often supported one of two particular positions. One heavily rests on supporting the work of Philippe Ariès. The other either looks at his work critically or rejects it whilst continuing to refer to his work. Whatever the stance, his *Centuries of Childhood* (1962) has had a lasting effect. In a volume published by Becchi and Julia in 1998 (2004 edition for this work) to celebrate 30 years since publication of Ariès's work, Julia (Becchi and Julia 2004:85) identifies three emblematic representations of childhood that emerged at the end of the eighteenth century and persisted well on into the twentieth century. Those three figures of childhood are the abandoned child who is reared by animals (i.e.: Victor,[1,2] Mowgli or Tarzan), child prodigies (Mozart is again the obvious one) and child

[1] Victor was the 'wild' boy found in Aveyron in southern France in 1797 who has become the subject of several books (e.g. Lane 1979) and films (see also note 16 in Chap. 8).

[2] See Mills and Mills (2002:27).

heroes (Petit Gavroche,[3] Jack Dawkins[4] or Huckleberry Finn). These characters and their effect on the image of childhood, which reminisces back to a time when children were considered indistinguishable from adults, will be more closely examined in turn. However their role in delivering a romanticised version of young lives has a key place in this brief introduction to the creation of a golden age.

This research thus aims to revisit many of the histories, philosophies, fiction and other sources that have contributed to the generation of a romantic view as well as providing clues to a realistic view. However, this is complemented by use of more prosaic sources that may have been discarded or overlooked because they offered no optimistic or 'resplendent' contributions about a perfect past that provide data of equal import. In all cases, direct or indicative reference to children, childhood or the status of young people is the most basic source.

There is, of course, no attempt to write a full *vademecum* of the many different histories, philosophies and so forth where children or reference to childhood may appear. There are limitations on the length of this work. Thus there are always going to be questions remaining to be answered. Nonetheless, in the space permitted, this work will examine the question to be resolved in as much depth as possible without leaving too many very obvious lacunae.

[3] Petit Gavroche is the street boy who fights in the French Revolution and dies delivering grapeshot to comrades manning a barrier in revolutionary Paris in Victor Hugo's *Les Miserables* (1862).

[4] He is better known as The Artful Dodger, the pickpocket and 'natural' leader of Fagin's boys who has earned his nickname for his skill and cunning, in Charles Dickens' *Oliver Twist* (1838).

Chapter 2
Methodology and Methods

This chapter describes the epistemological rationale behind and the choice of methods used to analyse material in Chaps. 4, 5, 6, 7, 8, 9, 10 and 11 that take us toward a conclusion to the original question regarding the *realism* or *romanticism* of the notion of children's citizenship. Stress is placed on examination of the past where evidence of a time when the status of adult and child was one and the same and takes account of the present to not only conclude but project a possible future.

Methodology

The original research was carried out on the basis of a quite short and in itself quite simple question: *Is the notion of children's citizenship a reality or romanticism?* This question looks at the status and extent of our knowledge of the position of children over a period of about 2,500 years in the past and toward an as yet unpredictable point of time in the future. In so doing, it looks at not only 'ourselves' but other cultures, traditions and beliefs that broaden the base of the question. It also considers particular branches of knowledge such as the social sciences, theology and philosophy. They have occupied the attention of those examining humanity with any amount of reference to children or childhood for at least as long as any of the disciplines included and philosophy most particularly have existed. The question, its parts and examination of those parts are subjected to the rigours of epistemological scrutiny. However, it is acknowledged that to consider only the theory of knowledge to the exclusion of practice gives little indication of what is at issue in seeking conclusions.

As the introductory paragraphs of this chapter have already shown, the fact that one of the answers this book must conclude with is what the differences between a romantic and real view are. This places a great deal of weight on the essential difference between the romantic or 'thought' against real or 'evident' use of data which makes my own point of view an important part of analysis. This suggests a potential for a pretentious or uninformative research that makes only disingenuous

B. Milne, *The History and Theory of Children's Citizenship in Contemporary Societies*,
DOI 10.1007/978-94-007-6521-4_2,

assumptions rather than reach scholastically proven conclusions. However, it has been accepted that human beings have very particular general capacities that are used in the acquisition of knowledge. Some of them are my own prejudices, perceptions and wish to achieve a particular end, thus must be parts of the epistemology that are employed positively and objectively in the choice of method.

Much of this is dependent on a rhetorical stance which reminds me of the Sophist philosopher Gorgias' extant rhetorical work *On Non-Existence* (McComiskey 2002: 32ff). It was a topic taken up by my school debating society in the 1960s. I recall he claimed three things. Firstly, nothing exists; secondly, if it did we could not know of it; and thirdly, even if we did know of it then we could not communicate that knowledge to others. Naturally this research does not reflect Gorgias in the strictest sense. It is reflective on the point that rhetoric itself has the weakness of being the root of more inconclusive debate such as 'nothing exists' than of a conclusive thought such as 'everything exists'. Use of rhetoric is intended to stimulate the potential for the development of this thesis into a wider discourse. That is to say, instead of attempting to be conclusive to the point of being definitive and in any sense irrefutable. However, the parallel with Gorgias for me is that we do not know whether or not children are citizens. We often assume they are citizens because they (usually) have a nationality. Despite assuming they are citizens because they have nationality, the lack of substantive rights such as electoral franchise to give them full citizenship shows they are not. So, as Gorgias might have asked: what are they?

Thus, a key part of the rhetorical course is the possibility of looking at children as 'citizen becomings' or 'potential citizens'.[1] That bears a remarkable degree of similarity to ideas expressed long ago by Aristotle and more recently by Qvortrup that that children are 'human becomings' which will be visited several times in this work.

Both questions seek to make sense of childhood. We have sought to construct a view of what the 'child' is throughout the long history of thought. Moral, political and social theorists have looked at the adults they will become through the lens of particular social environments and their concept of the future of their society. This appears to have lasted from the early Socratic dialogues through to more recent examinations with an occasional very clear statement of what little we do in fact know. In his Preface to *Émile* Rousseau (1979: i) stated that:

> We know nothing of childhood; and with our mistaken notions the further we advance the further we go astray. The wisest writers devote themselves to what a man ought to know, without asking what a child is capable of learning. They are always looking for the man in the child, without considering what he is before he becomes a man.

Thus, in the longer term and particularly bearing policy making and the eventual inclusion of young citizens in governance, the hypothesis out of which this research has developed its aims and objectives is as follows. The question of whether or not children are citizens or not and whether it is at all possible normally has its

---

[1] 'Potential citizens' assumes that children will survive to be adults and also overcome any possible barriers to them assuming full citizenship such as not having nationality of the country they live in.

origins in only a very small set of bases. That is to say that it is usually based on a Western neo-liberal understanding of citizenship. Whilst there are influences from civic republican and feminist perspectives, they are still firmly based in Western discourse. Furthermore, part of this perception makes assumptions around an idealised version of democracy to the exclusion of other forms of social organisation. Subequently, it has hitherto been culturally very narrow sighted and dismissive of what appears not to contribute to the argument.

History has provided a basis for much of the existing thought, however that often appears selective. Much the same can be said for philosophy, theology and social scientific theory. Law is also so widely open to interpretation that a rights-based examination using the CRC as a basis includes numerous possibilities. However, it is not only selection of what already exists, but also the narrow vision of what has thus far been used to project toward the future that is limited. Children's rights are a key component at the base of this work. However, that is used in a more substantial way than using a blossoming interest in 'children's participation' that is largely rationalised as a children's rights issue. This research placed emphasis on the fact that participation and citizenship is absolutely not one and the same thing.

The intended outcome foresaw analysis of data toward conclusions that direct the possibility of children enjoying the full benefits of the status of citizenship. Those have potential direct input into social policy development and indeed political discussion of the means to achieving that end. It examines and questions two and a half thousand years worth of focus on children to the widest possible geographical extent. It also aims to open the path for a prolonged and thorough discourse that will contribute to a resolution of the possibility of children's citizenship being realised.

Methods

Following on from the methodology described above, the choice of methods for the research included analytic induction, morphological analysis and also elements of content analysis with an eye toward symptomatic reading. The choice of methods was governed by the fact that the larger parts of all data used were in the form of printed texts. A very few of those texts are also my own work, some of which has been field based and other parts entirely theoretical. Those reflect my interest in this topic which emerged after an initial related piece of work in 1993. Thereby texts were used with a very small amount of previously unused field data where those sources are relevant to the aims and objectives, thus provide arguments and evidence for this examination.

Thus said, using a wide range of materials that set a very broad range over a relatively long period of time that concentrate on the collation of data that relate to *children* and *childhood* and *citizenship* eliminated the higher risk of subjective analysis that may have come with a smaller sample in every sense. The support the hypothesis provided for the conclusion was dependent on the number of constituent parts in and the careful selection of the sample. Here, if a more substantial library search had been made for *all* possible data, the task would almost certainly have been unmanageable. The balance there was use of a wide range of sources chosen purposefully which was sustained by supporting materials that ensured even-handed analysis.

Analytic Induction

Analytic induction was used first because it is a systematic examination of similarities between various social phenomena out of which concepts can be developed. It is most frequently used to search for similarities across a number of data sources that can then be used to flesh out sub-classifications. One goal of this research is to make general statements chapter by chapter that may need to be modified later, especially in the event of exceptions being discovered. In due course it may reflect fairly exhaustive knowledge of what is being researched. However, this is mindful of the fact that no analysis should ever be considered final, since reality is 'infinite' and thus constantly changing. Classifications occurring as an outcome of this method are often theories in themselves rather than being groundwork for theory.

The intention was that it would draw together a fairly exhaustive knowledge of the question researched. An example of how that might be used is when a social scientist examines the category of 'people who ride bicycles'. He or she then develops subcategories such as 'uses a bike for pleasure', 'uses it to get to work', 'uses it for health reasons or getting fit' or 'other uses'. If no relevant similarities can be identified, then either the data need to be re-evaluated and the definition of similarities changed or the category is too wide and heterogeneous and should be narrowed down.

Within that knowledge classifications occurring as an outcome are often theoretical rather than being groundwork for theory. There are also superficial similarities between fields such as history and philosophy where phenomena and subjects described have common origins. Although philosophers are very good chroniclers of their time, there are also different points of view that produce different versions of same histories. Beside that there is the bias that comes with the desired outcome the author is searching for that conditions the interpretation of texts. Induction is a process of reasoning in which the basis of an argument is believed to support the conclusion without leading to it, in other words does not ensure its integrity. It is thus a form of analysis that makes generalisations based on individual examples.

However, this form of inductive work does not work alone in the case of a question such as this. Coaxing out data from similar types of source should generate a linear process in which, for instance, chronological progression should help to draw out conclusions. Then again, the research was cognisant of superficial similarities that exist between, for example, history and philosophy where phenomena and subjects described have common origins. Behind the apparent there will always be the extreme of position to which the author belonged and how that conditions interpretation of texts.

Children and childhood occupy a relatively small niche in most of the areas that were examined. History, philosophy and theology have most certainly seen children as marginal, although the work of historians of childhood is probably ascending the way to a more prominent place in their discipline. As yet the historical work is largely limited to the western world with Western Europe at the forefront. Likewise, within the social sciences there are a few economists, an increasing number of anthropologists, steadily growing number of sociologists and clearly many psychologists. With exception of the latter, much of the work looks primarily at the western world. However, anthropologists are gradually beginning to cast their net wider. Some of the data these disciplines offer are repetitive because they often come from relatively small pools of experience and knowledge in which individuals are not infrequently working within close proximity to each other intellectually. To some extent that reduced the scale of the inductive task.

History provided at least a relatively certain starting point since in the Hellenic world citizenship was well enough described by Aristotle in the *Politics* (1908), early childhood in *Nicomachean Ethics* (1999a), a notion similar to *tabula rasa* in *De Anima* (1987) and the transition from childhood (youth) to adulthood and citizenship in Plato's (2005, see also Stokes 2005) *Crito*. In contrast to the Athenians, Spartans and Stoics saw human beings as something less status bound although neither set children in a position equal to that of adults. They were clearly not full citizens. Socrates' contemporary K'ung Fu Tzu saw the primary relationship between adult and child as being the first link between individuals within the state. That is to say through the 'filial piety' of children toward parents which we can justifiably assume has been the norm for many generations. He was probably the first philosopher to record the expectation that individuals 'became' through study and practice of appropriate behaviour. They could then take their place within a distinct hierarchy in which one was treated with humanity. Fatherhood was the highest value in Chinese society and each person a subject of the father and the emperor was the father of all subjects. A child was said to be 'cut, carved, filed and polished', describing something comparable with the Aristotelian 'becoming' process.

The *tabula rasa* notion is a constant throughout history, reappearing very clearly in the writings of Aquinas (1981) and reaching its probable maturity in Locke's (1971) work. Of all themes it is the single most pervasive view of infants until recent work such as Alderson et al's. (2005a, b) research on premature neonates.

Philosophy has contributed much to the stage we are at in the present where children are seen as individuals with rights rather than as merely an extension of their parents or family. In the seventeenth century Hobbes (1651) regarded childhood a period of servitude comparable with slavery in the modern world whereby the children are absolutely subject of parents as servants are to masters. They were property until age and maturity delivered privileges and the freedom of adult citizenship. It was part of his view of the moral obligations of state towards *citizen* members in which the notion of *best interests* is emergent. Locke challenged Hobbes' notion of property when he said that they are:

> …not born in (…) full state of equality, though (…) born to it. (…) parents have a sort of rule and jurisdiction over them when they come into the world, and for some time after, but it is but a temporary one. (Locke 1965:127)

About 120 years after Hobbes, Kant (1996) wrote that a child is not property of parents but instead argued having brought a child into the world they "…incur an obligation to make the child content with his condition so far as they can…" (*Ibid.*:64). Furthermore: "…this duty there must (…) arise the right (…) to manage and develop the child" (*Ibid.*:65). That describes *duty of care* comparable with present day obligations, but which stems from a child's satisfaction without the necessity of consent. Kant was also considering the child's *best interests*. He thought children were born without reason and were educated to become rational agents by parents. It is a view comparable with the human becomings thesis that also recognises the innate liberty each individual enjoys.

Hegel (2001) believed that there was a proper moral life achieved through absolute obedience to the laws of the state within which there are two subordinate levels of social activity to which people had to commit themselves: the family and economic contribution to civil society. He distinguished between individuals as 'economic man' (bourgeois) and 'political man' (citizen). However, children are potentially free and life was the quintessence of potential freedom. They were, he believed, not things and do not belong to anyone whether parents or others.

> As it is with children, so is it with nations under paternal government (…) not looked upon as self-dependent or of age (…) services required (…) must bear upon their education and promote their good. To ignore (…) would destroy the ethical element of the relation, and make the child a slave. (Hegel 2001:148)

We see the coming together of some of these ideas when compulsory education begins. As Corrigan (1979: 33ff) says, it was designed to provide bourgeois moral and religious standards for the working class through basic education of their children to offset potential revolutionary activity. That moral and religious code would shape their behaviour and contribute toward there being a disciplined, punctual labour force and establishment of social order based on education which the working class would respect although at the bottom of that order. It has been that type of moral order that has shaped modern views of the child as 'inferior' to the 'citizen adult' until duties and responsibilities required for full membership of civil society are attained.

Zelizer's (1985) view of the sacralisation of childhood in the transition from the nineteenth to twentieth century and birth of child sciences along with progressively changing standards in child care, protection and other provisions such as education and health has seen childhood fully emerging as separated from adulthood. It is now well defined and anchored in legislation and whilst there have been liberal positions from as far back as Winstanley (1649b) and Spence (1793), they are far and few between. Likewise attempts to 'democratise' childhood the way Korczak (1992) attempted early in the twentieth century or children in organisations like *Hitler Jugend* in national socialist Germany or *Pioneers* in socialist states (that ostensibly offered direct contributions to society and nation) are generally short lived or more tokenistic than *bona fide* full membership.

Morphology

Morphological analysis is a method that enables examination across different sources of data, especially where the content of the sources in this research appear either similar or even repeated. It is a reliable method to use where there are several prevalent factors, most of which cannot be expressed as numerical time series data with which one might construct a mathematical or statistical model. The orthodox approach would be to break sources down into parts. One would then isolate key parts (whilst dropping minor or inconsequential ones) for their input into a wider picture of the generally disaggregated topics *children* and *citizenship*. One disadvantage in using this approach is that real world situations rarely behave rationally. It then becomes possible that analysis will fail if the input of less consequential components becomes too significant. This will be taken into account in the careful choice of what to include or exclude from analysis.

It is particularly used for the identification, analysis and description of the structure of words. While words are generally accepted as being the smallest units of syntax, it is clear that in most languages words can be related to other words by rules. For example, English speakers recognise that the words *student* and *student union* are closely related. English speakers recognise these relations from a tacit knowledge of rules of word formation in English. They infer intuitively that *student* is to *students* as *lecturer* is to *lecturers* and similarly, *student* is to *student union* as *lecturer* is to *lecture room*. Rules understood by authors or speakers reflect specific patterns (or regularities) in the way words are formed from smaller units and how those smaller units interact in speech and the written word. Thus morphology is the branch of linguistics that studies patterns of word formation within and across languages and attempts to formulate rules that model the knowledge of the messages of users of those languages. For a study crossing time, culture and language it offers a complementary but also contrasting approach to analytic induction.

This method has most commonly been used by modern linguists since the term *morphology* was first used by August Schleicher (1859). However, it appears to have existed in one form or another for around 3,000[2] years. A recent use has been to analyse folklore. Vladímir Propp (1968) analysed folk tales for the function each character and action carried out. He concluded that they were composed of 31 elements and eight character types. Although elements were not all required for all stories, when they did appear, it was in invariant order. The exception was that each element may be negated twice. The elements or 'functions' are assembled as the morphology. Theoretically, variant forms of the elements could be used to reconstruct an almost infinite number of new tales. Here some of this 'folkloristic' approach supports the linguistic analysis.

---

[2]See George Cardona's work (1998:260–267) on Pāṇini, the fourth century BC Indian linguist who is thought to have formulated 3,959 rules of Sanskrit morphology in the text of the Aṣṭādhyāyī (the eight chapters) of Classical Sanskrit by using a constituency grammar.

Using the morphology of a number of elements that will be sought in this research, a 'model child' across time and space could be constructed or reconstructed. It can also be used to take different components for different routes to analysis so that more than a single morphology is available for what Propp classified as *character* and *actions*.

Those taxonomies will especially well show what time and thought tell us a child was and, perhaps, still is. The second will look especially at recent observations on the development of individuals. It that respect, it is probably the most significant of the methods chosen. As a problem structuring and solving method, morphological analysis was originally designed for intricate, often unquantifiable problems where causal modelling and simulation do not operate especially well or at all. However, for the purposes of this research it requires a further supporting method for induction and morphology to gain greater substance.

Morphological analysis was used in my research to examine different sources of data, especially where their content appeared either similar or repeated. It was used to examine recurrent motifs rather than events that could be catalogued taxonomically in order to identify the simplest irreducible narrative elements or 'functions' that construct *child citizenship*.

The requirement is that these functions occur in a standard, constant sequence that can be reassembled as a wider picture of the generally disaggregated topics *children* and *citizenship*. By using narrative units, or *narratemes*, from texts it will be possible to arrive at a typology of narrative structures and also sentence structures that have been deconstructed into analysable elements or *morphemes*. Analysis of motif and event types will reveal how many generic narratemes can be found.

However, since the real world seldom behaves rationally, these analyses take no account of exceptional motifs that are narratemes and morphemes that do not repeat thus have no place in a taxonomy. For this reason, a further method that supports analytic induction and morphology was chosen to attempt to gain greater substance if and where it was available.

Content Analysis

Content analysis, here purely textual analysis, was chosen since it is a standard method for the study of content of communication used by social scientists. It is a scientific method that includes specific consideration of objectivity and subjectivity, consistency, validity, replication and testing the hypothesis but is not limited to variables measured or context in which communications are formed or presented.

It can be used for the study of recorded human communications including books, journals, websites, visual representation (film, paintings, photography, etc.) and other sources of communicable data. It is usually used as a summarising, quantitative analysis of communications. It relies on the scientific method that includes specific attention to objectivity and subjectivity, *a priori* research design, consistency, validity, replication and testing the hypothesis. For the purpose of my research, it was used not as a quantitative method but instead as a qualitative one. In this respect, use of the method qualitatively and critically makes it more closely resemble symptomatic reading which is one of the most universally used critical methods in literary studies.

Louis Althusser and Fredric Jameson were both fervent advocates of symptomatic reading. It is a depth and surface model of interpretation that defines the precise meaning of texts as well as taking into account what they do not say. Thus breaks, silences, distractions and omissions become indicative of missing causes and formative structures in and behind a text. The critic or reader is left to reconstruct and bring to light the other side of a history, philosophy or other form of communication in which exclusions construct the untold parts of the story conveyed. The real purpose of this method is to suggest which other readings are necessary or possible and what forms of interpretation of the textual source are implied. One might use the metaphor that one is *seeking the virus that causes the undiagnosed disease* whereby one looks at all other and especially similar viruses that show both commonalities and contrasts. When one reads, he or she has to seek information and is confronted with different views which force them to consider their own position. In this process the reader is subsequently converted to a 'writer' whether or not he or she writes or publishes his or her own ideas.

However, since my research was governed by a regulated maximum length, the interpretive aspect was used and the suggestion of other readings left to those to take the intellectual course of this work forward in their turn. To some extent this version takes that task forward.

The purpose in the research was to look for breaks, diversions and omissions that suggested missing causes and formative structures in and behind the text. It thus made it possible to reconstruct and elucidate the other side of history, philosophy or other forms of communication where exclusions and incomplete accounts put together untold parts of the narrative. Here its real purpose was to suggest other readings that might have been indispensable or essential and in which forms of interpretation sources should be embedded. In this case the objective of this final point is not to infinitely extend the range of the research for myself. It suggests, without specifying exact authors or titles, a direction for further examination that might be taken up by others taking the intellectual direction of this work forward.

An example of the kind of extrapolation of unwritten central parts of a narrative is Disney's animated film *Snow White*. In the original story collected by the Grimms (Grimm and Grimm 1984:300–310), *Schneewittchen* is a princess whose own mother, the queen, hates her. The mother attempts to kill her daughter, the king finds out and is so angry he has his wife executed. Bolte and Polívka (1913) tell us that in the original version the King kills her because he is angry about her three attempts to kill Snow White. She is put into a pair of red hot shoes and perishes in agony. The Grimms did not include this in their version. It was the Grimms who changed the mother into a stepmother and then introduced the prince as her 'prince charming' rescuer. He rescued her with a cart. The jogging dislodged the poisoned apple going over a pothole, but there is no kiss. We can guess she is a young woman because they marry soon after. Disney took the story a step further in 1937.

In the original story and the Grimm version, the dwarfs do not really feature very much at all. We simply know that they are seven kindly, small men who look after her. Walt Disney and his team looked for central absences in the story that would embellish it. The animated film version explored the possibility of giving names and came up with Doc, Dopey, Grumpy, Happy, Sleepy, Sneezy and Bashful. Snow White is a girl, probably in early teens. The queen took on a witch 'alter-ego'. The dwarfs became a key part of the story and eventually chase the queen/witch to her death when she plunges into the wind and rain swept ravine. Absurdly, what appear to be white-backed vultures normally found in East and West Africa follow her down to the bottom of the abyss. After the kisses that revive her Snow White rides off into the world, and whilst there is a 'happy-ever-after' ending we are not told explicitly the couple marry. The point in using this example is that what is not in the original story can be found in the morphology of other folk tales, thus exploited to fill out and modify an otherwise attractive but not very exciting story. Disney induced a story for his film from what was not there, borrowed from other motifs in folklore and intuitively filled out the rest for the 'perfect' storyline. This is exactly the potential this method offered to my research and to the support of induction and morphology.

The original research and this somewhat further developed version both set out to draw together conclusions drawn from those three analytical methods to find evidence for there ever having been an equal or at least comparable status for adults and children in the past or present.

Chapter 3
Citizenship

This book attempts to examine whether children's citizenship is either realism or romanticism. The Introduction has given a definition of childhood that, whilst there are a few riders, is relatively easily identified. However, the more complicated part of the question is to identify what citizenship is before moving toward the actual enquiry. This chapter sets out to make as compact an overview of citizenship itself and examine the possibility of there being a child specific definition that could henceforth be the locus of this research.

There is a tendency to take the simplest path to this 'definition' that is broadly speaking unsatisfactory when looking at children. However, the simple path is one that considers citizenship to be something that is intrinsically egalitarian in the modern world and applies to all people to one degree or another. It is inclined to use the language of a neo-liberal model such as that described by Thomas Marshall (1950) in his seminal work *Citizenship and social class*. The disadvantage of taking the simple path is that it looks at the present and has a propensity for omission of the many people who do not enjoy citizenship rights or have been deprived of some of them. Furthermore, it mainly focuses on western liberal democracies. The outcome is that history, with the exception of Athens from the fifth to fourth centuries BC, is generally overlooked, people with partial or no citizenship are marginalised and other versions of citizenship that are neither western nor modern simply passed over. Therewith claims of children's inherent right to citizenship with foundations in the past and its inevitability in the future tend to lack substance and owe much more to contemporary interest in a very narrow view of their participation in civil society.

Jess Cooney is an archaeology postgraduate in Cambridge who was among presenters at the 5th Annual Society for the Study of Childhood in the Past conference (see http://www.cam.ac.uk/research/features/prehistoric-pre-school/). The conference *Child Labour in the Past: Children as economic contributors and consumers* took place at the University of Cambridge from 30 September to 2 October 2011. Her paper revealed recent research into art by young children in one of the most famous prehistoric decorated caves in France which is a complex of caverns at

B. Milne, *The History and Theory of Children's Citizenship in Contemporary Societies*,
DOI 10.1007/978-94-007-6521-4_3, © Springer Science+Business Media Dordrecht 2013

Rouffignac in the Dordogne, *la grotte de Rouffignac* also known as the *la grotte des cents mammouths* (cave of a 100 mammoths). She explained how painstaking research that used methods tailor-made for that work had made it possible to identify both age and gender of children who contributed to the artwork in the caves using a simple art form known as finger flutings. The flutings are around 13,000 years old from the hunter gatherer period. Her paper described how some of the flutings studied were made by a 3 year old and how the most productive young artist was a girl aged 5. Archaeologists first realised that children had produced some of the finger flutings in 2006 and during fieldwork carried out during 2011 by Jess Cooney with Dr Leslie Van Gelder of Walden University showed exactly how young they were.

Cooney is drawing attention to the fact that children as young as three were active in those caves with adults and that there appear to be few, if at all any, boundaries between adult and child activity. In her own words this raised an important question for her: "What I wanted to do with my PhD was to allow prehistoric children to have a voice, since children are rarely talked about in academic discourse. What I've found in Rouffignac is that they are screaming to be heard – the presence of children is everywhere in the cave, even in the passages furthest from the entrance."

Of course this bears little relationship to the question of citizenship but it does contribute to an open question as to when the separation began. Of course, 13,000 years ago during the hunter gatherer period there was no notion of statehood that would have included a concept of citizenship. However, these people would have belonged to families who belonged in extended groups or clans, possibly even tribes. What archaeology and palaeontology do tell us though is that children were involved in an activity that had ritual or symbolic significance, perhaps as simple as believing it would make a hunt more successful or with greater spiritual value. In that sense, if the children were included in a relationship of belonging that could be at all compared with what we now regard citizenship to be, then when and how did that notion transform into what was established in antiquity 2,500 years[1] ago? This book does not set out to search for the enigmatic truth in that respect but simply acknowledges that it occurred. Whether and to what extent it is reversible is far more to the point here.

[1]The period of approximately two and a half thousand years is undoubtedly vulnerable to just criticism. We know enough about ancient civilisations such as those in Syria-Mesopotamia who very clearly had citizens to the extent that their membership of a state comparable to a modern concept existed up to 2,000 years before the ancient Greeks. However, we have far less knowledge of the detailed social construction of those civilisations. For a modern social scientist there is consequently too little substantial data for enough to be said for that to be a definitive starting point for my timeline. The Greeks, on the other hand, have given us far more data than actually required. Thus the choice is pragmatic rather than partial.

Citizenship and Nationality

Citizenship is commonly defined as *membership of a political community* but the basis of that membership is a matter of some debate. Complications begin with organisation and structure of that 'community'. Where do we find its boundaries and extent and what is within those limits? Then there is a whole series of questions about who may belong and who is included or excluded according to certain criteria. Furthermore, one needs to question whether it is only a political community, or may it indeed be something far bigger or even without observable limits?

The neo-liberal view of citizenship assumes each individual has membership in the political community (originally a city or large town but now usually a national state). It carries with it the right of political participation, usually through universal and democratic electoral rights but also including the notion that each individual has a right to be represented or be elected to represent others. It is most often assumed to be synonymous with *nationality* although it is quite possible to have nationality without citizenship or, indeed, to be without either. In the majority of nations a non-national is without citizenship rights as *Citizenship Laws of the World* (United States Office of Personnel Management Investigations Service 2001) shows very clearly. It describes types of 'citizenship' (pp. 4–5):

> Citizenship by Birth: Citizenship is granted due to birth within the country. The legal term for this is "*jus solis*." In most cases, there are few stipulations on citizenship being granted. Birth in the country automatically confers citizenship regardless of the parents' citizenship or status.
>
> Citizenship by Descent: Citizenship of a nation is passed on to a child based upon at least one of the parents being a citizen of that nation, regardless of the child's actual country of birth. The term for this is "*jus sanguinis*."
>
> Though most countries adhere to the principle of citizenship by descent, they differ on some factors (father's vs. mother's rights, citizenship of one or both parents, the marital status of the parents, and others).
>
> As a person reaches an age of maturity, continuing the condition of citizenship by birth (*jus solis*) or citizenship by descent (*jus sanguinis*) may depend on factors unique to the nation of that citizenship.
>
> Citizenship by Naturalization: This is a formal process by which persons may acquire the citizenship of a country. The process varies and citizenship is not guaranteed. Basic rules may include a period of residence, renunciation of other citizenship, and familiarity with the language and customs of the country.
>
> Citizenship by Marriage: By some nations' laws, upon marriage, a person is entitled to become a naturalized citizen of their spouse's country without having to fulfil other naturalization requirements. These laws are often different for males than for females.
>
> Citizenship by Registration: In some instances, a person may acquire citizenship by registration with the national government without meeting all naturalization requirements for that nation. Usually these persons possess blood ties to the country through immediate relatives who are citizens, or by marriage to a citizen of that country.

These definitions of citizenship are a summarised version of the details for the directory of countries that then follows. However, on closer scrutiny they actually only describe *nationality* since they lack both detail of exclusion from membership of a nation from within or the duties of citizens as bearers of full rights.

There is a very clear example of this in Germany where, until 2004, 36 % of Turkish citizens living in that country did not have German nationality despite being born there. Under the prior law, children born to foreigners in Germany were not entitled to citizenship (*jus sanguinis*) so that a large population of permanently resident non-citizens grew up with the outcome that over time even the third generation born there remained foreigners. In 2000 legislation was passed (Bös 2002:3–8) which allowed the possibility of German citizenship for German-born children of foreigners and the naturalisation process correspondingly made easier. Dual citizenship is not allowed and any person possessing it through birth to foreign parents must choose between ages of 18 and 23 years which citizenship she or he wishes to retain. Many people of Turkish origin have chosen to retain their nationality and probably others will continue to do so thus increasing the number of generations resident in Germany. However, the sting in the tail for German born Turks is that only those (often the first generation) actually born in Turkey have full rights anyway.

Derek Heater (1999:95) looks at the origins of citizenship as nationality:

> For two hundred years citizenship and nationality have been political Siamese twins. Before the late eighteenth century the relationship was much looser than we have been accustomed to assume, and the connection is loosening again in our own age as multiple and world citizenships become increasingly evident.

He furthermore describes four central ideas in European political thought in the mid-eighteenth century helpful for looking at how this came about. They are: cosmopolitanism, citizenship, patriotism and nation (*Ibid.*:95). He describes citizenship as 'an assertion of freedom from arbitrary power, and usually intimately bound up with patriotism, the sense of loyalty to and duty to defend one's state' and a 'nation was a group of people speaking the same language and not necessarily synonymous with the population of a state' (*Ibid.*:95–96). Certainly the 'loosening' Heater refers to is very apparent at present. In many countries it is normal that refugees and asylum seekers are considered to be *stateless* people and there are considerable numbers of 'Internally Displaced Persons' or IDPs around the world who are either refugees or migrants within their own country of birth and denied either nationality or full entitlements of citizens for a number of sometimes quite arbitrary reasons. There are also ethnic minorities who for one reason or another have never been given either status.

Heater (*Ibid.*:96) says that the word 'nation' was not commonly used until the mid-eighteenth century and describes its development in France as being especially instructive. '*Nation*' came to be synonymous with '*patrie*' and '*peuple*', connoting unity of the people and its territory, fusing classes and provinces as part of the conflict between '*roi*' (monarchy) and the masses to express the interests of the nation against monarchic abuse. Abbé Sieyes constructed the modern French definition of nation in 1788 by endowing a clear political connotation that is inextricably linked to the concept of citizenship (*Ibid.*:97).

The universality of citizenship has also been gender biased for much of history as will be described under the subheading 'Exclusion from citizenship and suffrage' later in this chapter. There we see examples such as Liechtenstein granting women electoral franchise as recently as 1984 and Appenzell Inner-Rhoden in Switzerland allowed them to vote in 1991, whilst Saudi Arabia still does not allow them full voting rights. Brunei offers suffrage to neither adult men nor women. Although women are citizens by nationality they do not always entirely share the full franchise that status usually offers men in their countries. Within children's rights circles the progress of women's political status has been used as a benchmark for how that might be used to argue for the extension of those rights to at least some children. The fact that Austria, Brazil, Cuba and the Isle of Man are part of a handful of nations who allow the vote at age 16 is a yardstick for the notion of this becoming the universal standard with the possibility of lowering that age further in the fullness of time.

Citizenship and Children's Rights

The CRC Articles 7 and 8 describe nationality thus:

Article 7

1. The child shall be registered immediately after birth and shall have the right from birth to a name, the right to acquire a nationality and. as far as possible, the right to know and be cared for by his or her parents.
2. States Parties shall ensure the implementation of these rights in accordance with their national law and their obligations under the relevant international instruments in this field, in particular where the child would otherwise be stateless.

Article 8

1. States Parties undertake to respect the right of the child to preserve his or her identity, including nationality, name and family relations as recognized by law without unlawful interference.
2. Where a child is illegally deprived of some or all of the elements of his or her identity, States Parties shall provide appropriate assistance and protection, with a view to re-establishing speedily his or her identity.

Approximately 10 nations (including the UK[2]) submitted reservations against full implementation of Article 7, however estimates of 'stateless' children begin with estimates of 50 million unregistered births worldwide annually (e.g. see annual editions of UNICEF *State of the World's Children* or UN World Development Reports). There are numerous reasons why children all over the world do not have a nationality. One particular cause stands out: lack of birth registration in countries

[2]The reservations were withdrawn in September 2008 during writing this work.

where government funds are insufficient or where poverty dictates priorities other than birth registration. Furthermore, children from poor families cannot always afford expensive child registration fees and other families from rural areas cannot always cover the cost of travel to urban centres where registration is typically carried out. Some parents simply do not understand the importance of birth registration or lack basic information on how to register their children.

There are also legal barriers to establishing nationality. That is especially the case in countries where nationality is determined by parents' nationalities or birthplace of the child. Examples of people who commonly fall under this classification of statelessness include Roma, Bedouin, Karens, Kurds, Palestinians, Tibetans and many other smaller groups who cannot obtain an official birth certificate or formal papers declaring nationality. Estimated percentages of annual births not registered in 2000 listed by region were Sub-Saharan Africa 71 %, South Asia 63 %, Middle East and North Africa 31 %, East Asia and Pacific 22 %, Latin America and Caribbean 14 %, Central and Eastern Europe Commonwealth of Independent States and the Baltic States 10 %, industrialised countries (including EU members, USA, etc.) 2 %. The worldwide total has been estimated at up to 41 % of births not being registered (UNICEF 2002).

The balance of included and excluded embraces an estimated 36 % of the world population below age 19 years, 32.9 million refugees, asylum seekers, IDPs and other stateless persons (2.6 %), many of the approximated nine million adult prisoners (0.7 %) and other people such as those with mental health and legal reasons for exclusion. Thus, using basic UN statistics and allowing for double counting of adults and children across all categories, an estimated minimum of 40 % (nearly three billion) of all people do not enjoy full citizenship privileges. Thus, despite over 180 nation states ratifying the principles contained in Articles 7 and 8 CRC without reservation the real situation does not describe a universal standard from which a definition of citizenship can be drawn.

Whatever the case, at present in most modern secular nation states there is a close legal correlation between the two statuses that usually applies, if only in principle, to people of all ages. However what is more specifically definitive of what makes modern citizens is found in the rights and duties of citizenship. There are often obligatory duties of citizenship that vary from one country to another but often include such things as paying taxes or serving in the country's armed forces when conscripted. There are also ethical and moral duties that tend to include demonstrating commitment and loyalty to the democratic political community and state. A citizen is allowed to constructively view conditions of and participate in the improvement of the quality of political and civic life through electoral franchise and obedience of the law. He or she should also respect the rights and opinions of others, defend their own and the rights of others against those who would abuse them and generally exercise their rights. Those responsibilities do not, however, extend to all people. There are countries where people who have broken laws are deprived of some or all rights and duties whilst imprisoned or for a limited, extended or permanent period after having offended. Similarly, people classified as incompetent by mental health legislation are often denied many or most privileges of citizenship.

The vast majority of nation states also demand formalities such as birth registration documents and a registered 'fixed abode'. Thus people who have lost registration papers or never held them or are without permanent or any accommodation and those who are 'in transit' are commonly excluded within their own countries. Beyond that, most rights and duties of citizenship do not extend to persons below the age of majority which is usually 18 years of age in most countries. Some may gradually or partially be extended over the period of up to 5 or 6 years immediately preceding majority and others occasionally extend even beyond that age. It is, for instance, not uncommon in the UK for legacies to be age determined and stratification of such things as insurance cover up until notional maturity well into the 20s.

Children and youth are thus almost entirely without genuine political and economic influence. Therewith they lack the key components of what allows effective participation in civil society. Their citizenship is thus, unless withheld for one of the kind of reasons already described, limited to nationality and some of the ethical and moral duties, even then often under the supervision of adults. Thus children, along with the stateless, nationality-less, criminal and mentally ill, disprove the assumption that it is intrinsically egalitarian.

Citizenship in History

The situation in the contemporary world probably is very different to any other historical period. To begin with, the status of women has changed radically. Moreover, serfdom and vassalage have disappeared and the decline from the late medieval to the ostensible end of slavery and similar forms of 'ownership' of human beings from the early nineteenth century onward has changed what would have been an entirely different picture. We now view citizenship as the political bond between all people in each state and tend to measure their value as 'good' citizens (Milne 2005a:277–83) against the less frequently articulated 'bad'.

There are two main sets of political ideas and values defining *good citizen.* One has origins in Greece during the period 500–300 BC. We usually refer to this as the *civic republican* tradition. It is concomitant with an ideal of direct democracy in which all citizens take part in political decisions. The second set of ideas and values is informed by ideas held in Roman law developed in the Roman Empire from the first century AD onward that was more fully formulated in the seventeenth and eighteenth centuries in Europe. This is the *liberal* tradition which is linked to the ideal of a parliamentary democracy in which citizens elect representatives to represent their interests.

The starting point for scrutiny of citizenship is most commonly found in examination of ancient Greece and Aristotle's first systematic attempt to describe it theoretically (Aristotle 1908, 1999b). The Greek *polis* citizenship was very different in form and function to 'modern' (western) citizenship. The *polis* consisted of small-scale organic communities. Citizenship was seen as a public matter that was separated from the private life of the individual. Obligations of citizenship were profoundly connected with each individual's everyday life in the *polis*. To be fully human, one had to be an active citizen to the community, which Aristotle (Aristotle 1999 b:6) has famously expressed: "…he who is unable to live in society, or who has no need because he is sufficient for himself, must either be a beast or a god: he is no part of a state". This nature of citizenship was based on the obligations of citizens towards community as opposed to rights given to the citizens of the community. This was not a problem since all had a strong affinity with the *polis*. Personal destiny and that of the community were strongly linked. Furthermore, citizens of the *polis* saw their obligations within the community as an opportunity to be virtuous as their primary source of honour and respect. In Athens *citizens* were both ruler and ruled whereby significant political and judicial offices were rotated and 'everybody' had the right to speak and vote in the political assembly (Jowett 1901).

An important facet of *polis* citizenship was the elitism that delineated boundaries between who *was* and *was not* one of 'everybody'. Citizenship in ancient Greece and later in Rome and cities that practiced citizenship in the Middle Ages was very exclusive and inequality of status was the norm (see Riesenberg 1956, 1992; Faulks 2000:14). Citizens had a much higher status than those who could not obtain the status of a citizen, such as women, children, slaves or 'barbarians'. Women were, for example, not considered rationally capable of political participation although some philosophers, especially Plato, disagreed with this principle. Children (boys) entered the citizenry by stages (see Chaps. 3 and 5). There were also other means used to determine whether someone could or could not be a citizen (see Riesenberg 1992:35; Manville 1994:24). At particular times this principally had to do with wealth, usually the amount of taxes a citizen paid, political participation and birthright. In fact, both parents had to be born in the *polis* for their child to become a citizen.

During the Roman Empire *polis* citizenship changed form (see Hansen 2006; Heater 1990, 2004; Faulks 2000). The extent of citizenship was expanded from small scale communities to a status throughout the Empire. The Romans found that granting citizenship throughout the Empire bestowed legitimacy on Roman rule over conquered areas. They also found that taxes were more easily collected and a necessity for expensive military power in areas where citizenship was reduced. Thus during the Roman era it was no longer a status of political agency but had been reduced to a judicial safety measure and articulation of rule and law. After the collapse of the Roman Empire the importance of citizenship became even less.

In the fifteenth century Niccolò Machiavelli described republican citizenship in Florence as a tool for asserting citizens' interests in hard contrast to Aristotle's view that it was a fundamental element of what is required to be human. Thomas Hobbes (1651) was one of the earliest political theorists to draw attention to the essential equality of individuals although they lived within a state in which he saw absolute power in the hands of sovereigns as the only conceivable means of holding society together. John Locke (1965) considered it necessary to balance the Hobbesian concern with the security of the state with the principles of the protection of life, liberty and property. Hobbes, and more notably Locke, saw the state appearing with the unification of all people in a social contract. Locke believed the individual should be sovereign and that the explicit role of the state is to defend all individuals' right to life, liberty and property. Thus Locke postulated a view that all men had the same liberties and obligations as well as the right to change their government. His ideas were very influential on the outcome and aftermath of the American War of Independence. The rights and powers of all citizens to vote and stand for office were guaranteed by the consequent constitution.

Once we reach the eighteenth century, in the wake of the American War of Independence came the French Revolution. Thereafter came the beginning of the end of colonialism as Spanish colonies fought wars of independence. This is when we find the citizenship-nationality correlation and identity beginning to emerge in more or less the form it is viewed today. Whilst slavery and feudal control of people was in sharp decline, it is very important to note that Hobbes, Locke and other political thinkers and philosophers normally meant *men* rather than literally all people. It was exceptional that a few changes for women and fewer for children were proposed.

The notion of citizens having liberties, power and equality in front of the law has eventually become the norm in the west and in due course nearly all women have gained full citizenship. This perception of political citizenship is now the orthodox or liberal interpretation but has been constantly challenged. This work accordingly contributes to the debate on two counts. Firstly, it examines the exclusion of children from the proposition that there is 'universal' citizenship in an essentially egalitarian society. Secondly, it allows for both the fact that the orthodoxy is itself limited to the West and to those places worldwide that have aligned themselves with that concept and the vast numbers of individuals including children who are excluded.

Modern Principles and Theories of Citizenship

Most contemporary, western examinations of citizenship begin with a point of reference chosen from one of two models: the liberal or civic republican traditions. The liberal model's origins are more or less recognisable back as far as the Roman Empire and early-modern analysis of Roman Law (see Walzer 1989:211). Expansion of the Empire had the consequence of citizenship rights being extended to conquered peoples. That profoundly transformed the connotation of the concept. Whereas it meant being protected by the law, rather than participating in its making or implementation, it now implies membership in a community of common law, which may or may not be a territorial community such as a nation state.

Thus the liberal tradition, as it developed from the seventeenth century onwards, expresses citizenship primarily as a legal status. Within that, political liberty is important as a means to protecting individual freedoms from interference by other individuals as it is from the powers that be. However citizens exercise these freedoms for the most part in the world of a more private sphere rather overtly than in the political domain.

Over the last half century a great deal of work on citizenship has been highly influenced by the work of Marshall (1950). His argument was that development of citizenship since the eighteenth century has included successive acquisition of civil, political and social rights. Civil rights include such improvements as the right to fair trial, freedom from arbitrary imprisonment and violence, freedom of speech, right to own property and rights of contract. Political rights have come to include the right to vote and to stand for election. Social rights embrace rights to health care, education and a benefit system that came about with the institutions of the welfare state. He considered social rights as of vital importance (in fact, his work was to a certain extent aimed at promoting development of the welfare state). He maintained that citizenship limited to civil and political rights would exclude many people from full membership of society. His argument was that people who were struggling with poverty or ill health or who were poorly educated would not have the time, resource or ability to exercise citizenship rights in practice.

Marshall, the work of his contemporaries and subsequent theorists of the same school of thought have given us what is now generally considered the dominant *neo-liberal* model of citizenship. Neo-liberal citizenship having promoted the importance of welfare state appears to be far more inclusive than its liberal predecessor or the civic republican model. In fact it is probably far more prescriptive of the position of children since it puts a great deal of emphasis on the protection of and provision for children in a fashion that is set aside from adult protection and provision. Some authors (e.g.: Liebel 2007b:32–43) have expressed far more faith in the civic republican model as a natural place for children to attain full citizenship.

The civic republican model's basis can be found in the writings of numerous authors including Aristotle, Machiavelli and Rousseau. It is also found in foremost historical accounts of examples of republicanism that include Athenian democracy or the Roman Republic through to the medieval Italian city-states and more recently workers' councils.

The principal republican value is political liberty which must be understood as non-domination or independence from arbitrary power. Pettit (1997) describes republicanism as an enterprise that embraces a notion of political liberty that he calls 'non-domination'. In line with this concept, we are free in as much as that we do not fall under the domination of others, subject to their will and become exposed to the vicissitudes of their desires. If we use Isaiah Berlin's (1969:118–72) taxonomy of liberty it would appear that Pettit's notion of republican freedom may be considered a 'negative' rather than 'positive' concept. That is especially so since that idea does not indicate the amount of control over which any individual or community exercises its own existence. To be free of domination by others is not equivalent to being one's own master because it is a condition which people may benefit from in various ways. Those may be in equal measure by allowing themselves to be carried away by enthusiasm or allowing themselves to fall under the rule of reason.

Pettit also describes republican freedom as 'dominion'. That is something close to the notion of a capacity to shape one's own life with a typical example being education. Because one version of the concept of education is of an institution that limits autonomy at the same time it improves the individual's life by informing the agent's ability how to shape his or her life. Most certainly one might argue that the imposition of compulsory education is that which shapes a child's future and moulds them into future citizenship.

One of a few variants of republicanism is civic republicanism which is essentially progressive and liberal with significant distinguishing features. Some of its policy propositions deviate from mainstream liberalism in specific ways so that civic republicans are sometimes also confused with communitarians. At the core of contemporary civic republicanism is the perception of political liberty as non-domination or independence from arbitrary power. Thus, the individual or group is free in a positive sense to the extent that they are able to exercise self-discipline or even self-indulgence without interference.

The key principle of the republican model is public self-rule that is deep-rooted in classical institutions and practices. Those include rotation of public offices underlining Aristotle's portrayal of the citizen as one capable of ruling and being ruled as and when opportunity allows. Citizens are first and foremost individuals who share holding office. Public self-rule is likewise at the heart of Rousseau's notion of co-authorship of the law making by way of the general will that makes citizens free and lends laws legitimacy. Active participation in negotiation and decision-making makes sure that individuals are citizens instead of subjects. Essentially, the republican model emphasises the second dimension of citizenship which is political agency.

Neither, however, offers more than a very limited overview of a global representation of citizenship that is based only on two originally occidental theses. There are other ideas about how citizenship is changing; for instance, feminist citizenship theory leads to an assumption that there must be the possibility of a feminist or female citizenship. Then there is the notion of global or world citizenship that fits in with the convergence of nations (globalisation) and gradual homogenisation of economics, business, manufacturing, international migration and so on. Both are far more theoretical than practicable at present.

Other ideas such as social and active citizenship have become 'buzz words'. They imply that citizens share a role in working towards the development of their communities through economic participation, public service, volunteering and other socially beneficial activities to improve life for all citizens. To this end schools in England have begun to provide lessons in citizenship and the educational model in Wales is referred to as Personal and Social Education. This trend is born of Home Office policy that is inclined toward inculcation of the idea the *duties* and *responsibilities* of full citizenship. Ideally it contributes to social cohesion rather than any altruistic desire to make individuals freer than ever before.

Of course, none of these typologies leads to an assumption of the egalitarian nature of citizenship since each operates on the basis of differences. The final one certainly assumes the need to learn the qualities of citizenship at school in order to join those who have already attained that status. Of course, equality relates to status and difference to individuality which are naturally quite compatible. For instance, they give us 'leaders' in a society that is considered to be entirely *egalitarian*. Leaders are *different* in that they possess special qualities of one or more type that allow them to assume their role.

Thus we can also consider communism which is the ideology that seeks to establish a classless, stateless social organisation of people based on common ownership of the means of production. It is typically considered to be part of the broader socialist movement, inspired by various political and intellectual movements that have a shared vision of an egalitarian social state. It is one in which the common rather than individual good and common rights and duties are ultimate goals. Despite the principle of egalitarianism it usually depends very much on leaders and supporters structurally, usually appearing pyramidal between base and leadership. Consequently, what has sometimes been considered more an 'experiment' than realisation of a communal principle, has usually turned into a centrally planned, monopolistic state in which anything resembling absolute egalitarianism has yet to emerge.

Extraordinarily though, work in Viet Nam (see van Beers et al. 2006) has revealed a degree of goodwill toward children that is partially a cultural trait but also driven by the Party machinery. However, one of the paradoxes in Viet Nam is that despite apparent absolute political control of the nation by the Communist Party, the modern business sector and emergent affluent wealthy elite operate absolutely along neo-liberal lines and some of the more remote ethnic minorities still live in a more or less feudal environment. It is where Party control is for the most part still strongest that children enjoy anything resembling adult citizenship. This is as much part of a 'tug of war' between the state and traditional family values as an altruistic attempt to change children's lives. Some ethnic minorities (particularly H'Mong and Van Kieu) give children an extraordinary degree of autonomy from very early in life. However this is largely because of their dependence on swidden agriculture in remote mountainous areas which requires absence from home for several days at a time. Then children are left to fend for themselves and look after the home. They also tend not to physically or mentally abuse or punish children. The Kinh (Viet) majority, on the other hand, is very Confucian and often treats children very harshly allowing them little autonomy. The Party has recognised the 'gift' of rights for children and their increased participation in matters affecting them as a medium for their inclusion in the state. In due course this directs much of their loyalty toward the benevolent Party and state, thus sustaining its continued existence. Whilst this is superficially democratic it also achieves and maintains domination by securing commitment through early activism.

There are of course some 'theocratic states' in which only members of the state religion are allowed full membership. Theocracy means literally 'the rule of God' whereby government rules by or subject to religious authority. In fact, what we often consider theocratic is a state where clergy rule in the name of God and should be called either an 'ecclesiocracy' or 'hierocracy' or is in fact a monarchy (i.e. Saudi Arabia). In all cases the definition of citizenship is in line with religious and older cultural values (often called 'tribal practices') with women and children usually under firm patriarchal control. Finally, there are also civilian and martial dictatorships which are by and large authoritarian and define citizenship in very controlled terms. Those often include the gradual initiation of children into adult membership through indoctrination, civil or military service thus excluding those who do not qualify for whatever reason.

Social Organisation and Citizenship

Whilst what are essentially Western ideologies and definitions of forms of citizenship dominate, other forms of social organisation within states or parts of states require some mention in consideration of the probability of children's membership of any form of citizenry. At present most of the 194 nation states in the world are described by one or another of the foregoing definitions. However, it also possible to examine historical examples of statehood, most particularly through those that were republics, thus had some kind of constitutional structure.

There was the Licchavi state in India in the Himalayan Gangetic region around present day Vaishali in Bihar (Ojha and Jha 1987; Sharma 1968). It was already a republic around 600 BC throughout the reign of 34 elected kings. The first was Nabhaga, who is said to have abdicated rule on account of a human rights matter. Licchavi, in common with the latter Greek republics (Athens, Sparta and Corinth), was a city state. City state republics are not entirely uncommon historically (for instance, see Finer 1999), the Phoenicians had Carthage, Sidon and Tyre, Central Asia saw Bukhara, Qaraqorum and Samarkand, Italy had Florence and Venice, Africa had Eko and Abadan, China had several city states during the Shang and Zhou dynasties and, albeit without clear evidence, there were the Mesoamerican and South American empires of the Aztecs, Incas and Mayans. Many of them have been said to have been as much in the hands of their 'citizens' as of their rulers who were often selected (but not elected) monarchs, priests or 'political' leaders.

However, as far as we know, those empires were mostly aggressively territorial, dogmatic and internally hierarchal. They also frequently conquered and dominated or enslaved enemies or inopportunely surrounding people in attempts to expand their territory. However, on balance there is little difference in some cases between examples such as Licchavi, Venice or Athens. In them democracy and imperialism were considered complementary qualities, which is where we often look toward the origins of the notion of modern citizenship. Thus, we see little evidence of a membership for all people within the bounds of republics throughout history, let alone children, although history may suggest a far more 'blurred' distinction between adult and child in some of them.

A further consideration should be the 'tribe' which has often mistakenly been attributed with the character of a 'nation' thus assuming a form of membership that may be compared with citizenship (for instance, see Selassie 2003:58–60 and 68–70). What has been supposed by some (e.g. Thoreau 2007) who attach romantic values to the concept, is that the tribe is organised as a form of primitive communism as the original, hunter-gatherer state of humankind out of which it is said to have come about. In fact a tribe is a small, more or less independent subgroup of a larger social system. Tribal societies have generally lacked organisational capability beyond the local tribe, with each consisting only of a small, localised population.

The internal social structure varies vastly although the small size of tribes has meant that they have relatively simple structures with few social distinctions between individual members. Some are considered more or less egalitarian with many traditionally having a weak concept of property and ownership, occasionally no concept at all. They have a strong sense of shared identity and kinship, albeit the latter may not describe intergenerational relationships as western people would recognise them. Despite a generally egalitarian structure, they normally have a clearly identifiable leadership and hierarchy. One aspect of the latter tends to be age hierarchy whereby children grow into full membership and often need to pass specific markers in life, many of which are celebrated on completion of initiation rituals.

Broadly speaking, adulthood and full membership tends to correspond with the years during which individuals are economically most active and are able to produce children, thus often occur far earlier than in western society. Attempts to compare citizenship within a larger society and tribal membership are predisposed to the criticism that the latter frequently exists within the former in the modern world. What we know about that historically often badly accounts for recent change. The emphasis in the contemporary world has switched to a focus on the duties and responsibilities of individual and collective citizens.

Duties and Responsibilities

The duties and responsibilities borne by citizens are perhaps the central cohesive source of support and stability within the society to which each individual citizen or collective of citizens is bound, although in practice each may be unaware of their role. To define 'duty' in this context means that whoever is duty bound has an actual, ethical or moral obligation toward individual or many fellow human beings, an organisation or body or perhaps society as a whole to complete a particular action without damage to any of them. It may, for instance, be to carry out day to day duties in the service of one's nation as a member of the military.

A 'responsibility', on the other hand, is an obligation that is binding according to some kind of 'tenet', which may be a non-statutory regulation or something as enforceable as a law, to complete an action or task that has been assigned to or is attributed to an individual or group. It may be taken on voluntarily or as an allocated task or function but the onus is on whoever is doing that thing to be accountable for its completion or failure to do so. The two are often confused for the other but the actual difference can be determined in terms of choice. When one has a duty the expectation is that it will be completed without question or evasion whereas with a responsibility there is an element of choice. If a person fails to fulfil a responsibility or chooses not to do so there would normally be no sanction whereas to not carry out a duty may well be formally reproached or punished.

For adults it is assumed that their socialisation will have given them the sense of both as part of their role within a unit as small as a family through to the role they play as individuals within the collectivity of an entire civil society. In both cases children may be excused for a dereliction of a duty or not to be responsible for an action. Whilst the notion of the sense of both, and in some societies a sense of duty particularly, is expected to be learned far more stress is placed on duties than responsibilities. It is assumed that in learning one the other will be acquired. It is presume that children are without the maturity and experience until they reach particular markers during early years and through youth to the point at which they achieve adulthood when they will be able to bear their duties and responsibilities as conscientious members of their society. They are, therefore, chosen qualities inherent to citizenship and therefore the ability to choose to accomplish or not the desired outcomes of duties and responsibilities informs that they possess agency within the structure they belong to.

In sociological terms *agency* refers to the ability of individuals to act independently and make own free *choices*. In contrast, *structure* refers to factors of influence such as class, gender, religion, gender, ethnicity, etc., that determine or limit the decisions and choices an agent makes. The relative difference in the influence of structure and agency is contentious in that it is uncertain to what extent an individual's actions are inhibited by the social system he or she belongs to. However, agency is one's independent capability or ability to act independently, in other words choosing to do something. This ability is influenced by the cognitive belief structure learned and formed through experience and views of the society and individual as well as the structures and conditions of the environment one is in. To disagree on the extent of personal agency regularly causes conflicts such as those that occur regularly between parents and children.

Thus, in philosophy and sociology, the term *agency* describes the ability of an *agent* (a person or other body) to act in the (their) world. In philosophy, agency is considered to *belong* to an agent even when an agent is actually a fictional character or other nonexistent entity such as an 'alien' in science fiction. The capacity to act does not of itself mean an explicit moral dimension to the capability to choose to act so that *moral agency* is consequently a distinct, separable concept. Sociologically, the agent is an individual *engaging* with a *social structure*. There is however debate about social structure against individual capacity regarding an individual's actions with regard to the level of reflexivity an individual (agent) may have the benefit of.

Therefore, human agency is the capacity for human beings to make choices and impose those choices on others. Therefore, agency is more or less distinct from the concept of free will which is the philosophical principle that choices are not produced by causal chains but are in fact extensively free or undetermined by others. Human agency includes the assertion that people make decisions and act on them in the world. The question as to whether humans make decisions of free choice or under other influences is an entirely other issue.

The capacity of an individual to act as an agent is personal to that person although consideration of the outcomes of specific acts of human agency for others can be believed to advance a moral element into a given situation in which that agent has acted. That is said to involve *moral agency*. If a circumstance is the outcome of human decision making, then an agent may be duty bound to apply a *value judgment* of the consequence of their decision and be held responsible for that decision. Human agency permits the bystander to ask "*Should this have occurred?*" in a manner that may be irrational, for example, asking whether a child should have been born after he or she has already been born.

The concept of social *structure* describes the relationships between different individuals, units or groups (all of which are agents) or as durable and relatively established patterns of relationship and emphasises the notion that society is grouped into structurally interconnected groups or sets of roles. Each has a different function, meaning or purpose. Thus, we have the idea that society is separated into different strata partly or entirely governed by underlying structures in that social system. Family, religion, law, economy and class are all social structures and the social system itself is the parent system of a range of systems embedded within it.

In terms of duties and responsibilities the assumption is that children must learn what those are and whilst they have agency just as every adult does, the assumption is that choice must be guided until learned. Thus agency is assumed to 'increase' with age and experience. This, of course, is in line with the human becomings notion of childhood. However, given that fictional characters with no ability and mechanical objects with limited ability to make 'choices' are said to have agency, and that the former most certainly have no capacity to learn and increase their capacities, the notion of *agent becoming* that could be interpreted out of *human becoming* is a contradiction in terms. It is that contradiction that stands between a child and his or her entitlement to be a full member of their society in which they may choose whether or not to bear the duties and responsibilities that go with citizenship.

Terminology

It is not only history and human organisation that is important when examining citizenship but the entire terminology which is part of the socio-linguistic understanding of what it is. The word *citizen* is itself part of understanding what citizenship is. Across Western European languages there are two dominant forms. As with the English, the French *citoyen*, Spanish *ciudadno*, and other essentially Latin originating words describe somebody who is an inhabitant (and member) of a city. That is very much in the way the Greek concept described a native of a city state such as Athens. Northern European languages such as German *Bürger*, Dutch *borger* or Norwegian *medborger* derive from the Germanic word *burg* meaning castle. Many towns grew up around castles thus coming to mean city although the German word for city is, in fact, *stadt*. Thus one differentiates between, for instance, *Staatsbürgerschaft* (citizenship) and *Stadtbürgerrecht* (civic rights) in German and similarly in other Germanic and Nordic languages. However, the understanding of citizen in (for instance) English and German is different because the latter has a broader application than the former in line with wider usage.

When looking at *nationality* as a part of citizenship we find similarly divergent forms, thus *Staatsanhörigkeit* and similar northern European forms describe belonging (*Anhörigkeit*) to a state rather than being of that state (*national*). With both citizenship and nationality English antonyms alone are complicated. In most English speaking nations a non-citizen is also a non-national and referred to as either *foreigner* or *alien*. This becomes more complicated in federal structures such as the United States of America. Since there is state and national citizenship *foreign* is the legal term for someone not a citizen of a state and *alien* is reserved for someone not a citizen of the United States. A New York company is foreign in Illinois while its Danish employee is an alien. In German there is *Fremder* that describes an alien, foreigner or stranger and is thus, all degrees between a local stranger and a non-national. Then there is *Ausländer* which is both alien and foreigner and is also the legal term for a non-national.

Language is very influential in how laws manifest themselves in other domains, thus how they may generally be understood when they are used within Anglo-Saxon 'common law', Roman law, Code Napoleon and other secular and religious legal codes. Beyond the complicated language of Western Europe there are thousands of other equally different and occasionally more complicated expressions. Beside those are laws, norms, mores, beliefs and practice which make the actual meaning of citizenship an extremely diverse possibility.

This is only the lingual '*juggling*' in what is actually culturally and linguistically a very small part of the world. The global picture is of a world in which there are over 600 prevalent languages, but 6,912 (see Gordon 2005) 'living' languages plus distinct dialects, across something in the region of 5,000 recognisable 'ethnic groups' in 194 independent nation states. This warns one of a more complicated task in actually reaching definitions. The many cultural, belief led and politically varied forms of citizenship and membership become overwhelming when the entire socio-linguistic issue is taken into account and, of course, the role of historical development wherever either convergence or divergence has occurred.

Children's Participation and Citizenship

A further issue to examine in this chapter is 'participation' although Chap. 9 will more explicitly visit the topic. Participation has become virtually a 'cottage industry' of the children's rights world since the adoption of the United Nations Convention on the Rights of the Child (CRC) in 1989. The state of participation at present is that there is neither constructive debate nor discourse. From the beginning of enthusiasm for children's participation it has been taken into vague forms of 'ownership'. This includes numerous authors who make assumptions based on their interpretation of the participatory articles of the CRC to state rather than prove that children are citizens. Much of this has used the medium of Article 12 to the exclusion of other articles as described by van Beers, Invernizzi and Milne (2007: vii–ix) in their introduction to a reader on children's participation.

Whilst Article 12 is unique to the CRC, Articles 13–16 are also 'participatory' but have been taken almost unchanged from Articles 18, 19, 21, 22 and 23 of the 1966 International Covenant on Civil and Political Rights. They thus fall in line with the base principle of 'the equal and inalienable rights of all members of the human family'. There has been an additional elusiveness of real explanation by use of the word 'participation' out of context instead of describing it as *participation in civil society*. It is frequently contextualised. Thus, by way of example, one finds that in the United Kingdom it is possible to find publications that refer to the participation of *looked after children* (see Chap. 8) within the welfare and social work domains but largely divorced from the rest of society. It is this segmentation of participation that removes rather than incorporates children into full citizenship that undermines its potential for resolution of the question this research addresses.

Child participation tends, in fact, to be a distraction and to move the issue away from citizenship. It appears to work counter to early liberal-democratic theory such as John Stuart Mill's (1869) forceful advocacy for the extension of political franchise to women. This was part of his belief in representative democracy whereby all people (the electorate: men and women) chose their (educated) representation and included direct action and participation as necessity demanded. The contemporary pro-child participation view tends to suggest separatism. Accordingly, children generally make decisions addressing the issues of children and are allowed to have a degree of opinion but no real political influence. There is certainly no real decision making capability in the world generally where adults are best placed to decide for them. In other words, children are allowed only partial citizenship through a veneer of playing a role in *their* part of civil society. In fact, as evidenced by children's role in the Palestinian *intifada*, protests and strikes in apartheid period South Africa and anti-war protests from the 1960s onward, the response by people in places of authority and power is largely negative and occasionally harshly punitive (see Coles 1986b). Thus, and as Chap. 9 will examine more extensively, it is intellectually influential at best but pragmatically of little value to the matter of children's citizenship.

Citizenship remains the bedrock of contemporary legal and social status whereby its natural foundation is the principle that citizens enjoy equal rights. However, under certain circumstances consideration of individuals' interests or actions are used to justify differential treatment by the state. That may include not considering the possibility that children might have the capability to fulfil the duties and responsibilities of citizenship. This will be considered later in this work where exceptions as well as rules will, of necessity, be examined.

Children's Citizenship and Political Power

A question also arises how persuasive the argument for children's citizenship might be in complex and internally diverse societies? This question is dominated by a tension that is difficult to resolve without popular support of the populace in general and evidence that corroborates the argument for inclusion. Whilst the USA played a central role in the drafting of the CRC, at the end of the second decade of it being in force they have still not ratified it. In the USA there are said to be moral, legal and religious reasons for not ratifying. Whereas the Constitution and Bill of Rights should produce a policy of open-mindedness and respect for all 'citizens', fundamentalists have turned to Christianity to emphasise the moral duties of the family. Those are raised to a level beyond the opportunity to protect personal rights that are ensured constitutionally. At the same time, the US Constitution never specifically mentions children as bearers of the rights it protects. Thus whilst the majority of the population may not be concerned either way, the outspoken fundamentalist Christian lobby has used moral and quasi-religious reasoning to support a legal argument against ratification. Rather than going into more detail here, this issue will be examined again in Chap. 10.

What we know about the pluralist nature of contemporary societies leads us to draw attention to the importance of general legal and political principles that include democracy, human rights and the rule of law. However, those are often in the most cursory fashion rather than unequivocally presenting the entire picture. Even the most advanced liberal democracy has a tendency to do this rather than look at traditional symbols of citizenship and nationality that every nation state sustains in its common history and culture.

The power of government to call a 'state of emergency' during which many 'rights' and democratic institutions may be suspended without recourse to obtaining a mandate to do so from an electorate through the ballot box bears witness to this Achilles' heel. The Egyptian people have lived under an Emergency Law (Law No. 162 of 1958) since 1967 except for an 18 month break that began in 1980. The state of emergency was invoked during the 1967 Arab-Israeli War. It was reintroduced following President Anwar Sadat's assassination in 1981. Since then it has been continuously renewed every 3 years. Under it police powers are extended, constitutional rights suspended and censorship was legalised. It very consequently restricts any non-governmental political activity so that street demonstrations, non-approved political organisations, and unregistered financial donations are officially prohibited. Several thousand people have been detained under the law and estimates of political prisoners (administrative detainees) run high. The briefest examination of either Amnesty International or Human Rights Watch's Egypt reports would show a rather grim reality. Power is apparently organised under a multi-party, semi-presidential system in which executive power is supposedly divided between President and Prime Minister. In practice power rests almost solely in the hands of a President who was until recently usually voted in by single candidate elections.

In 2001 the 'Concluding observations of the Committee on the Rights of the Child: noted that:

> 14. The Committee emphasizes the important role civil society plays as a partner in implementing the provisions of the Convention, including with respect to civil rights and freedoms. The Committee recommends that the State party consider a systematic approach to involving civil society, especially children's associations and advocacy groups, throughout all stages of the implementation of the Convention, including policy-making. In this regard, the Committee recommends that the State party ensure that legislation regulating NGOs conforms to international standards on freedom of association, as a step in facilitating and strengthening their participation. The Committee recommends that greater efforts be made to involve relevant State actors, such as local government officials and the police, in the dialogue with civil society and encourages the State party to support initiatives aimed at strengthening the role of civil society.

Egypt is an example of the extreme use of state power in a country that is seen as an important ally by liberal democracies involved in political mediations they hope will bring the long term crisis in the Middle East to an end. Normally, countries negotiating for peace with Egypt at the heart of their mission should be diplomatically protesting for improved conditions in that country. This 'balancing act' is political expediency that creates a permanent state of conflict between states who tolerate Egypt uncritically and the human rights lobby. The Committee comments reflect this tension. To recommend "strengthening the role of civil society" addresses both the increased inclusion of children but simultaneously acknowledges the fact that within an undemocratic system there are other underlying problems.

With such questions we are confronted with resolving where children stand in the complicated issue of citizens' political agency. Without resolution we would be simply adding the dimension of children to parts of the world that have only relatively recently included women in their political and social environments. That change was most certainly central to debates between liberals and republicans for several decades and probably political 'dust' has still not settled in those places. Inclusion of young people assumes an understanding of democracy in terms of civil self-government along civic republican lines or through the capacity to implement control over government in a liberal society. However, it is not easy to determine how and through which means citizens of varying competence and maturity exercise meaningful political agency in complex societies that are themselves at different stages of social and political development.

Overall, despite almost two centuries of gradual change it is a very incomplete change. At present we have the phenomenon of the CRC almost mirroring the view that women required the guidance and protection of men that was prevalent for centuries (e.g.: paragraph nine of the Preamble, Article 3 – 'best interests' and Article 5 – 'evolving capacities' [see Appendix I]). Thus part of the evidence for citizenship that is required is a convincing argument for children's competence as social actors in a number of domains including the economy, politics and social environment.

Exclusion from Citizenship and Suffrage

In a narrow sense citizenship is of intrinsic nature exclusionary. Therefore, exclusion can be better defined by looking at what inclusion itself means. It describes who is a citizen of a nation state and which *set of rights* an individual can exercise. In most constitutions the equality of all citizens is declared as a foundation. That means that they should be equally entitled to particular rights which are characteristically those associated with a democracy, thus include the right to vote, freedom of association, freedom of belief, etc. Thus *social inclusion* requires us to go further into realms of formal and substantive equality which are characterised by discrimination, exclusion and inequality. Social inclusion begins from the premise that it is democratic citizenship that is at risk when a society fails to develop the talents and capacities of all its members. Social inclusion is undermined when, for instance, the rights of minorities are not respected and accommodated so that they feel they belong to the 'other'. Social inclusion means there is, or at least should be, no contradiction between democratic citizenship and differentiated citizenship in which people can hold dual or even multiple loyalties. People under the age of majority are very often treated as a minority whilst in reality, in many nation states they are actually the greater part of a population and where discrimination and inequality are also present they are dual or multiple forms of exclusion.

Under some circumstances citizenship is in part or entirely denied, removed or suspended. This most commonly manifests itself as the removal or suspensions of suffrage so that whilst other citizens' rights still apply, persons may be without voting rights or eligibility for public office.

Religion has often been a reason for the partial or entire denial of removal of all or parts of citizenship, especially political rights (for instance, see Boyer 2001). Following the Reformation, throughout Europe it was common for people of discredited religious denominations to be denied civil and political rights. That included the right to vote, stand for election or take a seat in parliament. In the UK, Roman Catholics were barred from voting between 1728 and 1793 and could not sit in parliament until 1829. British Jews could not be naturalised. When an attempt was made to change that with the Jewish Naturalisation Act 1753, it provoked so many reactions that it was repealed in 1754 and remained thus until 1858. Following the Declaration of Independence in 1776, several states in the USA denied Catholics, Jews and Quakers voting rights and forbade them to run for office. In 1886 Romania made the provision in Article 7 of their first Constitution that only Christians could become Romanian citizens. Jews who had been in Romania for many generations were declared stateless. In 1923 a new Constitution was adopted, in which Article 133 extended citizenship to all Jewish residents as well as equal rights to all Romanian citizens. At present, in the Republic of Maldives still only Moslem citizens have voting rights and are at all eligible to stand for parliamentary elections.

Arising out of very similar moral roots to beliefs, the status of the illegitimate child has set some of them aside from the majority of members of their society. Despite decreased legal significance of illegitimacy, exceptions can be found in nationality laws of countries, which discriminate against illegitimate children in the application of *jus sanguinis*. That is especially the case where a child's putative tie with the country can only be claimed through the father whether he is the biological parent or has paternity only through marriage to the mother before the birth of the child without being the biological parent. To give one example, as in many other nations, the United Kingdom did not normally allow nationality to be passed on exclusively because the British father was not married to the mother. Formerly, it was held that fathers who remained unmarried to the mothers of their children did not usually have strong links with them. However, attitudes and laws have changed so that for nationality purposes the law changed on 1 July 2006. From this date on, as a rule, unmarried fathers became able to pass on British citizenship on the provision that he is proven to be the father of a child. Normally, this was through birth certification although other evidence including DNA tests and court orders are normally acceptable. The change in law was not retroactive, in other words, it does not apply to children born before 1 July 2006.

Ownership of property and being a tax payer were the qualification for full citizenship and political rights. Until the nineteenth century several Western democracies had property qualifications written into electoral law. For instance, only landowners could vote since at that time the only tax was property tax. Similarly, voting rights were weighed according to the amount of taxes paid, for instance the Prussian *Dreiklassenwahlrecht,* where men aged over 24 years were eligible to vote in 'classes' divided by their direct tax revenue into three classifications. Today such laws have largely been abolished and replaced by having a 'fixed abode' although the homeless are commonly unable to register because do not have permanent addresses.

Some electoral systems hold elections within sub-national jurisdictions that prevent persons who should normally be eligible to do so from voting because they are not resident within those jurisdictions or they reside in an area which cannot participate. In the USA residents of Washington DC, for instance, have no electoral representation in Congress although they have *de facto* full representation in presidential elections.

Sometimes citizens are ineligible when they longer reside in their country of origin. Australian citizens, for example, who are out of their country for more than one, but less than 6 years, are excused from an obligation to vote whilst they remain abroad. In Australia is normally compulsory for resident citizens to vote. In some countries naturalised citizens do not acquire voting rights or are allowed to stand for office, either permanently or for a definite period. In the Federated States of Micronesia, citizenship over a minimum of 15 years is the condition in order to be elected to parliament. In the USA the President and Vice-President must be natural born citizens whereas all other offices may be held by any citizen. The use of exile as a form of punishment or restriction has most certainly place limits on citizenship. Where a person in sent or deported into external exile, which is to say outside their own country, to all intents and purposes that individual is without citizenship. However, even internal exile often removes or reduces it. Permanent or life exile where the person or persons placed or sent out of their country of origin who are unable or who do not wish to take a new nationality are without citizenry of any kind for that entire period. Self-exile, all forms of international refugee and asylum seeking persons or diasporas tend to have much the same outcome. Many of them are given the status *stateless* to describe their situation.

Race has been used to limit not only the political element of citizenship but also to entirely withhold it to some extent. This may be indirectly whereby nothing in law explicitly prevents anyone from voting on account of their race. However, other laws and regulations are used to exclude people. In southern states of the USA before the *Civil Rights Act*, 1964 and *Voting Rights Act*, 1965 a combination of literacy and other tests frequently disenfranchised African-Americans. Property qualifications also disenfranchise non-whites, particularly if tribally-owned land is not allowed to be taken into consideration. Official laws and regulations were sometimes passed expressly to disenfranchise particular races such as in South Africa under apartheid.

In Canada, the Abella Report (1984) supported the notion that equality itself does not signify *sameness* but that we have to treat differences differently. It has been argued that minority rights have a 'corrosive effect' on citizenship since they politicise such issues as ethnicity and undermine the emergence of national identity. Moreover, that leads to separation that in due course only reinforce exclusions minority rights activists are struggling against. Those critics fail to understand the considerable power and privilege enjoyed by a majority that denies that to others because of their gender, disability or race. Preceding the Abella Report, Morton Weinfeld referred to the fact that: "…the ideals behind the rhetoric of multiculturalism have not been attained…Canadian native people and other non-whites continue to be victimized, a fact reflected in economic inequality or in patterns of social exclusion, abuse, and degradation" (Weinfeld 1981:29).

It is the pervasiveness of intolerance aimed at disadvantaged individuals and groups and prevalence of discrimination that contribute to the disintegration of social cohesion, thus causing separation and disparity. Main contributing factors in what Reginald Bibby (1990) called *mosaic madness* is not the demands of minorities, but is in fact the continued existence of racism and sexism. The Supreme Court of Canada noted that minority rights do not erode democratic citizenship, rather "The accommodation of differences is the essence of true equality" (see Kymlicka and Norman 2000:33).

Many countries restrict or entirely remove the voting rights of convicted criminals and those classified as criminally insane.[3] A few countries, including some states in the USA, withhold that right to vote people convicted of serious crimes after their release from prison. In some countries the removal of the right to vote is automatic with conviction, whereas in other cases such as France and Germany[4] (see Seifert 1976 for the example of German law) withdrawal of the vote is only

---

[3]An insanity defence is used by criminal defendants and its most common variation is *cognitive* insanity. Under the test to prove the plea a defendant must have been so impaired by a mental disease or defect at the time of the act that he or she did not know the nature or quality of the act. Furthermore, if a defendant did know the nature or quality of the act, he or she did not know that the act was wrong. Most countries allow defendants to plead a cognitive insanity defence. That defence should not be confused with *incompetency*. Accused persons who are incompetent to stand trial are held in a mental institution until they are considered capable of participating in the proceedings. This kind of defence reflects a generally accepted notion that persons who cannot understand the consequences of their actions should not be punished for criminal acts. It's origins as *complete madness* were first established by common-law courts in late thirteenth century England. By the eighteenth century it had developed into the *wild beast* test whereby that defence was available only to a person who was 'totally deprived of his understanding and memory so as not to know what he [was] doing, no more than an infant, a brute, or a wild beast' (Feigl 1967:161). All people judicially committed to institutions have all citizenship rights withheld or removed until such time as they are assessed as being *capable* of making informed judgement which may be well after a release back into the community.

[4]Federal Electoral Law (*Bundewahlgesetz*, BGW), Section III *Franchise and Eligibility*, Article 13 Disqualification from Voting, enacted on 7 May 1956 (Federal Law Gazette I, p. 383). In the version

applied for certain crimes such as offences against the electoral system. In a majority of countries in the modern world, prisoners are allowed to vote but are ineligible to stand as candidates for office.

Age and gender are the final areas that require examination. One of the most forceful arguments for the continued political exclusion of women was always their incapacity to direct their own lives. Whilst the Pitcairn Islands granted them suffrage as early as 1838, one of the last European countries to grant women equal voting rights was Liechtenstein in 1984. The Swiss Federation for Women's Suffrage had to campaign from 1909 to 1971 before women were allowed to vote in national elections and it was still not until a 1990 decision by the Federal Supreme Court of Switzerland that women in the Appenzell Inner-Rhoden Canton were allowed to vote as of 1991. At a meeting of the Committee on Elimination of Discrimination against Women (CEDAW) in January 2003 it was said that a number of experts 'were concerned over the pace of change, noting that Switzerland had ratified the Convention relatively late and had only given the vote to women in 1971' (CEDAW 2003:4). The Convention on Elimination of Discrimination against Women had come into effect in 1979 but Switzerland had only ratified in 1997. With regard to women's role in political and public life a report to the Committee said that women had only won the right to vote and be eligible for election at national level in 1971. Some cantons had granted that right earlier, however Appenzell Inner-Rhoden was the final canton to grant women the right to vote.

A few countries like Saudi Arabia are still in the process of introducing franchise and there are countries where economic rights allowing only property owners to have voting rights still work against the majority of women. In 2011 King Abdullah announced that women in Saudi Arabia are to be given the right to vote and run for office in future municipal elections which are the only public polls in their country. They will also have the right to be appointed to the consultative Shura Council. The number of countries where religious edicts such as *Sharia* stand in the way of universal franchise is however gradually but inexorably decreasing.

Economic rights have also often been biased against women whereby wage differences, even in countries with equal pay regulations, are very common. Those women have problems caused by a lack of economic power in areas such as

---

promulgated on 23 July 1993 (Federal Gazette II p. 1288, 1594) most recently amended by the law of 15 November 1996 (Federal Gazette I p. 1712) it states:

A person shall be disqualified from voting if

1. he or she is not entitled to vote owing to a judicial decision.
2. a custodian has been appointed not only through a restraining order to attend to all his or her affairs ; this also applies when the custodian's sphere of duties does not include the affairs set forth in Article 1896, Paragraph (4) and Article 1905 of the Civil Code (Bürgerliches Gesetzbuch),
3. he or she is accommodated in a psychiatric hospital under an order pursuant to Article 63 in conjunction with Article 20 of the Penal Code.

See also: Seifert (1976).

property ownership and renting where those who choose to live without men may be disadvantaged by not have that form of capital.

Thus, turning age and the denial of full citizens' rights that entails, which is also mainly based on an assumption that children also lack the capacity to direct their own lives. One of the issues not at stake here is their rights. The fact that all but two nations in the world at the times this is being written are states parties to the CRC bears that out. There is though the tacit assumption that children are not ready for the duties and responsibilities that come with full citizenship.

The initial question this chapter raised was what a specific definition of citizenship might be for the purpose of my research. Citizenship is different things and at a vast range of stages of development from one nation to another. The ideal model for this examination would be to assume that it is essentially egalitarian and to search for arguments from history to the present to substantiate the case for inclusion. On the other hand, to do so would be to place emphasis, as is already often the case, on western liberal democracies where the predominant political culture is far more likely to view the notion positively. Thus, the option remaining is to apply an adaptable, wide ranging definition. The proposition my research raised was then incorporated and conclusions could be reached that were not only identifiable with a single political culture or nation state.

Democracy and Citizenship

The two preceding topic areas have examined children's citizenship and political power and then their exclusion from citizenship and suffrage. Both are part of a political dimension that since the advent of the CRC in 1989 and a burgeoning interest in their participation in civil society have been placed in particular contexts. Those are mainly areas in which one can freely talk about contexts such as 'Demeny voting' whereby voting rights would be extended to everyone including children regardless of age. This does not mean that they could stand for election but within the 'child participation' field would almost certainly entail alternative and complementary bodies and institutions being set up. Thus there would be 'children's parliaments' and their like, who whilst having no lawmaking powers or real contribution to the entire range of political decisions, may at least have advisory or consultative status in a few forwarding thinking nations. Notions of political power and suffrage carry with them another favourite topic of participation specialists: democracy.

Before developing arguments for citizenship further it is almost unquestionable that the subject of 'democracy' be addressed. The first point must be that there is no absolute link between the two since citizenship in one form or another exists in even the extremes of absolutely totalitarianism and apparent lack of political cohesion. Indeed the twentieth century saw several examples of child and youth 'participation' with the *Deutsches Jungvolk* for boys and girls aged 10–14 years, then *Hitlerjugend* for boys and *Bund Deutscher Mädel* for girls up to 18 years. It was created in 1922 and finally disbanded with the German defeat in 1945. The Всесою́зная пионе́рская организа́ция и́мени В. И. Ле́нина (*Vladimir Lenin All-Union Pioneer Organisation*, also known as the *Young Pioneer Organisation of the Soviet Union*) for children of ages 10–15 years in the Soviet Union between 1922 and 1991 was a model for numerous either erstwhile or at present extant child and youth organisations. Whilst they have frequently been prerequisite for access to full citizenship, they actually have little to do with any form of democratic or democracy-like input into the societies in which they exist.

The second issue is that the choice of approximately 2,500 years used is also the most conventional timeline used in work on democracy when, for instance, Athenian 'assembly democracy' is the starting point. Here, and without question, the fact that Keane (2009) gives a large part of the early chapters of his work over to dispelling that argument draws attention to frailties in my own timeline. Keane tells us that the ancient civilisations of the Assyria-Mesopotamian region were more or less experimenting with what we might now consider popular assemblies up to 2,000 years before the Athenians. Athens stands out historically for their almost narcissistic sense of destiny far more than their innovative democratic institutions. There is, thus a view, that we expend too much time concentrating on the *demos* (δῆμος 'people') in Athenian democracy and not enough taking apart the *krátos* (κράτος meaning 'force' or 'power' but used more often than not as 'rule'). On top of that we are also hampered in associating what the word was with what it means now along its assumed trajectory from Greek *dēmokratía*, understood as popular government, through Late Latin *dēmocratia* to roughly sixteenth century Middle French *démocratie* and then fairly directly to what it has become in probably the most frequently used context of 'representative democracy'.

Here we very quickly correlate with the 'franchise' issue which describes the input of citizens into a democratic system. When we look at democracy in terms of gender particularly and also in other forms of exclusions from democratic principles such as class, race and economic status, the modern timeline tends to correlate very closely. However, in the case of children it may well be argued that things that gave them a more citizen-like status such as their labour being given in very similar terms to older people before legislation began to change their position are also undemocratic. They are without choice because they are not allowed to work and, arguably, that has been decided entirely by adult legislators without inclusion of any kind of countervailing argument by children ever being taken into account. Child labour legislation, for right or wrong, in point of fact precedes an evidential point in time at which either citizenship or democracy emerged. Since, on a 'cart and horse' argument basis, we can always only accept that a civilisation with a notion of belonging will always have preceded the kind of social innovation early democracy was we can, with some safety, speculate on children having been more like adults in general in that they shared many of the economic, social and cultural duties and responsibilities in their society. If anything, since on balance when we look at the history of democracy it is where they have been almost unquestionably excluded from the privileged groups who inevitably possessed it, they are still amongst those waiting for access to it.

It is because this is a study of children's citizenship specifically that this short insertion has been included rather than a lengthy analysis that will not be developed on. The hypothesis that in the fullness of time, once children have gained full citizenship would be followed by a progression to eventual full democratic inclusion is assumed rather than treated as part of the question. Above all else, when looking at democracy and citizenship anyway, there is absolutely no good reason for presupposing children's progress could be substantially different from that of adults anyway in either case or in how one relates to the other.

Chapter 4
The Emergence of Childhood – From the Ancient World Until the Dawn of the Enlightenment

The objective of this work and Chaps. 4 and 5 *more* specifically, is not to painstakingly re-examine the history of childhood. That is already a relatively thoroughly thought through aspect of social history. Whilst most of the easily accessible literature looks at Western European children since at least the late medieval period and Britain is exceptionally well covered, interest in other parts of the world is gradually falling into place. Archaeologists have fairly recently begun to contribute complementary data that increase our knowledge of how children lived in the past (for instance, see Sofaer Derevenski 2000 or Jess Cooney's work described earlier). Their work is extremely interesting and beginning to broaden our knowledge of children's everyday lives. Despite that, as with historical data from most sources, we learn very little about children's position in civil society.

There are notable exceptions like boy pharaohs, girl queens, child priests and other high ranking children whose remains and occasionally stories of their lives are discovered. They are, however, almost always exceptions to the rule and contribute little at best to a social history of childhood. Likewise, comparably recent developments in both biological and social anthropology have increased interest in children in all branches of the discipline. They now examine childhood from the prehistoric to contemporary world. History itself is often highly dependent on other disciplines. It is frequently interwoven with the descriptions of children or family life that were described by philosophers, theologians and poets. Whether these are selective or distorted by idealised descriptions is not as important as the fact that they are written and may be the only data available. Thus Socrates,[1] Plato, Confucius, Cicero, later on Thomas Aquinas, St Anselm and more recently John Locke, Jean-Jacques Rousseau are among the many proxies for exact historical sources.

This brief examination of history has thus been divided into two chapters. This chapter looks at the ancient world until the sixteenth century then Chap. 4 continues on to the present day. The former, rather more than the latter, attempts to present

[1] Nothing written by Socrates survives so that whilst much is attributed to him, all of 'his' work is either the work of Plato, Xenophon or a later interpreter.

B. Milne, *The History and Theory of Children's Citizenship in Contemporary Societies*, DOI 10.1007/978-94-007-6521-4_4, © Springer Science+Business Media Dordrecht 2013

a world overview. There are good reasons for this. Many of the perceptions of childhood we find today owe origins to older traditions that have only partially changed more recently. Thus it may be said that in a large part of the world the influences of Ibrahimic religions have been carried over into the modern world. To one degree or another, Christianity has not moved so very far from what Socrates was saying of children and in other places Hinduism and Confucianism have retained traditions from time well before inclusion would be at all relevant here.

However, it should be noted here that both Africa and the Americas particularly, but also other parts of the world receive scant, if any attention, in this history. In fact, those are the least influential parts of the world in a bigger picture. Africa, with exception of Islamic regions, has almost too many different histories. The great empires that include Ethiopia, Ghana, Mali and Munhumutapa (Zimbabwe) all comprised of many different people whose social organisation, beliefs and traditions were more diverse than would be practicable here. The many smaller nations, indeed even the smallest ones we sometimes refer to as 'tribes', are far too many to consider.

Nonetheless, apart from some exceptions, such as what we may know about child monarchs, little of substance about childhood is known. Much the same can be said for the pre-Columbian Americas and once we begin to have a picture of the great civilisations such as Aztec, Inca, Maya or Toltec again we lack real knowledge about children there. Those who survived the conquest of the Americas following Colombus' voyage of 1492 were originally described in what are often extensive accounts of 'savage' people written by missionaries and pioneer colonists. More recently they have been studied by mainly anthropologists and archaeologists who also tend not to say very much about children. Thus, seen historically neither Africa nor the Americas have a great deal of substance to offer in the context of this work although knowledge of older societies is an ongoing process that may well tell us more in years to come.

There are notable exceptions. Lee and DeVore's (1976) work on the !Kung San of the Kalahari is used in Chap. 8 because an entire section of their book (Part III) appears under the heading 'Childhood'. They were looking at the !Kung San as they were in the early 1970s, when they remained essentially a nomadic hunter-gatherer society as they had been for many centuries. The childhood observed by those anthropologists was almost certainly little changed over most, perhaps all, of the period covered by this chapter.

One of the common strands in historical study of western childhood is either notion of an 'emergence' or a 'disappearance'. It has been expressed in various ways. Cunningham (2006) calls it '*The Invention of Childhood*', Pollock (1983) uses '*Forgotten Children*', Ariès (1962) '*Centuries of Childhood*', Buckingham (2000) '*…Death of Childhood*' Postman (1982) '*The Disappearance of Childhood*' and deMause (1974) '*The History of Childhood*'. It is the question that arises out of either proposition that allows for an assumption that there was and is again a time when adulthood and childhood are inseparable that is more interesting. It is that possibility and its implications that justify the inclusion of history. It is thus a chronological examination of what is known and has been said about childhood rather than a reconsideration of historical data. One of the obvious difficulties is to know exactly where to begin in a roughly chronologically ordered examination of childhood. The ultimate aim of this work is to look at the possibility of children's full citizenship. Thus the question arises as to whether or not this has arisen in one form or another in the past. Any line of enquiry that pursues an exact answer to that question also needs to take into account different forms of citizenship or the absolute absence of a concept of a common membership of a society that can be understood as a form thereof.

The Classical Period

In order to not to move too far away from the intended outcome of this work into the realms of another equally intricate intellectual task, a starting point has been chosen to the exclusion of whatever is known about the period preceding that time. This beginning is sometime after 470 B.C., the birth of Socrates, and as it was recalled by Plato in his *Crito* (Κριτων).

In the *Crito* there is citation of Socrates explaining the passage of membership into citizenship thus: "…having granted the indulgence to any of the Athenians who may desire to use it as soon as he has arrived at the years of discretion and become acquainted with the business of the state…" (Stanford 1834:104). In his annotation Stanford notes that "At what age children were … enrolled does not appear; some suppose at one, others at three or four years old. …second enrolment was at eighteen" and again at "twenty years old". The process through which a child became a citizen was, in effect, entry in the register (*κοινόν γραμματεϊον*) of the ward (*φρατρία*) in which they resided along with an oath by both parents that the child was legitimately born or adopted, thus entitled to enjoy the full privileges of citizenship. The second enrolment was for ephebi (*εφηβος*) who were the young men, usually 18–20 years old, undergoing military training. The final enrolment was in a further register (*ληξιαρχικόν γραμματεϊον*) that entitled them to full civil rights that included freedom from the will of parents or guardians and to inherit from their fathers.

What we also learn from Plato in the *Crito* is that Socrates expressed a view that the state is to us as a parent is to a child. Given that it is always wrong for a child to disobey a parent, it is commonsense that it is always wrong to disobey the state. We could, of course, raise serious doubts about the legitimacy of an analogy between parents and the state. Obedience to our parents is after all only a temporary obligation we ultimately grow out of by learning to make decisions for ourselves. His argument was that obeying the state is an obligation for an entire lifetime (for instance, see Emlyn-Jones 1999).

Plato, again citing the assumed words of Socrates, wrote about differences in his Republic. In the Greece of his time it was assumed that natural differences between adult male and female members of the human race results in a significant segregation into appropriate social roles. Children, in Plato's view, should be further segregated from adults. His view is that the best interests of the state are served if children are brought up and educated by society as a whole rather than by natural parents. He proposed a simple scheme for the breeding, development and education of children of the guardian class.

Plato believed that the supposed pleasures of family life are among benefits that higher classes of society must be willing to relinquish. It is those children who in due course become guardians of the state. Their accomplishment at this level of education correctly ascertains whether they are qualified to do so and, if so, whether they deserve to be a leader or a soldier. Society should accordingly design its educational system as a measure by which to discriminate among those future citizens whose functions will be at variance and thus educate them appropriately to the capability of each. Thus we see that some children are allowed to watch and listen to 'dangerous' art whilst others are encouraged to directly observe the violence of war. Of course this is specific only to a particular class and does not extend to, for example, artisans or labourers who are citizens who should be ruled by the higher classes. Again this is example of an early example of recognition of children as future citizens rather than as being already part of their society.

Apart from Plato we know enough about the status of children to understand that it was not entirely dissimilar to what it is in the modern world.[2] However, Greek children tended not to go to school. Many children in ancient Athens, Corinth and other cities were, in fact, slaves therefore could not go to school in the first place. They would never be citizens anyway. Poor boys, including those who were free, could not go to school since their families could not afford to pay teachers. They usually needed sons at home to work, especially those of tradesmen who would be learning their future skill from fathers. Girls normally stayed at home with mothers until they were married. They either worked in the home or, among agriculture people, in the fields. Apart from that, there were no public schools.

Parents who had enough money did try to send their sons to school since not learning to read and write and having some general education meant there would have been little opportunity to participate in politics when they grew up. Boys began school when they were about seven and attended until about 13 years old. At school they generally learned to read and write and learned large amounts of Homer's *Iliad* and *Odyssey* by heart. Therewith they had basic skills for access to the political sphere which was always limited to those with literature and cultural skills and more often than not to those who were born privileged to begin with. They furthermore learned to play the lyre and pipes and also to sing (see Beaumont 2006; Golden 1990; Kamp 2001; Tames 2002).

The exception to other children in Hellenic antiquity was among the Spartans (see Cartledge 2001, 2002) whose family was quite different from that of the other city-states. The word 'Spartan' now describes a life of abstinence and minimalism

[2]This very brief description of children in Ancient Greece has been drawn together from the four texts listed where Plato and Socrates are not used. The fourth book was written for children as an educational text and provides much of the substance for this 'thumbnail sketch'.

in our terms, which is what Spartan life was essentially about. Their notions of family, childhood and citizenship were very different from modern, western understanding of these terms. Men and women did not live together although they married, but met occasionally for procreation. A wedding comprised of a ritualised physical fight which resulted in the man tossing the woman over his shoulder and taking her away. By the end of the fourth century BC there were more men than women in Sparta so that there was often more than one father of children or several men might even share a wife. Connubial love was discouraged and progeny were born children 'of the state' rather than of parents, raised to be soldiers or wives of soldiers, staunch supporters of the state and expected to be strong and self-disciplined. A mother's 'softening' influence was in fact deemed harmful to a boy's education.

When a baby was born, soldiers examined it assiduously to determine its strength. The child was bathed in wine instead of water to see how it reacted. If it was frail it was left on a hillside (to die) or taken away to become a slave (*helot*[3]). When a boy reached his seventh birthday he was enrolled in the *agoge* (military training) under the authority of the *paidonómos* (*παιδονόμος*), or 'boy-herder', a magistrate who supervised education. Nurses who did not indulge them took immediate charge of them. Boys were housed in a dormitory and began the first of the three stages of the *agoge*: *paides* (ages 7–17), *paidiskoi* (18–19) and *hebontes* (20–29). The boys lived in *agelai*, ('herds') under an older boy leader and were expected to give their loyalty to the communal mess hall rather than families. Boys were given one piece of clothing per year and made beds of reeds from the Eurotas River. They suffered austere physical discipline and denial to make them robust. They marched unshod, going without food for lengthy spells. They were intentionally underfed to master skills essential for foraging or stealing food. However, they were severely punished if caught. They developed their acumen as fighters, bearing pain and in survival skills. Older boys beat younger boys to toughen them up. Abstinence, frugality, the soldier's code, and loyalty to the city-state were their *raison d'être*. They were taught stories of courage and resilience.

At around age 12 boys entered into an institutionalised sexual relationship with a young adult male Spartan. It was a form of pederasty, whereby older soldiers would engage promising youths in long-lasting relationships with ostensibly educational objectives. Boys were expected to ask for these relationships which were seen as a means of passing on knowledge and upholding loyalty in war. At *paidiskoi*, around age 18 students became reserve members of the army. Promising students were taken to the *Crypteia*, a kind of festival to test skills by declaring war on *helots*, encouraging them to slay any who were out at night and steal their food. At the stage of *hebontes* they became full part of the *syssitia* and Spartan army after passing a rigorous test to graduate as full citizens. Only soldiers were received into the

[3]Helots farmed land owned by Spartans to remove the burden of sustaining Sparta from citizens of the city-state. This left them free to commit themselves to the art of war. Helots accompanied Spartans in battles and provide support as archers who Spartans thought of as not true warriors. They also set up camps and performed other work for the Spartans during campaigns.

'aristocratic' citizenry. If they failed tests they could not become citizens, but *perioeci*[4] which in contemporary terms was a kind of middle class. Thus to some extent class was based on merit rather than birth. When they passed, young men continued to live in barracks, train as soldiers and compete for a place among the Spartan *hippeis*, the royal guard of honour, and also required to marry to produce new young Spartans. The state gave them a piece of land which was cultivated by *helots* to provide income for their support so that they could remain full-time soldiers for another 10 years.

Girls were also removed from home at age 7 and sent to school where they learned dance, wrestling, gymnastics and underwent other physical training together with other subjects such as reading, writing and war education. Spartans believed that robust mothers produced strong children, thus young women competed in athletic events and probably partook nude as men did. Qualities such as grace and culture were frowned upon in favour of physical disposition and moral integrity. They wore the old-fashioned *peplos* (*πέπλος*) that was open at the side, leading to teasing by other Greeks who nicknamed them *phainomerides,* (*φαινομηρίδες*) or 'thigh showers'. During religious ceremonies, holidays and physical exercise girls and women were naked. When they passed citizenship tests at age 18–20 and when they were emotionally mature and closer to the age of future husbands they were expected to marry. In preparation for her wedding a woman's hair was cut short and she was dressed in male clothing. Afterwards the husband returned to his all-male barracks.

Thus childhood was seen as a preparation for particular roles in Spartan society. Those who were rejected perished or were enslaved early in life. Those who failed tests never achieved full citizenship and only those who fulfilled all criteria for full membership enjoyed all privileges. Childhood was preparation for adulthood which was more or less synonymous with citizenship. Thus childhood was 'potential citizenship' but not 'citizen-becomings' because achieving full recognition was not ensured. However those who became *helots* almost certainly became like other slaves who had no exact status in this regard. *Perioeci* were probably far more comparable with a modern European 'blue collar class', although those who had failed tests were probably a very different kind of adult to those born *perioeci*.

From these early descriptions of the transition from childhood to adulthood in the Hellenic world of around 400 BC we learn two important things. Firstly, when children are referred to it most frequently means male children rather than both sexes. Secondly, what Plato tells us about is a transition that gives only partial citizenship at the first stage which is a notion that will be revisited at a later stage when looking at Locke, later Durkheim and more recently Qvortrup. In further examination of

---

[4] *Perioeci*, or perioikoi, were the members of a self-governing group of free but non-citizen inhabitants of the Perioikis (*Περίοικις*) territory that belonged to the Lacedaemonian State within Sparta. They were the only people allowed to travel to other cities, which Spartans could not without permission. They had the right to own land and belonged to the army without being part of the aristocratic warrior class. They could neither participate in political decisions nor marry Spartans.

antiquity there are various conditions that we can roughly compare with class structures in the modern world and the privileges enjoyed by a minority in upper echelons until the nineteenth and early twentieth century.

Asian Philosophies and Beliefs

An emergent culture almost contemporary with the philosophy of Socrates and Plato is Confucianism (Oldstone-Moore: 316–332, 362–371 and 406–15). Its founder K'ung Fu Tzu (Latinised as Confucius) lived from 551 until 479 BC. He was a social philosopher in China whose teachings have profoundly influenced East Asia for at least the last 24 centuries, albeit it is sometimes held that the relationship between Confucianism and Confucius is for the largest part tenuous.

One of the central themes of Confucianism is that of relationships and various duties arising from different statuses held by individuals in relation to others. Those individuals are held to concurrently have different degrees of relationship with different people. Notably, they are junior in relation to parents and elders and senior in relation to their own children, younger siblings and all other people of lesser age. It is considered that juniors owe strong duties of veneration and duties to elders. They, in turn, have duties of benevolence and responsibility toward juniors. In one form or another, contemporary versions of this belief permeate many aspects of East and Southeast Asian culture to the present day.

There are extensive filial obligations on the part of children toward parents and elders and profound sense of responsibility of parents toward their children. Filiality (*xiào* or *hsiao*; 孝) is considered among the greatest of virtues and must be shown towards both the living and dead. Filial itself means 'of a child[5]' and represents the respect and obedience that a child should show to parents and especially his or her father. This relationship was described as a sequence of five principal relationships (*Wŭlún* 五倫). Those are between ruler and subject, father and son, husband and wife, elder and younger brother and finally between friends. Particular duties were prescribed between participants in each of these relationships. Those duties also applied to the dead since the living are considered children (sons) of their ancestors. Stafford (1995) describes two different paths to adulthood in Confucian society. By the first, children are 'persons' from the moment of conception and growing is a natural process that needs to be protected as they grow and mature. The second sees them as formless and without competence and as growing persons who must learn the Confucian ideal of filial piety and deference to arrive at full adulthood. Stafford explains thus:

> There is not so much a problem with Chinese children *becoming* something, as with them *remaining* something. The underlying assumption is that children are, were, and will forever be persons... The emphasis is (...) not on making them social, but instead on protecting

[5]Literally it is 'of a son' but has become a generic term much like the use of 'he', 'him' and 'his' that have been used as generic for children, even where the gender is known, for many years and, indeed, 'man' for the human species.

> a natural process and on emphasising certain forms of identification. …this exists alongside another more "Confucian" view (…) in which children are in the process of becoming persons (Stafford 1995:18)

In the fullness of time, filiality was incorporated into the Chinese legal system. A criminal was traditionally punished more severely when somebody had committed a crime against a parent. In general, fathers have always exercised great power over children. The same tends to be found in other age biased relationships where elders are involved. Thus, we again see that in the most populous areas of Asia children have not occupied a position in which a notion of the child citizen finds substance. In fact, as we also see in the Occident, they are 'human becomings'. Indeed, a great deal of what has survived for well over 20 centuries tells us what a society which now appears to be increasingly assimilating life in the western world was like historically (see also: Ivanhoe 2000; Yao 2000).

Siddhārtha Gautama (*circa* 556/563-476/483 BC) who we know as the Buddha (*Gautama Buddha*), founder of the Buddhist philosophy (see Eckel 2000:110–29) was a contemporary of Confucius who died in 478. Buddhism and Confucianism often coexist and have shaped life in much of East and Southeast Asia. Buddhism itself does not itself precisely describe an ethos of intergenerational relations but initially introduced practices from the older Hindu ideology. Siddhārtha was himself born into that religion and incorporated numerous other tribal practices into his doctrine. Thus we find beliefs about family values that may sometimes appear to contradict each other elsewhere but correspond or occasionally overlap throughout the Buddhist, Confucian and Hindu world.

However one of the most pervasive values in all three philosophies is that the main purpose of marriage is to make and raise children. They are not only important in their own right but ensure extension of family lineage and are there to perform last rites for parents. In general, Hinduism places emphasis on children being loved and never neglected. Indeed, the first part of the ancient *Bhagavad Gita* touches on moral and social problems caused by unwanted children (see Coburn 1984 or Cornille 2006). Hindu texts expressed disapproval of contraception, proposing that children be wanted rather than sex being primarily for pleasure. Children, therefore, have always been most certainly very much included in the sense that for a parent duty is to their child to provide a home, warmth, food, clothes and education. In return, a child is duty bound to show gratitude to parents, work hard to make the best of his education and respect the people who provide for him or her.

Despite a great concern for the well-being and benevolent rearing of children there is little to suggest that in the past, or indeed in the development of these philosophies up to the present day, that children have ever enjoyed any manner of position that may be understood as making them in any way comparable with or equal to adults. Needless to say, where caste systems such as Hindu *varnas* with further classifications such as *jati* have ever shaped social status or are still present, it is not remarkable that the adult-child distinction is less obvious given that a child of a specific caste status may be of higher social rank than an adult of a another caste. Furthermore, Hinduism is complex and really refers to people of particular caste, community, region and language rather than a single religion or ideology. Narayanan (2005:11) says that:

> In Indian law, the term 'Hindu' may even include those who belong to traditions usually thought of as theologically distinct from Hinduism. It is generally applied to anyone who lives in India and accepts the Hindu tradition – which is not defined – in any of its forms or developments. This therefore embraces Buddhists, Jains, and Sikhs.

Thus, when looking at India rather than Hinduism itself a combination of caste, community (ethnic group) and region together with particular Hindu practices provide example without the complexity of attempting to portray a single typology. Fuller (1976) and Agarwal (1994) describe the Nayars of Kerala, a Hindu upper caste who were traditionally prominent in medicine, education, law, politics and government service. Prior to British occupation of Kerala in 1792 the region contained small, feudal kingdoms. Each had royal and noble lineages, a militia and most land administrators were exclusively drawn from the Nayars and related castes. At the beginning of the British occupation their armies were disbanded. Partly as a result of that, their tradition of plural marital unions gradually died out by the end of the nineteenth century. Laws passed in the 1930s imposed monogamy on them and permitted division of what had traditionally been matrilineal estates among male and female members. Thereby children were also given full rights of maintenance and inheritance from the father.

Thus the very different practices that had described an entirely different form of social organisation changed. It was one in which we would identify a very different kind of 'citizenship' that was determined by and included brothers and sisters, the latter's children, and their daughters' children and lineage. The oldest man was always legal head of the group. By the middle of the twentieth century it was increasingly common, especially among urban families, for nuclear families to form separate residential and economic units away from matrilineal joint-families. Furthermore, Fuller (*Ibid.*) draws particular attention to other issues such as the impact of the changing modern market economy, disappearance of traditional military training and assimilation of new values through the late and post-colonial system of education. A new consciousness was engendered by lower castes with their demand for equality and equal constitutional rights. Thus, Nayars began to adapt to the modern world.

To all intents and purposes they often appear part of contemporary, rather westernised life. However, beneath the veneer of modern ways many of the old practices and rituals define who they are. Children are less 'free' than we understand in western terms, thus usually experience lives that are ranked by traditional structures, governed by practice and are substantively unlike occidental standards that describe how and when full membership of society, citizenship, precisely begins. India, even today, with numerous differences of origin, caste, religion and understanding of their own democracy essentially bridges time between European antiquity and contemporary western civil society.

Whilst eastern philosophies and their cultural imprint have continued to shape the historical development of the family, the importance of the philosophy of western antiquity began to decline in influence. They were eventually to be a significant influence on each of the main Ibrahimic theologies as they increased in importance.

Whereas western philosophies tell us about the emergent socio-political world that continued to exist in one form or another throughout the Roman Republic and later Empire, their historians, social commentators and philosophers were little concerned with children or any other aspect of family and social life. Strabo (*circa* 63 or 64 BC to 24 AD), for instance, looked at people and social organisation in much of the world known to the Roman Empire to the degree that his description of the Indian caste system is reasonably recognisable today.

The Romans

What we do know about Roman childhood[6] is that it was more or less as connected with status and class as it was in Greece (Rawson 1991, 2005). When a child was born he or she was laid at the father's feet. If the newborn child was raised in his arms it was acknowledged as his and given access to all rights and privileges of membership in that family. Birth registration was a requirement from sometime during the reign of Marcus Aurelius (121–180; emperor from 161 to death) onward. The father was required to register his child's name and date of birth within 30 days (Schulz 1943). However, a boy was not enrolled as a full citizen until he put on a man's toga. When a boy came of age varied, depending to some extent to physical and intellectual development but otherwise on his father's decision. That also appears to have depended on the period in which a boy lived. By and large, a man's toga was donned between the 14th and 17th years whereby a higher age was customary in earlier times. In the classical period the boy's age was by and large about 16 years.

Girls, on the other hand, were as their mothers, women who were a class apart whose status in Roman society altered over time. Roman women were not allowed to vote or enter civil and public office since they were, theoretically, subject to the almost total power of their *paterfamilias*. In many respects they were little more than slaves although the interrelationship of social 'classes' would, in fact, add another dimension of this notion.

Social and moral education and training was largely carried out by parents. The emphasis was on moral rather than intellectual development. The most essential qualities for a child to acquire were reverence for gods, respect for the law, absolute and instant deference to authority, honesty and personal independence. Education (school) was left to parents' discretion and lasted until about age 7. Boys and girls were taught to speak Latin correctly and do elementary reading, writing and arithmetic. The 12 tablets of law were learned by rote.

[6]The brief recount of children in the Roman Republic and Empire has been drawn together from seven texts: Albasi (1991), Dixon (2001), Evans (1991), Rawson (1991, 2005), Schulz (1943) and Wiedemann (1989). In fact, most of them are primarily concerned with *patria potestas*, whereby as head of the family a father had power over his wife, slaves, house and other personal and family property including the power to sell a child into slavery as well as holding power over life and death known as *ius vitae ac necis* in the early Empire. Although most titles infer direct reference, little is said about children themselves leaving a very selective précis the most appropriate means of examining all that may be salient for this work.

In the early period of the Empire, education was left to both parents but gradually became more a duty of mothers and sometimes specially hired slaves. Additional education was limited to wealthier families who could afford a tutor and keep the child from working. Whenever possible, a boy would go to a regular teacher but a girl became her mother's companion. Formal education was nearly always discontinued because girls married early and needed to learn about home management. Girls learned to sew, spin and weave from mothers. Boys were trained by fathers. If a father was a farmer, a son would learn to plough, plant and harvest. When fathers were of high status their sons stood beside them in the *atrium* when visitors were received. That facilitated them acquiring first-hand knowledge of political affairs that would enable them to be full citizens. Fathers also trained sons in use of weapons, military exercises, riding, swimming, wrestling and a form of boxing for manhood and time they would probably spend doing military service.

Full citizenship was effectively dependent on one hand on age and gender and on the other on status such as social class and whether or not an individual was free in the first place. However, in the later days of the Roman Empire Christianity began to shape the organisation of the family that would eventually become the modern model for a large part of the world. It had developed for the most part from the family structure of the ancient Hebrews that was patriarchal and monogamous. The type of family that emerged from Greco-Roman culture was also patriarchal and governed by strict religious principles. As Greek and later Roman civilisations declined so did their highly ordered family life but what remained was the importance of the union of man and woman and their children as the 'nucleus' of the social unit. Christianity made marriage and procreation central concerns in religious teaching. Children became the issue of the sin that made them. Other influences and several centuries during which we know little about childhood came at the end of the Western Roman Empire in 476. The Byzantine Empire retained Roman legal and cultural traditions in a markedly Christian form for about a further 1,000 years until giving way to the Ottoman Empire in 1453 when Constantinople fell. Therewith over 2,000 years of continual 'Roman' history[7] came to an end (Treadgold 1997).

---

[7]The Latins are estimated to have settled in the wider area of Rome around 1000 BC. The Greeks were settling southern Italy, founding cities like Cumae and Tarentum, brought their form of civilisation to the country and it was from them that the Romans learned basic skills such as reading and writing with even religion derived from Greek mythology (i.e. Jupiter is Zeus, Venus is Aphrodite, etc.). The Etruscans to the north of Rome in Etruria (modern Tuscany) were primarily an urban society. Their substantial wealth came from seaborne trade. Although the Romans considered Etruscans to be decadent and weak they were highly influential in formation of Roman society. Although a distinct society the Etruscans owed much of their culture to the Greeks. Around 650–600 BC the Etruscans crossed the Tiber and occupied Latium (part of modern Lazio). Latium is considered to be the cradle of the Roman Empire and Rome. The Islamic Turks considered themselves proper heirs to the Byzantine Empire until the demise of the Ottoman Empire in the early twentieth century. However, the heirs to the Eastern Orthodoxy who became the Tsars of Russia (*tsar*, or *czar*, derives from the Latin *caesar*) held a view that Moscow was the rightful successor to Rome and Constantinople. The notion of the Russian Empire as the 'Third Rome' continued until the Russian Revolution in 1917 thus extending the possibility another 460 or so years.

The purely religious nature of family relations that was once Roman, but later became the Roman Catholic Church's dogma, more or less persisted until the Reformation. Given the continued patriarchal structure of the family, despite lack of precise knowledge about children's lives there are few reasons for assuming they assumed any form of status that one could describe as adult-like.

The Early Middle Ages

With the end of the Western Roman Empire, the influence of the ancient order in Europe declined. The period known as the European Early Middle Ages, from about 476 to roughly 1,000, is one of the periods we know least about. All of the Eurasian landmass saw change through migration, invasion and historically speaking rapid transition that had a profound effect on social structures. A corresponding period, known as the Migration Period (also called 'barbarian invasions' or 'Völkerwanderungen'),[8] largely occurred within a period from about 300 to 700 during the transition from Late Antiquity to the Early Middle Ages. During the latter years of Roman occupation much of Western Europe had been Christianised. This was maintained by Germanic Visigoths who conquered much of Spain, France, southern Germany, the Alpine region and Italy.

Eurasian Huns who occupied large parts of the eastern Empire displaced Christianity and the established social order of centuries of Roman occupation. From about 360 onward 'pagan' Germanic people began to invade and settle in parts of Roman Britain. After the Roman Emperor Honorius withdrew the last legions from Britain in 410, 'Anglo-Saxons' progressively consolidated their foothold in the British Isles. During eighth to tenth centuries, although not customarily counted as part of the Migration Period and despite being within the Early Middle Ages, new waves of migration of the Magyars, later Turkic peoples and then the Viking expansion from Scandinavia threatened the newly established order of the Frankish Empire in Central Europe.

In East and Southeast Asia a great deal of movement and change similarly affected social environments. The Khmer Empire was consolidated in 802 (Dagens 1995, 2003). There the next 600 years were to see the wide variety of belief systems and tribal practices brought closer together to form a relatively cohesive regional culture lasting until colonialism began in the nineteenth century. At first the empire's official religions included Hinduism and Mahayana Buddhism until Theravada Buddhism became more significant after introduction from Sri Lanka in the thirteenth century. Confucian influence was also very strong since large parts of the region south of the modern Chinese border were under Khmer control until well into the tenth century.

---

[8]The migration included the Ostrogoths, Visgoths, Huns, Vandals, Franks, Alans, Suebi and other Germanic, Persian (Iranian) and Slavic groups.

In China[9] the Tang Dynasty (618–907) gave way to the Five Dynasties and Ten Kingdoms until the Song Dynasty (960–1297) reunited much of what is modern China. Song Neo-Confucian philosophers found particular integrity in the imagination of ancient classical texts and wrote commentaries on them. The most influential was Zhu-Xi (1130–1200) whose blend of Confucian thought with Buddhist, Taoist and other ideas became official imperial ideology from the late Song period until the end of the nineteenth century (Berthrong 1998:109ff). His philosophy evolved into an uncompromising official doctrine placing emphasis on the one-sided obligations of acquiescence of each subject to the ruler. Under that nomenclature child to father, wife to husband and younger brother to elder brother were all subject to the same principles. This inhibited societal development in pre-modern China that affected the position of children through to the present day. Neo-Confucian doctrines also came to play a dominant role in intellectual life in Japan, Korea and Viet Nam with strands of influence throughout Southeast Asia into parts of modern Indonesia and Malaysia.

During the seventh century the Prophet Muhammad founded Islam (see Graham 2006; Nasr 2003). *Sharia* law ('well trodden path') determined by traditional Islamic scholarship and using the Qur'an as the principal source of jurisprudence reinterpreted older Jewish and Christian principles and established an Islamic family life in which children are categorically subject to adult, particularly paternal, authority. In fact there are very few significant sources shedding light on how and what medieval Muslims thought about children and families. What little is available tends to offer insights into physical needs of children, actions for fulfilment of those requirements and advice for parents grieving the loss of children. However legal treatises on marriage offer a few details obliquely related to childhood. The most useful ones integrate Qur'anic pronouncements and the word of the Prophet on marriage, women, children and family life. There is no apparent paradigm of the child and childhood in the classical period of medieval Islam. Indeed, if anything Islam appears to have generally been more concerned with adults and where children are mentioned tends to see them as beneficiaries of the actions of parents.

The Middle Ages

During the lengthy period described thus far, relatively little is known about childhood generally, most certainly less about the status of children. In Western Europe, England particularly, a little information survives to tell us about adult attitudes toward children during the Anglo-Saxon period from about 500 to 1066. Some archaeological work found burials where children had grave goods like adults.

[9]Trying to condense China's history into appropriate form for this work, thus covering approximately 5,000 years with comparatively little reference to children appears a Sisyphus task, therefore a single book, John King Fairbank's *China: a new history* (1992) has been used for this and later chapters except where any direct reference to other authors may be required.

Knowledge about adult attitudes develops when we examine the twelfth century which was an age of law-making by both the Roman Church and lay society. Law making included specific arrangements for children who could not be expected to bear the same responsibilities and penalties as adults. Medieval law-makers usually demarked the transition from childhood to adulthood at puberty. Through baptism a child was received into the Church and freed from the burden of original sin. Infancy lasted up to the age of 7 years, *pueritia* or childhood traditionally until age 12 years for girls and 14 years for boys.

The Church usually led the way in deciding the distinction between childhood and adulthood based on notions inherited from Greek and Roman authorities on the stages of life. It regarded pre-pubertal children too immature to commit sin or comprehend adult concepts. Accordingly they were not allowed to marry, exempted from confession to priests and excluded from partaking in the sacrament of the Eucharist. Secular justice developed a similar concept of age of legal accountability beginning about puberty, although there are accounts of children receiving adult punishments (see Crawford 1999).[10] There is generally little that leads to believe that children really may have been considered 'little adults' as some historians maintain (e.g.: Ariès 1962; deMause 1974). Childhood was not thought as imperative as we now consider it in formation of personality and character. Nevertheless, there was scope for consideration on how it was best to bring up a child.

One account gives a sketchy insight into an example of how children were seen. It tells how St Anselm, Archbishop of Canterbury from 1093 to 1109 (Southern 1972), came to be considered a 'pioneer' of child protection. The story tells how an abbot told Anselm about difficulties he was having raising boys entrusted to his care. The abbot was authoritarian and beat boys for every transgression. Anselm could not restrain his distaste for their treatment and chastised the abbot for unjust and violent treatment of the boys, saying that kindness and reason would always prevail. Anselm's views were commonly quoted into the late Middle Ages. The resultant debate 'spare the rod and spoil the child' persisted until the late twentieth century and subsequently prohibition of corporal punishment in schools in an ever increasing number of countries. That tells us very little about childhood itself beyond the treatment of boys. It at least contributes to putting paid to the idea that in the Middle Ages and much of the time thereafter children were essentially 'little adults'. They were very clearly not and childhood was undoubtedly identifiable as being unambiguously a set of stages in the life cycle.

When we come to *conduct books* about two centuries later, the contradictory nature of the 'little adult' stance becomes clearer. Whilst children were expected to behave *like* adults, probably contributed a great deal to the economic survival of most households and had particular responsibilities, a conclusion we may

[10] This naturally depended on the nature of the offence and who was trying a child. However, for crimes such as arson, burglary, theft, murder or treason the only punishment was death and forfeit of property to the king. The Church advocated mutilation, as this gave the guilty person a chance to make amends for a crime in this world and thus save his soul. Children were occasionally mutilated or put to death for the most serious crimes.

extrapolate from an example like Anselm is that children were then as now being 'brought up'. There was clearly a notion of transitions from infancy to adulthood that may be obscured behind the reality of contributing to domestic tasks, possibly other non-domestic work and the measure of responsibility (Icher 2002) they bore that probably demanded more 'adult-like' behaviour in many situations. These perceptions are also very culturally conditioned and where a thesis such as Ariès tends to be right is within a narrow European context among those whose lives were observed and recorded who tended to have belonged to an equally narrow social stratum of their society. Exactly as in the contemporary world, childhood would always be different from one place to another and in accord with conditions at particular points in time.

The Mongol Empire

Across Asia and parts of Europe the Mongol Empire (1206–1405)[11] extended influence from Western China and Japan to the eastern edges of Hungary, Poland and Lithuania, across the north of Russia and Siberia and down well into the Levantine, Persia, India and Southeast Asia. The Mongol Nation began as a group of disparate tribes in what we now call Mongolia. The man who united them was born with the name Temüjin (*circa* 1167–1221) in the Borjigin clan. At around age 9 his tribal leader father, Yesugai Bat'atur was poisoned, after which his household was driven away by his clan who thought he was too young to rule. He became leader of his family under his mother's guidance. At one stage in his childhood he was carried off by a rival clan but escaped after a few months. At age 16 he married and began his career as a leader.

Whilst Temüjin was still 16 the Merkid tribe attacked his family and carried off his wife. With his small force of five men he could not retaliate, so turned to one of his father's old allies, Toghrul Khan of the Kereyid tribe. He, in turn, enlisted Jamugha and his men. Together they defeated the Merkids so that Temüjin recovered his wife. It was over 20 years later aged over 40 that he brought the clans together to form the Mongol nation. By then he had been given the title Genghis Khan. Whilst he had been a young leader, most of his famed leadership accumulated in adulthood. There is little to suggest that among the Mongols or in their areas of influence children enjoyed any great privilege. However the influence of the Mongol Empire was that three great religions, Buddhism, Christianity and Islam, were permanently to be the most influential across the entire landmass. With them their moral influence was formative in how societies were structured (Marshall 1993; Weatherford 2004).

[11] There are many versions of the story of the Mongols and Genghis Khan. This brief examination uses spelling as per Marshall (1993), and uses a combination of that work with Weatherford (2004), rather than a more exhaustive examination of a large number of books. The purpose here is an example rather than an 'exact' history.

Urban Awareness

Italy was very influential in the development and change in Europe (see Duggan 1994:31–59). After the fall of the Roman Empire there was concerted urban awareness in northern Italy that had declined in importance in other parts of Europe. Some Italian cities and institutions were survivors of earlier Etruscan and Roman towns which had existed within the Roman Empire and the republican institutions of Rome had also survived. There were still some feudal lords with well-ordered labour forces and vast territories. By the eleventh century a number of cities such as Florence, Genoa, Milan and Venice had become large trading conurbations which had been able to win independence from monarchies. Italy between the twelfth and thirteenth centuries had been very different from feudal European countries to the north of the Alps. It was essentially a peninsula, geographically divided into many small regions by mountain ranges that made inter-city communication difficult and a patchwork of cultural and political territories rather than a unified state.

The city states that survived longest were in the least accessible and best defended regions, such as Florence and Venice. Since attacks over the Alps were complicated, Teutonic invaders found it difficult to apply sustained control over Italian vassal states so that they were largely free of Germanic political incursions. Thus strong monarchies did not emerged as easily as they did in the rest of Europe. The independent city state emerged instead. While Roman, urban and republican feelings endured there were numerous movements and changes taking place. Italy had initially felt the changes in Europe from the eleventh to thirteenth centuries. The influences borne on Italy were rise in population which doubled during the period and emergence of vast cities (Florence, Milan and Venice each had over 100,000 inhabitants and others such as Bologna, Genoa and Verona exceeded 50,000) by the High Middle Ages.

There was considerable rural to urban migration making Italy the most urbanised place in the world when the urban population arrived at around 20 %. There was also an agrarian revolution and rapid development of commerce. It has been estimated that *per capita* income in northern Italy nearly tripled from the eleventh to fifteenth century. It was a very mobile, demographically expanding society that was invigorated by rapidly growing trade throughout the Renaissance. By the thirteenth century, northern and central Italy had become the most literate society in the world. At least one third of men and a smaller but nonetheless significant number of women were able to read in vernacular languages.

During the eleventh century in northern Italy the city state or commune had emerged as a new political and social structure. The civic culture that arose in those cities was extraordinary. In other places such as Britain and Flanders where communes had arisen they usually were merged into powerful monarchies as they emerged. Almost exceptionally they survived in northern and central Italy to become independent and powerful city states. Their breakaway from feudal lords had occurred in the late twelfth and early thirteenth centuries during the Investiture Controversy between the Pope and Emperor. Milan led the Lombard cities against the Holy Roman Emperors to gain independence. Meanwhile Genoa and Venice were able to establish powerful naval empires on the Mediterranean. By the end of the twelfth century a new and distinctive society had emerged that was rich, mobile and expanding. It had a mixed aristocracy that was interested in urban institutions and republican government. However many city-states had within them a violent society that was based on family, association and affiliations that destabilised cohesion. By 1,300 most of these republics had become principalities dominated by a Lord (*Signore*). The exceptions included Florence, Lucca and Venice that remained republics despite an increasingly monarchic Europe.

The Children's Crusades

At about the same time as waves of Mongol hordes were sweeping through Asia, the fifth to ninth, and final, 'Crusades' were fighting against Islamic rule of the 'Holy Land'. The Crusades were, in fact, a series of military campaigns of a religious character waged by Christians from 1095 to 1291 (Riley-Smith 2001:66; Setton et al. 2005) and usually sanctioned by the Pope in the name of Christendom. The objective was to 'liberate' Jerusalem and the sacred 'Holy Land' and bring them back under Christian influence. They were originally called for[12] in response to a plea from the Eastern Orthodox Byzantine Empire to help quell expansion of the Islamic Seljuq dynasty into Anatolia.[13] In the thirteenth century there were several crusades, two of them in 1212 were said to be 'children's crusades'.

Children's Crusades were not exactly military campaigns but something more of the nature of popular uprisings that began in France and Germany. The probable intent was to march to the Holy Land in order to peacefully convert Moslems to Christianity. There appear to have been two movements of (young) people in France and Germany. Similarities between the two led to later chroniclers and consequently historians merging them into a single account. The first appears to have been led by Nicholas, a German shepherd from near Cologne, who led a group across the Alps into Italy during spring 1212 (Raedts 1977:279–323). About 7,000 young crusaders reached Genoa in late August. Unfortunately their plans fell apart when the waters of the Mediterranean failed to part as they expected and the crusade disbanded. Some went home, others possibly to Rome and some allegedly travelled down the

[12] Pleas for help from the Byzantine Emperors began in about the 1060s although the first actions against the Islamic forces were against the Moors by Iberian Christians in what is now Spain. Pleas made during the 1070s after the fall of most of Anatolia (modern Turkey) except for the area around Constantinople and another small part of western Anatolia. The first Crusade was preached in 1095 after the first successful reoccupation of Toledo by the Iberians.

[13] Pleas from Byzantine Emperors who were threatened by the Seljuks originally fell on deaf ears. When in 1074 Emperor Michael VII appealed to Pope Gregory VII and again in 1095 Emperor Alexios I Komnenos appealed to Pope Urban II the position changed and may have adopted a stance similar to 1063 when Pope Alexander II, had blessed Iberian Christians' for their wars against Muslim Moors.

Rhône to Marseilles. It is said that some were sold into slavery. Only a few returned home and none ever reached the Holy Land (Munro 1914).

During the same spring the story has it that in the middle of a field near Cloyes in France, a boy of 12 years called Stephen was tending sheep (see Runciman 1951: 139–144). A stranger who he recognised was Jesus, approached and spoke to Stephen. Jesus explained that the (adult) crusades had failed because the hearts of the soldiers were impure. He told Stephen to lead a new crusade of the most pure of believers – children. Stephen was promised that his crusade would succeed because the waters of the Mediterranean would part so they could cross directly to the Holy Land. Stephen went to Saint-Denis where he began to tell his story to anyone who would listen. The story had a profound effect. Crowds gathered, listened and allegedly had no problem believing that past crusades were tainted by impure hearts. They found the proposition that children might succeed where bad adults had failed reasonable.

By June 1212 30,000 children had gathered in Vendôme located on a Roman road leading to the port of Marseilles. The large number of children appears to have marched to and fro in France until disease, exhaustion and disillusion depleted them to about 700. Two merchants 'rescued' the crusade and provided seven ships. During the voyage a storm wrecked two ships and all children including Stephen were lost. The remaining children were taken to Alexandria and sold into slavery. It was approximately 30 years before news of the children reached France, by which time it was far too late for them.

By some accounts it was said that as many as 50,000 children set out in the combined French and German crusades, of those only around 10,000 were ever accounted for again. Nicholas was hung (Runciman 1951:142). Of course, we know little about the children. One possibility is that they were not children at all. In the early thirteenth century bands of wandering poor appeared throughout Europe (see Zacour 2005:332–41; Raedts 1977). They were peasants displaced by economic change which compelled many poor people in France and Germany to sell their land. They were often referred to as *pueri* (Latin for 'boys') in a disdainful fashion by chroniclers which may have lent much of the substance to many of the stories. It would appear that bands of itinerant poor may have merged into a religious protest movement, thus transforming their enforced march into a 'religious journey'. If the *pueri* marched behind the Cross and associated themselves to Christ's journey in the Bible then it would have been very easy to call them 'Crusaders' in line with popular imagination of that time. In reality there is little consistency in any account of the Children's Crusades and less to suggest they were children if any part of either account is at all true.

Medieval Children

Some of the most valuable explanations of how children and youth lived in Western Europe appear in *conduct books* mainly written between 1300 and 1500. They tell us that two dominant behaviours of children are either 'behaving' or 'misbehaving'. The books give an overview of how children and young people were perceived in various social and domestic situations since the literature describes the propagation of representative perceptions of the 'ideal' child. In early fourteenth century literature particularly, emphasis was on courteous behaviour and conduct of children as they carried out specific tasks. Those included serving in privileged households, how they used public spaces such as the street and how they interacted socially. That literature develops the notion of ideal behaviour of children characterised by the figure of male child servants who lived and worked within elite households. They generally expressed concern with behaviour through repetition of rules on manners, public conduct and how to follow a consistent set of procedures. Those would combine to exemplify the model 'courteous' child. A very good example is *How the Goode Man Taght Hys Sone* (Salisbury 2002) that illustrates particularly well that sons were subject to the will and wishes of fathers rather than being, by any means, little adults. Another example is *Symon's Lesson of Wisdom for all Manner of Children* (Opie and Opie 1959) from *circa* 1,500 that very precisely described how children were expected to conduct themselves and, above all, "worship they father and thy mother".

St Anselm, Thomas Aquinas (1225–1274) as well as other theologians and Christian philosophers gave rise to implications that filter right on through into the work of Kant and later Hegel. Is this a clear historical point for the end of the notion of 'little adults' and separable childhood and adulthood? Probably not, since the readership of those books was limited to the essentially small number of people who were literate and had access to books in the first place.

There were boy bishops and Festivals of Misrule throughout the occidental Christian world. The custom of electing a boy bishop on the feast of St Nicholas dates (see for instance ecclesiastic website sources such as *The Catholic Encyclopedia*) from very early times and was in vogue in most Catholic countries, although chiefly in England. It prevailed in all larger monastic and scholastic establishments as well as many country parishes with the full consent of civil and ecclesiastical authorities. A boy bishop was selected from a monastery school, cathedral choir or pupils of a grammar school. He was elected on St Nicholas's Day, 6 December, dressed in clerical vestments, followed in procession round the parish by his companions in priest's robes to bless the people. He then occupied the church to officiate at all ceremonies and offices until Holy Innocents Day on 28 December.

In Scotland the Abbot of Unreason and in France the *Prince des Sots* was an officer appointed during Advent to preside over the Feast of Fools or Festival of Misrule. The Lord of Misrule was a boy appointed to be in charge of Christmas revelry, including drunkenness and wild parties as in the pagan *Saturnalia*. In England the custom was abolished by Henry VIII in 1512, restored by Queen Mary and again abolished by Elizabeth I. In practice it lingered on longer. Across mainland Europe it was suppressed by the Council of Basle in 1431 but revived in some places from time to time until as late as the eighteenth century. It was essentially no more than a symbolic office preceding Holy Innocents Day that conferred no real power on any boy.

We know very little about young people as individuals during this period. One of the exceptions is Joan of Arc (Jeanne d'Arc) who was a peasant girl born in Domrémy in eastern France who laid claim to divine guidance to lead the French to victory during the Hundred Years War (1337–1453) between England and France for the throne of and which in turn lead to the foundation of what has become modern France (for instance see Warner 1983, Part One, Chapters 1 and 2). Joan was born in 1412[14] and lived only to the age of 19 years[15] when she was executed. At age 16 it is said that she asked a relative to bring her to see a garrison commander, Count Robert de Baudricourt to gain access to the French royal court at Chinon. She was initially refused, but returned a few months later and gained support of Jean de Metz and Bertrand de Poulengy. With their backing had a meeting at which she made an extraordinary prediction about the reverse in French military fortune near Orléans. The prediction came true. She successfully turned the long-standing Anglo-French conflict into a holy war.

Her military 'career' lasted only 12 months between May 1429 and the May of the following year when she was captured. One year later on 30 May 1431 she was burned at the stake in Rouen for heresy. Since then she has since been pardoned, declared a martyr and later canonised and is considered a model of French patriotism. In fact, her cause was neither of loyalty to her country or people but to God in the pursuit of justice for France in his name. She was also on the upper edge of what we would consider youth at the time of the events that shaped her story. However, the visions she claimed to have had clearly began at a lower age thus a little more justifying her inclusion here. In October 1429, after Joan lead in taking Saint-Pierre-le-Moûtier, she was granted nobility which should have given her what would have served as full citizen's rights at that time. There are, unfortunately, no historic accounts as to whether or not that played any significant role in her life. For the purposes of this work she is more anecdotally that substantially interesting, mainly because of her being at the upper age limit. Despite that, she is one of the few young lives recorded during this period and thus serves as an exemplar of the potential young lives held at that time.

The Black Death

However, other forces contributed to change. A ruinous *bubonic plague* pandemic began in south-western Asia and spread to Europe where it appeared in Sicily in 1347. It became known as the Black Death. Each successive wave of the plague killed between a quarter and two-thirds of Europe's population[16] and, including the

---

[14] Some authors avoid giving an exact date and rely on estimates made at the time of her execution in 1431 (e.g. Warner 1983) whereas others accept 6 January 1412 on the basis of a letter written by Lord Perceval de Boullainvilliers in 1429.

[15] See note 11.

[16] The exact numbers are contentious. To give two examples of the range of estimates, Stéphane Barry and Norbert Gualde (2006:45), say "between one-third and two-thirds" whereas Gottfried (1983: 257), claims the lower number of "between 25 and 45 percent". Demographic historians note a considerable amount of geographic variation. On the whole the balance is probably in the range of in Mediterranean Europe, Italy, the South of France and Spain where the plague reoccurred during four consecutive years and was probably close to 80–75 % of the population whereas in England, Germany and the Lowlands where the space between outbreaks was longer it was probably closer to 20 %.

Middle East, India and China is said to have killed at least 75 million people. The Black Death is thought to have reappeared in Europe roughly every generation with varying intensity and numbers of fatalities until disappearing from Europe during the eighteenth century. The Black Death had a drastic effect on Europe's population, irrevocably changing Europe's social structure.

The plague brought radical reorganisation of the economy in its wake and in due course changes in the organisation of European society. In emergent urban centres the disasters of the fourteenth and early fifteenth century and consequential labour force shortages caused rapid drive for economic diversification and scientific innovation.

Subsequent to the Black Death the loss of life, famine and desertion of entire communities and previously productive agricultural land contributed to an intensification of capital accumulation in urban areas. This stimulated trade, industry and rapidly increasing urban populations in fields as diverse as banking, textiles and weapons. The Hundred Years' War brought about a boom in production of armaments which also brought about growth in the making of iron and steel and thus the materials required for their manufacture. As recovery and success advanced the population grew back to its former levels by the early sixteenth century.[17] A combination of a more than ample labour supply and improving productivity were a 'mixed blessing' for many sections of European society. Regardless of tradition some landlords began to remove peasants from 'common' and unenclosed land.

The Emergence of Mercantile Capitalism and the Reformation

During the fourteenth and fifteenth centuries the most powerful Italian city states (Duggan 1994: 60ff), Florence, Milan and Venice, had been able to conquer other weaker city states thus creating regional states. In 1454 the Peace of Lodi had ended the struggle for hegemony in Italy and brought about a balance of power that was to largely persist until the unification of Italy in the nineteenth century. By the beginning of the sixteenth century and the period pertinent to this chapter only Venice was still able to fully preserve her independence and compete with the European monarchies of France and Spain or the Ottoman Empire. Nonetheless, the experiences of the Italian republics and the mercantile capitalism that had arisen and thrived within them were to be of great influence on economic development.

As trade became more successful landowners progressively moved away from the feudal economy. Wool production greatly expanded in England, France, Germany and the Netherlands and new textile industries began to expand. With the new 'mercantile capitalism', the 'humanism' of the Renaissance enjoyed unprecedented academic

[17] European history from the fourteenth century onward here and for most of the rest of this chapter is based on a synthesis of the work of Braudel (1973), McNeill (1963), Ogg and Sharp (1926) and Rice (1970).

interest. With it came disquiet about the lack of academic freedom. Intense theoretical debates came about in the universities that seriously questioned the nature of the church, the authority of the Pope and Vatican Councils and also of monarchies.

The Catholic Church faced a crisis in theology that commenced with William of Ockham (*circa* 1288–1348) in England during the fourteenth century that was taking place alongside communal discontent. Again in England, John Wycliffe (1320–1384) made an English translation of the Bible and spoke out against the authority of the Pope and monasticism. A little later, In Bohemia, Jan Hus (1369–1415) a follower of Wycliffe's teachings challenged the authority of the papacy for which he was excommunicated in 1411, then tried and burned at the stake in 1415.

With the gradual collapse of philosophical fundamentals of scholasticism, *nominalism* replaced it with a doctrine that regarded abstract concepts or universals to have no independent existence other than as 'names'. They threatened the existence of the established church whose legitimacy was based on its institution and clergy being the only mediator between man and God. A new argument emerged that preferred the notion that no religious doctrine can be proven by philosophical arguments. It thus made inroads into the previously unchallenged alliance between reason and faith expressed by Thomas Aquinas that had taken firm root in the medieval period. The Reformation was the outcome.

Martin Luther (1483–1546) finally inspired the Reformation and his theological work gave life to several major traditions that have collectively come to be known as Protestantism. With those changes the Peasant's War (1524–1525) began as a response to his teachings. Peasants' revolts had occurred periodically since the fourteenth century. However some peasants erroneously believed that Luther's attack on the established church would also lead to the downfall of the social hierarchy on the basis of his condemnation of the close relations between secular princes and those who were called princes of the church. Small revolts in Swabia, Franconia, and Thuringia in 1524 gained support among peasants and nobles disaffected with their power and influence, often influenced by debts owed to both groups of princes.

The New World

At the same time the world was both changing and opening up very quickly. In Spain the Islamic Moorish conquest and occupation that began in 711–18 came to an end with the union of Castile and Aragón in 1479. The ensuing conquest of Granada in 1492 and Navarre in 1512 brought most of Spain together as a single country. Spain and their neighbour Portugal also began extensive exploration of the globe.

In 1453 the Ottoman Empire under Mehmed II conquered Constantinople which became Istanbul, the capital of the entire empire. It was at its height of power during the sixteenth and seventeenth centuries, particularly during the rule of Süleyman I (the Magnificent) from 1520 to 1566. The Empire covered three continents, dominated much of south-eastern Europe, the Middle East and North Africa. It extended from the Strait of Gibraltar (and in 1553 the Atlantic coast of North Africa beyond

Gibraltar) in the west to the Caspian Sea and Persian Gulf in the east. It northern limits were the edge of Austria and Slovakia and the hinterland in the region of Ukraine to Sudan and Yemen at its southern limits. The Ottomans inherited aspects of both Roman and Islamic traditions with a 'unification of cultures' that to this day directly influences large parts of the 'Mediterranean world'.

At its eastern edge was the Islamic Mughal Empire, which at its greatest territorial extent ruled most of the Indian subcontinent, known then as Hindustan, and parts of what are now Afghanistan and Pakistan. It was established in 1526 by the Timurid prince Babur, a descendant of Genghis Khan, expanded and consolidated until about 1707 when it was at its zenith. It was a dominion of Islamic rule over Hindu and Buddhist subjects that shaped much of the region and incorporated values from each to form many of the social structures and values that persist to the present day.

Throughout the fifteenth century Portuguese explorers had already sailed the coast of Africa and set up trading posts as they searched for a route to India in order to bring back spices which were in high demand throughout Europe. During 1498 Vasco da Gama finally round the Cape of Good Hope, reached India and thus brought economic prosperity to Portugal. In 1500 Pedro Álvares Cabral landed in Brazil and claimed it for Portugal. Ten years on Afonso de Albuquerque occupied Goa in India, Ormuz in the Persian Strait and Malacca in what is now Malaysia. Consequently the Portuguese empire held dominion over commerce in the Indian Ocean and South Atlantic. Don Cristóbal Colón (Christopher Columbus) set out on voyages across the Atlantic in order to find the Indies from the opposite direction and began a determined European venture to explore and colonise the Americas. Although history places great emphasis on his first voyage of 1492, he did not in fact reach the mainland until his third voyage of 1498. At more or less the same time Ferdinand Magellan, a Portuguese explorer in the service of Spain, led the first successful attempt to circumnavigate the world. Thus, not only the social environment but also the space in which changes would occur began to become greater.

The Changing World of Children

The impact on children was little visited by contemporaries and generally largely unknown. What is certain is that very few of them made noticeable impact as Protestantism took hold and more devout groups such as those known as 'Calvinists' flourished. Children became more subject to adult authority than previously since it was the duty of adults, out of whose sin children were born, to teach them righteousness and piety. In the Protestant world, Marianism was mainly discarded with its veneration and admiration of Mary as the spiritually immaculate and eternally giving mother of the Christ child and the baby Jesus who was the embodiment of godliness and purity. Thus one a cornerstone of belief that had once guided the view of what and how children should be became unfashionable.

On the other hand, conduct books and changing values of 'behaviour' and 'misbehaviour' indicate a shift in perceptions of childhood in late medieval Europe as the Reformation began. Compared to the idealised behaviour of the type the conduct books prescribed, late fifteenth century literature shows growing concern with identifying misbehaviour as an indicator of the child's moral nature and character. That was combined with a diminution of the importance of superficial 'courteous' behaviour in children's overall actions.

Throughout much of the world little is known about children, although we can often see that many traditions have continued for almost as long as the entirety of history covered in both periods. With exploration, conquest and eventual Christian missionary activity vast parts of the 'New World' were drawn under the influence of a Western notion of childhood and, thus, what a child should be and how they conduct themselves as children. This, in turn, has also had varying amounts of influence on parts of the world that were not themselves under the power of European colonial powers. There are no precise universal standards to describe citizenship which makes this manner of search for what may at the very least provide a clue to a shared understanding of children as citizens. However there are also no apparent local standards other than those measured against occidental principles.

The transition from fifteenth into sixteenth centuries marks the end of the ancient to pre-modern period in which about 2,000 years of childhood has been considered. There have been a very few children who have found a place in history about whom we have a consistent and comprehensive knowledge. There are many more who are of uncertain provenance (e.g.: the rise of Genghis Khan as a 'young' leader or the Children's Crusades). There is little to suggest that in whatever form citizenship can be extrapolated out of the societies considered in this 'thumbnail' history that it was ever inclusive of children. Where there is divergence from modern-day standards is in that the transition from childhood to adulthood was often earlier. Thus, age 14 years would perhaps not refer to a child but a young adult which may colour contemporary versions of those we remember for their youth. Nevertheless, when we look at the ancient European world particularly, childhood in Greek and Roman civilisations does not look so much different to the modern world when we look at when (and occasionally how) the transition from youth to full adulthood actually occurred.

Chapter 5
The Emergence of Childhood – From the Enlightenment to Modern World of Childhood

There was a changing perception of children during the sixteenth and seventeenth centuries in Europe. During the sixteenth century the Protestant Reformation supplanted the Catholic Church and its rituals with a sterner form of faith that emphasised the sinfulness of children. Therewith children and parents no longer had the reassurance of understanding that baptism would spare children the torment of Hell if they died in infancy. Devout parents were urged to bring children to acknowledge their sins and the need for salvation by clerics. They were born out of sin into sin and needed to be taught the ways of righteousness. The increasing availability of the printed word made catechisms the preferred method of bringing children to the knowledge of God. Adults posed questions and children learned appropriate responses by rote. Parents could never start this too early with a catechism even for children "*that are not past the breast yet*" and behaviour books of around 400 pages for 5 year olds.

Some parents consequently lived in a situation of *angst* unequalled until the present. That was without considering the situation of children themselves (for instance, see deMause 1974:51; Ariès 1962:379). Parents' unease about bringing up children was greater than in the past and undoubtedly began to mark out different ages at which childhood ended and conflicts this could cause. Many poor children would then have been earning a living full time at 6 or 7 years of age although 'better off' boys might still be in full-time education at age 14. The period saw the expansion of boys' education and an astonishing *volte-face* in attitudes to girls' education that defied the established (Roman Catholic) Christian doctrine.

Economic Expansion

There was a great deal of change in Europe which in economic history is known as the Commercial Revolution. It was a period of European rapid economic expansion, colonialism and mercantilism that lasted from approximately 1520 until 1650. This

B. Milne, *The History and Theory of Children's Citizenship in Contemporary Societies*, DOI 10.1007/978-94-007-6521-4_5, © Springer Science+Business Media Dordrecht 2013

change was partially influenced by the commercial success of the Italian city states but also by a policy of expansion through acquisition of new territories that earlier voyages of discovery had opened. The voyages of discovery of the late fifteenth into sixteenth centuries allowed some European nations to begin to accumulate vast networks of international trade. In turn that generated a great deal of wealth that went into circulation throughout Europe. Initially the rapidly growing global economy was based on silver which allowed the purchase of goods (for instance: silk, spices and other goods from the Far East) that Europeans wanted. However, they possessed nothing of comparable valuable for which to exchange it until vast amounts of silver coinage and bullion were found for payment. This drove exploration of newly discovered territories in which silver and gold could be found. An important outcome of Europe's commercial revolution was accrual of the basis of the wealth that led to the Industrial Revolution.

The large amount of money caused widespread inflation, widening the already wide gap between rich and poor. Inflation was worsened by a growing population but stagnant production, low wages and a rapidly rising cost of living. This, when combined with overpopulation, affected agriculture profoundly. The landholding aristocracy also suffered under inflation because they were dependent on fixed rents paid by peasant tenants who were fast becoming poorer and unable to pay. Botched attempts were made by the aristocracy to offset diminishing income by setting up short term leases of land in order to allow periodic reassessment of rent. The manorial system dwindled and aristocratic landowners were forced to sell pieces of land in order to maintain their standard of living. This attracted a new rich bourgeois who wished to buy land to improve their social status.

Common land was gradually being enclosed by landed bourgeois who increased the efficiency of stock breeding. Enclosure made food production more efficient and less labour intensive, thus forcing the surplus population who could no longer find employment in agriculture into cottage industries such as weaving. In the longer term, this pushed them into growing towns and cities and newly developing factories. Initially, wool from growing numbers of well husbanded sheep fed quickly expanding textile production. That eventually became one of the most important components of the impending Industrial Revolution.

The European economic centre relocated from the Islamic eastern Mediterranean to Western Europe (Portugal, Spain, France, the Netherlands and England). Following circumnavigation of the Cape of Good Hope, the new eastern trade ended the monopoly of the Ottoman Turks and their competitors the Italian city states. Portugal came to control trade between east and west and later the (then) Dutch city of Antwerp which had one of the first currency exchanges in Europe.

One of the outcomes of this rapid expansion was the growth of something that was to shape parts of the modern world. That was the transatlantic slave trade. The traffic of slaves from Africa to the Americas originated around 1500 during the early modern period of European exploration of West Africa and setting up colonies in the Caribbean, South and North America. It is estimated that 11–12 million men, women and children were transported in ships across the Atlantic to various ports in the New World. Most went to South America and the Caribbean between 1500 and

1850. In the Americas, slavery played an important role in economic development, with slaves planting and harvesting cash crops and working on construction of buildings and roads as well as performing domestic duties.

As the early exploration of the New World moved forward the conquest of native people and often their enslavement followed. In the Spanish Americas the native population dropped when diseases they had never previously suffered arrived and rapidly depleted them. That is when the importation of African slaves began. The liberalisation of trade from a large merchant base may have allowed parts of Europe to produce and utilise emerging scientific and technological developments more effectively than countries with robust monarchies and aristocracies who were still essentially feudal. For children also, the changes in distribution of people around the world, the conversion of many of them to Christianity and introduction to European economic, social and political structures as well as social and economic changes in the Western world were bringing changes. Those were to give the world the beginnings of what universal notions of childhood are considered to be today.

A Period of Unrest

People were beginning to show disquiet with their situation in Europe. In the spring of 1517 the *Bundshuh* movement arose and rebelled on account of a harsh period of by the aristocracy. Castles were ruined, aristocrats slain and expanses of the countryside devastated throughout 3 months of uprisings. The Emperor Maximilian stayed his hand throughout the episode and appeared favourable to the cause of the peasants as long as they only punished the most avaricious aristocrats. Thereafter as peasant 'armies' disbanded and the remainder degenerated into marauding bands he sent a few hundred knights to end the disorder. Little compassion was shown to fugitives and brutal executions followed. Additionally, heavy reparation was demanded from the entire peasantry in the form of a perpetual tax. The conflict was mostly in southern, western and central areas of what is now Germany and parts of modern Switzerland and Austria. At its height in the spring and summer of 1525 it involved about 300,000 peasant rebels. Contemporary estimates put fatalities at 100,000. The revolt in the Krain (Slovenia) lasted longest and was suppressed with most bloodshed. Those in Styria and Karinthia (Austria) came to an end sooner with far less disastrous results for people who had been involved.

The bad feeling was to continue in Europe. During 1524 and 1525 the Peasants' War began. It was Europe's most massive and widespread popular uprising before the 1789 French Revolution. The strife consisted of a series of economic as well as religious revolts by peasants, townsfolk and the aristocracy without common objectives. It was not only in Germany or elsewhere in Central Europe that discontent was perceptible among peasant populations at the beginning of the sixteenth century. In England expropriation of land to make room for sheep farms gave occasion for periodical local disturbances that culminated in 1549 in Wymondham in England where Robert Kett led a rebellion.

The Period of Economic Hardship and Recovery

At that time much of Europe was facing severe economic hardship. In England, in the region of 80 % of income was used to purchase food. Wages were lower than before and falling. In 1559 they were 60 % less than in 1509. There were consecutive harvest failures following heavy rains in 1556 and 1557 and an outbreak of 'sweating sickness' during 1551 and 1552. Epidemics in 1556 and 1558 reduced the population by 200,000 (6 %), with the death rate at twice its normal level (see Livi-Bacci 2000). It has been argued by historians (for instance, Rosenwein 2001) that the long period of population expansion during the Middle Ages was brought to an end by either a Malthusian 'positive check'[1] at the end of the thirteenth century or by the 'exogenous' intercession of the Black Death in 1347–1350. However, population expansion is part of a continuum that lasted up to the end of the nineteenth century during which there were obstacles, some of them direct consequences of development. When labour was depleted after an epidemic, famine or war starvation, malnutrition and lower birth rates, there was often a relatively immediate outcome. However, as the situation improved, standards of living and wages rose. Labour shortages demanded increased use of all available people including children. In rural economies all labour inputs were required to maintain economies. Much has been made of the situation of working children in the early part of the Industrial Revolution. Large scale industrial manufacturing and mining appeared only in the late eighteenth century and children began to be removed from workplaces by the mid-nineteenth century. In fact, children in Western Europe were only engaged in heavy industrial labour for around a century, which is only a small part of the period this research looks at. Here we find what such authors as Ariès may have misread as periods when it was difficult to distinguish between adults and children.

During the fifteenth century, European recovery became general with rapid population growth and relative prosperity. Urbanisation increased exponentially and mercantilism replaced what had previously been a more sedentary rural economy. Religious war, plague and economic upheaval changed much of that. The Italian city states never recovered and the ascendancy passed to Northern Europe particularly the Hanseatic cities of the North Sea. Growth was steady until 1700 when improving technology, expanding sea routes and growing cities began to change rural agrarian production systems toward capitalism and imperialism. The Netherlands, Great Britain and France became powerful and increasingly ambitious about acquisition of new colonies. Between 1750 and 1845 there was extensive population growth, with

[1]Malthusian 'positive checks' were famine, misery, plague and war that were necessary because 'preventative checks' had not limited the numbers of the poor. Malthus thought that positive checks were indispensable for that task. He believed that if positive checks were unsuccessful, famine would inevitably be the consequential means of keeping a population down. Moral discipline, vice and birth control were primary preventative checks. Moral restraint was the means by which higher ranking people limited family size so as not to dissipate wealth among too many heirs. For lower ranking people vice and birth control were means by which numbers could be contained although he believed they were insufficient to limit vast numbers of poor people.

about half of the world population in Europe (250 millions). Spain at first and then Portugal began to decline in influence beginning with liberation wars throughout Latin America in the nineteenth century.

New Philosophies That Include Children

In the middle of the seventeenth century Hobbes, the philosopher and political theorist turned his attention to the evils of 'the state of nature' in his argument for absolute rule in his best known work *Leviathan*. The problems of social organisation included some consideration of the 'ownership' of the child. His work, including his consideration of children, exerted a continuing influence on later thinkers (see also Chap. 6).

Children finally became the focus of new thought as the seventeenth century ended and the eighteenth century began. The impact of two great philosophers, John Locke and Jean-Jacques Rousseau, on children and their vastly differing views of childhood began to change perceptions of whom and what children were. In 1693 John Locke published *Some Thoughts Concerning Education* which was for many years probably the most influential British book on childhood. Its origins hardly suggested this.

Locke had been tutor to a number of aristocratic children and on the basis of this experience wrote some letters to a relative on child rearing. These circulated and eventually Locke was persuaded to publish them. Locke, unlike the Puritans of the sixteenth and seventeenth centuries, was not apparently concerned with children's salvation. His concern was with suggesting ways of inculcating good habits into children that would last for life. The way to do this was neither through corporal punishment nor through frightening them, but taking reason as the means: "the Principle of all Vertue and Excellency lies in a power of denying ourselves the satisfaction of our own Desires, where Reason does not authorize them" (§ 38.). The first thing infants should learn, according to Locke, is that they should not have something simply because they like it but because it is deemed good for them. He also thought that learning should be fun and children and they "…must be tenderly us'd[2]…" (Locke 1971:19). He also appreciated that each child should have his (or her?) own "natural genius and constitution" (Locke 1971:27).

John Locke's book was comparable with the work of Benjamin Spock in the twentieth century in that he comforted parents and described a clear schema. In that he claimed that "nine parts of ten" (Locke 1971:4) of how a child develops into the adult, for "Good or Evil, useful or not" (*Ibid.*), will be the result of education and upbringing. This was the age of the development of a gentler and more affectionate type of family life. The life of the child in the bosom of the 'protective' family was established.

For something in the region of half a century Locke's book held a place of enormous influence throughout Europe and North America as well as in Britain. It was

[2] 'us'd' is *used*.

eventually challenged by Jean-Jacques Rousseau's *Émile* (1762). Rousseau believed that the problem with Locke rested in his fixation on the adult-to-be rather than on the child. He was conceivably the first intellectual to be at least convincingly 'child-centred'. He wrote that we should not reason with children but let them learn from things, ideally from nature rather than teachers. Rousseau therewith laid a foundation for the Romantic poets in the late eighteenth and early nineteenth centuries and for a number of philosophical and moral stances on children during the twentieth century. It was only a single small step from arguing that a child should learn from nature to postulating that a child might gain access to the natural world in a manner that was normally inaccessible for unhappy adults.

New Economic Thought

Economic analysis of the period generally disregarded children however Adam Smith (1723–1790) noticed the conditions of some in his native Scotland. He was one of the major figures in the intellectual movement known as the Scottish Enlightenment and for his treatise: *An Inquiry into the Nature and Causes of the Wealth of Nations* (1776, here '*The Wealth of Nations*', 1973) It was one of the earliest attempts to methodically study the historical development of industry and commerce in Europe and attempt a sustained attack on the doctrine of mercantilism. His work was a foundation of the modern academic discipline of free market economics. It offered one of the best-known components of the intellectual *raison d'être* for capitalism, free trade and libertarianism. His treatise was so successful that it led to the refutation of earlier economic schools. Much of his work reflected his knowledge of the Scottish economy and it is here he noticed the situation of children: "poverty (…) is unfavourable to the rearing of children" (Smith 1973:182).

He was critical of working conditions of the common people that did not allow them a state in which children would grow to maturity. In what is essentially an argument for better pay and a larger labour force that child survival would bring, he says that: "(The) liberal reward of labour (…) enabling them to provide better for their children, and consequently to bring up a greater number…" (*Ibid.*). Later economists such as Malthus refined his theory into what is now known as classical economics.

Thomas Malthus (1766–1834) was an avid disciple of Jean-Jacques Rousseau and David Hume, both of whom he knew. In his *Essay on Population* (1798) he hypothesised that *unchecked* population growth always exceeds the growth of the means of subsistence. Actual, or 'checked', population growth is kept in line with food supply growth by 'positive and preventive checks' both of which are exemplified by 'misery and vice'. His hypothesis inferred that actual population always has a tendency to exceed food supply. Thus any attempt to improve the condition of lower classes by increasing incomes or improving agricultural productivity would be futile. The additional means of subsistence would be entirely absorbed by the boost in population it caused. He saw three elements at the root of this situation: the overproduction of children, incapability of resources to remain abreast of the rising human population and recklessness of the lower classes. He suggested the family size of the lower class ought to be regulated so that they did not produce more children than they could support.

That, of course, does not conform to Smith's proposition and certainly countervails Rousseau's ideas. In contradiction to his views it may be argued that a high rate of population that is rapidly increasing meant a high rate of innovation. The extreme exception in his time was Ireland. It had the fastest growth in Europe in eighteenth century following the introduction and widespread cultivation of the potato. In the nineteenth century that was to see its greatest ever population crisis during the Great Famine. Starvation, disease and mass emigration saw the population of Ireland reduced by 20–25 % between 1845 and 1852. About a million people died, many of them children, and a million more emigrated to England, Scotland, Australia, Canada, and the USA.

One of the harshest critics of Malthusian principles was Robert Owen (1771–1858) who believed in far more positive ways that people were the product of their environment. That nurtured his support for education and labour reform making him a pioneer in the promotion of investment in human capital. A general malaise and trade stagnation as a consequence of the end of the Napoleonic Wars was gripping the United Kingdom. Thus he considered the special causes connected with the wars that led to the execrable situation. He noticed that the permanent cause of distress could be found in the contest between human labour and machinery with an effective remedy in the united action of men and subordination of machinery.

He advocated social inclusion and early intervention at the beginning of the nineteenth century when he stated that the community he created would accommodate more than just the children of New Lanark. Anyone in nearby Lanark or thereabouts who could not afford to educate their children would be able to send them to his school whereby (Owen 1816) said:

> They would receive the same care and attention as those who belong to the establishment. Nor will there be any distinction made between the children of those parents who are deemed the worst, and of those who may be esteemed the best members of society: indeed I would prefer to receive the offspring of the worst, if they shall be sent at an early age; because they really require more of our care and pity and by well-training these, society will be more essentially benefited than if the like attention were paid to those whose parents are educating them in comparatively good habits. (Address to the Inhabitants of New Lanark, 1 January 1816)

This was part of his proposition on the remedy of poverty. Communities of about 1,200 persons would need to be settled on parcels of land from 1,000 to 1,500 acres. Everybody lived in a large building in the form of a square that had a communal kitchen and dining rooms. Families would live in private apartments and have care of the children until the age of 3. Thereafter they should be brought up by the community, although parents could see them at mealtimes and on other occasions. The notion was that the communities could be established by individuals, parishes, counties or state. Supervision would be by suitably qualified persons. Work and its rewards would be a common good. Education and inclusion were the keys to the success of this plan:

> It is therefore, the interest of all, that every one, from birth, should be well educated, physically and mentally, that society may be improved in its character, – that everyone should be beneficially employed, physically and mentally, that the greatest amount of wealth may be created, and knowledge attained, - that everyone should be placed in the midst of those external circumstances that will produce the greatest number of pleasurable sensations, through the longest life, that man may be made truly intelligent, moral and happy, and be thus prepared to enter upon the coming Millennium.
>
> (A Development of the Principles & Plans on which to establish self-supporting Home Colonies, 1841)

What he was describing was what should be referred to as an intentional community. It is a planned residential community planned and operated so that it has a higher degree of collaboration amongst members than other communities. They usually share responsibilities and resources. Members typically hold common social, political or religious beliefs and are often considered part of alternative society.

Those communities include co-housing communities and cooperatives, communes, eco-villages, residential land trusts, retreats, kibbutzim and ashrams. Members are selected by a community's active membership and whilst many attempt to live in a 'different' and 'improved' circumstance to the rest of society they do not tend to claim to be 'Utopias'. Children are often treated very much as in Owen's vision, indeed are often far more autonomous and allowed to share decision-making. However there is often a great deal of emphasis on a childhood unspoiled by adult influences (for instance see McLaughlin and Davidson 1990:187–216). Owen's ideas were to be of great influence on Karl Marx. Apart from a few idealised and usually short lived communal experiments from that time to the present, those egalitarian and inclusive ideas have never really come to fruition.

Children in Literature

With the end of the eighteenth and beginning of nineteenth centuries the impact of British poets on childhood through works such as those of William Blake and William Wordsworth further 'softened' hearts and minds toward children. When we examine the transition into the Victorian age, we find a period in which some children were allowed to live out the dream of a romantic childhood. On the other hand, the conditions of life in a rapidly industrialising and urbanising Europe gave an appearance that many were 'children without childhood'. Those children were predestined to long hours of work and their lives were far from the nature that the Romantics so highly valued.

Critical authors such as Mayhew, Dickens, Kingsley, Twain, Anderson and numerous others used fiction and/or journalism as a means of exposing the situation of children. Briefly mentioned in the Introduction is a related trend whereby Dominique Julia (Becchi and Julia 2004:85) identifies three illustrative representations of childhood that emerged toward the end of the eighteenth century and was to endure well on into the twentieth century.

In literature and current affairs three romantic figures of childhood were drawn into popular imagination. The first was the abandoned child who is reared by animals (i.e.: Victor,[3] Mowgli or Tarzan). Victor's discovery fortuitously came toward the end of the Enlightenment when many intellectuals were debating what exactly distinguished man from animal. A prevalent enquiry of the time was about the human ability to learn language. It was hoped that by studying Victor they might discover the answer. Mowgli[4] and Tarzan[5] are examples of the same genre who also possess extraordinary powers and skills much like those in the third group.

The second group was child prodigies. Wolfgang Amadeus Mozart (1756–1791) is perhaps the most well known example in general. The German mathematician Carl Friedrich Gauss (1777–1855), Irish mathematician and physicist, William Rowan Hamilton (1805–1865) and English composer, organist and artist William Crotch (1775–1847) are probably his equal in their respective areas and creativity. In the oriental world child priests and deities such as Tibetan lamas and living gods have been attributed similar prodigious spiritual qualities. Siddhārtha Gautama (the Buddha) is said to have had the enlightenment that led to his later life as a youth and in Hinduism more than a few gods such as Rama appear to have become divine whilst they were still very young.

The third was child heroes who were mainly fictional figures, including such characters as Petit Gavroche,[6] Jack Dawkins[7] or Huckleberry Finn[8] who often possessed extraordinary skills and occasionally almost superhuman powers. They do things that adults would not normally do or dare that are both considered childish

[3]Victor (of Aveyron) also known as the Wild Boy of Aveyron seemingly lived his childhood naked and alone before being found wandering in the woods outside Saint-Sernin-sur-Rance, near Toulouse in France in 1797. He escaped soon after being captured but was captured again and placed in the care of a local woman for a few days before escaping again. On 8 January 1800 he came out of the forest alone and stayed in human care until he died in 1828. His age was unknown but local people estimated that he was about 12 years old. The fact he could not speak and his food preferences suggested that he had been in the wild for most of his life. His story has become the subject of several books and films.

[4]Mowgli originally appeared in Rudyard Kipling's short story 'In the Ruk' in *Many Inventions* (1893), then became the main character in *The Jungle Book* (1894) and *The Second Jungle Book* (1895). He is the child of British parents in the Indian jungle lost during a tiger attack. The human baby is adopted by wolves who call him Mowgli (Frog) because he has no fur. Kipling tells us some of the stories about his childhood until he returns to human society where many other adventures begin.

[5]Tarzan (Tarzan of the Apes, Edgar Rice Burroughs, 1914) is John Clayton, born in western equatorial Africa to John and Alice Clayton, a marooned couple from England, who are also Lord and Lady Greystoke. The infant child is adopted by Kala the she-ape after his parents died and named 'Tarzan' ('White Skin' in ape language) and raised by the band of apes. In his youth he feels alienated by his peers because of physical differences and then discovers his human parents' cabin where he finds out about others like himself from books which he teaches himself to read.

[6]Petit Gavroche is the street boy who fights in the French Revolution and dies manning a barrier when students revolt and erect barricades in the narrow streets of Paris in Paris in Hugo's *Les Miserables* (1862).

[7]Dawkins, aka the Artful Dodger, appears to possess very mature qualities.

[8]Huckleberry Finn first appeared in Mark Twain's *The Adventures of Tom Sawyer* (1876) but was so successful that *Adventures of Huckleberry Finn* followed in 1884 with Huck as the hero.

because of the risks but heroic and mature because of their courage and fortitude. Surprisingly, there are few accounts of real 'child heroism' in the seventeenth to twentieth centuries. It appears that with exceptions of examples like Hugo's fictional Petit Gavroche, children usually take the role of victim and frequently the nameless victim.

Despite the number of wars and the role of the hero as a model for society, it would seem that heroism was a matter for adults and reserved almost exclusively for men. Jack Cornwell, although 16 years old when he died (Unknown author 1918), volunteered to serve in the Royal Navy and became Boy Seaman First Class after basic training. He received further training as a Sight Setter or Gun Layer. After the Battle of Jutland in which his ship, the *Chester*, was engaged and seriously damaged, Cornwell was found to be sole survivor at his gun. There were shards of steel in his chest, but he was still looking through his gun sights and waiting for further orders. He died 3 days later in Grimsby General Hospital. Later that year his mother received his posthumous Victoria Cross. His example is quite unique and has also something of the boy hero that has been used to describe a particular British type of courage and devotion to duty. It has, however, little apparent appeal outside of the sphere of British influence.

Crossovers like Mowgli or Tarzan bridge the gap between the 'wild' children and 'heroes' and have some of the promise of the prodigies. Various forms of this vision of childhood persisted well into the twentieth century when film stars such as Jackie Coogan, Shirley Temple, Judy Garland and Mickey Rooney often seemed to bring many of those characteristics together through both their acting skills and the characters they portrayed. This is part of the history of childhood that has implanted a notion of a 'golden child' that supports an earlier view of the indistinguishable nature of children and adults espoused by those who believe in a 'golden age'.

At the other end of the spectrum were children whose lives were less exciting and certainly neither privileged nor exceptional. Literature also contributes here. Henry Mayhew[9] described many urban children's miserable lives as a critical journalist and Dickens contributed very revealing caricatures of lives and attitudes in several of his books.[10] In the harsh industrial world in particular, Victorian reformers such as Lord Ashley, Mary Carpenter or Dr Barnardo in the UK set themselves the undertaking of rebuilding childhood for those who were effectively missing out on it (for instance, see Selleck 1985).

In the USA 'child savers' were more concerned with delinquency but also contributed to changes in attitudes and practice toward young people (Platt 1977).

[9]His four volumes of *London Labour and the London Poor* appeared between 1851 and 1861 chronicled the lives of the poor in London and gave a graphic account of children's lives as they probably were throughout Europe and probably elsewhere in the world at that time.

[10]In *Bleak House* (1853) his descriptions of the life and fate of Jo the crossing sweeper are a stark portrayal of a miserable life and many attitudes toward such children and the fictional headmaster of Dotheboys Hall school, Wackford Squeers, in *The Life and Adventures of Nicholas Nickleby* (1839) illustrates, whilst also exaggerating to an extent the cruel attitudes toward them.

It was felt that children should be protected from the adult world of work and responsibility. They should become and thus remain dependent on adults with their time apportioned between home and school.

The ideal was that they should be *happy*, which was something that has since been particularly associated with childhood. Childhood was idealised as a kind of garden that was protected by walls and hedges and where nature throve flawlessly. In reality few parents attained or even wished for this kind of childhood for their children. The better off put their children into the care of governesses and later sent them to boarding schools. For the majority of working classes poverty meant that a child had to contribute to the family economy as soon as possible, which the law allowed.

Although there was a removal of children from the labour force from about the 1850s onward, compulsory and universal education from the 1870s onwards generally had to be imposed by force of law (for example, see Davin 1996). The economic value of children was changing from one of the child as a contributor, to one of the 'property' of the parents and, to a point, the state who invested in the child as a future asset (Zelizer 1985).

Education

Education was another key element in the changing status of children. It is not an exclusively European notion, but in its present form largely owes much to western formats. When the Church of Scotland was established in 1560, a year later it followed up by setting out to provide schools in every parish controlled by the local kirk session. Education was to be provided free for the poor and it has hoped that pressure by the church would assure that all children took part. In 1633 the Scottish Parliament introduced a local tax to fund it. Schooling was not free for everybody, however the tax kept fees low and the church and charities financed poor students.

This was substantially successful, although late in the eighteenth century some parishes had grown so much that there was a growing role for 'adventure schools' that were funded through fees and religious charities. In 1872 education for all children aged 5–13 was made compulsory through 'public schools' (in Scotland that meant for the general public) run by local school boards. Leaving age was raised to 14 years in 1883 and a Leaving Certificate Examination introduced in 1888 to set a national standard for secondary education. General school fees were brought to an end in 1890 (see Smout 1972; Devine 2006:389–412).

In 1833 the United Kingdom government budgeted for the construction of schools for poor children which was when the state became involved with education in England and Wales unlike Scotland that began in 1561. The Elementary Education Act 1880 made education compulsory from age 5 to 10 years. The Elementary Education (School Attendance) Act 1893 raised leaving age to 11 and a little later to 13. The Elementary Education (Blind and Deaf Children) Act the same year gave compulsory education to blind and deaf children with provision for special schools (Green 1990).

During the eighteenth century Prussia was probably the first country in the world to introduce free and universally compulsory primary education. Historically, Lutheranism had a strong influence on German culture including education and Luther himself had advocated compulsory schooling. It consisted of 8 years of primary schooling (Volksschule). It provided the skills needed in the early industrialised world through reading, writing, and arithmetic but also a strict education in ethics, duty, discipline, and obedience. At that stage the general population had almost no access to secondary education. In 1810, after the Napoleonic Wars, the Prussians introduced state certification of teachers which considerably raised standards. The leaving examination (*Abitur*) was introduced in 1788, compulsory in all Prussian secondary schools in 1812 and extended to all of Germany in 1871. With unification in 1871 the school system was centralised. More secondary schools were opened and the state assumed the sole right to set standards and supervise recently established schools. At the beginning of the twentieth century, four types of schools were given equal rank and privilege, thus ending what had previously been a class based system. Even then, the different types did not mean that they were of equal prestige. The divisions were retained in order to allow a small corridor of difference in which the distinction between those educated to be the ruling elite varied, down to those destined to be the rump of all echelons of the national labour force.

With the enthronement of the Meiji in1868, the new leadership of Japan set out on rapid course of modernisation. It included establishment of a public education system designed to enable Japan to catch up with the rapidly industrialising West and develop a modern nation. The influence of education in England, Germany and the USA and initially the 'liberal' education of the latter shaped what was to become a conservative but dynamic system by the end of the nineteenth century.

Italy had a state-wide school system from 1859 when the *Legge Casati* (Casati Act) authorised educational responsibility for the imminent Italian state (unification was completed in 1861). The *Legge Casati* made primary education compulsory with the prime intent of reducing illiteracy. Control of primary education was devolved to single towns and cities, secondary education to *Regioni* (counties) and the universities to the State. Part of the task was to standardise Italian identity through education using a common language which had hitherto consisted of dialects and distinct languages. It was also very progressive and whilst very slow in achieving education for all Italian children, it was equally delivered to boys and girls and attempted to offer schooling to others previously excluded.

In 1898 Maria Montessori gave a lecture at an Educational Congress in Turin on the topic of education and training of the disabled. The serving Minister of Education was at the lecture and was so impressed by her compelling arguments that the same year he appointed her director of the *Scuola Ortofrenica*. It was an institution dedicated to the care and education of the mentally backward. She accepted the post so that she could put her theories to proof. Her first outstanding success was that several of her 8 year old pupils applied to take the state examinations in reading and writing.

The 'defective' children not only passed but did so with marks above average. After her success with these children she was invited to start a school for children in a poor housing project in Rome in 1907. She called it the *Casa dei Bambini*

(Children's House). The *Casa dei Bambini* was essentially a child care centre in an apartment building where she focused on teaching her pupils ways of developing their own skills at their own pace. It was a principle she called 'spontaneous self-development' (see Montessori 1964). The success of the *Casa dei Bambini* prompted the opening of many others and worldwide interest in her methods of education and philosophy of the meaning of childhood. She was very well informed about educational developments and the ideological propositions behind many other nations' views of children and uniquely for her time saw children as bearers of rights.

The Century of the Child

This was followed by the twentieth century that was loudly proclaimed at its outset to be 'the century of the child' (see Ariès 1962). What this meant, was acknowledgment of the future of any nation being dependent on the wellbeing and preparation of its children. There were numerous positive facets to this new creed of 'welfarism'. The so-called child sciences that included paediatrics and parts of psychology and psychiatry came to be publicly acknowledged and formally established practical and theoretical disciplines. Child health received serious attention. So did education. There were some ambitious campaigns to relieve children from poverty with measurable success in the Family Allowances Act of 1946 in the UK. Elsewhere children began to receive equally successful attention as the principles of welfarism disseminated universally (Shinwell 1963:167). One of the initial responses was the reaction to the suffering of children during and in the wake of the First World War and a growth in charitable work with children (see also Chap. 7 on Englantyne Jebb and Save the Children).

Early in the twentieth century, science was held forth that the key to the future could be seen through such examples as the work of child psychologist Cyril Burt. In the 1920s he claimed that: "superintending the growth of human beings is as scientific a business as cultivating plants or training a race horse" (see Chap. 7). It was a notion that bore the hallmark of Freud's acceptance of the *tabula rasa* idea. Many parents then seemed badly prepared for the task. Burt, at roughly the same time, notably ascertained that girls were equal to boys in general intelligence which was a change from beliefs prevalent since the Edwardian era.

Thus, throughout the 1920s and 1930s behaviourism dominated child rearing with the stress on producing obedient children. A backlash against behaviourism during the 1940s that has lasted to the present probably did little to alleviate the fear of consequences of 'maternal deprivation' and relieve the trepidation of parents (see *The Curtis Report* 1946). However, rising standards of living mid-century permitted parents to commence investment of hopes and resources in children on a previously unprecedented scale. A question arises about this period's influence on where children stand today. For instance, does it contribute to an assumed understanding of '*the evolving capacities of the child*' expressed in Article 5 of the CRC or in a broader view of what children can and cannot do?

The relationship between authoritarian parents and children changed so that from the 1960s onwards children began to acquire new rights in relation to the state and families. What had happened was that childhood itself appears to have in numerous ways become longer and somehow 'safer' and children attained better status within both family and society generally. However, in its distinctness childhood has become so very different from adulthood. The notion of the child as a *citizen* with rights, responsibilities and any form of contribution comparable with those of adults was clearly an aspiration rather than a possibility. The early part of that period saw some efforts toward changing the *status quo*. The 'children's liberation' movement was overtly occupied with establishing equal status between adults and children. What was at first covert, became increasingly evident very quickly, which was that it was occasionally very manipulative. Advocacy of sexual liberation, for example, of children sometimes blurred into attempts to justify paedophilia. That probably had far more to do with the power relationship between knowing and occasionally 'predatory' adults and learning and 'vulnerable' children in many cases.

Child Protection

The backlash against the negative aspects of children's liberation and also the growth of greater attention to abuse and neglect phenomena that owed much to Henry Kempe's work began to more sharply define the need for protection. In 1958 Kempe and his colleagues Elizabeth Boardman and Betty Elmer created the Child Protection Team at the Colorado General Hospital in Denver. In 1961 Kempe, Brandt Steele and other colleagues made their first presentation entitled *The Battered Child Syndrome* (see Kempe and Helfer 1974; Kempe et al. 1962) in Chicago at a meeting of the American Academy of Pediatrics. It was also a very open acknowledgement of the universal nature of the phenomenon, something borne out by the extent of membership and regional sub-grouping of the *International Society for Prevention of Child Abuse and Neglect* (ISPCAN) in 1977. However, despite the widespread concern with the topic, the 'discovery' of child abuse has had some negative consequences for children.

The true nature and extent of the 'new' discovery during the 1960s and 1970s is exemplified by the English experience. In 1884 the Reverend Benjamin Waugh had founded the *National Society for the Prevention of Cruelty to Children* (NSPCC) in England. George Staite had begun this work in Liverpool in 1883, which in turn had been inspired when Thomas Agnew had visited the *New York Society for the Prevention of Cruelty to Children* in 1881 (see also Chap. 7). Harry Ferguson (1993) completed his doctoral thesis, *Protecting children in time: a historical sociological study of the abused child and child protection in Cleveland from 1880 to the 'Cleveland Affair' of 1987*, that charted over a century of usually unpublicised data about children held by the NSPCC. 1993 was also the year that the murder of 3 year old James Bulger by two 10 year old boys on 12 February had attracted world media to focus on the UK.

In fact, these English examples can very easily be matched by contemporary cases of violence against children, the 'home alone' phenomenon, working children, child soldiers, trafficking, international adoption and other events that have had the effect of reinforcement of child protection legislation internationally. In 1982 Neil Postman described a gloomy picture in which he noted the disappearance of games, food and clothes that were specifically for children. His vision of childhood was one in which children should be deferential to adults and committed to preparing themselves for adulthood rather than being a time in which relative free will and happiness are paramount. He saw this phenomenon as an aspect of an age of consumerism in which children are targeted as economic actors rather than having the kind of 'traditional', unbridled childhood that is embedded in folk memory.

This is very much part of the state of childhood we have at present and where the dividing line between how far they appear to need protection and how far they can actively play a role in civil society with all or most rights, duties and privileges of full citizenship is reliant on the success of children's rights.

Children and Human Rights

Throughout the twentieth century the development of human rights has been rapid, the 1924 *Declaration of the Rights of the Child* was to be reworked several times. It eventually inspired the 1979 International Year of the Child and subsequent 10 year long drafting process that produced the CRC in 1989. That, in turn, has come to be the most universally adopted United Nations convention ever.

In theory, if not yet in practice, it should be a counterbalance to redirect some power back toward children. Thus, whilst much of the CRC is concerned with protection and provision, the inclusion of a judicious but comprehensive set of participation rights notionally redresses the tension between parental anxiety and the route toward increased inclusion in civil society.

There is tension between the perceived need for greater protection, a nostalgic perception of an unbridled but safe childhood in the past. There is also an ideal of increased shared responsibility and decision making for our world and mounting fear of the apparent lack of restraint of children and youth that marks the present state of play in the history of children's role in society. That does not generally describe a move toward inclusive citizenship as either the restoration of an earlier state of being or as a seriously considered proposition for the future supported by adults in general.

Chapter 6
Intellectual Discourse, Beliefs, Moral and Ideological Positions on Children from Antiquity Until the Present – Children from Antiquity to the High Middle Ages

Chapters 6 and 7 go beyond notions explored in the preceding chapters drawn from history. Some require further development and others supplementation through examination of philosophies, theologics and beliefs that affect the position from antiquity through to modernity. Thus, to follow the time line set in the examination of children in history, this begins with Hellenic philosophers such as Aristotle (i.e.: *Politics* and *On Youth and Old Age*) and Plato and their approximate contemporaries.

Both philosophers named already were included in Chap. 3. They are chroniclers of events as well as thoughts during their time and in the immediate earlier period and are therefore themselves contributors to history. However in this chapter their work will be developed further to take in the intellectual contribution rather than the record of events as substance for this work. Other cultural areas will also be examined, including the great Eastern religions and ideologies that differently describe adults and children and the relationship between generations, as too other aspects of the three main Ibrahimic religions.

This and the following chapter follow a passage through time to the Middle Ages, on to Hobbes, Enlightenment philosophers, Rousseau, Smith, Kant, Hegel and Marx. They pass on into theoretical sociology as a precursor to modern sociology in Chap. 7 through the influence of authors such as Tönnies, Durkheim, Simmel and Weber, then on toward mid and late twentieth century thought. It includes moral and ideological positions of the period of history that shaped their work where that has any connection (however tenuous) with childhood. Likewise, it includes where they describe notions such as citizenship and human rights that were born in philosophy mainly and theology to some extent if they relate in any sense to children and childhood. Thus, the following chapters give much of the basis of that which follows.

B. Milne, *The History and Theory of Children's Citizenship in Contemporary Societies*,
DOI 10.1007/978-94-007-6521-4_6,

European Antiquity

Whilst history tells us about the position of children in different places and at particular points in time recorded in sufficient detail for us to recreate a picture, it does little to tell where they belonged. Much of the content of what made history has often been best recorded by those who have observed it or shaped it intellectually. Thus, this work turns to thought, particularly as it is expressed by philosophy, theology and other intellectual expressions of who and what a human being is and where parts of humanity belong in the social order the authors of those views saw about them. At first impression, children are not always immediately evident and seldom acquire the importance male adults hold, indeed much early philosophy often leans toward older people since they have accumulated wisdom over a whole lifetime.

Socrates was certainly of a mind that adults above the age of 30 would be best situated to begin to learn dialectic and to begin to learn philosophy one should be 50 years old. Having thus learned it by old age the person, by virtue of knowing philosophy, became interesting. However, Matthews (Turner and Matthews 1998:12) tells us that Plato found it "entirely appropriate for Socrates to engage older children and young people in philosophical discussion". It is, of course, difficult to extrapolate from this which ages he meant but it does at least show that for him there was a lifelong learning course in which preparation for 30 and 50 were permissible. However it does separate adulthood and childhood very clearly.

Only a few of the several stages of childhood are interesting for most ancient philosophers. The birth of the new child is both enigmatic and apparent, depending on whether one believed the continuum began with conception and birth or as a transition from a 'spiritual' existence to an essence or soul that entered the person at birth. For those whose focus on childhood includes a belief that life begins at birth there is a 'clean slate' view. The *tabula rasa* concept is an early appearance in philosophy. Aristotle certainly gets very close to identifying it in *De Anima* (*On the soul* or *Περι Ψυχης*):

> What the mind thinks must be in it in the same sense as letters are on a tablet (*grammateion*) which bears no actual writing (*grammenon*); this is just what happens in the case of the mind. (Aristotle 1987:3.4.430a1).

He wrote of the mind as the unwritten tablet in *De Anima*, which one might possibly consider the first text that could be described as psychology by modern western standards. He also did so more explicitly in *History of Animals* (Balme 1991:587a228-b9) in which he observed children neither laugh nor cry for 40 days, usually do not laugh when tickled and have no attachment to their parents. In *Nicomachean Ethics* (Aristotle 1999a:[VIII.12]141) he wrote: "parents love their children as soon as these are born, but children love their parents only after time has elapsed and they have acquired understanding or the power of discrimination by the senses." For him they begin life without knowing anything of the world around them. They are incomplete beings, a principle that was at odds with the earlier held Platonic notion of the human mind as an entity that already existed somewhere in the heavens before its consignment to corporeal existence. Despite bearing the knowledge of existence before corporeal life the young human being still needed to be educated in the skills of citizenship:

> Plato: what we have in mind is education from childhood in virtue, a training which produces a keen desire to become a perfect citizen, who knows how to rule and be ruled as justice demands. I suppose we should mark off this training from others and reserve the title 'education' for it alone. (Plato 1970:73)

In the Aristotelian process of 'becoming', paternalism is necessary for the progression from powerlessness, immaturity and lack of knowledge in childhood. Thus it can be seen in terms of ownership since the child, having no faculties for independent life, requires the unconditional control of the father until he (more so than 'she') learns to make own choices and be responsible for his own actions. Aristotle describes paternal exercise of constraint over a child thus:

> The justice of a master and that of a father are not the same as the justice of citizens, though they are like it; for there can be no injustice in the unqualified sense towards things that are one's own, but a man's chattel, and his child until it reaches a certain age and sets up for itself, are as it were part of himself…
>
> …justice can more truly be manifested towards a wife and chattels, for the former is household justice… (*Ibid.*: [V.6.] 82)

He also saw achieving membership of the *polis* as part of a process of learning citizenship whereby:

> …children must be trained by education with an eye to the constitution, if the virtues of (…) them are supposed to make any difference in the virtues of the state. And they must make a difference: for the children grow up to be citizens… (Aristotle 1999b:22)

Aristotle (384–322 BC) has in fact some points in common with what Socrates' contemporary K'ung Fu Tzu (*Confucius*, 551–479 BC) saw as the primary relationship within the state. That was 'filial piety' (*xiao*) (Coogan 2005:324) of children toward parents. It had probably been what had been expected for many generations. However, Confucius was the first philosopher we know to write down the expectation that a person 'became' through the study and practice of appropriate behaviour, thus takes their place within a well-defined hierarchy in which one would be treated with humanity (*Ibid.*:363–65). Fatherhood was the highest value of Chinese society, each person a subject of the father whereby the emperor was the father of all subjects. It was said that a child was 'cut, carved, filed and polished', which one might take as a somewhat more poetic manner of describing the Aristotelian 'becoming' process. The notion of citizenship was very much different to the understanding we have in the present world. Similarly, children were not born with any equivalent to our understanding of citizenship but, as Confucius described, grew into it. His work has remained the cultural foundation of much of East and Southeast Asia including where Buddhism, Tao, Shinto or, to a lesser degree, Hinduism and Islam are the dominant beliefs.

Asian Philosophy

During the sixth century BC in China Laozi (sometimes written Laotse) was author of a classic Chinese book called the *Tao Te Ching* (道德經). Tao (or Dao (道)) is a Chinese character that also means 'path' or 'way'. Although already an existing philosophy (see Oldstone-Moore in Coogan 2005:221–24) Laozi is considered the founder of Taoist philosophy as we now understand it. A common thesis running throughout the *Tao Te Ching* is that a head of state should not meddle with society. The people should be left to their own devices. When, for example, referring to government in Chapter 58 of the *Tao Te Ching* he wrote: "That which is meddling, touching everything, will work but ill, and disappointment bring". Laozi viewed the happiness of the individual as the primary goal of society.

The Taoist concept of *wu wei* ('non-action') is expanded on in Laozi's text to express *wei wu wei* ('action without action' or to 'do without doing') and is held to be an equivalent of the modern Western concept of *laissez-faire*. That is 'let do' literally, but has come to be largely based on the notion that all individuals have equality of and in rights in liberal political theory.

Laozi's position is quite unique among East Asian thought since it does separate the individual from the collective and also puts the interests of private people (citizens in our terms) before those of his or her ruler and also appears to do so without direct reference to age and gender in a classless framework.

Buddhism is more or less as far removed from Confucianism and Taoism as Aristotle was from Plato. Siddhārtha Gautama taught a doctrine of *samsara* (wandering) that describes a process of 'rebirth' whereby a person is born, ages, dies and is reborn to begin the same process in another body as animal, deity, spirit or human being. Those who have been corrupt or evil in the last life may alternatively be reborn in Hell. Whatever form is taken, after death the cycle continues. The assumption is also that in human form the experience of the former life is carried over until the *karma* is exhausted and *nirvana* is achieved. One might extrapolate from that succession that since life is a continuum that a child is born in full wisdom of previous lives, thus whatever form citizenship took comes with life.

In reality the teachings of the Buddha are only based his understanding of older Hindu beliefs, of which there are many forms with vastly different social and hierarchal practices. It is also highly influenced by other older beliefs, tribal and social organisation of different groups who became Buddhists.

There are likewise numerous differences between the main forms of Buddhism: Mahāyāna practised in China, Tibet, Viet Nam and parts of Japan, Theravāda in Sri Lanka and South East Asia, Vajrayāna which is a Tibeto-Mongolian form. Each is also divided, some are heavily influenced by Han Chinese culture, particularly in China and Viet Nam, and also very Confucian in character. There is also Chan (禅) Buddhism (commonly known by the Japanese name *Zen*) which developed as an amalgam of Mahāyāna Buddhism and Taoism (*Tao* (道). That has ancient origins and whilst the first scripts are believed to be those of Laozi from the fourth or fifth centuries BC, there are both older and more recent influences although its basic principle is of *wu wei* (無為) or 'non action' (meaning 'harmonisation' rather than 'passivity'). The passage of Buddhism into China was, in fact, by way of a 'discourse' with later Taoism that transformed both. Over several centuries of interface, Buddhism progressively found itself transformed from a philosophical rival of Taoism to a fellow denizen of the Chinese cultural ecosystem along with Confucianism, other lesser beliefs including Judaism and localised social organisation. Across the Sea of Japan, Mahāyāna Buddhism, eventually challenged the indigenous religion Shinto, eventually also bearing elements of Confucianism and Tao with it. As elsewhere and common to other cultures and beliefs, the outcome has been co-existential philosophies with no single or simple position on children.

Buddhism, despite Siddhārtha Gautama developing on older Hindu beliefs that shaped their cultural and social environment, has no precise philosophical statement about children anywhere. The adoption of the Hindu belief in *karma* that has an underlying theory of spiritual immortality gave it the notion of rebirth. For Hindus it meant spending periods of undefined time in Heaven or Hell before reincarnation. Life is thus a cycle in a longer existence and, if only notionally, the previous existence is carried over into the new, thus age is a corporeal concept. Childhood is only a stage.

However, Hinduism is a collective name for many beliefs that are at the outer extremes quite dissimilar. As elsewhere in South, East and Southeast Asia, local practice is very diverse. Thus in Hinduism children may be born as reincarnations of gods, saints or other holy people and be venerated from infancy on, thus enjoying far more privileges of his or her society than most other people of all ages. Buddhism has taken on some of that in the rebirth of *living buddhas* and priests (such as *lamas*), however it also tends to 'educate' young reincarnations into their roles by early adulthood. It is where the filial piety of Confucianism has entered or influenced Buddhist practice that children have a role that is well defined but always subordinate to that of adults.

Thus, when we look at the early period of the growth of these world religions and some of the key aspects of their philosophies that are more or less contemporaneous with ancient Greek philosophers, very few clues to a notion of an ancient egalitarianism across ages are apparent. Indeed, children are often only apparent in exceptional circumstances as child monarchs, reincarnations or their like and in no way portray anything typical of childhood.

From Antiquity to Early Christianity

Returning to European antiquity, the Stoics advocated the brotherhood of humanity and the natural equality of all human beings and became the most influential school of the Greco–Roman world. They embraced a view of the individual as a citizen of the world that reflected what Socrates is held to have said (attributed to Plutarch) that "I am not an Athenian or a Greek, but a citizen of the world." Lawrence Becker (Turner and Matthews 1998:45–61) says that the Stoics were "…theoretically committed to rejecting any form of sexism, racism, slavery, or elitism that imposed developmental defeaters" (*Ibid.*:52). However, practice seems to have been a more pragmatic approach to the moral development of children that depended on the quality of care given by adults. The Stoics were also quite opposed to Plato's view that life was a continued existence of an entity that took human form at birth, thus saw the beginning of development at the point of birth. Therefore, clearly where a theoretical space for a notion of lifelong citizenship may otherwise have been offered, in fact the Stoics are far closer to the position of modern child development than to other thinkers of their time.

Stoicism was highly influential in the Roman world which, in turn, grew as the Empire eventually occupied large parts of the Mediterranean and Western Europe but as a philosophy did not always disseminate beyond Romans themselves. One of the cultures taken into the Empire but that retained its older traditions was Judaism. Whilst the exact origins of many Jewish beliefs and teaching are difficult to precisely place, what is certain is that the inherent nature of *being* a Jew has changed very little from the earliest time to the present.

Early Jewish philosophy and theology are overshadowed by Old Testament and Torah biblical teachings. However, during the medieval period when philosophers had direct access to Arabic philosophical and scientific writings and referred closely to the Greek works of Plato, Aristotle and the Stoics, their philosophical repertoire developed and opened up. Jewish responses to Greek ethics may be seen in major rabbinic work such as the teaching of Maimonides (see Fox 1990) who propounded a Jewish interpretation of Aristotle through Islamic writings. In turn, his work was to influence Thomas Aquinas who was to be one of the leading figures in Catholic ethics and the natural law tradition of moral theology in the medieval world.

Children already had a very firmly fixed place in Jewish society. The Torah requires children to honour their parents and to care for them in old age. Childhood is also relatively short but well defined and ends with the *b'nai mitzvah*. Jewish Law says that every Jewish girl becomes a *bat mitzvah* (הוצמ תב, 'daughter of the commandments') which happens automatically reaching age 12 years. No ceremony is required, although the Reconstructionist Movement introduced the idea of celebrating *bat mitzvah* in 1922 thus ending the carried over ancient practice. A Jewish boy becomes a *bar mitzvah* (הוצמ רב, 'son of the commandments') at age 13 years because boys mature later than girls. *Bar mitzvah* is celebrated by a ceremony in both synagogue and as a secular event. As a *bat mitzvah* or *bar mitzvah* the child becomes duty-bound by God's commandments as specified in the Torah and interpreted by Moses, the Prophets, the Sages and the Rabbis. Before reaching that transition parents take all responsibility for their children following Jewish law and traditions. Thereafter they are allowed to participate in all areas of Jewish community life and bear their own responsibility for Jewish law, tradition and ethics as adults.

Judaism and the Roman Empire were eventually to have a major influence on western beliefs and where children belonged in Christian society. In fact, between the early Stoics and lifetime of Jesus Christ children appear to have attracted little intellectual attention. In Rome during the first 8 days of a baby's life there were different religious ceremonies (see Dixon 2001; Rawson 2005). A child was named on a day of purification (*dies lustricus*) but was not enrolled as a citizen until a boy put on a man's toga at a coming of age ceremony according to the birthday that came nearest to the *Liberalia* (the festival of *Liber*) on 17 March. No special ceremony marked a girl's transition into womanhood. When a boy attained majority, he discarded the childhood red edged toga (*toga praetexta*) and put on the pure white toga of a man (*toga virilis*) at some time between the 14th and 17th years. The boy's name was added to the list of citizens and official congratulations were offered (Albasi 1991; Wiedemann 1989).

As Christianity developed, Jewish and Roman purification rituals merged into baptism, at first a total immersion (of adults) in a *mikveh* (a pool where water has gathered) but later a place in a synagogue or temple. Immersion was not intended for physical cleansing since that would have been done beforehand but for spiritual cleaning in a purification ritual. Jesus Christ was immersed in the River Jordan by John the Baptist (Matthew 3:13–15 in Unknown 1971:3) and Romans practised purification and naming in early infancy. In the early Christian churches immersion was still practiced and later Roman Catholicism translated the *mikveh* into the sprinkling or smearing of water from a font onto the head of the child as an initiation into the Christian family during early infancy. However, whether Christian, Jewish or Roman ritual none of them makes a child a full member of his or her society. There was still a period of transition between initial membership, naming, purification until full membership donning the *toga virilis*, *b'nai mitzvah* or confirmation and first communion that symbolically if not legally represented admission into adulthood.

Christianity has a particularly important role in the development of the predominant modern view of children. The origins of seeing the child as weak and need of protection are to some extent based on the premise that they are born out of original sin. Pelagius (*circa* 354–420) (see Rees 1988) taught that original sin did not denigrate human nature because that was a divine quality given by God.

In his view Adam's sin set a bad example to his offspring and descendants (everybody) but had none of the other consequences attributed to the Original Sin. He taught that mortal will is able to choose between good and evil with divine intervention. Thus Jesus Christ set a good example that nullified Adam's bad. Thereby humanity has full control over its actions and bears responsibility all sins and thus is also responsible for its own salvation. Pelagius taught that since human beings were responsible for those things they did not need God's grace, thus Christ's self-sacrifice was free of the quality of deliverance from sinful transgression.

His follower Caelestius, a monastic lawyer, is said to have ascertained that even if Adam had not sinned he would have died and that his sin harmed him only but not the entire human race. He believed that the image of God is present in each newborn child and that sex is a facet of our essential creation given by God. Consequently, children are born in the same state as Adam before his fall.

Augustine

Pelagius and Caelestius' teachings were opposed by Saint Augustine (354–430) (see Saint Augustine 1998:26ff. and Defarri 1955) who taught that salvation ultimately comes through the grace of God and that individuals must also perform freely chosen benevolent works. He also believed in a form of limited predestination that did not impinge on mankind's free will. However nobody could earn salvation through these good works since that was an endowment of God's grace. Augustine saw humanity as essentially evil and corrupted by the sexual activity that brings about conception. He was shocked that Pelagius and his followers were not denounced as heretics thus summoned the Council of Carthage in 418 and at which he declared nine beliefs of the church in opposition to the principles of Pelagianism:

> Death came out of sin but was not of humanity's physical nature.
> Infants must be baptised in order to be cleansed of original sin.
> Extenuating prayer covered past and helps prevent future sins.
> The blessing of Christ gives strength and will to carry out God's commandments.
> No benevolent works are possible without God's blessing.
> All of us must confess that we are sinners because we believe it is true not do it as an expression of humility.
> Saints must also ask for forgiveness for their own sins.
> Saints must also confess being sinners since that is what they are.
> Children who die without having been baptised cannot enter the kingdom of heaven or enjoy eternal life. (*Pelagius' letter and statement of belief showing himself to be orthodox to Pope Innocent I*:417)

Each of Augustine's principles was accepted as a universal belief of the church henceforth and all Pelagians declared heretics. It was to influence the position of children in western society as the church's dogma until the twelfth century which was in part to persist until at least the views of Hobbes and Locke began to redefine their place in society. To one degree or another they have a resonance today that is still retained in secular legal views of children across all beliefs and political systems.

The Rise of Islam

Two centuries after the zenith of the moral influence of Augustine a new religious force changed the position of children in what had at first been largely a Jewish and Christian world. It eventually spread to other parts of the world where it displaced Buddhism, Hinduism, Zoroastrianism and many older, minor religions. Islam is usually dated from 622 (Kramers et al. 1954) when Mohammed and his followers arrived in Medina.

In pre-Islamic Arabia children were considered the property of fathers. Infanticide was practiced as a form of postnatal birth control, often in situations of familial destitution (boys and girls), as sacrificial offering to gods or in the advent of being disappointed or stigmatised by having a daughter. As Islam displaced other religions infanticide became a serious sin. Arabs also had a custom of using a form of adoption whereby a child was assimilated into a family legally as though through a property transfer. Under Islam the notion of children as property was discarded and the custom of adoption ended. However, Islam continued to consent to child slavery under certain circumstances (Levy 1969:79ff) such as when the children of married slaves were born enslaved they became the property of the woman's owner. Even if a free man married a female slave he did not own their children. They would be the property of the woman's owner. The same went for a child born of a slave parent from an 'irregular union'. If a child is born of an owner and slave that child is automatically free although his or her inheritance is reduced by an amount representative of the (re) sale value of his or her parent.

The Qur'an uses a variety of terms for children (Arabic words and expressions that include: *dhurriyya*, *ghulām*, *mawlūd*, *sabī*, *saghir*, and *walīd*) (see McAuliffe 2006) although the context usually does not make clear whether it is specifically referring to the maturity or age of children. Quranic assertions are more commonly connected with adoption, breast-feeding, infanticide and orphans and have traditionally been of a normative moral significance for Islamic jurisprudence that laid down the foundations of Islamic law.

However, in Quranic law children have a set of well defined rights that also describe their status in society. They have the right to be fed, clothed and protection until adulthood and to have the benefit of love and affection from their parents. They also have the right to be treated equally with siblings whenever receiving financial and material gifts and parents are expected to provide adequate inheritance for their children. Children likewise have the right to education. In return parents have very clear rights, of which the first and foremost is to be obeyed and respected by their children. A mother has particular privilege in receiving the best treatment accorded to any person and the right of custody of a child under normal circumstances.

Historically, parents had the right to physically punish children over 10 years old who neglected prayers and also had the right to admonish their children as well as protect them from physical or moral harm. They have always had the right to be looked after by their children and be given material, financial or personal physical support as required. That is most especially so during old age, although 'offspring' will probably no longer be strictly speaking definable as 'children' by age by that stage in life.

Children, it would appear, were always and are in fact still well defined by their roles and maturity and, if anything, may historically have remained children by status far longer than today. With such a fluent definition and the legal roles of children being clearly described, there is no clear reason why it may be assumed that an Islamic child could be seen as a citizen in any comparable sense to adults and, in many parts of the Islamic world, male adults especially.

One of the greater problems that always accompanied Islam has been the difficulty of differentiation between Quranic law and older, persistent cultural practices such as tribal traditions that have even persisted for the 1,400+ years in Arabia (see Kramers et al. 1954). As increasing numbers of people with different customs and traditions came under Islamic rule it came directly into contact with the theological systems of Judaism, Christianity and Zoroastrianism. It also took in the ancient philosophies of

India and Greece. Islamic theologians increasingly began to use philosophical ideas and principles to interpret Quranic doctrines. Thus, in the early medieval period, Islam itself went through an intellectually rich period in which the Greek and Roman philosophers, Jewish and early Christian theologians such as Augustine and the influences of each of the other great religions it came into contact with influenced its development. Indeed, the exchanges between the three main Ibrahimic religions were extremely fluent although very much more concerned with examination of God and belief. Relatively little energy was dedicated toward the laity.

The Influence of Ibrahimic Philosophy and Theology

Medieval thought was less philosophical than generally theological. The Ibrahimic religions were seeking divine truth through logic, dialectic and analysis to discover the truth. Underlying that was the principle of reasoned argument that was highly respectful of the positions of ancient philosophers, particularly to Aristotle, with high esteem for their intellect. The common commitment was to bring together the standpoints of philosophy with theological teaching and revelation. The latter was important above all else. Probably no other single issue concerned medieval thinkers more than the relation of faith to reason. This pursued the manner of classical Platonic ideal principles and scholasticism, particularly in Christianity, thrived throughout the medieval era. Islamic theology or *Kalam* was the rational reflection on Allah and his holy word, the Qur'an, really began at the end of the seventh century, or first century in the Islamic calendar, with debates about divine and human freedom. One school of thought was the *Qdariyyah* who defended a comparatively strong view of human freedom, although later medieval thought began to become far more rigid and seek many of the divine solutions the other faiths sought.

It was a contradictory world where compassion for the worldly was almost absent from Christianity despite it being one of the main messages of Christ to humanity. Typical of the period was that in 1095 Pope Urban II had priests' wives sold into slavery and their children were simply abandoned. Indeed, Christ's view of children as innocents deserving of compassion was relegated to little more than words in the Bible: "Suffer the little children to come unto me, and forbid them not; for of such is the kingdom of God", *Mark* 10:14, (see also Unknown 1971:101). Priests were increasingly being pressed toward devotion to piety rather than worldliness. Nonetheless, it would still not be until during the early Reformation before the Roman church eventually stopped most priests[1] marrying and having families.

Rhazes, also known as Al-Razi, (862-*circa* 925) defended the views of Plato against Aristotle, considering the latter a falsifier of philosophy. Aristotelianism was

[1]In fact priest marriage in the Roman church has never entirely disappeared for a number of reasons irrelevant to this work and the question of male priests fathering children and occasionally even through to extraordinarily 'scandalous' relationships with nuns who bear children, is a history worthy of a thesis in its own right.

maintained by Al-Farabi (870–930) and Abū ‘Alī al-Husayn ibn ‘Abd Allāh ibn Sīnā, also known as Ibn Sina (often known by the Latin name *Avicenna*), (980–1037). The Ash’arite theologian Al-Ghazali (1058–1111) denounced Aristotle, Socrates and other Greek thinkers as non-believers and characterised whoever made use of their methods and ideas to be corrupters of Islam. Islamic Aristotelian thought reached its height with Ibn Rushd (known as *Averroes*) (1126–1198) with his commentaries on Aristotle of which Hebrew translations had a lasting impact on Jewish philosophy and theology. Medieval Jewish philosophers and theologians at that time were divided into three categories. There were those primarily concerned with commentary on the Talmud, those whose main interests were more in the area of philosophical theology and others who were part of a movement that rejected the Talmud.

Thus medieval philosophy is typically viewed as theological due to the seriously debated topic of that age which was *faith* versus *reason*. Ibn Sina and Ibn Rushd were both inclined more towards the side of reason. However, Augustine and Anselm both supported a view on the ascendancy of faith. The Augustinian solution to the faith against reason problem was to believe and then search for understanding. Thus there is an abundance of philosophy in the works of medieval thinkers who used the ideas and logical techniques of ancient philosophers to tackle challenging theological questions and clarify points of doctrine.

The Graeco-Roman Hipprocratic tradition divided childhood into three stages (Heywood 2006:14). *Infantia* was birth to 7 years. Girls were *pueritia* from 7 to 12 and boys 7 to 14. *Adolescentia* lasted for both until 21 years. Ibn Sina’s *Canon* was highly influential in the Christian west, to the point that his Latin name Avicenna was preferred. He described life in stages, the first being birth to age 30 (*Ibid.*) divided into five stages that described details such as the ability to use legs through to full physical growth. Doctrinally these arguments established the unready state of the infant to be participant in the spiritual setting, which in the medieval world was considered more or less equally important across the Ibrahimic religions.

The intellectual influence of the Arabic world was especially important since it included works by classical authors that had been preserved by Islamic scholars and penetrated the Christian West through Islamic Iberia and influenced theologians like Gerbert d’Aurillac (*circa* 950–1003) who was later to become Pope Sylvester II (999–1003). Outstanding theological activity was happening in some European cathedral schools giving birth to universities such as Bologna and Oxford. The intellectual examination of faith prefigured the upsurge of theological argument that began to take place throughout the twelfth century and take philosophic enquiry even further away from worldly issues.

Aquinas

At its zenith in the thirteenth century, Thomas Aquinas (*circa* 1225–1274) sought after concord between faith and reason. Although normally regarded to be a theologian some of his work is distinctly philosophical by nature. His name for philosophy was *ancilla theologiae* (theology's handmaiden). However, he also said that theology is the guidepost of philosophy. He wrote that philosophy and theology are in harmony because both were created by God and that if philosophy conflicts with theology that would be erroneous, so that such a philosopher must revisit his or her work and look for the error within. As a consequence he was confirming a common rapport between philosophy and theology. He also brought the Aristotelian concept (see *Summa Theologica*, Volume I, Treatise on Man, 'Of the Intellectual Powers') back to the vanguard of 'modern' thought.

For Aquinas the human mind was the lowest in the order of forms of intelligence and furthest removed from the perfection of the Divine intellect. It is, he cites Aristotle having said, at first "like a clean tablet on which nothing is written" (Aquinas 1981:396). It contrasted with the Platonic notion, supported by his contemporary St Bonaventure, that since the person existed as an entity before human birth, that the intellect naturally came with the 'spirit' and was, thus, innate. However, it was the Aquinas view that was to become received wisdom. Henceforth it was held that the normal way of looking at personal development was that the full store of knowledge is built up gradually from experiences and sensory perceptions of the world into which each individual is born. With that he brought back an examination of the worldly that included what was considered the conventional way of looking at infancy and early childhood for several centuries.

By and large supporters of the *tabula rasa* thesis championed what we now consider the 'nurture' quality of the *nature versus nurture* debate whenever it comes to explanation of the development of the characteristic of an individual's personality, their emotional and social behaviour and intellect. Aquinas's views on the *tabula rasa* theory stood untried and without development until at least the time of Rousseau in the eighteenth century. However, he had an impact on political theory that Heater (1990:22) describes as 'revolutionary'. Certainly the renaissance of Aristotelian political theory, to which he contributed, accelerated the return of the concept of citizenship into the political world in the thirteenth and fourteenth centuries. These, in turn, would see the ages of liberal civic consciousness and secularism emerging during which the child would in time achieve 'personhood' and the possibility of considering citizenship would begin to be a reality.

DeMause (1974:1–74), Lyman (DeMause 1974:75–100) and McLaughlin (DeMause 1974:101–182) portray the Middle Ages in which childhood was by modern standards a nightmarish period of life (see also Alexandre-Bidon et Lett 2004). Religious belief dictated that children were born innocent but weak and had to be trained and corrected in order to enter the social order of adulthood. However it is also the period when some points of view have been expressed that probably follow the Platonic rather than dominant Aristotelian thesis. Although generally discredited on account of a very narrow view of life in the Middle Ages, Ariès (1962:15–32) analysis of the period was that once a child was weaned, he or she was regarded as a small adult whose life was little differentiated from the adults around him or herself. In his conclusion to the first part of *Centuries of Childhood* (*Ibid.*:128) he says that:

> In medieval society the idea of childhood did not exist: this is not to suggest that children were neglected, forsaken or despised. The idea of childhood is not to be confused with

> affection for children: it corresponds to an awareness of the particular nature of childhood, that particular nature which distinguishes the child from the adult, even the young adult. In medieval society this awareness was lacking.

Of course, one must draw attention to the fact that he was looking at children above age 6 years and that infancy is little more than a passing note throughout his work. The main focus of his work is also France. However it has been a highly influential thesis since it appeared in 1960. It was almost certainly the first ever social history of childhood, thus still holds sway for many other authors today.

The more important point is that as with history, even the authority of the spiritual leaders who shaped moral life has not been interpretable either way. Thus, even if the Ariès thesis was proven in everyday life, it was religions that shaped much of life and had immense power in 'political life'. They determined the exclusion of children from anything resembling modern citizenship. It was largely on the basis of doctrinal views of childhood and the role of children that with relatively few exceptions nothing substantial changed from the time of Augustine (*circa* 430).

The doctrine of original sin emerged out of the Pelagian heresy, despite not being entirely unsympathetic to children (Lyman in deMause 1974:88). That view persisted until the twelfth century when the notion of child innocence became a more acceptable view (Heywood 2006:33) although Augustinian fervour resurfaced in the Reformation (*Ibid.*). Martin Luther preached a position that original sin was as deeply implanted in children as in adults.

To all intents and purposes, the Augustinian view was orthodoxy for over 1,200 years until Thomas Hobbes (*circa* 1650) began a process of intellectual examination that moved children out of the position of total subjugation. It might also be argued that Ibn Sina and Thomas Aquinas placed markers on the route to change that began to really accelerate with John Locke in 1693.

If Ariès draws attention to any particular point, it must include the fact that in medieval feudal[2] Europe very few individuals were truly free. Education was the privilege of the small elite. Economic activity was the duty of the masses, including children from the age at which any particular child could be made to contribute within the family. It was an age when vassalage, bondage, slavery, serfdom and thraldom were the norm, where fealty to an entire secular hierarchy from local 'lords' to monarchy made the majority of people more property than free citizens. Moreover they were heavily taxed by secular lords and usually through tithes, alms and other forms of church taxes by their priests. It was also the spiritual duty of all believers of a religion to build, maintain, feed and support the places of worship, spiritual retreat (i.e. monasteries) as well as pay priests in their communities.

---

[2] *Feudalism* is used more or less as it was described by Karl Marx as the dominant economic situation before the inexorable rise of capitalism. It was defined as the power of the ruling class (aristocracy) based on their control of farming land, leading to a class society whose structure was predicated on exploitation of peasants who farmed these lands as serfs or similar. I am quite aware that it is a term that entered into common usage after European feudalism had virtually ended. It is, thus, used as a disambiguation, thus describing pre-modern (pre-capitalist) economic and social organisation that bears characteristics of what European feudalism was held to have been with emphasis on fealty and serfdom.

Whereas Ariès draws us toward a limited view of the world, in fact history holds that there was a great deal of change worldwide. Single but lengthy events such as the Mongol invasions of the thirteenth and fourteenth centuries or relatively rapid spread of Islam from Arabia to much of the known world from the seventh century on changed entire cultures, transferred parts of cultures elsewhere and integrated cultural practice into the larger event. Within such upheavals the real social and economic conditions and values of people changed.

By the time of the Mongol invasion of Europe feudalism was beginning to come to an end with material and monetary values gaining ascendancy and capitalism emerging in its earliest mercantile forms. The upshot of the Black Death in the fourteenth century was radical reorganisation of the economy leading to widespread change in European society. In the flourishing cities labour deficits brought about the momentum for economic diversification and technological innovation. The initial loss of life due to famine in the wake of the plague pandemic contributed to intensification of capital accumulation in cities, thus stimulating trade initially, then the rapid increase of other sectors as diverse as banking, textile and clothing manufacture and trade, iron mining for the flourishing armaments industry. The accumulation of surplus and overproduction increase competition to take full advantage of economic advantage bringing about civil war, peasant uprisings and uncompromising militarism. This was to lead to moves toward centralisation from the thirteenth century to its successful conclusion in England, France and Spain by the end of the fifteenth century. All constitutional restrictions on the exercise of the authority of kings and other rulers were removed although the power of the church remained by and large steadfast.

However, Europe recovered from the worst of the Black Death and prosperity advanced thus allowing the population to regain former levels by the late fifteenth and into the sixteenth centuries. The combination of both a plentiful labour supply and rapidly improving productivity promoted the move away from manorial rural economies towards industrialisation in growing urban centres.

Humanism during the Renaissance led to new theoretical discourses on the nature of the church, the authority of the papacy and royalty and most especially in universities that were seeking academic freedom. One of the innovations that advanced the intellectual cause was the growth of biblical literacy that came with the invention of movable type (*circa* 1439) and translation of the Bible in the wake of the first printed version (*circa* 1450) by Gutenberg. In parts of Europe there was dissent in the established church. In England the Lollards led protests against the authority of the church under the leadership of John Wycliffe during the 1350s as too the Hussites in Bohemia and Moravia, founded by Wycliffe's follower Jan Hus, from 1420 to 34. A century later, in 1517, Martin Luther began the protest against doctrine and authority in the church that began the Protestant Reformation.

Although Luther in point of fact revived Augustinian values, which effectively diminished and worsened the situation of children for the immediate future, it was to lead to reconsideration of their position during the Age of Reason and later to the Enlightenment. Theology that had held the dominant intellectual position among the Ibrahimic religions from at least the early medieval period was in sharp decline and to be once again superseded by philosophy. The work of such men as Descartes, Hobbes and Locke, later Hume, Rousseau and Kant would lead to a discourse that would have an enormous impact on the increasingly material and secular world. Much of the rest of the world remained broadly speaking culturally unchanged and socially and economically conservative from the medieval period until the sixteenth century. However, it was the beginning of the colonial and early capitalist period where European influence began to dominate the world and would soon begin to reshape the entire political and economic landscape.

Chapter 7
Intellectual Discourse, Beliefs, Moral and Ideological Positions on Children from Antiquity Until the Present – Children from the Middle Ages Through Early Modern to the Present

When the medieval world became the early modern, new concepts of 'humanity' began to manifest themselves in the work of European intellectuals. The influence of the Renaissance, Reformation and relatively recent historical experiences such as the peasant uprisings and Italian city states had contributed to new ways of thinking in Europe. The world was opening up as exploration, conquest and colonisation of vast areas of the world that had largely been socially and economically isolated from Europe had western values imposed on them.

Machiavelli and Erasmus

Machiavelli's best known work *The Prince*, which was written in 1513, but appeared posthumously in 1532 (Machiavelli 1532), brought about a debate that has continued to the present day. He documented the generally violent means by which political power was gained, retained and lost with detail of the public works and private morality of people involved. An explanatory footnote by the editor (*Ibid*.:103) to his inclusion of 'citizens and subjects'(*Ibid*.:37) describes them thus:

> *citizens and subjects*: Machiavelli generally distinguishes between the members of a city-state who have rights and privileges and participate in the municipal government, on the one hand, and those people who live in the surrounding *dominio* (territory or dominion), and who have fewer, if any, rights of the citizen.

Throughout the entire chapter (IX *Of the civil principality*) (*Ibid*.:34–37) he goes to length to describe who may be a citizen which includes, under two different circumstances, the 'common people'. Whilst not explicitly describing who he means by age and gender, it is probably safe to assume that men are meant from the overall language of his work. It was at the very least a move away from the narrower view Plato had expounded. That was broadly speaking all what those who were aware of such ideas knew about civic republics and citizenship. Moreover, it begins to address

B. Milne, *The History and Theory of Children's Citizenship in Contemporary Societies*,
DOI 10.1007/978-94-007-6521-4_7, © Springer Science+Business Media Dordrecht 2013

the issues that eventually contribute to liberal definitions of citizenship that included the *rights* and *privileges* of *citizens* and *subjects*.

In the Netherlands, Machiavelli's contemporary, Desiderius Erasmus van Rijn (1466–1536) was an advocate of the emergent doctrine we now know as humanism. It was a critique of ingrained and unshakeable interests and the preponderance of irrationality and superstition. In response to Erasmus's critique, Erasmusian societies formed across Europe. That was to some extent a response to the insecurity caused by the Reformation. Erasmus considered freedom of will to be a crucial point in forming a view of humanity. His discourse *De libero arbitrio diatribe sive collatio* (1524) analyses the Lutheran overstatement of obvious limitations on human freedom with enormous intelligence and good humour. Thus we see notions of citizenship and individuality emerging from what had hitherto been suppressed by religious intolerance of secularity, personal uniqueness and ability of individuals to hold their own beliefs, have free will and contribute to change of the established social order.

Hobbes

Thomas Hobbes (1588–1679) was an early political theorist occupied with the problems of government. He held that social institutions, of which he viewed government as one, were the outcome of measured agreement between free individuals. His great work *Leviathan* appeared in 1651 at the end of the three phases of war between Parliamentarians and Royalists from 1642 until 1651 commonly referred to as the English Civil War. The political *status quo* was rapidly changing and where monarchy had ruled more or less absolutely until 1642, by the end of the Civil war and following the deposal and execution of Charles I, governance and the role of common people was very much changed. Hobbes' argument was that in the absence of a social or political organisation it would be rational individuals of relatively equal status who would enter into an agreement on setting up a government. They would hold the monopoly of use of force. This innovative view heralded the beginning of modern political philosophy and the liberal state:

> A Common-wealth by Acquisition, is that, where the Soveraign Power is acquired by Force; And it is acquired by force, when men singly, or many together by plurality of voyces, for fear of death, or bonds, do authorise all the actions of that Man, or Assembly, that hath their lives and liberty in his Power. (Hobbes 1651 (1976):196)

That power acquired by force is called 'dominion' (…'this kind of Dominion, or Soveraignty, differeth from Soveraignty by Institution'… (*Ibid.*)). Hobbes says it comes in two forms which are *master over servant* and *parent over child*. The rights of sovereignty occurring out of institution and acquisition are the same (*Ibid.*:197) and also dominion:

> …is acquired two wayes; By Generation, and by Conquest. The right of Dominion by Generation, is that, which the Parent hath over his Children; and is called PATERNALL. And is not so derived from the Generation, as if therefore the Parent had Dominion over his

> Child because he begat him; but from the Childs Consent, either expresse, or by other sufficient arguments declared. For as to the Generation, God hath ordained to man a helper; and there be alwayes two that are equally Parents: the Dominion therefore over the Child, should belong equally to both;... (*Ibid.*)

In other words, the child is as absolute a subject of the parents as a servant is to the master. Hobbes viewed childhood as a period of servitude we would consider slavery in the modern world. Throughout *Leviathan* (1651) he expressed his views of children as follows:

> There be beasts, that at a year old observe more, and pursue that which is for their good, more prudently, than a child can do at ten. (71)
>
> Children therefore are not endued with Reason at all, till they have attained the use of Speech: but are called Reasonable Creatures, for the possibility apparent of having the use of Reason in time to come. (86)
>
> ...Children, Fooles, and Mad-men that have no use of Reason, may be Personated by Guardians, or Curators... (170)
>
> The Master of the Servant, is Master also of all he hath; and may exact the use thereof; that is to say, of his goods, of his labour, of his servants, and of his children, as often as he shall think fit. (199–200)

It is an expression of the incapacity of children to raise themselves above the level of animals ('beasts' or 'creatures'), be more reasonable than the psychologically deficient ('fooles' or 'mad-men') or those lacking reason to be their own person ('servants'). The final citation also expresses very well the fact that they were, in fact, essentially property until age and maturity delivered the privileges and freedom of adult citizenship. Hobbes was thus more than clearly stating a view that children, like slaves, were *owned* by their parents.

Hobbes did not believe that this authority over children simply emanated from generation but came:

> ...from the Childs Consent, either expressed, or by other sufficient arguments declared. (197)

It is a view with its foundations in a belief that authority functions only with the consent of the subject. However, given the preceding examples of views describing children as lacking rationale it is very hard to understand how that consent in fact operates. Hobbes argued (*Ibid.*:199) that force is congruent with consent in that agreements made under threat or in fear are morally binding especially in the state of nature. For him political theory itself begins in this state of nature. There is no actual need for an obligation to consent or the social contract but he assumes that people are equal in the state of nature, therefore the need for consent is foregone:

> Nature hath made men so equall, in the faculties of body, and mind; as that though there bee found one man sometimes manifestly stronger in body, or of quicker mind then another; yet when all is reckoned together, the difference between man, and man, is not so considerable, as that one man can thereupon claim to himselfe any benefit, to which another may not pretend, as well as he. For as to the strength of body, the weakest has strength enough to kill the strongest, either by secret machination, or by confederacy with others, that are in the same danger with himselfe.
>
> And as to the faculties of the mind, ...I find yet a greater equality amongst men, than that of strength. For Prudence, is but Experience; which equall time, equally bestowes

> on all men, in those things they equally apply themselves unto. That which may perhaps make such equality incredible, is but a vain conceipt of ones owne wisdome, which almost all men think they have in a greater degree, than the Vulgar; that is, than all men but themselves, and a few others, whom by Fame, or for concurring with themselves, they approve. For such is the nature of men, that howsoever they may acknowledge many others to be more witty, or more eloquent, or more learned; ... But this proveth rather that men are in that point equall, than unequall. For there is not ordinarily a greater signe of the equall distribution of any thing, than that every man is contented with his share.
>
> From this equality of ability, ariseth equality of hope in the attaining of our Ends. (*Ibid.*:141)

In *The Elements of Law* (1650 (1994):85–86) Hobbes described:

> ...already subdued... or gotten into his power any other, that (...) by infancy, or weakness, is unable to resist him, by right of nature may take the best caution, that such infant, or such feeble and subdued person can give him, or being ruled and governed by him for the time to come... ...Out of which may also be collected, that irresistible might, in the state of nature, is right...

Thus ‘might’ is ‘right’ is justified without need for any form of agreement. For the child there is filial obligation as he describes it in *De cive* (1642 (1983):167):

> ...whoever is freed from subjection, whether he be (...) a son (...) promises at least all the external signs by which superiors are honoured by their inferiors – from which it follows that the precept about honouring parents belongs to the natural law not only under the heading of gratitude but also of contract...

His proposition is that filial obligation itself derives the obvious inequality of power between adults and children within a state in which ‘citizen’ obligations reflect the consent of individuals to be governed. The obligation itself exists in the best interests of the individual. Thus we find what is essentially a political enquiry addressing the question about the moral obligations of the state towards its citizen members and who decides what *best interests* are emerging. This is an ongoing theme that will be addressed in other parts of this work and most especially when children's rights are examined. Of course, whilst Hobbes used the status of children as a means of expressing a particular relationship between generations there is no specific interest in changing their status in his work.

Changing Philosophy

At this early point in liberal theory it essentially attempted to see people as citizens of a state rather than as subjects of a monarch whose rule over them was generally accepted as a divine right conferred on the ruler by God. As the notion of absolute and divine rule over subjects declined and intellectual moves toward the individual citizen who consented (or dissented) to political authority advanced, another strand of thought questioned the dominance of patriarchal authority. Those such as slaves, servants and wives had been thereto considered to have lacked reason to be citizens but children had the potential of *becoming*. The child was seen to be capable of developing rational capacities that would ultimately lead to a point at which *he* could *become* a citizen.

In England the Civil War had brought about new perceptions of how social stratification was received. The Levellers and True-Levellers (better known as the Diggers) movements whilst relatively short lived saw a new philosophy sometimes referred to as Christian Communism. Gerrard Winstanley (1609–1676) was one of the leaders of a group of True-Levellers who began a short lived commune at St George's Hill near Weybridge in 1649 and a shorter lived commune at Little Heath in Cobham in 1650 after eviction from the first settlement.

Winstanley was very acutely aware that the Civil War would secure a bigger share of power among the merchant class and landowners, thus, quite rightly, foresaw the deprivation and corruption that would follow. He was an archetypal radical who was able to identify the obsession of those with access to capital with ownership and private property as the major root of social discontent. He was determined to put an absolute end to this form of materialism in favour of common ownership and justified this in God's word through Solomon that mankind: "… may enjoy the free use of the earth, with the fruits thereof" (Winstanley 1652; see 'Chapter 1'). As in two of his earlier pamphlets (1649a, b), his phrasing tends to imply gender equality and whilst not inclusive of children most certainly advocates the preparation of children and youth for citizenship in which very modern notions of participation and internationalism are evident:

> Mankind may be considered in a fourfold degree, his childhood, youth, manhood and old age. His childhood and his youth may be considered from his birth till forty years of age; and within this compass of time, after he is weaned from his mother, who shall be the nurse herself if there be no defect in nature, his parents shall teach him a civil and humble behaviour toward all men. Then send him to school, to learn to read the laws of the commonwealth, to ripen his wits from his childhood, and so to proceed in his learning till he be acquainted with all arts and languages. And the reason is threefold:
>
> First, by being acquainted with the knowledge of the affairs of the world, by this traditional knowledge they may be the better able to govern themselves like rational men;
>
> Secondly, they may become thereby good commonwealth's men, in supporting the government thereof, by being acquainted with the nature of government;
>
> Thirdly, if England have occasion to send ambassadors to any other land, we may have such as are acquainted with their language; or if any ambassador come from other lands, we may have such as can understand their speech.
>
> …children may not quarrel like beasts, but live in peace like rational men, experienced in yielding obedience to the laws and officers of the commonwealth, everyone doing to another as he would have another do to him. (Winstanley 1652; see 'Chapter 5')

Essentially the same kind of idea had been expressed a few pages earlier when he had explained how young people should be prepared for responsible adulthood:

> A father is to cherish his children till they grow wise and strong, and then as a master he is to instruct them in reading, in learning languages, arts and sciences, or to bring them up to labour, or employ them in some trade or other, or cause them to be instructed therein, according as is shewed hereafter in the education of mankind.
>
> A father is to have a care that as all his children do assist to plant the earth, or by other trades provide necessaries, so he shall see that everyone have a comfortable livelihood, not respecting one before another.
>
> (*Ibid.*: see 'Chapter 4')

He was also warned against creating a ruling elite who would rise in status above those of lesser ability and access to power:

> But one sort of children shall not be trained up only to book learning and no other employment, called scholars, as they are in the government of monarchy; for then through idleness and exercised wit therein they spend their time to find out policies to advance themselves to be lords and masters above their labouring brethren, (…) which occasions all the trouble in the world.
>
> Therefore, to prevent the dangerous events of idleness in scholars, it is reason, and safe for common peace, that after children have been brought up at schools to ripen their wits, they shall then be set to such trades, arts and sciences as their bodies and wits are capable of; and therein continue till they come to forty years of age.
>
> For all the work of the earth, or in trades, is to be managed by youth, and by such as have lost their freedoms. (*Ibid.*)

However, the underlying message was adherence to Christian biblical teaching and very much a reflection of the message of the prophets of the Old Testament. They would thus, had Winstanley's arguments ever become the accepted form of governance, been very closely aligned to the authority and overview of the church. It was also, and as history has tested, tried and proven, at odds with and less influential than Hobbes' views.

Critics of religious intolerance at about this time were, however, increasingly encouraging the separation of religion and secularity. In the Netherlands, Baruch Spinoza (1632–1677) wrote the *Tractatus Theologico-Politicus* and *Tractatus Politicus* as proto-liberal defences of the notion of the separation of church and state as well as describing types of democracy. In the former he expressed an early critique of religious intolerance and defence of secular governance. He was a meticulous determinist who held a view that absolutely everything occurs out of necessity. He held that even human behaviour is fully determined with freedom being our capacity to know that we are preordained to do and understand how and why we act as we do. Thus Spinoza said that freedom is not just the option of saying 'no' to what happens to us but must also entail the possibility of saying 'yes' with full comprehension of why things inevitably happen that way. The growing influence of theological positions such as John Calvin's view that all people are entirely at the mercy of God were the core of great intellectual authority and were to have a major role in the confessional and ecclesiastical debates throughout the seventeenth century. Even so the influence of developing liberal perspectives was nonetheless bringing enormous change as well.

The Enlightenment

John Locke (1632–1704) posited a theory of *mind* that is often cited as the origin of modern concepts of identity and 'self' which came to feature significantly in the later works of other philosophers such as Hume, Kant and Rousseau. He was the first philosopher to define 'self' through a continuity of 'consciousness'. He expressed the view that the mind was a 'blank slate' or *tabula rasa* without inborn ideas. That was contrary to the Cartesian philosophy, which initially arrived at a single principle: thought exists. This was a position that thought cannot be separated from the self therefore one exists.

Descartes is famously quoted as saying "*cogito ergo sum*" ("I think, therefore I am") although it is more precisely "*Dubito, ergo cogito, ergo sum*" ("I doubt, therefore I think, therefore I am"). Thus, drawing on Descartes' conclusion that if he doubted something or someone must be doubting, therewith the fact that he doubted proved his existence. The Cartesian philosophical position implies, since it is not explicitly expressed, that thought (and also doubt) are innate and thus the human mind has the foundation upon which it builds rather than beginning from nothing. Everything we experience becomes in a sense part of us, becomes an intimate component of our mental and physical being.

The contemporary appeal of Enlightenment theory is often credited to Locke's demonstration of the 'becoming' idea. In his philosophy the epistemological notion was that of the *tabula rasa* expressing the view that the human mind is a 'clean slate' at birth without rules for processing data, which are gradually added and the specific rules for progressing formed exclusively through corporeal experience. This thesis is central to Lockean empiricism. For Locke *tabula rasa* meant not only that the mind of an individual was born 'blank' but he also placed a great deal of emphasis on the individual's freedom to cultivate his or her own soul. Each individual is thus free to define the substance of his or her own character although his or her elemental identity as a member of the human race can never be changed. It is from this presumption of a free, 'self-authored' mind that is combined with an unchangeable human nature that the Lockean principle of 'natural' rights is drawn. It is, in fact, only a small step to move on from the *tabula rasa* notion that draws the 'becoming' thesis into the contemporary argument that contends that free will and choice is born into the individual although capacities and experience do indeed evolve with age. It exists in children's rights as part of Article 5 CRC that uses 'evolving capacities' as an expression for justification of adult authority over and responsibility for children.

In his *Second Treatise of Government* Locke also challenged the authority of patriarchy (1965:126–37) in which he saw the child as 'becoming' but still subject to parental authority:

> Children (…) are not born in this full state of equality, though they are born to it. Their parents have a sort of rule and jurisdiction over them when they come into the world, and for some time after, but it is but a temporary one. (127)

and:

> …the power that parents have over their children arises from their duty to take care of their offspring during the imperfect state of childhood. What the children need, and what the parents are obliged to provide, is the forming of their minds and the governing of their actions; that is while the children are still young and ignorant; when reason comes into play the parents are released from that trouble. (129)

also that:

> …we are born free as we are born rational; not that we have actually the exercise of either: age that brings one, brings with it the other too. And thus we see how natural freedom and subjection to parents may consist together, and are both founded on the same principle.

A child is free by his father's title, by his father's understanding, which is to govern him till he hath it of his own. (130)

Unlike Hobbes, Locke believed that human nature is typified by reason and tolerance, although like Hobbes he believed that it allowed men to be selfish. The latter explains why he was not an advocate of bringing children up to be only reasonable and tolerant, thus generating 'ideal' citizens. Archard (Turner and Matthews 1998:91–92) describes Locke's important contribution to political theory thus:

…his insistence that legitimate authority is founded upon the freely given consent of those individuals over whom the authority is exercised. Human beings, in a state of nature, enjoy a freedom subject to the laws of nature and are, "as Creatures of the same species and rank," entitled to equality of recognition. It is only by means of consent, their contracted agreement, that they quit this state for "the bonds of Civil Society." The rights – to life, liberty and estate – enjoyed in the state of nature are not given up with the creation of the State; it is only the power to enforce and protect these rights which is transferred from individuals to government. Civil government retains its legitimacy only in so far as continues to secure and protect these rights.

For Locke it is adult human beings who make the contract, and consequently enjoy the protection of their rights under civil government. Children are neither parties to the contract nor right-holding citizens of the government thereby agreed to.

However (*Ibid.*:92):

For Locke, children are not born *in* the full state of equality enjoyed by their parents, but they are born *to* it.

(…)

The condition of children (…) justifies parents in acting on behalf of their children, but it also constitutes (…) tutelage as a duty.

Furthermore (*Ibid.*:93) he:

…specifically rejects the view that natural parents enjoy rights over their children because the *own* them.

(…)

…he denies that parents own their offspring in virtue of having produced them.

To use 'selfish' in a very literal sense, in Locke's view although children lack the capacity to decide for themselves they are individuals with the potential that is to be developed. Thus by placing them in the setting of work that examines the origins and development of civil government and the foundations of knowledge itself he opened the door to the possibility of an inclusive stance on children in civil society. Of course, since Locke did not generally (the exception being *Some Thoughts Concerning Education* in 1693) write about children specifically it is difficult to use his work to evidence a substantial step forward in the direction of a changing position of children either intellectually or in early modern civil society.

Rousseau

Jean-Jacques Rousseau (1712–1778) was to change the established perception of childhood with *Émile, or On Education* (*Émile, ou l'education*) (1762) (here: Rousseau 1979). It was a work that drew on his own early experience of employment as a tutor and musician long before taking up his literary career in his 40s. It is a semi-fictitious work describing the growth of Émile who is a young boy being brought up under Rousseau's tutelage. In this fictional setting he is bringing him up in the country where he believes people are better suited than being in a city. That is where we learn both physical and intellectual bad habits. The purpose of education is, in his view, to learn how to live which is achieved by following a custodian or guardian who can direct one on the way to good living. The growth of a child is divided into three parts with the first from birth to the age of about 12. At that stage calculating and complex thought is not possible so that children, he deeply believed, live more like animals. The second stage is from 12 to about 16 years when reason begins to develop. The third and final part of childhood is from age 16 onwards at which stage the child develops into an adult. Émile then finds a young woman who complements him, Sophie.

By and large the book is based on Rousseau's ideals of a healthy life. The growing Émile has to work out how to follow his own social instincts and protect himself from the vices of urban individualism and self-consciousness. Émile is not an account of education of a gender-neutral 'child' since the education he suggests for Sophie, who Émile is destined to marry, is significantly different to that of Émile. Mary Wollstonecraft responded to Rousseau's assertion about men and women: "In what they have in common, they are equal. Where they differ, they are not comparable" (Rousseau 1979:358). She devoted a considerable portion of one chapter, 'Animadversions on Some of the Writers who have Rendered Women Objects of Pity, Bordering on Contempt' (Wollstonecraft 2004:99–143), to attack his arguments in *A Vindication of the Rights of Women* (1792).

The authorities made a great deal of effort to suppress Rousseau's works and the ideas they expressed, along with those of Locke, although they were to be of great influence during the French Revolution. Thus it was many years before his proposed changed educational vision would become more widely known and his 'revolutionary' ideas to be associated with the 'emergence' of children.

Some of the key elements that we can still see in his work include a view of children being very different to adults since they are innocent, vulnerable, mature slowly and are entitled to freedom and happiness. In his terms, children are naturally good. Then there is the notion that people develop through the stages above and that different forms of education may be apposite to each. There is also the guiding principle that what will be learned should be determined by understanding of an individual's nature at each stage of development. Thereto there should be appreciation of the fact that individuals vary within those stages and that education must consequently be individualised as he says 'Every mind has its own form'. All children have a fundamental impulse to partake of activity. Restlessness is eventually replaced by curiosity with mental activity being a direct development of their physical activities. Because of his views on a healthy life, the power of the environment determined the success of educational experience. It was crucial, which John Dewey would later recognise, that educators pay attention to the environment. The more they were able to control and use it, the more effective education would be. Rousseau also argued that children should be kept in complete ignorance of ideas beyond their grasp. This is the controlling function of the educator which he saw as a fundamental principle. There was also the importance of developing ideas for oneself in order to make sense of the world in one's own way.

In short, Rousseau is seen as a turning point at which children find a more pronounced place in civil society, characterised by 'primitivism' and 'irrationalism'. It was a view that gained little credence until the twentieth century and certainly adds little to an argument for children's citizenship as part of a revolutionary process such as the French Revolution to which Rousseau contributed. In fact, two of his seminal works, *Discourse on the Origin of Inequality* (1754; here 2004) and *The Social Contract* (1762; here 1998), do little to pursue the case for a changing status of children in France or elsewhere (e.g. Russia and Cuba) where his work was to contribute to revolution.

Indeed Rousseau's influence is highly evident in one of the great works in the process of achieving a universal notion of human rights, Thomas Paine's *Rights of Man* (1791 and 1792; here 1999) which is a call for democracy and egalitarianism. However, as most documents of its time, it is a call for social reforms that included reform of wage policy, public provision for those in need of work and social security for *men*. In essence it excludes women, children and slaves who are still seen as generally under the 'dominion' of men.

Kant

Around 120 years after Hobbes, Immanuel Kant (1724–1804) developed parts of his argument further. Kant's view was that a child is not property of parents. Instead he believed that having brought a child into the world they "...incur an obligation to make the child content with his condition so far as they can..." (Kant 1996:64) and that from "...this duty there must necessarily arise the right of parents to manage and develop the child" (*Ibid.*:65). It is an expression of the duty of care that broadly speaking persists to the present day but that this obligation derives not out of the child's consent but depends on his or her satisfaction ('content').

Kant was also very clearly considering the child's best interests. This in part derives from his theory that there is a single moral obligation. He called it the 'Categorical Imperative' and described its derivation from the concept of *duty*. He thus defines the exigencies of the moral law as 'categorical imperatives'. They are principles that are inherently valid and are good in and of themselves, must be obeyed under all circumstances and situations so that our demeanour is to comply with the moral law. All other moral obligations emanate from the Categorical Imperative, as too the means by which all moral obligations can be examined. Kant furthermore stated that moral means and ends may be applied to the categorical imperative, thus rational beings may pursue certain 'ends' by application of the appropriate 'means'. Those *ends* are based on physical needs or wants that will always apply for purely hypothetical imperatives. The categorical imperative, however, may be based only on something that is an 'end in itself'. That is, an *end* that is a *means* only to itself but not to another need, desire or objective.

Kant's view was that moral law is a principle of reason in itself and is not based on conditional details such as what might make us happy. Hence, for example, a human being acts on the moral law which has no further motive than the 'worthiness' of being happy: "…all happiness awaits us, except in so far as we have diminished our share in it through our unworthiness of being happy, is a practically necessary idea of reason" (Kant 1996:428). Accordingly, he believed that moral obligation applies to all and only to rational agents. However, since Kant believed children were not born with reason but had to be tutored toward being rational agents by parents, we have again a thesis that tends toward the 'human becomings' but that is cognisant of the essentially inborn liberty of each individual.

There we have what appear to be intellectual steps toward the nature of recognition of the child as an individual and bearer of rights and also the development of the concept of citizenship that may well have given children extensive rights (and duties) in civil society. Perhaps it came as a development of an event such as the French Revolution or American War of Independence, another force most certainly contributed to delaying that possibility. This was the emerging idea of 'nationhood'. Rousseau and Kant were both to contribute intellectually to this notion through their common goal of resolving the issue of bringing an end to the affliction of war on the world, in their case Europe.

Rousseau's notion of citizenship was almost Aristotelian (see Heater 1990:54) but with an inclination toward the development of a sense of national cohesion rather than global citizenship.[1] Kant, on the other hand, advocated a cosmopolitan citizenship[2] that transcended national and international laws. It thus looked toward

[1] *Global citizenship* applies to the entire world being committed to achieving absolute world peace and a concept of citizenship that is literally global and strongly connected to the concepts of globalisation and cosmopolitanism. *World citizenship* can normally be distinguished from global citizenship although sometimes the two concepts are merged. A range of ideas what a global citizen is exist. Global citizenship is also defined as an ethical and moral outlook which may guide individuals or groups in both local and global contexts in order to remind them of their respective responsibilities within a range of communities. There is a notion that during the present century children and students will become *global citizens* through education. This is held to be possible through an amalgamation of scientific and technical skills as well as traditional academic disciplines. The main canons of global citizenship include respect for all fellow global citizens, regardless of race, religion or creed, which should give rise to universal sympathy beyond the obstacles nationality has hitherto maintained.

[2] Recently the notion of cosmopolitan citizenship has been used in the form of *cosmopolitan* childhood. It is all apparently derivative from Kant whose notions of cosmopolitan law and world order essentially shaped his notion of cosmopolitan citizenship. To begin with, his interpretation of a right of universal hospitality was rooted in the natural right to carry out trading activity. That is to say, on that is in the temporary, random and trade focused exchanges between foreigners a state and its citizens. Only foreigners who passed through or resided in another state for the specific purpose of trading would be permitted to have cosmopolitan rights. Then his repudiation of the need to institutionalise cosmopolitan law beyond the state meant that pledges for the generation, execution, enforcement and maintenance of cosmopolitan rights relied principally on a state's ethical commitment to cosmopolitan ideals instead of the sovereignty of supra and super-national institutions. Consistent with these two conditions a state's duty towards non-citizens was merely to provide the conditions of the hospitality necessary in the form of a limited civil protection to

a future with something approaching world government. However, the concept of nationhood assumed a fundamental political significance that came with the rise of political ideology and the doctrine of nationalism.

Those who came to be regarded *nationalists* saw a 'nation' not merely in terms of a descriptive term for a group of people with a 'common' identity, but as an entity endowed with the right of sovereignty. If necessary, this could be achieved by the conquest or absorption of non-national territories. There is no consensus among the theorists of nationalism on whether nations were a significant political factor before the eighteenth century. Some of them see the nation state as a nineteenth century phenomenon that came about as the result of the political campaigns by nationalists or as a top-down construction of pre-existing states.

The doctrine of nationhood was that all human beings are divided into groups called nations which gives rise to the ethical doctrine of nationhood and is the foundation of nationalist ideology. The members of a 'nation' are distinguished by some kind of common identity and almost always by a common origin which is frequently expressed in terms of a sense of shared ancestry. National identity refers to the distinctive features of the group and to an individual's sense of belonging to the nation. People may be separated by differences in personality, belief systems, geography, temporality or language yet they may regard themselves, and also be seen by others, as members of one nation. Members of that nation are deemed to share certain characteristics, values and behaviour and feel a sense of duty toward other members and take a degree of responsibility for the actions of other and all members of the same nation. The nation state, however, whilst possessing many of those characteristics tends to exist in a state of political cohesion that binds people to a single 'national' identity within geographically defined boundaries which may divide literal nations.[3]

---

allow their economic activity. He believed that the right to hospitality derived from the ancient and natural right to "free access to all for the purpose" to "establish community with all". Moreover, it meant that the rights of citizens and foreigners were separate. Regardless of his expression of its global and universal extent, cosmopolitan law was not considered competent to overrule domestic law and grant foreigners access to civic and political rights linked with state citizenship. His cosmopolitan citizenship was more an idiom of global collective identity than a legally prescribed politico-legal status of universal belonging. Thus, whereby the cosmopolitan ideology and the modern paradigm of citizenship are founded on liberal principles of individualism, egalitarianism and universalism, Kant's cosmopolitan rights are limited in their content and in terms of access (see: Kant 1781, 1795).

[3] Beyond universalism and liberal nationalism, some theorists (for instance, see Delanty 2006) have identified post-colonialism. Post-colonialists argue that the nation and national identity are in essence hybrid categories in which the national, transnational and global domains are implicated concurrently. That is to say that nationalism and cosmopolitanism neither compete nor are within distinguishable frameworks for the political and social organisation of human beings. It is different to the notions of universalism and liberal nationalism since it rejects the modernist legacy of political thought generally and opposes Eurocentric and liberal individualistic ideologies entailed in other analyses of cosmopolitanism. How far this can be applied in the field of childhood remains to be seen but for this work is too new and untested to attempt to draw in.

Spence

With the emergence of the modern nation state the status of the 'citizen' and 'national' (member of a nation) began to appear. As a political status it also brought with it a new emphasis on the roles of citizens and their duties and responsibilities within their nations. In his pamphlet *The Real Rights of Man* (1793), later republished under the title *The Nationalization of the Land* (1882), Thomas Spence (1750–1814) advocated the kind of absolute change in social organisation that would have brought about an almost universal citizenship. He was a Radical democrat and advocate of the common ownership of land who strongly believed the role of the state was to provide for its members was through taxes.

His proposal was not that land be nationalised but that self-contained parochial communities be established and in which rent paid to that parish, which had absolute ownership of the land, should be the only form of taxation in that state. Profits from rents would to be used to support local government, public libraries and schools in that area. Each parish would choose a representative for the country's national assembly and every adult male would be a member of the militia. His *The Rights of Infants* (1796) is an early English language declaration of the natural rights of children. In fact, it broadly speaking addresses the question through the 'voice' of a woman in the form of a dialogue between the aristocracy and a 'mother of children'. In his own appendix to *The Rights of Infants*: 'A Contrast between Paine's Agrarian Justice, and Spence's End of Oppression', he argues that:

> ...both young and old share equally alike of the parish revenues, children and aged relations living in a family will, especially in rich parishes, where the dividends are large, through high rents or the production of mines etc., be accounted as blessings.

It is an early appeal for equality of all across boundaries of age and gender. It is a sign of the gradual move toward a new attitude on the road to the disestablishment of usually economically distinguishable (i.e. property owning) men as the only people with access to citizen's rights and duties. Spence's idea was that all people retain control and oversight of governance very locally. Whilst nationhood was one pillar of a unified society, the interdependence of members of communities with devolved control over essential resources gave both equity and stability to the other pillar of that society.

Hegel

Georg Wilhelm Friedrich Hegel (1770–1831) believed that individuals can only lead a proper moral life through absolute obedience to the laws of the state. Within that state there are two subordinate levels of social activity to which people had to commit themselves: those are the family and economic contribution to civil society. Hegel went to some lengths to distinguish between the role of individuals as 'economic man' (the bourgeois) and 'political man' (the citizen) (for instance, see Hegel

2001:76–83). He also gave great credence to the notion of nationalism as an attribute of membership of the state that thus gave identity and meaning to the citizen of that state. Within that state the family was the basis of the 'unity' which cemented overall membership and wherein children are of great importance:

> The unity of marriage which, as substantive, exists only as an inner harmony and sentiment, but, so far as it exists actually, is separated in the two married persons, becomes in the children a unity, which has actual independent existence, and is an independent object. This new object the parents love as an embodiment of their love. — The presupposition of the direct presence of the two people as parents becomes, when taken on its merely natural side, a result. This process expands into an infinite series of generations, which beget and are presupposed. (147)

Within the family, children were naturally subject to the authority and decision making processes of their parents, thus:

> Children have the right to be supported and educated out of the common family means. The right of parents to the service of their children, as service, is limited to and based upon family cares. The right of parents over the free choice of their children is just as clearly limited to correction and education. The purpose of chastisement is not mere justice; it has a subjective moral side, its object being to restrain a freedom, which is still bound to nature, and to instil the universal into the child's consciousness and will.
>
> Addition.—Man does not possess by instinct what he is to be, but must first of all acquire it. Upon this is based the child's right to be educated. As it is with children, so is it with nations under paternal government; the people are supplied with food out of storehouses, and are not looked upon as self-dependent or of age. The services required of children must bear upon their education and promote their good. To ignore this good would destroy the ethical element of the relation, and make the child a slave. A prominent feature in the education of children is correction, intended to break their self-will, and eradicate what is merely sensual and natural. One must not expect to succeed here simply with goodness, because the direct volition of children is moved by immediate suggestions and likings, not by reasons and ideas. If we give children reasons, we leave it open to them whether to act upon them or not. In this way everything depends upon their pleasure. In the fact that parents constitute the universal and essential is included the necessity of obedience on the part of children. When no care is taken to cherish in children the feeling of subordination, a feeling begotten in them by the longing to be big, they become forward and impertinent. (*Ibid.*:147–48)

Therefore children are also seen as comparable to membership of the state itself ("As it is with children, so is it with nations…"), wherein they are also bearers of rights:

> Children are potentially free, and life is the direct embodiment of this potential freedom. Hence they are not things, and cannot be said to belong to any one, their parents or others. But their freedom is as yet only potential. The education of children has with regard to family life a two-fold object. Its positive aim is to exalt the ethical nature of the child into a direct perception free from all opposition, and thus secure that state of mind, which forms the basis of ethical life. The child thus passes his earlier years in love, trust, and obedience. Its negative aim is to lift the child out of the natural simplicity, in which it at first is, into selfdependence and free personality, and thus make it able to leave the natural unity of the family.
>
> Note.—That the children of Roman parents were slaves is one of the facts which most tarnishes the Roman law. This wounding of the ethical life in its most intimate quarter is an

> important element in forming an estimate of the world-historical character of the Romans, as well as of their tendency towards formal right.
>
> The necessity for the education of children is found in their inherent dissatisfaction with what they are, in their impulse to belong to the world of adults, whom they reverence as higher beings, and in the wish to become big. The sportive method of teaching gives to children what is childish under the idea that it is in itself valuable. It makes not only itself ridiculous, but also all that is serious. It is scorned by children themselves.
>
> Since it strives to represent children as complete in their very incompleteness, of which they themselves are already sensible. Hoping to make them satisfied with their imperfect condition, it disturbs and taints their own truer and higher aspiration. The result is indifference to and want of interest in the substantive relations of the spiritual world, contempt of men, since they have posed before children in a childish and contemptible way, and vain conceit devoted to the contemplation of its own excellence. (*Ibid.*)

Whilst he was not advocating intergenerational equality, he expressed a mild critique of the irrationality of some of the notions normally considered as defining what is suitable for children and their capacity to express opinions. It is a step forward in the longstanding notion of the child as being in a state of becoming that is far from offering a full role in civil society. It certainly offers a chink of light through a previously closed door of opportunity that had moved relatively little from Hobbes, despite some interpretations of what Locke and Rousseau said as great steps. It is most certainly measurably less Aristotelian than Rousseau's positions. However, Hegel's position on the subservient role of the citizen within a very strong state denies the degree of individuality that is attached to contemporary concepts of citizenship in which children would be able to make choices independent of the will and supervision of adult caretakers.

Mill, Marx and Engels

Then there is John Stuart Mill's (1859) argument for a broader 'weak' autonomy. He postulated a view that people (adults) do not necessarily make wise and right decisions but that the highest value is liberty. People possess the right to choose for themselves. Mill (1806–1873) included women but not children because he assumed that they are too immature to be liable for the risk of making personal decisions. For him, the 'age of consent' divided adulthood from childhood. Along the lines of a view held by Jeremy Bentham, Mill relocated morality away from duty toward utility and cost effectiveness.

He considered that in democracies the highest value is the right of choice and to vote when the freedom to choose matters more than whatever value or an alternative is chosen. People generate their personal destiny that is based on their own risk-benefit reckoning. In Mill's world, contracts replace trust and thus reduce risk. However, it should be borne in mind that civil rights were only really extended to working men in the nineteenth century and to women and other 'minority' adult groups in the twentieth century as the outcome of often embittered campaigns. Thus the history of the 'liberation' of women plays an important role in concluding the argument for the extension of citizenship to children although the inclusion of children was unacceptable for theoretical and practical reasons. Citing Mills' *Principles of Political Economy* (Turner and Matthews 1998:139):

> …classing together, for this and other purposes, of women and children appears to me both indefensible in principle and mischievous in practice. Children, below a certain age cannot judge or act for themselves; up to a considerably greater age they are inevitably more or less disqualified for doing so…

Given the influence of Mill's work, it is most likely that it has had at least some lasting influence on the modern view of childhood which separates children as immature and vulnerable. In Mill's view they are subject to the care and protection of adults who also bear responsibility for their moral and social preparation for adult life. That view holds sway to the present day. If viewed through a contemporary equivalence of his position on women's right to equality then it may be possible to extrapolate a view that children deserve moral and political equality with adults.

In examination of the intellectual progress of children from antiquity to the present day, it would be almost natural to assume that Mill's contemporaries Marx and Engels would contribute. Indeed, the latter in his most famous work *The Condition of the Working Class in England* in 1844 Friedrich Engels shows a great deal of concern with English children. However that is more or less confined to critical appraisal of their working conditions, broadly speaking that they worked at all, and somewhat less to their broader role in civil society. He does, however, say that schools had the role of teaching "… educational skills, (…) not only occupational skills, but also the nature of (…) domestic and social relations, (…) position in society, and the moral and religious duties appropriate to it" (1999:157).

Karl Marx likewise shows some degree of concern for the economic exploitation and poverty of children in parts of his large body of work. On the other hand he does not look at them as important social actors so that in his examination of civil and human rights where political and social emancipation is separable from an essentially economic thesis there is relatively little. Indeed, the only really substantive work is *On the Jewish Question* (1844) which was a critique of the situation of civil and human rights at the time he was writing. It is mainly a critical view of Judaism and Christianity seen from his position on social emancipation. In his *Foundations of the Critique of Political Economy* (1857), sometimes known as *Grundrisse* (*Grundrisse der Kritik der politischen Ökonomie*) (1993), he said that: "Die Gesellschaft besteht nicht aus Individuen, sondern drückt die Summe der Beziehungen, Verhältnisse aus, worin diese Individuen zueinander stehn." (Society does not consist of individuals but articulates the sum total of relationships [and] conditions that describe the relationship of individuals to each other). English translation loses a great deal of the nuance of the word *Gesellschaft* which has greater depth in its original form as used in Ferdinand Tönnies' 1887 work *Gemeinschaft und Gesellschaft* (Tönnies 2005) that has become part of the vocabulary of modern sociology.

Whilst Tönnies was of the view that distinction between social groupings is based on an assumption that there are only two basic forms of an actor's will to express approval of other actors, that approval is by no means self-evident (see Tönnies later in this chapter). It is rather more an idea in line with what Hobbes is saying than Marx, thus there is a very little room for a view that Marx's *Gesellschaft* is an inclusive version in which children might have a distinct role. Indeed, Marx, whilst giving little consideration to children is often cited as having written that "Children should educate their parents" in an article for the New York Daily Tribune in 1857. In their joint works such as *The Communist Manifesto* (1872) there is a great deal of reference to gender disparity and only fleeting attention paid to age and then usually with reference to labour exploitation by bourgeois entrepreneurs. Thus, despite a tendency to look toward Marxism for suggestion of highly influential social changes there is very little of any notable value for this work.

The Philosophy of Education and Welfare as Social Control

In fact education and welfarism, and more explicitly emergent 'philosophies' of each, were to have a far greater role in influencing how children were seen. In England and Wales the 1870 Elementary Education Act introduced compulsory universal education for children aged between 5 and 13 years. The 1880 Education Act better regulated school attendance laws. There is some debate whether or not this was for the best interest of children depending on whom one reads. Some authors such as Corrigan (1979), Goodman (1971) and Illich (1971) occasionally use the example of nineteenth and early twentieth century political argument for the introduction of compulsory education as a means of removing idle, unemployed youths from streets and public places. It is highly possible that what appears a propitious move toward the protection of children and bringing about an improvement of their living standards was almost always inclusive of the element of increased control over them thus more ideological than altruistic.

What is apparent from political history is the real fear of potential disruption by young people. That was to lead to every consideration of one of the more important products of education which was turning out people who would be part of a disciplined, punctual labour force, as Corrigan (1979:33) says:

> In looking at the inspectors' reports over thirty years we can see that there were a number of strands in (…) 'education' and that these were very directly linked to fears of insurrection.
>
> 1. The provision of bourgeois facts and theories to counter both 'revolutionary' facts and those facts that were derived from the material conditions of working-class existence at the time.
> 2. The provision of a bourgeois moral and religious code, which once it had been taught to the working class, would shape their behaviour.
> 3. The creation of a disciplined, punctual labour force.
> 4. The creation of a hierarchy of civilisation based on education and refinement which the working class would respect and of which they would find themselves at the very bottom.

It is a view that reflects Engels' simpler analysis of the reason for compulsory education. It was designed to provide a bourgeois moral and religious code for the working class within basic education for their children that would offset the potential for revolutionary activity that was an embryonic force under the material conditions of the working class way of life at that time. Therewith the position of children when they grew up and took their place in the social hierarchy would be an outcome of the subtlety of educated-ness that schooling with its routines and disciplines inculcated (see Corrigan 1979:29–43). This was the educational ideology that was disseminated through the entire British Empire as public education began to be widespread.

Social Reform

Education was part of the wider provision of welfare that was developing quickly in industrialising Europe. The welfare state is a 'double-edged' provision that requires something back from the people it looks after. It is the outcome of a long process of social reform that not only bestowed greater freedom and privileges on people but also demanded more of them.

From the late eighteenth and throughout the nineteenth centuries social reform was a fast moving component of the changes of the status and situation of children especially. Two particular *forces majeur* that contributed to change that led to the creation of the welfare state have had long term effects that resonate to the present day: philanthropy and literature. In 1807 when the abolition of the slave trade was being debated in Parliament, a campaign that had lasted two decades ended and saw the age of philanthropy come into its own. The House of Commons voted by 283 to 16 to abolish the slave trade. Acquisition, transport and the sale of enslaved Africans became illegal although slavery remained legal in Britain's colonies.

When the driving force of the abolitionist movement, William Wilberforce retired from Parliament in 1825, younger MPs like Thomas Fowell Buxton took over the Parliamentary campaign. In July 1833 the bill abolishing slavery was finally passed. The Buxtons were to continue to campaign for what we would call 'human rights' today. The end of slavery is probably the single most distinct marker on the way to a rights based social state in which most people are entitled to the benefit of welfare provisions. The extension of rights was also a political expediency that reflected a genuine fear of the possibility of the masses rising up in revolution.

Philanthropy

People like the Buxtons were part of a new group of educated, well-heeled people who became known as philanthropists. Philanthropy describes endowment of money, goods, services, time or effort in support of something socially beneficial. It has a defined objective but offers no financial or material reward for the donor. It usually includes any unselfish activity aimed the improvement of the improvement of the quality of life of humans or animals. It is essentially a liberal, intellectual pursuit that must always be converted into practical and material outcomes. Children were early beneficiaries. Mistakes were also made, as examples of the expatriation of children to the colonies that follow illustrate.

Toward the end of nineteenth century greater attention was paid to the specific needs of children. Mary Carpenter (1807–1877) opened a small school for girls with her mother in Bristol. It has been said that her interest in the problems and experiences of children living in poverty began when she was out with a philanthropist, Dr Joseph Tuckerman, in 1833 and saw a small ragged boy in the street. He said that "…the boy should be followed to his home and seen after…" (Young and Ashton 1956:166).

In 1846 Mary Carpenter opened a 'ragged school' in a poor neighbourhood of Bristol where: "…she was faced with the riotous behaviour of untamed and poverty-stricken children, yet she succeeded in holding their interest by her ability and enthusiasm" (*op. cit.*). She thus began to focus on the needs of the 'difficult' children who were often also offenders because she was shocked by the way they learned criminal behaviour at such an early age. She began to study the situation in other countries.

In 1851 she published an essay on reform schools *Reformatory Schools for the Children of the Perishing and Dangerous Classes and for Juvenile Offenders* and organised a conference in Birmingham on the institutional care of young offenders. There was a great deal of interest in her ideas and in 1852 she opened a reformatory for boys and girls. Her work was influential, influencing the writing of the Youthful Offenders Act 1854 that acknowledged the role of the reformatory schools.

Her lobbying contributed to the passing of the Industrial Schools Acts 1857, 1861, and 1866. Young and Ashton (1956:169–172) described six of her methods and principles:

1. Treatment should be based on the love of the child. Thereby the trust, affection and sense of security 'normal' child expected within the family can be stimulated. After visiting the Rauhe Haus in Hamburg she believed that a reformatory should be as close in size to a family as possible so that individual needs could be dealt with and an appropriate environment created.
2. Change necessitated the cooperation of a child. She believed it difficult to do any consequential work unless children were ready and willing to change and believed that progress was possible. Without their active participation she believed that change would not be forthcoming.
3. Work was only a means to an end instead of an end in itself and never forced work since she believed it had no instructive quality. She felt: "It would be better for a child to be idle, even refused access to work, so that when he was tired of his idleness work could be made available as a favour."
4. Recreation was as important as work and children needed sport which was stridently opposed to the dominant thought of her day. She thought that teachers in schools had better opportunity to determine "the true nature of the boy in his periods of recreation than at any other time."
5. Corporal punishment was reduced to a minimum because she felt that relentless harshness and intemperance were counterproductive. When children earned money for work and had own possessions they would be more prone to respect the property of others.
6. The approach should be educational whereby Christian and moral teaching had to be parallel to learning a trade.

In contrast to other practitioners she also had no fixed idea of how long a reform process might take believing that: "Each case should be dealt with on its merits, release dependent on the progress made, and decided by the school managers under a government inspection" (*Ibid.*:171). Whilst the emphasis was for work with children who broke laws, the undercurrent was always the social environment in which they lived and seeking a better quality of life for children generally (see Manton 1976).

A 'child-saving movement' emerged in the USA during the nineteenth century (see Platt 1969) that was very similar to the work of Carpenter and was to be very influential in the development of the juvenile justice system. The 'child-savers' emphasised the value of redemption and prevention through the early identification of deviance with intervention in the form of education and training. They were reformers who developed programmes for disturbed and troubled youth rather than for all children. Contemporary critics say that they were far more interested in control of the poor rather than their welfare. However, the development of juvenile justice has contributed to giving children a well defined place in society that whilst separating them from adults also introduced a notion of proportionality and practice that can be compared with the 'evolving capacities' principle at the core of present day children's rights (Article 5, CRC).

Poverty was nonetheless an issue that drew attention to children. Thomas Barnardo (1845–1905) noticed the plight of homeless and destitute children in 1866 whilst working in the East End of London during a cholera epidemic. He opened his first home in the East End in 1870. His homes were started to search for and to receive waifs and strays who were then fed, clothed and educated and wherever possible given industrial training. The principle was of free and immediate admission with no restrictions on age, sex, religion or nationality.

Children were accepted irrespective of whether they were physically healthy or incurably ill with one necessary qualification of destitution. Infants and younger girls and boys were usually 'boarded out' in rural districts. Girls over 14 years of age were sent to industrial training schools to be taught useful domestic occupations and boys over 17 years of age tested in 'labour homes', then placed in employment at home, sent to sea or emigrated. Boys between 13 and 17 years of age were trained for various trades for which they were assessed to be mentally or physically suited. There were also other institutions including a rescue home for girls in serious danger, a seaside convalescent home and a hospital for the chronically ill. At the time it was generally felt that the most useful of all work introduced by Barnardo was the emigration system. Thereby thousands of boys and girls were sent to British colonies, mainly Canada.

Other organisations began to send British boys and girls overseas. One, the Fairbridge Society, was established specifically to relocate young children to populate the Empire with 'Good White British stock'. Other British national charities such as the Church of England, the Methodist Church (through the National Children's Homes), the Salvation Army and the Catholic Church played major roles in forced migration. In New Zealand children were frequently placed with foster parents whilst in Canada children were placed with farmers, often without sufficient preparation and supervision. Some farmers were later charged with manslaughter due to the extent of their cruelty.

Only few children were ever legally adopted overseas with the majority spending entire childhoods in large, impersonal institutions or farm schools that accommodated over 300 children. These migrations were motivated by a diversity of objectives although none of them gave priority to the needs of children. Accordingly, child migrants were later seen as a propitious source of cheap labour for Canada's farms, as a measure to boost Australia's post-war population and means of safeguarding a white, professional elite in former Rhodesia. Considering it had begun as a philanthropic principle, the sad truth for many child migrants was appalling standards of care that fell well below accepted standards found within British institutions. Nonetheless, it was to persist until the 1960s.

In 1881 the Reverend George Staite wrote to the *Liverpool Mercury*: "…whilst we have a Society for the Prevention of Cruelty to Animals, can we not do something to prevent cruelty to children?" (NSPCC 2005:4). Social attitudes made very clear distinctions between the public and private lives of Victorians so that the famous reformer Lord Shaftesbury said to Staite: "The evils you state are enormous and indisputable, but they are of so private, internal and domestic a nature as to be beyond the reach of legislation" (*Ibid.*) A Liverpool banker, Thomas Agnew, visited the *New York Society for the Prevention of Cruelty to Children* whilst on a trip to New York in 1881. On his return he set up a similar project in Liverpool in 1883, the *Liverpool Society for the Prevention of Cruelty to Children* that was eventually followed by the *London Society for the Prevention of Cruelty to Children* in 1884 under the his guidance (*Ibid.*:7). In 1889 the London Society had 32 branches that were known as *aid committees* throughout England, Wales and Scotland. Each branch raised funds from donations, subscriptions and legacies that supported an inspector whose task was to investigate reports of child abuse and neglect. At the 1889 Annual General Meeting the Society changed its name to the *National Society for the Prevention of Cruelty to Children* (*Ibid.*).

Josephine Butler was a Victorian 'feminist' whose work was especially concerned with the welfare of prostitutes. As an outcome of her efforts, international organisations including the International Abolitionist Federation began a campaign against state regulation of prostitution and the traffic in women and children between 1869 and 1886.

Throughout Europe and North America other philanthropic works were to be influenced by the reforms in Britain. However it was the other major force for change that was to be more universally influential. That was literature. It would be more likely that a separate thesis examine the role of literature in order to do its diversity and importance justice. This brief visit attempts only to give only a small sample.

Literature and Children

In the early nineteenth century Romantic poets and novelists 'discovered' children. William Wordsworth's *Ode: Intimations of Immortality from Recollections of Early Childhood* (1807) epitomises the direction of this development. It is a deeply philosophical work thematically ranging from the Platonic belief in pre-existence to the poet's own belief that children have an instinctive wisdom that adults lack. His interpretation of Plato's pre-existence was that the soul existed in an 'ideal' other state prior to corporeal existence and that it will return to the ideal other state after death. The immortality the title refers to is that of the soul which he believed is felt or alluded to during infancy; thus his famous opening line to the *Ode*: "The Child is the Father of the Man."

Samuel Taylor Coleridge, John Keats, Walter Scott, James Hogg and Lord Tennyson all wrote about children, whereas others including the Lambs, Edward Lear, Heinrich Hoffmann and Lewis Carroll (Charles Lutwidge Dodgson) wrote for them. Much of the work of Romantic poets was largely sentimental and more trivialising than contributing to any significant steps forward in civil society. On the other hand, the authors writing *for* children had made a large step forward to recognition of children as an audience capable of enjoying their work.

Charles Dickens tends to be the first author who strikes a critical chord generally. His *Bleak House* appeared in 1853 is one of the sharpest parodies of social injustice of its time. One of the main characters is Jo the crossing sweeper, a rootless child who has nobody and nothing. He is a forlorn, hopeless character who lives in a decaying part of London known as Tom-all-Alone's. Jo's character and history are only briefly outlined by Dickens.

He presents Jo thus:

> Here he is, very muddy, very hoarse, very ragged (Dickens 1853:108).
> …Jo the outlaw with the broom… (*Ibid.*:160).

When he appears in court as a witness for his one and only friend he cannot comprehend the coroner's quite ordinary questions about his identity, so that Dickens tells us:

> Name, Jo. Nothing else that he knows on. Don't know that everybody has two names. Never heerd of sich a think. Don't know that Jo is short for a longer name. Thinks it long enough for him. He don't find no fault with it. Spell it? No he can't spell it. No father, no mother, no friends. Never been to school. What's home? Know's a broom's a broom, and it's wicked to tell a lie. Don't recollect who told him about the broom, or about the lie, but knows both (*Ibid.*:10).

Dickens very graphically portrays children of his time in a number of books. In *Oliver Twist or the Parish Boy's Progress* (1838), *The Personal History of David Copperfield* (1850) and *Great Expectations* (1861) there are children who could have as easily be rewritten versions of observations from journalist Henry Mayhew's four volume *London Labour and London Poor* (1851) or *London Characters* (1874) who visited the poorest parts of the city. However it was not only England where we find rootless, dispossessed children. In the USA Mark Twain (Samuel Langhorne

Clemens) wrote two books with boys as main characters: *The Adventures of Tom Sawyer* (1876) and *The Adventures of Huckleberry Finn* (1884). *Huck Finn* was a development on *Tom Sawyer* and demonstrated a more serious quality than its antecedent. The main assertion behind *Huckleberry Finn* is the young boy's (Huck) confidence in 'the right thing to do' although the majority of people believe that what he did was wrong (Bennett 1974). It is a very moral story that examines the situation of children in the society Twain lived in and recorded as a journalist.

Hans Christian Andersen's short 'fairy tale' *The Little Match Girl* (1846) used a short story to describe the hopeless plight of an impoverished child who would die rather than fail to sell her matches in the freezing streets of a Danish city on Christmas Eve. She dies unseen and uncared for by celebrating people around her.

Charles Kingsley wrote *The Water Babies* (1863) categorically as a 'fairy tale'. It naturally has the moral, even though Kingsley was explicit rather than tacit as is the norm in more traditional tales. The morphology of the story owes a great deal to contemporary writers and is to a degree a social comment on injustice against children in his time although traditional elements are present. His inspiration was Charles Darwin's *The Origin of Species* and is a modified version of the theory of evolution for children. It shows that survival of a species is determined not only by the condition of the physical being but also the condition of the soul. It was a critique of the materialism of the Victorian age as a vehicle for adaptation of Darwin's theory. In fact, he was heavy influenced by reporters of his age like Mayhew and thus reflects portrayal of the real world in which he lived.

Although the story is set earlier, Petit Gavroche is one of Victor Hugo's main characters in *Les Misérables* (1862) the street boy is a powerful image who Hugo dedicates six subchapters to. He took almost eight pages (Hugo 1994:396–402) to introduce the notion of the Parisian 'gamin' before turning to Petit Gavroche himself. In a footnote he tells us:

> This word 'gamin' was printed for the first time, and passed from the popular language into that of literature, in 1834. It was in a little work entitled *Claude Gueux*[4] that the word first appeared. It created a great uproar. The word was adopted. (Hugo 1994:396).

It is, in fact, a social comment on the lives of children of his own time including children he would have seen around him in France and later in exile in other places including Jersey.

The preoccupation of Victorian authors was with poverty and injustice, however their portrayal of young characters is usually independent, competent, moral and reasoned (Jo is generally all of those things despite his general ignorance of the world about him). Thus literature was not uncommonly used in campaigns for anti-cruelty

---

[4] *Claude Gueux* is a short story written by Hugo in 1834. It is regarded as an early example of 'true crime' fiction and is written around his early thoughts on societal injustice which 30 years later he brought to life in *Les Miserables*. *Gamin* appears on the second of the three page story in this sentence: *Rien ne pouvait faire que cet ancien gamin des rues n'eût point par moments l'odeur du ruisseau de Paris*, and describe Claude Gueux as an 'old (former) street urchin'.

laws and the raising of the age of sexual consent and marriage were amongst many laws that came either side of the change of century in Europe, parts of the USA and South America, as also in large parts of the European colonial world.

The Emergence of Child Sciences

The early twentieth century was, though, to be undoubtedly the beginning of real change for children. Child 'sciences' including developmental psychology, paediatrics and child psychiatry were to become formally accepted disciplines. It was an era during which, as Zelizer (1985) describes in the USA but applied almost comparably throughout the Western world, efforts to capitalise and in some ways assign a financial value to children and increasingly sentimentalise them to the degree of making them almost 'sanctified'. It is this period when the child ceases to simply be a chattel of parents, especially the father, toward becoming an individual bearer of rights. The knowledge of the importance of the life stage 'childhood' also began to develop. Undoubtedly some of the greatest steps toward what we recognise as modern child protection and welfare occurred at that time.

Thus, one might say that, childhood had finally emerged as a distinctly identifiable life stage in a way that absolutely separated them from adults. Even then in many respects it was a position that had travelled only a very short step forward from the view held by Hobbes in 1651. Zelizer's title *Pricing the Priceless Child: the changing social value of children* encapsulates all of the components of childhood that was on the threshold of becoming what it is at present. That includes the nature of the contradiction between (over-) protection and the potential for participation in society as full citizens. This theme will be developed on in the next chapter.

Sociology

Toward the end of the nineteenth and early in the twentieth century sociology emerged as a discipline in its own right. Its roots were deeply embedded in moral philosophy although its proponents and those beginning to advance the discipline were looking at how society was organised, from whence it came and where it might be going. Pre-eminent among sociologists at the time were Ferdinand Tönnies, Émile Durkheim, Georg Simmel and Max Weber.

Ferdinand Tönnies (1855–1936) was a Hobbesian sociologist best known for his contribution to sociology that made the distinction between two types of social grouping: *Gemeinschaft* – often translated as *community* – is a form of social integration based on personal relations, thus more a community than association as in *Gesellschaft*, and conceivably historically epitomised by a family or neighbourhood in pre-modern (rural) society. *Gemeinschaft* is characteristic of small scale, localised societies and is in contrast to *Gesellschaft* which refers to complex, impersonal societies.

Gesellschaft – often translated as *society* – is a form of social integration based on impersonal ties thus attributed to large scale, complex societies, with strict division between private and public spheres of life and contrasting to community-oriented life. *Gesellschaft* relationships arose in urban and capitalist settings embodied by individualism and impersonal pecuniary connections between people.

The distinction between social groupings is based on an assumption that there are only two basic forms of a social actor's will. His *Wesenwille* (essential will) describes an actor seeing himself as a means of serving the goals of social grouping, which he considered to be an underlying subconscious force. Group around *Wesenwille* are called a *Gemeinschaft*. The other is *Kürwille* (arbitrary will) whereby the social actor sees a social group as a means of advancing individual goals thus decisive and future-oriented. The groups are called *Gesellschaft*. Whereas membership in *Gemeinschaft* is self-fulfilling, *Gesellschaft* is instrumental for its members. In theoretical sociology the two types of will are strictly separated, whereas in applied sociology (thus empirically) they are mixed.

Émile Durkheim (1858–1917) was primarily concerned with how societies could maintain integrity and coherence in the modern era. He believed that things such as common religious and ethnic background should no longer be assumed. So as to study social life in modern societies, he set out to establish one of the first scientific approaches to social phenomena. Under the influence of Herbert Spencer, he was one of the first people to describe the existence and quality of different parts of a society by reference to what function they served in maintaining the *commonplace* or *every day*, and sometimes seen as a forerunner of functionalism. He insisted that society was more than the sum of its parts. Unlike his contemporaries Tönnies and Weber, he focused not on what motivates actions of individuals but instead the study of *social facts* which describe phenomena with existence in and of themselves not bound to actions of individuals.

Durkheim argued that social facts had independent existence, better and more objective than actions of the individuals who composed society. They were only explained by other social facts instead of, for instance, society's adjustment to a specific climate or ecological location. In his view, the phenomenon of society is not itself dependent on the personal nature of individuals (Durkheim 1963:36) and also that "…individual natures are (…) indeterminate material that the social factor moulds and transforms" (Durkheim 1966:24). This view is developed a little further in the following chapter.

Georg Simmel (1858–1918) referred to "all the forms of association by which a mere sum of separate individuals are made into a 'society'" (Simmel 1949:157) that he describes as a "higher unity" (*Ibid.*) composed of individuals. He was particularly excited about the "impulse to sociability in man" (*Ibid.*) which he described as "associations… (through which) …the solitariness of the individuals is resolved into togetherness, a union with others" (*Ibid.*:158). It is a process he described by which "the impulse to sociability distils, as it were, out of the realities of social life the pure essence of association" (*Ibid.*) and "through which a unity is made" (*Ibid.*) and is "free-playing, interacting interdependence of individuals" (*Ibid.*). He defines sociability as the "play-form of association" (*Ibid.*) motivated by "amicability, breeding, cordiality and attractiveness of all kinds" (*Ibid.*). So that free association can occur "the personalities must not emphasize themselves too individually… with too much abandon and aggressiveness" (*Ibid.*).

Simmel also elucidated a "…world of sociability… democracy of equals… without friction" provided that people interact in a spirit of fun and affection that would "bring about among themselves a pure interaction free of any disturbing material accent" (*Ibid.*:159). Since numerous social interactions are not exclusively of this agreeable disposition, one must conclude that he described a rather idealised vision of the best types of human interaction which are absolutely not the most representative or common type.

Max Weber (1864–1920) considered ultimate values and their consequent political values to be subjectively determined. He believed that particular communities are able to provide conditions for not only *bourgeois* values such as citizenship and true democracy but "…also much more intimate and yet eternal values, including artistic ones" (Lassman and Speirs 1994:76). Language used to characterise the two types of values led to the interpretation that he understood them to be a subjective matter. As regards the first set of values, labelling them *bourgeois* revealed their conditional nature in which they are the product of a class. The second set of labels *intimate* and *eternal* explicitly set them apart from any objective basis. An *intimate* value is by definition personal such as an opinion. Furthermore, it carries the implication of emotion and *eternal* likewise. In his *Economy and Society* (Weber 1992), he looked at society in terms of 'Status Groups and Classes' (*Ibid.*:302–309) and 'Household, Neighbourhood and Kin Group' (*Ibid.*:356–369). He thus moved on from Durkheim's concern with how societies maintain their integrity and coherence to how society is structured in capitalist society and also developing on the *Gemeinschaft* and *Gesellschaft* ideas expounded by Tönnies.

He was also very interested in religion. His *Religion of China: Confucianism and Taoism* (1951) was his second major work on the sociology of religion. He focused on aspects of Chinese society different from those of Western Europe that particularly contrasted with Puritanism. He also asked why capitalism did not develop in China. He viewed extended kinship groups in China that were based on the religious importance of family ties and ancestry as the means of protection of members against economic hazards. They thus approved or disapproved accumulation and payment of debts, work discipline and rationalisation of work processes. They also opposed development of an urban *status* class, slowed down development of legal institutions, the codification of laws and the emergence of a lawyer class.

He believed that Confucianism and Puritanism represent two comprehensive but mutually exclusive types of rationalisation in which both endeavour to organise human life according to specific definitive religious beliefs. They both encouraged moderation and self-control and were well-suited to accumulation of wealth. Confucianism strove to attain and preserve a cultured status position and used education, self-perfection, courtesy and familial piety as means of tuning into the world. Puritanism used those means to create a tool of God thus generates individuals who would serve God and thus succeed in the world.

Whilst none of these, or indeed, other early sociologists contributed directly to the substance of this work in respect of children, they were to be highly influential through the social sciences and, in due course, to what became most recently known as the *new sociology of childhood*. On the other hand, none of them is to be excluded in any examination of citizenship.

Children's Rights Pioneers

Philanthropy, education and even literature were also to contribute to changes that came with the twentieth century. One of the vanguards was Janusz Korczak (1878–1942). Korczak was the pseudonym of Henryk Goldszmit who was a Polish-Jewish paediatrician, educationist and children's writer. It is uncertain when he seriously began to give children's rights any form of consideration but what is known is that in 1911–1912 he was director of a Jewish orphanage, Dom Sierot, in Warsaw. Until serving as a military doctor in 1914 he created a simple children's republic with its own parliament, court and newspaper in the orphanage. After 1918 he returned to the orphanage and helped found a second (Catholic) one. In 1926 he helped children start their own newspaper that was eventually published as a supplement to a national Jewish newspaper. His work ended in August 1942 when he was taken to Treblinka with the children and presumably gassed on arrival. However, in the fullness of time his work would become a driving force for children's rights.

At the end of World War I Dorothy Buxton started a group that began to campaign for European children whose misfortune was to have been on the losing side. She was married to Charles Roden Buxton, great grandson of Thomas Fowell Buxton the anti-slavery campaigner. She was also related to William Godwin the anarchist philosopher and atheist dissenter against religious tyranny and his daughter Mary Shelley, wife of the poet anarchist Percy Bysshe Shelley. It was a family with a good 'pedigree' in campaigning for social change.

Eglantyne Jebb, Buxton's sister, was a member of the group. Buxton launched the Save the Children Fund in 1919 to raise money for children affected by war throughout Europe. Jebb was a sickly but mentally energetic woman who went to live in Geneva where she began the Save the Children International Union. Jebb was eventually the figurehead of the group founding a second Save the Children charity in Sweden. Her best known contribution to children was in 1921 when she wrote a 'Children's Charter' that the International Union would adopt in 1923. In 1924 it was adopted almost to the letter by the League of Nations as the *Declaration of the Rights of the Child*, often called the *Declaration of Geneva*. It was the starting point for what has since become the CRC.

Modern Philosophy

John Dewey (1859–1952) probably made the most considerable contribution to the development of educational philosophy in the twentieth century. His pragmatism, interest in interaction, reflection and experience and furthermore his fascination with community and democracy came together as an evocative educative form. He is often misrepresented and erroneously linked to child-centred education. In fact his work is not simply inserted into curricular traditions that have dominated North America and UK over the last century. His importance for informal educators arose out of his belief that education should engage with and increase experience, which has become a significant element in informal education. In addition, exploration of thought and reflection (and the associated role of educators) has continued to be an inspiration. He also had great enthusiasm for democracy and education for all that provides a *raison d'être* for practice in the settings in which informal educators work. In his *Democracy and Education* (1966) he attempted to combine, criticise and expand on the democratic or proto-democratic educational philosophies of Plato and Rousseau.

He saw the former as overemphatic of the society and the latter overemphasising the individual. He viewed the mind and its formation as a communal process in which the individual is only a significant concept when viewed as an inextricable part of his or her society which has no meaning apart from its realisation in the lives of individual members. It was crucial that education should not be the instruction of facts and that the abilities and knowledge students learned be fully integrated into their lives as persons, citizens and human beings. The key concept of his view of education was greater emphasis placed on the enlargement of intellect and development of problem solving and critical thinking skills instead of simply memorising lessons. He believed a school was much like a repair part or accessory to the 'organism' of society. Education thus opened a door to a society in which children already belonged but in which they grew into their proper place.

Throughout the twentieth century to the present few other philosophers have seriously contributed directly to significant change in the position of children toward their inclusion as full citizens. Some authors (e.g.: Philip Shields: Turner and Matthews 1998:161–88) have attributed more than is possibly due to Ludwig Wittgenstein. In fact his contribution is limited to his experience of the Austrian Reform School Movement. It is thus a worthy but essentially small contribution to the kind of area where Alexander Neill's work at Summerhill offers something of greater significance. Similarly there is an almost inexplicable enthusiasm for John Rawls (e.g.: Freeman 1983; Archard 1993, 2003, 2002 [with Macleod]; O'Neill 1994; Brennan and Noggle 1998 [Turner and Matthews 1998:203–32]) that in reality is limited to examinations of rationality through the medium of autonomy and self-determination and a theory of justice (Rawls 1971). Both are valuable assets in an argument for social justice for children. That, in chain, has a key role in delivery of well reasoned argument for children's citizenship, although Rawls never categorically touched on that subject.

Piaget, Kohlberg and Vygotsky, whose work will be examined in this chapter, are not uncommonly placed under the rubric of intellectual input, however whilst they have all contributed to a view of a culture of childhood they would all be misplaced here. Their part in this work is of a more practical nature and their real contribution better measured in terms of their input into theoretical areas (e.g. the sociology of childhood and 'childhood studies') and practical domains (psychology particularly but also education and child care).

Some important guidance can be extrapolated from the work of Paulo Freire (1921–1997) who contributed a philosophy of education with roots in classical approaches derived from Plato and also modern Marxist and anti-imperialist thought. In some respects his *Pedagogy of the Oppressed* (1972) is a development on a theme embarked on in Frantz Fanon's *Les Damnés de la Terre* (1961) [*The Wretched of this Earth* (2001)] emphasising the need to provide indigenous populations with education that was both new and modern (instead of traditional) and anti-colonial. This is one of the few approaches not expressly western and inward looking. Freire is renowned for his fervent critique of what he called a 'banking' concept of education.

This is where the student was seen as an empty account that was to be filled by teachers. The key critique was not new since it developed on Rousseau's concept of a child as an active learner. That was a considerable step away from Locke's *tabula rasa* that is essentially the same as a 'banking' concept and closer to such thinkers as Dewey who were ardently critical of the transference of 'facts' as the goal of education. However he brought the concept up to date and placed it in line with contemporary theories and educational thereby laying a foundation for what came to be 'critical pedagogy'. It most certainly incorporates a notion of *inclusion* that presents a strong argument for children's citizenship.

Elise Boulding was a Quaker peace campaigner whose view of the world imagined a 'global civic culture' that is not simply composed of nation states but is a global community of human beings. She believed that a civic world order could become a reality despite acknowledging the discord that exists. To create peace she believed that we must all be teachers and develop new learning communities in which everyone, old and young, will teach. Generations will teach each other from the perspective of their respective generations. Her belief was that we understand events unique to our own generation which shapes how we each perceive later events. In order to achieve this we must think 'outside of the box'. She believed that for most of us education is stymied by the maxim 'stick to facts, no need for imaginative thinking'. To the contrary she believed we need to harness both intuition and imagination to solve world crises. Whilst writing *Children's Rights and the Wheel of Life* in 1979 she noted that:

> As I studied the UN Declaration of Human Rights and the Declaration of the Rights of the Child, I became more and more aware of ageism as a phenomenon that excluded both the young and old from participation in society according to their abilities, and established them instead as a vast protectorate inside the social order (xiii–xiv)

In her book she looked at chronological age and maturity, children and youth as shapers of the future world and extension of human rights to people under 21 (still the age of majority in many nations at that time) with a great deal of focus on civil participation of all in which children were the equals of older generations. It is a text that has brought a certain amount of credence to an *ideology* of children's participation. It is also one of few texts that essentially theoretically describe what citizenship might be for children. It is perhaps a 'naïve' view that has far greater faith in the ability of humanity to form inclusive community than take account of the tendency of individuals to defend personal territory and spheres of influence.

Other authors have contributed other arguments. Although better known for her works on Kant and Rawls, Onora O'Neill has made brief visitation to the issue of childhood and especially given good account of the then impending change that would come with the CRC in 1989:

> If we care about children's lives, we will have a number of good reasons not to base our arguments on appeals to children's fundamental rights. Some of these reasons are the theoretical difficulties of theories of fundamental rights. To look at rights is to look at what is ethically required indirectly by looking at what should be received. Constructivist accounts of what should be received are radically indeterminate, hence blurred. All rights-based approaches are incomplete in that they tell us nothing about what should be done when nobody has a right to its being done: they are silent about imperfect obligations. The view we get from the perspective of rights is not merely indirect, but blurred and incomplete. (O'Neill 1988:463)

Since rights has to be the foundation on which a concept of citizenship must be constructed, O'Neill's counsel in the closing words is the caveat that reminds that whilst Hobbes is a watershed in change of the status of and thought about children, in reality little intellectual progress has been made. It is difficult to view more than a small amount as sector and overall in this context it is mostly a newly emergent and unfinished concept that is still often more elusive than conclusive.

The entirety of this chapter is 'Western' with little exception, reflecting a global view of citizenship that is broadly speaking a neo-liberal notion with occasionally some strands of influence from the civic republican tradition. Most modern nation states have secular constitutions and basic laws that consolidate the concept of nationality and the nature of belonging within a political state. Within those states the family is still viewed as the benchmark of basic structure within community that has remained hierarchically conservative. It thus understands children as typically deferential to adult (primarily parental) authority and protection. Most intellectual clues that may be drawn from about 2,500 years of thought tend to offer only limited indication of how to move the notion of children's citizenship even the first few steps forward.

Philosophy has offered the greater argument for advance whereas theology that began by cementing societal cohesion within its doctrines appears to have offered little guidance. Indeed the position on children has little changed across beliefs since Augustine's time. Despite the tendency of child researchers to emphasise the importance of Locke and Rousseau, their role is probably better appreciated as 'liberal' educational theorists rather than as pioneer thinkers for the rights of children. Perhaps Kant's belief in the inborn liberty of each individual and Hegel's position that children are potentially free and that life is the direct embodiment of this potential freedom are far more significant. This is a question raised by Renaut (2002:229–313) in his chapter '*Avec ou contre Rousseau*' as he moves toward examination of children's rights in the contemporary world and includes a brief examination of the question '*L'enfant citoyen?*' (*Ibid.*:341–46). His view tends toward the Kantian inborn liberty in which the ethics of the position of children is for him of greater but never entirely resolved import rather than the contestable issue of their rights.

One should also not overlook less universally regarded figures like Winstanley, Spence and their ilk in the formation of ideas that have given life to a tradition in which the likes of Montessori, Neill, Korczak and Freire could give us the foundation for a vision of children's inclusion in the modern world. Literature has often drawn attention to the unequal situation of children and has a probable future role. Those whose work was both moral and practical at least gave a *raison d'être* to the 'voluntary sector' in which advocacy and action for change in children's lives takes root. None have insignificant roles but have as yet to play a momentous part in an unforeseeable future.

Chapter 8
The 'Child Sciences', Social Sciences and Childhood Studies

The preceding four chapters have looked at children in a more or less chronological sequence that began with the 'emergence' of childhood in history then moving on to intellectual discourse, beliefs, moral and ideological positions on children from antiquity until the present. The following three chapters look at how children are seen now. With the advent of studies of childhood in the nineteenth century that we can follow through to the wider range and more thorough examination of today it would be difficult to be all inclusive. Therefore these chapters are essentially an insight through use of examples or 'snapshots' rather than a comprehensive analysis. Several particular topics such as child labour, street children or child soldiers that could be used as 'substantiation' of arguments have not been included. Whilst a far more comprehensive examination would be very easy to justify, it remains available for future work, particularly where specialists in key topic areas such as feminist theory could develop themes beyond the background this work offers. Chapters 4, 5, 6 and 7 thus provide a backdrop for such deeper examinations, beginning with 'child sciences' in this chapter.

The late nineteenth and early twentieth centuries saw 'child sciences' such as paediatrics, child psychiatry and developmental psychology emerge and come into their own as disciplines with academic and practical components. They are generally considered to be very contemporary disciplines. In fact, the provenance of 'child science is older as this chapter shows by very early on by giving mention to Hippocrates (*circa* 460–370 BC) in passing when introducing medicine's interest in children as a starting point. Paediatrics appeared in written form in the tenth century. Child care, which has become virtually a 'science' only recently is historically richly described if one includes the story of Moses' discovery by the Pharaoh's daughter (Boswell 1988:145–46) in a reed basket or Romulus and Remus cared for by a wolf until a shepherd found them (*Ibid.*:76). Mary Carpenter, Dr. Barnardo,

B. Milne, *The History and Theory of Children's Citizenship in Contemporary Societies*,
DOI 10.1007/978-94-007-6521-4_8, © Springer Science+Business Media Dordrecht 2013

Charles Dickens (e.g.: Jo the crossing sweeper) or Victor Hugo (e.g.: Petit Gavroche), as described in the previous chapter, briefly examine similarly 'dispossessed' or 'abandoned' children.[1]

Although child care is a theme that will not be developed extensively in this work, it deserves a mention here in the context of what has become (residential) social work. It has a close relationship with child psychiatry and developmental psychology and more recent developments in child sciences. Whilst they contribute little to the actual nature of what children's citizen might be, they tell us much about the way we see the intellectual development of human beings from infancy to adulthood. Therein we also find clues to the way the possibility of children gaining equal rights with adults that they are competent to possess are perceived. That perception has also been examined closely by sociologists.

The sociology of childhood is therefore a more pertinent and relatively recent arrival for this work. We can see some of its theoretical roots in Aristotle's notion of the *tabula rasa*. That was also used by Ibn Sina in the eleventh century, Aquinas in the thirteenth century, Locke in the seventeenth century and Freud in the nineteenth century before its emergence as a notion of 'human becomings' at the end of the twentieth century. The sociology of childhood focuses particularly on the ways societies conceptualise and organise childhood. The two central themes are the child as a *social actor* and *generational order* with socialisation in practice and through institutions central themes in research. They are being examined in an innovative, more sociological way than before that analyse socialisation processes by reconstructing historically and culturally shifting concepts and processes. Other concepts such as the strategies of the formation of *habitus* and the practice of *status* production and reproduction are being taken into account. In this chapter the 'genesis' of this branch of sociology, its influence on the social sciences and the closely related area of childhood studies[2] are examined up to the most recent point in time when a significant contribution to this work arises where it begins to refer to citizenship.

Sociologists had already studied children as learners or as what were at first considered to be *adults-in-the-making* for several decades. The means to this end was to use the concept of socialisation. Talcott Parsons, was particularly influential during the 1950s and 1960s. He theorised social systems as smoothly

---

[1] I have visited the *Ospedale degli Innocenti* in Florence on numerous occasions (the UNICEF Innocenti Research Centre is in the Ospedale) and have seen the carefully kept records of children taken in since the fifteenth century. I also know the door with the rotating horizontal wheel that took babies into the Innocenti without parents being seen and was used until the foundling hospital closed in 1875.

[2] Childhood Studies is a relatively new academic discipline. It is interdisciplinary and consists of areas of contemporary study that ask questions, attempt to resolve problems and find the solutions that contribute to improving the quality of childhood experienced by the all children. It draws on the social sciences (anthropology, criminology, economics, history, human geography, social psychology and sociology), the humanities (especially literature and religions with some input from fine arts) and the behavioural sciences (chiefly psychology but also appropriate domains of education, socio-linguistics and medicine).

functioning wholes. As he saw it, initially family, then schools and other institutions shape the growing child. That child learns, internalising the rules and values of adult society into which he or she is born (e.g. Parsons and Bales 1955). During the 1980s, a number of European and American scholars in particular drew attention to the virtual absence of children in the social sciences. Their argument was that children needed to be studied as full social actors rather than previously being seen mainly as adults-in-training or as problematic and disturbing for the adult social order which an extensive interest in juvenile delinquency had portrayed them as being.

In the closely related field of anthropology, Schildkrout (1978) put forward an early critical view when she observed that children only infrequently entered in accounts of social systems and made the previously unheard proposal that they should be understood as children instead of being viewed as the next generation of adults. The 'new social studies of childhood' began to draw attention to children as social actors with diverse and distinct lives and experiences. These 'childhood studies' gained momentum in the 1980s and 1990s.

Sociologists of childhood very frequently credit the French historian Ariès (1962) for making the first step in the early 1960s. However, Zelizer (1985) also drew attention to changing perceptions of children and childhood during late nineteenth and early twentieth century in the USA from an economically *useful* child to an economically *useless* but emotionally *priceless* individual. This came as they were taken out of paid labour and placed in cosseted spaces of families and schools. Her work probably set in motion the interest initially raised by Ariès. Increasing awareness of international political and economic changes during the late twentieth century also increased awareness of the wide-ranging lives and circumstances of children. With some reference back to what had been seen historically, street children, child workers, children in war and child abuse began to attract greater attention.

These contributed to new approaches in the social study of childhood. Firstly, the comparative analysis of the political economy and social structuring of particular childhoods moved emphasis away from previous Eurocentric views. Then the study of symbolic or discursive constructions of children and childhoods lead the way to drawing attention to children as social actors, creators and interpreters of (their own) culture. Whilst each approach overlaps it also they also draw on a distinctive set of theoretical tools and research methods. In turn these are now beginning to contribute to research and practice in the field of 'children's participation' and the more recent interest in children as citizens in their own right.

This very brief insight into the child sciences is followed by Chap. 9 in which one of the key areas, children's rights, emerges. This is treated as part of the broader human rights field. Human rights itself has roots in much of the substance of Chaps. 4, 5, 6 and 7. There is very clear correlation between the latter and this chapter that can be very plainly seen in the 'humanism' of modernity and the path pursued by philosophers such as Kant, Locke, Rousseau and then through the influence of some of the major contributions by social scientists from the nineteenth through twentieth centuries.

What is often called the 'rights revolution' has become a focal point of modern political consciousness and has brought within a proliferation of theories about the real status of children's rights. Mainstream thought of the kind examined in the last chapter and liberal theories particularly in which children's rights have been theorised have seldom taken children's rights as citizens seriously. The standard position in liberal theories is that children are 'not-yet-citizens' or 'citizens-becoming'. The analysis has tended to be located within anti-racist, feminist, gay, lesbian and transgendered theories of citizenship that are mainly concerned with difference (see Moosa-Mitha 2005:369–88). The emergent analyses generally look for an alternative, difference-focussed expression of children's citizenship rights through an analysis of their rights to liberty and equality.

With the 'rights revolution' there has been an expansion of liberal, normative concepts of liberty that have been defined around the exercise of individualised, autonomous decision-making and participation in civil society. There is also a notion of 'equality-as-same' that allows for treating children as 'differently equal' members of society in which they are full participants but more similar to others who are 'different'. There are some people who argue that children's rights will sufficiently transform societies at the point in time when the notion of 'human rights' is reconstructed in the light of childhood rather than of difference. Should that ever occur, human rights would thus be understood as grounded but not in modernist perceptions of autonomy, liberty, privilege or agency, but within a post-modern flow of responsibility to each other. This interpretation of rights is constructed through inspection of diverse forms of child-centred ethical theory in Western history. That theory has had impact on the major human rights theories since the Enlightenment and persists until the present.

Alternative visions implicit in twentieth century international children's rights treaties have allowed new theoretical bases to arise out of post-modern ethics which, in turn, allow the possibility of human rights genuinely including all humanity (for instance, see Wall 2008:523–543). The sociology of social inequality is an important area of study for sociologists of childhood and also central to the development of the recently emerged 'children's-rights-as-human rights' argument.

In the areas this chapter examines it is difficult to locate any exact point in time when children became a separable topic or any particular branch of scholasticism entirely concerned with them became a formal part of a distinct discipline. It is somewhat easier to turn to child protection, age of consent, political franchise, education, employment and other social and civil reforms for points of entry (for instance, see Milne 2008:44–45) however scientific study generally came many years after those provisions were in place. Whilst there is by no means an extensive source of literature that sheds light on a solution to the children's citizenship question, it is simultaneously extraordinarily difficult to choose what to use.

By and large the early twentieth century was the point in time when serious interest turned to the methodical and academic as a possibility. In Viviana Zelizer's seminal work, *Pricing the Priceless Child: The Changing Social Value of Children* (1985), she draws attention to the fact that so-called child sciences such as paediatrics, child psychiatry and developmental psychology became formally accepted disciplines with academic and practical components within the areas each belongs to. However, each also has older provenance that gives a degree of insight into attitudes about children. It is, thus, why this chapter begins by examining them because of the cumulative knowledge of children they belong to.

Paediatrics

Paediatrics has a particularly long history. Most of the short history here is synthesised from Still's (1931) *A History of Paediatrics: The progress of the study of diseases of children up to the end of the XVIIIth century*. He used a predominantly biographical method in which he traced the growth of medical interest in children chronologically from Hippocrates to Jenner during a period of about 2,200 years up to about 1800. Here it is used to trace much of the later period where that sheds any light on the status of children. The period after 1800 draws on Roy Porter's *The Greatest Benefit to Mankind: A Medical History of Humanity from Antiquity to the Present* (1997:397–524) whereby the latter part begins to contextualise psychiatry (493–524) as an emergent science. This has been supplemented by a chapter by J.A. Walker-Smith in Irvine Loudon's (1997) *Western Medicine: An Illustrated History*. Beyond these sources, website searches tend to repeat only what is found in the foregoing texts and add little further detail. One problem that arises here is that medical history appears to be more concerned with biographies. Furthermore, the gradual increase of scientific knowledge and understanding with particular conditions and diseases is given greater prominence than detail about the patients. However, despite this, these histories do help to map the 'emergence' of children as a defined social group and gives some expression of their status.

During the tenth century Rhazes (Muhammad ibn Zakarīya Rāzi also known as Rhazi or Al-Razi: 862–925) wrote *The Diseases of Children* (see, Browne 2001: 44), the first book that deals with paediatrics as an independent field of medicine. Medical historians occasionally refer to Rhazes as the 'father of paediatrics.' His teacher Ali ibn Sahl Rabban al-Tabari was a pioneer in the field of child development which he earlier discussed in his *Firdous al-Hikmah* (*Paradise of Wisdom*) (*Ibid*.: 37–38) that is still referred to as the first encyclopaedia of medicine. The first work on paediatric medicine in Europe appeared nearly six centuries later; the *Boke of Chyldren* by Thomas Phaire (1510–60) was published in 1545 (here the 1955 facsimile edition) and was itself inspired by the works of Rhazes and Abū 'Alī al-Husayn ibn 'Abd Allāh ibn Sīnā (Ibn Sina or Avicenna).

Paediatrics as a separate area of practice in the Western world principally began in the nineteenth century. The Hospital for Sick Children in Great Ormond Street, London, was established in 1852 adjacent to Coram's Fields which is the site of the earlier Foundling Hospital established in Lamb's Conduit Fields from 1742–1745 by Thomas Coram. He was shocked by the presence of many abandoned, homeless children living in the streets of London. In 1739 he obtained a Royal Charter to establish a 'hospital for the maintenance and education of exposed and deserted young children' which is said to be the world's first incorporated charity. Great Ormond Street Hospital, as it is now more commonly known, has continued a close relationship with the Thomas Coram Foundation. Its work continues today and goes beyond medical and social issues into academic areas examining adoption, parenting and research into many more aspects of childhood as a social phenomenon including direct input into the sociology of childhood.

During the middle nineteenth century demographic research in England revealed that 15 out of every 100 babies born died during the first year of life. The main causal factors were malnutrition, bad hygiene and lack of knowledge about how infants should be looked after. In 1880 the first organised infant welfare work began in Paris with the work of Dr. Baudin. Important evidence emerged that was to have a major influence on the health of young children. He established that infant mortality was highest in industrial towns. Working mothers were unable to breast feed infants at industrial workplaces. He found that the only recently available glass bottles and rubber teats should be adequately sterilised for safe use. He furthermore found that poor hygiene and changes in the seasons contributed to diseases like summer diarrhoea.

The outcome of his work combined with increasing awareness of preventable child health problems and thus the first international Child Health Conference was held in Paris in 1905. Progress in practice and research accelerated rapidly thereafter and a marked downturn in the numbers of childhood deaths can be measured from about that point in time onward. Today paediatric medicine is a discipline in its own right with numerous specialised branches. It also has links with other child sciences that include social studies which give insights into the causes of child health issues, including child psychiatry.

Child Psychiatry

A significant precursor to child psychiatry emerging as a discipline was the social recognition of childhood as a specific stage of life (for instance, see Zelizer 1985; Timimi 2002; Porter 1997[3]) with its own developmental stages that began at neonatal and lasted through adolescence. In 1899 the term 'child psychiatry' appeared in Dr. Marcel Manheimer-Gommès' monograph 'Les Troubles Mentaux de L'Enfance', *Précis de Psychiatrie Infantile*. In 1933 Moritz Tramer (1882–1963) in Switzerland was in all probability the first person to define the parameters of child psychiatry so that there could be formal diagnosis, treatment and prognosis within the medical discipline. In 1934 he founded *Zeitschrift für Kinderpsychiatrie* which later became *Acta Paedopsychiatria*. The first use of the term 'child psychiatry' in English was when Leo Kanner published *Child Psychiatry* in 1935, focussing on psychiatric problems of children. The discipline probably had its zenith in its earliest days but

[3]Most of the account of child psychiatry has been drawn together from Porter (1997) and Timimi (2002), with a limited amount of examination of websites describing early child psychiatry.

during recent times has received a great deal of critique (see Timimi 2002, 2006). Psychiatry also occasionally appears to work against the nature of inclusion that full citizenship implies.

By its nature the discipline is concerned with deviation from the norm that has behavioural or (mental) health reasons for diagnosis of a number of conditions. Whoever displays symptoms of these conditions to a degree that requires psychiatric intervention is a then subject of diagnostic evaluation of the nature of the condition. This may result in responsibility for their life and decision making being taken away from the individual. He or she is almost certain to be confined in an institution, with many of the rights, duties and other qualities of citizenship withdrawn. This may be temporarily or permanently enforced according to the degree to which an individual is diagnosed as being psychiatrically ill.

One of the critiques of both medical areas, paediatrics and child psychiatry, has been 'medicalisation' (see Timimi 2002) of childhood whereby young patients become very much passive recipients of diagnosis and treatment in which they have little or no say. In the case of psychiatry in particular, children diagnosed as 'abnormal' early in life have often been taken out society and placed in institutions. Occasionally this has been for much of and all of life. The British royal family has given good example of the extremity of this approach. Under the Mental Deficiency Act of 1913 two of the late Queen Mother's cousins were incarcerated as too was the so-called 'lost prince' who was in fact Queen Elizabeth II's uncle John.

In 2002 a BBC television film, *The Lost Prince*, written and directed by Steven Poliakoff (see Cardwell 2006), told the boy's story. During boyhood he was diagnosed epileptic and suffered from autism-like learning difficulties. He was unable to participate in public life and became increasingly isolated from his family and the world at large. John was easily lost in history because he died when he was only 13 years old and also because it happened in 1919. From 1916 until his death he lived in isolation at Wood Farm at Wolferton near Sandringham in Norfolk. He was cared for by a nurse Mrs. 'Lalla' Bill and a male orderly well out of the public eye.

The Queen Mother's cousins (see Summerskill 2000) were Nerissa Bowes-Lyon (1919–1986) and Katherine Bowes-Lyon (1926–1986). Both of them were diagnosed developmentally disabled and consequently institutionalised for most of their lives. They had simply been listed as deceased in various publications thus causing something of a scandal when discovered living and fairly neglected in the Royal Earlswood Hospital during the 1980s. Burkes Peerage incorrectly reported Nerissa as having died in 1940 and Katherine in 1961. Both were recorded as 'mentally impaired' from birth. Both were confined to the hospital in 1941 aged 22 and 15 respectively where they both remained until their almost anonymous deaths in 1986.

In the USA President John F. Kennedy's sister, Rose Marie (1918–2005) commonly known as Rosemary (see Gibson and Schwarz 1995) was kept in an institution and eventually had a frontal lobotomy. Although she had been good-natured and easy-going as a child and teenager, Rosemary developed an increasingly aggressive personality. She was reported to have become subject to violent mood swings which some observers attributed to difficulties in keeping up with her active siblings. She was diagnosed as having the hormonal surges during puberty. Moreover the Kennedy family found it increasingly difficult coping with the tempestuous behaviour and her stealing away from the convent where she was being educated and taken care of in the night. At age 22 the lobotomy was performed in order to contain her embarrassing behaviour. Once in office John Kennedy brought about reform to allow people with learning difficulties to live in their communities.

In the UK the Mental Deficiency Act (1913) was rather typical of its time as interest in mental health became increasingly methodical and scientific. Whilst still crude compared with psychiatry today, it began to identify mental illnesses and also to categorise people in particular groups; accordingly those classified 'disabled' people were described as follows:

- *Idiots* were people with a mental defect of such a degree that they were considered unable to guard themselves against everyday hazards.
- *Imbeciles* were those in whose case there was a mental defect which did not equate with idiocy but was so apparent that they were thought incapable of managing themselves and their normal affairs or, in the case of children, being taught them.
- *Feeble minded* described persons in whose case there were mental defects which did not amount to imbecility but was nonetheless so pronounced that they required care, supervision and control for their own protection and that of others. In the case of children it was judged that they appeared to be permanently incapable by reason of those defects of benefiting from instruction in a normal school.
- *Moral defective* was used for individuals in whose case there were mental defects together with pronounced vicious or criminal propensities who required care, supervision and control for the protection of others.

Under the Mental Deficiency Act at least 50,000 children with communication and physical impairments were confined in institutions in the first half of the twentieth century. Many of them were only released as adults (some quite elderly) in the 1980s. Children with significant learning difficulties were deemed unfit to be educated whereby those with less significant learning difficulties went to educationally sub-normal schools until 1973 when the law changed.[4]

Critics of child psychiatry have frequently argued that diagnosis lacks objectivity. This is especially so when comparing it with diagnoses in other medical areas. However, in psychiatry, as in all branches of medicine, there is an irreducible element of the subjective that is difficult to overcome. Traditional models of child psychiatry have been criticised as being deep-rooted in a medical model which conceptualises adjustment problems in terms of illness. Critics say that these normative models unambiguously characterise problematic behaviour as representing a disorder within the child or young person. They emphasise a view that the role of environmental influences on behaviour have become progressively more neglected. This, in turn, has lead to a decrease in the popularity of non-psychiatric therapies. There is

[4]In fact I was a residential social worker with the National Children's Home at a residential school in the mid 1970s when ESN and SSN were still the standard classification of such children.

also criticism of the medical model from within and without the psychiatric profession. It has been said that neglecting the role of family, cultural and environmental influences, also not accepting the psychological meaning of behaviour and 'symptoms' in order to promote a view of a 'patient' as thus dependent and in need of a 'cure' or be cared for undermines any sense of personal responsibility for conduct and behaviour. It is then used to endorse a normative notion based on conformity to societal norms whereby the 'ill' person must adapt to society. These assumptions are based on defective foundations of a notion of reliance on a classificatory system that has been proved problematic to validate and unreliable and especially so in the field of child psychiatry (for instance, see Timimi 2006).

In point of fact, in the UK, throughout the British Empire and similarly elsewhere[5] many people remained in the hands of psychiatrists for many years into adulthood. For some, most or even all of life, they were deprived of many of the civil, social and political rights we normally associate with enjoyment of full citizenship.[6] The discipline has become less radical in its application of labelling and inflexible diagnosis since the 1980s and gradually many more countries are ceasing to stigmatise sufferers of mental health problems for life. Nonetheless, there is still a degree to which ignominy remains part of the problem that makes a normal transition from childhood to adult, thus full citizenship, problematic. However, patients of closed psychiatric institutions with the most serious and especially unpredictable conditions in many countries remain isolated from their communities and are often still detained under legal orders that also remove normal civil rights from them.[7]

Developmental Psychology

Developmental psychology has had a far more positive history and constructive contribution toward a contemporary view of childhood than psychiatry. It is a scientific study of the progressive psychological changes that take place in individuals as they age. Its modern form has roots far back in history taking in influences from a wide range of sources that include Aristotle, Tabari, Rhazes and William Shakespeare (1952:70). From the latter, the melancholic Jacques in *As You Like It* describes the 'seven ages of man' of which three stages are childhood and four adulthood. Jean Jacques Rousseau (1979) described three stages of childhood as *infans* (infancy),

[5]At the extreme end and not included here was the treatment of many people with any form of physical or mental abnormality in National Socialist Germany between 1933 and 1945.

[6]During fieldwork in Iraq, Kyrgyzstan, The People's Republic of China and Viet Nam I have visited mental health institutions where children are still placed – some of them were street children who were classified as though 'ill' or 'unstable' because of their 'deviant' lifestyles and others simply there for relatively minor, adolescent behavioural problems at school or home.

[7]In the USA, for instance, many people under mental health orders have virtually no civil rights and the transition from age of minority to majority may well only be marked by transfer from one class of accommodation to another.

puer (childhood) and adolescence in *Emile or On Education*. His ideas were strongly supported by educators at that time. Toward the end of the nineteenth century, psychologists conversant in Darwin's evolutionary theory began to look for an evolutionary description of psychological developments. Prominent among them was Granville Stanley Hall (see Partridge 1912, chapter one) who attempted to correlate ages of childhood with previous ages of mankind.

A more scientific approach was initiated by James Mark Baldwin (see Gregory 1987:721) who wrote essays on topics that included a step by step theory of cognitive development. It was to become highly influential in the more widely-known developmental theory of Piaget. In 1905 Sigmund Freud (1996) described five psychosexual stages of development and later Rudolf Steiner (2006) expounded stages of psychological development throughout human life. The first three stages correspond closely with Piaget's stages of childhood that were described some years later. By the early to mid twentieth century the work of Vygotsky and Piaget came to dominate the discipline.

Cognitive development is primarily concerned with the ways in which infants and children acquire and develop internal mental capabilities such as problem solving, memory, and language. Major topics in cognitive development are the study of language acquisition and the development of perceptual and motor skills. Piaget was one of the first influential psychologists to study the development of cognitive abilities. His theory suggests that development proceeds through a set of stages from infancy to adulthood and that there is an end point or goal. Other accounts, such as that of Lev Vygotsky, have suggested that development does not progress through stages, preferring the argument that the development process that begins at birth and continues until death is too complex for such structure and finality. Rather, from this viewpoint, developmental processes proceed more continuously, thus it should be analysed, instead of a product to be obtained. Furthermore, modern cognitive development has chiefly moved away from Piagetian stage theories. It is influenced by descriptions of domain specificity that argue that development is guided by innate evolutionarily specified and content-specific information processing mechanisms.

Vygotsky

Lev Semyenovich Vygotsky (Лев Семёнович Выготский) (1896–1934)[8] worked comprehensively on ideas about cognitive development particularly in regard to the relationship between language and thought. His written work emphasises the roles of historical, cultural and social factors in cognition using the central argument that

[8] Most of the biographical detail has been taken from Kozulin (1990), Wertsch (1985), and Van der Veer and Valsiner (1994), with further detail added from a brief examination on the 1987 edition of *The Collected Works of L. S. Vygotsky*.

language is the most important symbolic tool afforded us by society. He was a prolific author with his major works extending over six volumes that were written over about 10 years beginning with *Psychology of Art* (1925) to *Thought and Language* (1934) (see Vygotsky 1987; Van der Veer and Valsiner 1994). His interest in the fields of developmental psychology, child development and education cover a wide diversity of issues. His ground-breaking work in psychology included several key concepts including psychological tools, mediation, internalisation and the 'zone of proximal development'. He explored child development and how this was directed by the role of culture and interpersonal communication. He studied how higher mental functions developed historically within specific cultural groups as well as individually through social interactions with significant people in a child's life, especially parents but also other adults. These interactions aided a child to learn the habits of mind in her or his culture which included speech patterns, written language and other symbolic knowledge through which a child derives meaning and thus shapes a child's construction of her or his knowledge. This is the key premise of Vygotskian psychology that is commonly referred to as cultural mediation. The specific knowledge acquired by children through these interactions also represents the shared knowledge of a culture. This is the process known as internalisation.

This can be understood in one sense as 'knowing how'. A typical example would be riding a bicycle which is a 'tool' of the society that is initially outside of and beyond the child. The mastery of such a skill is acquired through the activity of the child within society. A further aspect is appropriation in which a child takes a tool and makes it their own even in a way limited to her or himself. Internalising the use of paints allows a child to use them for their own ends rather than paint what others in society have painted beforehand.

His less well known research is on play as a psychological phenomenon and its role in the child's development. It describes how through play a child develops abstract meanings separated from the objects in the world which are critical features in the development of higher mental functions. Play is a transitional stage which as children get older diminishes. A further aspect of play Vygotsky referred to was the development of social rules that develop when children play particular games such as house whereby they adopt the roles of family members. The rules of behaviour children acquire that go unseen in daily life are consciously acquired through play. Beside that social rules they acquire are what we now refer to a self-regulation.

However his most important contribution probably concerns the interrelationship of language development and thought. That concept, explored in *Thought and Language*, (sometimes under title: *Thinking and Speaking*) (Vygotsky 1987) established an explicit and profound connection between speech (both inner [unspoken] speech and oral [spoken] language), and the development of mental concepts and cognitive awareness. Vygotsky described inner speech as being qualitatively different from normal (external) speech. Although he believed inner speech developed from external speech via a gradual process of internalisation, whereby young children could only really 'think out loud', he maintained that in its mature form it would be unintelligible to all but the thinker and does not resemble spoken language as we understand it because it is compressed. Therefore, it follows that thought itself develops socially. An infant learns the meaning of signs through interaction with carers so that pointing, cries and babble can express what is meant. How verbal sounds (words) are used to carry out social interaction is learned thus and children learn to develop this ability by using names for objects, etc.

Thus language begins by being a tool external to a child used for social interaction. He or she guides personal behaviour by using this tool for a kind of self-talk or 'thinking aloud'. Initially, self-talk is a tool of social interaction although used at low levels when a child is alone or perhaps with deaf children. Progressively self-talk is used increasingly as a tool for self-directed and regulated behaviour. By the time a child starts school speech has been learned and internalised so that self-talk is seldom present. Inner speech then develops through its differentiation from social speech.

Speech thus develops along two routes, social communication and inner speech, by which the child mediates and regulates an activity through thoughts which are mediated by the semiotics or meaningful signs of inner speech. This is not to say that thought cannot take place without language but rather more is mediated by it and thus develops a higher level of sophistication. The form of inner speech is not comparable with external speech which is the process of turning thought into words. Inner speech is the opposite being conversion of speech into inward thought. Inner speech appears to consist of predicates and subjects are redundant. A word in inner speech may be so full of sense for an individual that it takes many more words to express external speech, thus words are used economically. If we take Vygotsky's ideas as a measure of how children develop articulate language and thought then some of the debates on articles 12, 13 and 14 CRC having application for young children's participation in civil society tend to be less persuasive.

Piaget

Jean Piaget (1896–1980)[9] began work as a *malacologist*[10] and later became professor of psychology at the University of Geneva between 1929 and 1975. He became best known for reorganising cognitive development theory into a series of stages. It expanded on earlier work with four levels of development corresponding approximately with infancy, pre-school, childhood and adolescence. Each stage is characterised by general cognitive structures that affect children's thought (which is a structuralist view predisposed to Kantian philosophy). The stages represent children's comprehension of reality during that period. Development from one stage to the next is produced by the accumulation of errors in the child's understanding of the environment whereby the accumulation ultimately causes disequilibrium to such a degree

[9]See Miller (1993), Chapter 1, and Gruber and Vonéche (1977).

[10]Malacology is the branch of invertebrate zoology that studies molluscs.

of cognitive that thought structures require reorganisation. He described the four development stages as:

- Sensorimotor stage: birth to age 2 years when they experience the world through movement and senses and learn object permanence;
- Preoperational stage: from ages 2 to 7 years when motor skills are acquired;
- Concrete operational stage: from 7 to 11 years when children begin to think logically about concrete events; and
- Formal operational stage: after age 11 years and the development of abstract reasoning.
  (Piaget 1936)

He gave no exact description of the development process as a whole. It consists of a cycle which begins when a child performs an action that has an effect on or organises objects and the child is aware of the characteristics and consequences of the action. Through repeated actions with variation, different contexts or different kinds of objects, a child becomes able to differentiate and integrate its elements and effects. This is the process of reflecting abstraction (described in detail in Piaget 2001b). At the same time a child is able to identify properties of objects through how different kinds of action affect them. This is what he described as the process of empirical abstraction. Repeating the process across a range of objects and actions enables a child to establish a new level of knowledge and insight. This leads to formation of a new cognitive stage.

Once a child constructs new kinds of knowledge, he or she begins to use them to create still more complex objects and carry out more intricate actions. Accordingly, a child begins to recognise more complicated patterns and construct even more complex objects. Then a new stage begins which is concluded when a child's activity and experience have been entirely re-organised on this higher level.

The process is not entirely gradual since once a new level of organisation, knowledge and insight proves to be valuable it will promptly be disseminated to other areas. Thus transitions between stages tend to be quick and radical with most of the time spent in a new stage used to refine the new cognitive level. Once knowledge that has been acquired at one stage and experience leads swiftly and radically to a higher stage of insight, a '*gestalt*' (more comprehensively explained in Piaget 1936) is considered to have occurred.

Since the process takes this dialectical form, whereby each new stage is created through the further differentiation, integration, and synthesis of new structures out of old, the sequence of cognitive stages is logically necessary rather than merely empirically correct. Each new stage emerges once a child can take achievements of precursors for granted and there are other sophisticated forms of knowledge and action still to be developed.

Piaget's model of development explained some features of human knowledge never previously researched. For instance, showing how children progressively augment understanding as a result of which by acting and reflecting on the outcome of their previous knowledge, they are able to organise knowledge about increasingly complicated structures. Simultaneously, by reflecting on their actions children develop ever more sophisticated understanding of 'rules'. He explained their increasing awareness of notions such as 'right', 'wrong', 'necessary', 'appropriate' and so on. In other words, through objectification, contemplation and abstraction children construct principles through which actions are not only successful or correct but are also acceptable.

Originally Piaget did not study younger children, since if at 4 years old a child could not cope with quantity how could a child who is younger? Thus he examined the question and one of his best known studies (recounted in Mehler and Bever 1967:141–2) looked at the discriminative abilities of children between the ages of two and a half and four and a half years old. Piaget took children of different ages and laid out two lines of M&M sweets. One was with the sweets in a line spread further apart and the other had the same number of sweets laid out closer together. He found that, "Children between 2 years, 6 months old and 3 years, 2 months old correctly discriminate the relative number of objects in two rows; between 3 years, 2 months and 4 years, 6 months they indicate a longer row with fewer objects to have 'more'; after 4 years, 6 months they again discriminate correctly" (*Ibid.*). It proved that children of less than 3 years and 2 months have quantity conservation but as they get older lose the quality which is recovered at about four and a half years old. The skill may be lost due to temporary inability to solve it caused by overdependence on perceptual strategies that correlate more sweets with a longer line of sweets or else the inability of a 4 year old to reverse situations.

By the end of the experiment several results were established. Firstly, younger children have a discriminative ability which demonstrates a logical aptitude for cognitive operations that exists earlier than previously received. It also revealed that young children may be capable of possessing particular qualities for cognitive operation that depend on how logical the construction of the task is. It also showed that children develop explicit understanding at age 5 and consequently will count M&Ms to decide which line contains more. Lastly, the study found that generally quantity conservation is not a basic characteristic of humanity's native inheritance.

Using Piaget's research one might surmise that the evolving capacity passim in the CRC (Articles 5, 12, etc.) may be prejudicial on the basis of subjective rather than objective assessment of a child's abilities. However, there is a problem in that Piaget's samples were very small and localised and may be substantively disproved, for instance by using large, cross-cultural samples.

Kohlberg

Other developmental psychologists have had a great deal of influence on how we view children as individuals. Lawrence Kohlberg's (1927–1987) work on the stages of moral development (see Kohlberg 1981a, opening chapters and 1981c) offers an interesting contribution to the question of reasoning that plays an important part in describing what makes citizens. His stages of moral development are planes of moral adequacy that explain the development of moral reasoning. The theory was inspired by Piaget's work and his interest in children's reaction to moral dilemmas.

The theory regards moral reasoning as the basis of ethical behaviour which has six identifiable developmental constructive stages. It goes through the stages sequentially without omissions. Movement through these stages is not natural, which is to say that people do not automatically move from one stage to the next as they mature. Movement is caused when cognitive dissonance occurs, which is when a person notices inadequacies in his or her present way of dealing with a particular moral dilemma. According to this theory, individuals cannot understand moral reasoning more than one stage ahead of where they are. Thus, someone in Stage 1 may understand Stage 2, but not beyond that. Kohlberg's proposition is that we should present moral arguments one stage ahead of a person's present level to stimulate movement to higher stages (see Colby and Kohlberg 1987 and Walker 1989). The six stages are set out in three levels thus:

Level One *Pre-conventional Morality*	Stage 1: Punishment-Obedience Orientation Stage 2: Instrumental Relativist Orientation
Level Two *Conventional Morality*	Stage 3: Good Boy-Nice Girl Orientation Stage 4: Law and Order Orientation
Level Three *Post-Conventional Morality*	Stage 5: Social Contract Orientation Stage 6: Universal Ethical Principle Orientation

At Stage 1 the individual might ask: How can I avoid punishment? In Stage 2 it becomes: What's in it for me? Stages 3 and 4 are when social norms such as the good boy/girl attitude, followed by a law and order morality lead on to Stages 5 and 6. That is when a social contract orientation and universal ethical principles complete the moral development of the individual.

Kohlberg followed the development of moral judgment beyond the lower ages originally studied by Piaget who also maintained that logic and morality develop through constructive stages. Kohlberg believed that that the process of moral development was principally concerned with justice and that development continues for life. The philosophical implications of that research go well beyond Piaget's simpler predisposition for Kantian ideas. Kohlberg's theory is not value neutral but is initiated with a stake in particular perceptions in the area of meta-ethics that include a view of human nature and some comprehension of the form and content of moral reasoning. It contains notions of the right to and scope of moral reasoning across different societies. Moreover it includes the correlation between morality and the world and also between morality and logical expression and furthermore the role of reason in morality. It then examines a view of social and mental processes involved in moral reasoning.

Kohlberg's basic premise is that humans are inherently communicative and capable of reason in addition to possessing a desire to understand others and the world around them. His stages refer to qualitative moral reasoning which people espouse and do not translate directly into praise or blame regarding the actions or character of individuals. So that he could argue that his theory measures moral reasoning but not particular moral conclusions, he contended that the form and structure of moral arguments is independent of the content of arguments, a position he described as 'formalist' drawing on Kant.

His theory enfolds the notion that justice is the essential attribute of moral reasoning. Likewise, justice relies strongly on the notion of meticulous reasoning on principles. Thus despite being a justice centred theory of morality, Kohlberg considered it to be congruent with credible formulations of *deontology*[11] and *eudaimonia.*[12] His theory therefore understands values as a key component of the right or just. Whatever the right is it must be universally valid across different societies (be morally universal) and there can be no relativism. Furthermore, morals are not natural features of the world but are prescriptive and moral judgments can be evaluated in logical terms of truth and untruth.

His work most certainly correlates well with Thomas Marshall's notion of duties and responsibilities. Given that he looked at moral development at a lower age than Piaget, it could support an argument for early access to full citizenship although falling short of a notion of lifetime (from birth) citizenship. Kohlberg lowered the threshold at which the evolving capacities argument is an absolute value and in his arguments on moral reasoning the question of the 'best interests' principle (Article 3 CRC) in the same context is open to further scrutiny.[13] Deontological theory emphasises duty as the basis of moral value in which there is a principle of the right over good. In the case of a moral judgement in respect of an issue affecting a child or children in their best interest, no decision should be reached without full inclusion of children to absolutely establish their capacity as morally reasoning individuals. This is entirely compatible with a justice centred

[11]Deontological methods of ethics are normally those opposed to consequentialist methods whereby they insist that the moral value of an action is wholly independent from the consequences of an action. Rather than focusing on consequences, deontological methods emphasise duty as the basis of moral value. Deontological theories emphasise a principle of the right over good. Two well-known deontological theories are Kant's *Formalism* and William Ockham's *Divine Command Theory*. Both base a conception of right action on a conception of duty for duty's sake. Deontological theories are often criticised for being too legalistic and not providing an accurate account of human impulses.

[12]*Eudaimonia* comes from the Greek and is usually translated as happiness or well-being, but it has some of the same connotations as 'success', since in addition to living well it includes doing well. For example, it can be devalued by events that happen after the subject's death and it is not a state that children can possess. It is complete and self-sufficient, to be attained for no other end than itself, thus includes all other ends that are pursued for themselves and includes pleasure but goes beyond it. In the *Nicomachean Ethics* Aristotle extols the life of study as the essential realization of *eudaimonia.*

[13]In *Childhood and Society*, Erik Erikson (1950) claimed that every human being goes through a number of stages to reach full development. He theorised eight stages that somebody goes through from birth to death (however, his widow Joan Serson Erikson added the ninth stage, old age, later). Erikson was developing Sigmund Freud's theory of a genital stage through to adolescence to which he added three stages of adulthood. Neo-Freudians will almost certainly argue that this justifies and evolving capabilities thesis.

theory of morality (see Article 3, CRC[14] which places the 'best interests' of the child in everybody's hands except those of the children themselves).

Likewise, Kohlberg's formalist approach using Kantian philosophy (see Chap. 7) is most certainly more engaging for advocates of full citizenship for children who normally have only pro-children's rights structuralists to support their view. This is particularly the case for those who place greater emphasis on participation than on a broader application of social justice through a range of civil and human rights. There are countervailing forces in vexing questions about the rights of children. This is especially so with regard to the precarious territory in which those rights conflict with traditionally accepted rights of parents to raise their children as they choose without intervention by outside authority or influence.

Pro-children's rights structuralists attach a very precise meaning to children's participation that is produced and reproduced within a children's rights culture through various activities which serve as systems of association within which there is only a partial participation in civil society. Those are largely based on children's activities mainly disassociated from equivalent adult activities. Thus meaning is produced and reproduced within a separatist (different) culture that assesses only children's participation without balancing adult and children's comparable pursuits (including adult choice to bring children up in a particular way).

Kohlberg offers Kant's theory that there is a single moral obligation which is derived from the concept of duty. Kant defined the exigencies of moral law as 'categorical imperatives' which are principles that are inherently valid. The moral subject needs to be able to transcend his particular preferences, thus must act according to the moral law as a law given by the subject itself but which is also universally applicable. Those principles are good in and of themselves, so must be obeyed under all circumstances if we are to observe moral law. Since Kohlberg believed children acquire and possess moral reasoning at a relatively low age (see Kohlberg et al. 1983:101–189), the logic must follow that they belong within the same social order as all other moral beings, thus enjoy citizenship in which duty derives from the ability to reason and understand and contribute to what is just.

Among the many other psychologists who have looked at children's moral development, Robert Coles (1986a, b, 1997) has gone a step forward with his *The Political Life of Children* (1986b). That book looks at children struggling with their own political concepts among influences as diverse as nationalism, religion, ideology, language, culture, class and political morality. His fieldwork took in accounts including those of children in then *apartheid* South Africa and violent Northern Ireland. In those places children had grown up within conflict and were still only 10 years old expressed mature views, albeit laden with prejudices but also well reasoned and full of hope for change. Developmental psychology has undoubtedly a significant role to play in designing and justifying change for children.

[14] See Appendix I.

Sociological Research

Other disciplines have drawn heavily on theories in developmental psychology particularly sociology and social anthropology. However those disciplines have only very recently begun to look at children inclusively and seriously. There are still doubts about the viability of anthropology to achieve that end without far greater development of the work that (for instance) Vygotsky, Piaget, Kohlberg and others have done to set the agenda that has been questioned by Hardman (2001; originally published in 1973), Buehler-Niederberger (1998) and Milne (1997b) although in recent years children are beginning to attract greater attention. Until the recent focus on the topic both anthropological and sociological field studies tended to overlook children without even actually appearing to realise that that was the case.

It was felt that children were part of communities, therefore they were ultimately included. There were studies in which children were included that became seminal works for future research. The study of 'Middletown' in the USA has come to be considered an exemplary example of this kind of work. In 1924 Robert and Helen Lynd went to Muncie, Indiana (Middletown's real name) to research American institutions and values. The results of their work are the classic studies *Middletown* (1929), a case study of a typical American town of the 1920s, and *Middletown in Transition* (1937), which is an analysis of social and economic trends in that community during the Depression.

In the late 1970s a team of social scientists, Theodore Caplow, Howard M. Bahr, Bruce A. Chadwick and a number of research assistants, revisited Middletown to test changes that had taken place over the 50 years since the Lynds' first visit. The Middletown III Project replicated the earlier work, in some instances using the same questions and gives an extraordinary portrait of a small American town as it adapts to changing times. The first report, *Middletown Families*, was published in 1982.

The main findings of Middletown III were numerous. The class system the Lynds had observed in 1924 had not entirely disappeared but its importance was considerably reduced. This was partly because most industry upon which the class system was based had gone elsewhere, closed or gone entirely out of business. The new employers in Middletown were service industries so that the resulting pattern of class relationships was less clear. Unlike other commentators then, Caplow, Bahr and Chadwick discovered that the 'Middletown family' was not disappearing and religion remained vitally important to the majority of the townspeople. However, some substance of both institutions had changed. Families were more often fractured by divorce and religion had lost its essentially dogmatic character and become an optional part of people's lives. The study has continued on to become Middletown IV and so it was seen that by 1999 only half of Middletown's high school students lived with both birth parents although those living with their children spent more time with them than previously. Whereas in 1924 parents wanted children to be respectable churchgoers and be deferential, in 1999 parents wanted children to be broad-minded and independent.

Whilst it is a remarkable longitudinal study of a 'typical' community the family is never really examined from any other perspective than that of adults.

Caplow et al.'s (1982) first book includes a chapter under the heading 'Parents and children' (136–58) in which children are only accounted for in terms of the relationships and roles of their parents and there is only brief mention of how some children independently earn pocket money. The closing chapter, 'The myth of the declining family' (322–43) also focuses on adults with little attention paid to children. Recent findings on the Middletown website (see http://www.bsu.edu/middletown/history/) give little more emphasis on children themselves and continue to almost marginalise them despite the greater concern with what will come of them in a changing world.

In the UK Michael Young and Peter Willmott's (1957) *Family and Kinship in East London* has similarly been used as a seminal work.[15] They were surprised that the extended family was alive and well and also that neighbourhoods were microcosms of the world at large. Three generations lived close to each other and knew 'everybody' in Bethnall Green. It was a safe place to live because family and friends ensured that. If one was to examine the index (Milne 1998:70) there is little reference to children and none of the entire content at all describes any aspect of childhood whatsoever. Their follow up study focused on Woodford (Willmott and Young 1968), a suburb with a higher middle class population, and compared the nature of family and communal life with Bethnal Green as it had been. They found that kinship ties were much looser in Woodford, for instance:

> When a couple marry they set up a genuinely independent household; relatives' homes are more often connected by occasional missions, not by the continuous back and forth which make two homes into one in Bethnal Green. Kinship matters less, friendship more. (*Ibid.*:108)

Whereas in the first book they had concluded that 'the mother-daughter tie' was a widespread and probably universal phenomenon in urban areas of industrialised countries among manual workers, the Woodford study revealed that it was also a significant feature of middle class family life (*op. cit.*:111). However, it told nothing about daughters as children.

Michael Young revisited Bethnal Green with two other researchers (Dench et al. 2006) about 50 years after the area had gone into vast decline and was comprehensively redeveloped. Half a century had seen the traditional families mostly leave and replaced by a massive influx of Bangladeshi families. Many of them are now into the second or third generation. This study looks at how the community is coping with radical change. It especially examines relations between the old white and new Asian populations and how government policy affects racism. It is a comprehensive examination of life in a fascinating part of London. Like the 1957 study, children are notable for their absence. The index (*Ibid.*:266–74) give no direct reference to

[15] *Family and Kinship in East London* appeared as a key reference in studies of urban communities in the 1960s and well into the 1970s; however it still appears in such countries as Brazil and Peru where life in cities is constantly in flux and what the authors saw over 50 years ago is still relevant although notably one annotated bibliography I know does so beside references to Mayhew and Dickens.

children or youth, in fact only two brief entries on pages 12 and 118 on child rearing appear to cover this aspect of the study.

Peter Willmott's *Adolescent Boys of East London* (1969, originally published in 1966 by the Institute of Community Studies) was one of a small number of sociological examinations of youth in the mid 1960s. The post second world war sociological literature focussing on experience of young people was limited to two main contributors, Pearl Jephcott (1942, 1948, 1954, 1967) and John Barron Mays (1954, 1962, 1965). In the early to mid-1960s a number of authors including the Eppels (Eppel 1966), Downes (1966), Jackson and Marsden (1962) and Musgrove (1968) studied youth. Much of this work appeared to have been influenced by William Whyte's (1943) Street Corner Society. Willmott was unique amongst them in that able to communicate something of the essence of their experience and lives. He studied 200 or so youths and classified three wide-ranging typologies:

> First the 'working class' boy who went to a secondary modern or comprehensive school and left school at 15 to go into a semi-skilled or skilled job – comparable with Whyte's 'corner boys'. Then there was the 'middle class' boy whereby in Bethnal Green where the majority were working class this described those who went to grammar or comprehensive school and left school at 16 or over then entered white collar employment – Whyte's 'college boys'. Finally, the 'rebel' described boys who went to secondary modern school but left at 15 and went into unskilled or semi-skilled manual work, probably going through several jobs. (Willmott 1969:171–6).

He noted that: "...during adolescence most boys withdraw from the mixed-age society of childhood into a one-age society of their fellows, and that as they mature and particularly as they move toward courtship and marriage, they rejoin the mixed-age society as adults" (*op. cit.*:177). He saw that the peer group was of obvious significance as too the local community. It was still "...important to the great majority of boys and becomes even more so as they move into adulthood" (*op. cit.*: 182). Whilst his subjects were youths, little suggests that they were at all capable of assuming full 'adult' or citizens' duties and responsibilities. Perhaps, in terms of how we saw children then and now, our perception then of youth of around age 15 was that they were on the threshold of adulthood. That has changed somewhat. More recent studies of childhood emphasise children's agency, that is to say, their capacity to help shape circumstances in which they live rather than being shaped by their social, cultural and physical environment. This is a an issue that some sociologists and anthropologists with the experience of observing children in the field have recorded which will be shown in the next section but has been extensively examined and developed in the section thereafter that looks at the sociology of childhood.

Social and Cultural Anthropology

Anthropology has no markedly greater success being inclusive of children. Christopher Fuller (1976) in his study (see also Mencher 1965:163–191) of the Nayars in Kerala, India was particularly concerned with the disintegration of the matrilineal joint-family system (123–50) noting that at the time of his study the nuclear family had emerged as the dominant type of household and economic unit.

Children were seen in terms of maternal and paternal authority, marriage ages and the value of virginity before marriage. Economic change was driving change in which the economic importance of children was becoming defined by education and the future value in the labour force. The Nayar had three principal marriage and *rite de passage* ceremonies. First was the *thaali* tying rite that happened before puberty. During the ceremony a girl was married to a man who was ideally a Namboothiri Brahman. The ritual husband had no additional duties to the girl after completion of the ritual although she was required to observe a period of death impurity when the ritual husband died. The *Thirandukalyanam* ceremony was the puberty ceremony during which femininity was celebrated and when women were allowed to occupy parts of households usually occupied by men. The *Sambandham* ritual was less auspicious than the *thaali* and puberty rites, literally meaning 'relationship'. It was the traditional institution that described casual marriage alliances within what is called *marumakkathayam*, which is a matrilineal system of inheritance.

The ritual was held on the union of bride and groom but was not necessarily a permanent arrangement. *Sambandham* denoted hypergamy between Nayar women and Namboothiri men as well as reciprocal marriage among Nayars. However, the bond was not recognised as constituting marriage by Namboothiri Brahmins or colonial courts but seen as immoral, allied with polyandry, comparable to concubinage or even prostitution. It was nothing like that for Nayar girls since *sambandham* essentially gave the liberty to initiate, consent to or terminate a sexual relationship with any man and thereby formed one of the foundations of matrilineality. Despite that virginity was considered a very high value and also the legitimacy of children paramount. The degree of competence in making moral decisions and keeping what were essentially very rigid rules was entrusted to females particularly, however in our terms these would have been children.

Formal marriage more or less marked the passage into adulthood and a more stable and in some ways less regulated relationship. Unfortunately, beyond this complicated betrothal and marriage system there is little else said that gives a measure of the rest of the girls' roles in society and even less about boys. Thus, whilst in moral terms very big decisions were made as a matter of course, there is little more information about the broader societal role of these young people.

In examination of the transition from childhood to adulthood such authors as Arnold van Gennep (1966) and Victor Turner (1969) tell us much about initiation (*rites de passage*) and liminality but as in other areas we learn little about children themselves. Van Gennep's seminal work (1966) on initiation had two chapters, IV. Pregnancy and Childbirth (*Ibid.*:41–49) and V. Birth and Childhood (*Ibid.*:50–64), that looked at early years. For him childhood ended slowly as individuals go through rites of passage that are transitions when individuals move from one social status to another in a three-phased scheme of *separation*, *segregation* and *incorporation*.

It appears that society guides individuals from one status to another as though going from one room to another, whereby they always pass over thresholds. The spatial constituent is important since changed status often implies changing place. The 'magico-religious aspect of crossing frontiers' (*Ibid.*:15) absorbed van Gennep for whom religion signified abstract ideas or dogma and magic meant ritual action.

'Magico-religious' was his idiosyncratic explanation for practical religious acts unlike Durkheim's distinction between religion as collective activity and magic as privately selfish activity.

According to van Gennep, the dynamic transitions depend on 'the pivoting of sacredness' (*Ibid.*:12) during the middle liminal phase which underlines why *door* and *threshold* (Latin: *limen*) were important for him in both literal and metaphorical senses. The fear inherent in changing status and responsibility was dealt with ritually even if not concurrent with adolescent biological changes. The rites designate the journey through life indicating physical change and altering responsibility.

Victor Turner explored a threefold structure of rites of passage (1969:94–130) and broadened theories about the liminal phase. Van Gennep's structure consisted of the pre-liminal phase (separation), a liminal (transition) and a post-liminal phase (reincorporation). Turner observed that in liminality, the transitional state between phases, individuals were 'betwixt and between' thus did not belong to the society they were previously part of and were still not reincorporated into society. Liminality is like limbo which is an ambiguous stage characterised by humility, isolation, trials, sexual indistinctness and *communitas* (*Ibid.*:131–65) which he defined as an unstructured community in which members are all equal.

Van Gennep and Turner were highly dependent on the language of psychology and psychoanalysis, although neither used either discipline as a research tool. However, we have the possibility of comparing Jean Piaget and Margaret Mead as psychologist and anthropologist who used both psychology and psychoanalytical method as tools to reach their respective conclusions. Piaget's research (1929) in developmental psychology and genetic epistemology set out to discover how knowledge grows. His answer was that it comes about through progressive construction of logically embedded structures that replace each another through a process of the inclusion of lower, less powerful logical means that become higher and more powerful as the individual grows to adulthood. He concluded that children's logic and modes of thought are wholly different from those of adults at the outset. During the first half of the twentieth century, he claimed (*Ibid.*) that his subjects, all Swiss children, were *animistic*[16] in their thinking.

In contrast, Mead combined psychological sciences with anthropological fieldwork for the first time. She believed that study of children was vital to developing an understanding of ourselves and improving our futures. She was one of the first anthropologists to study child rearing practice and its effects on various societies. Her theory of *imprinting* was a method through which she believed children learn.

[16]Rudyard Kipling's Mowgli, the 'wild boy of Aveyron' (Lane 1979) and similar accounts of children raised by animals have sometimes given credence to the notion of animism. Mowgli and other fictional characters were held to possess almost superhuman qualities that came from the animals they grew up with. Victor, the 'wild boy of Aveyron' was found in 1800 when he emerged from the woods of the Aveyron District. He was naked and behaved like an animal, probably aged about 12 years, it was estimated that he had lived wild since about age 4. Dr Jean-Marc-Gaspard Itard invented a programme of training for him but with only limited success. Children with learning difficulties who attend Montessori nurseries are taught the method of hands-on play devised by Itard for Victor that tends to maintain if not reinforce the 'animal nature' argument.

She presented evidence (1967) demonstrating that Pacific island children were not *animistic* although her title describes them as 'primitive children'.

Mead and Martha Wolfenstein (1955) tried to put childhood into a broader social context. Wolfenstein's chapter in their collection, 'French parents take their children to the park' (99–117), recounts how in Paris she observed the behaviour of parents and children in parks. She noted that French children quickly learned that any display of physical aggression was not permissible and also that verbal clashes are substituted by other means of expression.

Her conclusion was that French childhood and adulthood are very distinct so that the correlation between childhood and adulthood were almost completely opposed in the USA and France. In the former, childhood is viewed as an almost ideal time with adults nostalgic about their own childhood. Adulthood is an interminable life of work in which immediate gratification is virtually absent. For the French, the opposite is true since adulthood is when one can live for the moment and that passions become ends in themselves; and preoccupation with such pleasures and resourcefulness in achieving them is an ongoing issue as an adult. French children have to learn to be adults by diligent attention to the world around them, unlike the American children who grow out of blissful times into the austerity of adulthood.

Whilst the topic seems grave, Wolfenstein had written *Children's Humor: A Psychological Analysis* (1954)[17] only 1 year earlier and did see a profounder competence in children. Analysis of their use and creation of humour focussed especially on the child's view of the ludicrous. She drew data on what children regarded funny from interviews with children between ages 4 and 12 years who were asked to tell funny stories, jokes they already knew, recall funny things in class and other things that made them laugh. She noted that, banal and unfunny as adults might find children's humour, ultimately the same rules defining and constructing what was funny applied to both adults and children.

Richard Lee and Irven DeVore's (1976) work on the !Kung San of the Kalahari includes an entire section of the book (Part III) under the heading 'Childhood'. It is a relaxed childhood that consists of seasonal comings and goings in which there are child marriages (Draper 1976:199–271). The menses and attendant rituals are of great symbolic importance as too is childbirth (see also: Konner 2005:19–64). That is usually in the bush and unattended for women who by western values would be considered young girls. The transitions are shorter but very clearly marked and celebrated. This is more clearly shown in Hewlett and Lamb's (2005) work on hunter gatherer childhoods in which they look at what they regard as 'evolutionary' developments and a range of cultural perspectives in which we find childhood very clearly defined and recognised.

Enid Schildkrout's work with the Hausa in Nigeria (Rodgers and Standing 1981:90–5 and 103–06) looked closely at the socio-economic role of children. It is a study of work that challenges many previous assumptions. It particularly shows

[17]Wolfenstein was a psychoanalyst who used ethnographic methods, especially observation, for her studies unlike Mead who was an anthropologist who used psychoanalysis as a complementary research method for analysis of her field data.

how women's economic responsibilities in Islamic society are dependent on the work of children who have greater freedom of movement. She looked at their daily activities, including play and self-care, as well as their work. They are ranked by age and gender without their role in Hausa society really ever described. There is no real reference to their decision-making capabilities or, indeed, to particular skills.

Neither Fuller nor Schildkrout say much about the conditions in which childhood occurs or how children are valued. Likewise, they tell us little about children and their capabilities and importance to their society as the capital for the preservation of traditions in the former and part of the economic capital of family and community in the other. Lee and DeVore are a little more concerned with aspects of childhood that indicate the need for extensive use of individual decision making and competence.

Whilst these works give a wider perspective on the content of childhood one of the key themes that is repeated is the economic value of children. They very much support the view expressed by Zelizer (1985) in her two chapters on the labour value of children. Economic approaches to the value of children have largely been neglected by social scientists, although economist Joseph Spengler (1966a, b) saw them in terms of a controlled, desired birth rate as a response to industrialisation where economic and social changes influence income generation.

Each family, he believed, consciously or unconsciously weighed up the value and cost of each additional child against resources available to invest in that child. Thus family size shifts as income increases and the value of a child includes their labour contribution to the family economy. However, when a country industrialises, child labour laws, compulsory education and other factors such as social security provision reduce potential monetary value. The real costs of a child are outlays for their needs and the cost of parenting time against paid labour. Thus the cost of a child in a traditional society is low since he or she demands few resources against those of a rich, industrialised country where family size is a direct function of income.

The New Sociology of Childhood

Over the last two or three decades the sociology of childhood has gained increasing attention and generated numerous empirical studies as well as rigorous theoretical disputes within Scandinavia and English speaking countries particularly (for instance, see Alanen 1988; James and Prout 1990; James et al. 1998; Corsaro 2005; Mayall 2000; Qvortrup 1993, 1994). This sociology of children and childhood is essentially a study of social inequality, about children's 'nature', needs, interests, values, morals and capabilities. It is actually interdisciplinary rather than a single discipline, bringing together sociology, history, ethno-methodology and ethnography, cultural studies, pedagogy and law. It is an examination of the changing social circumstances of contemporary children's lives, social class differences in their life experiences, traditional and emerging perspectives on socialisation, gender and race, and methodological issues concerning children and children's peer cultures. It puts all aspects of children's lives at the centre of research.

Rather than assuming that children are passive participants in interactions involving adults, the assumption is that children are active participants who do not simply respond to the demands, instructions or explanation by adults. Children also make independent contributions to social life affecting adults. Until the late 1980s, sociologists tended to include children in the kind of sociological studies previously described in which they are passive objects in an adult led process of socialisation or are causes or victims of social problems. Now sociology approaches children and childhood from a mainly socialisation perspective in which the emergence of the new sociological paradigm was analogous to the feminist critique of sociological traditions. Childhood sociologists attacked 'adulto-centric' approaches and the 'separatist view' of sociology towards children.

The sociology of childhood is organised around two central discourses. The first is the child as a social actor in which the approach draws from youth sociology and ethnography. It focuses on everyday life and ways in which children take their place in society as too the social worlds they construct and take part in. Theory and research approach children as active participants and members of society right from the onset. Thus they are neither analysed as outsiders of society nor as merely 'emergent' members of society. The social actor has 'agency'. When agency is considered in the philosophical sense, it is the capacity of an agent to act in the world. The capacity to act does not at first imply a specific moral dimension to the ability to make the choice to act. Moral agency addresses this type of issue. Human agency describes the capacity of human beings to make choices and to impress those choices on the world. They are normally contrasted with natural forces which involve only impulsive deterministic processes.

It is therefore subtly distinct from a concept of free will, because it takes in the uncontroversial, weaker assertion that humans come to make decisions and whether that is by free choice or other processes is another issue. The capacity of a human to act as an agent is specific to that person, although considerations of outcomes flowing from particular acts of human agency for us and others may be considered to invest a moral element of a given situation wherein an agent has acted and thus involves moral agency. If a situation is the consequence of human decision making actors may be responsible for applying value judgements to the consequences of their decisions, thus held responsible for decisions. Human agency entitles the observer to ask whether it should have occurred. In some philosophical traditions, human agency is a shared, historical force instead of a function arising out of individual behaviour. In social psychology the term agency refers to the self-efficacy of a person and ability to act on his or her own behalf.

Philosophers suggest that only rational beings, thus people who are capable of reasoning and forming selfish (egotistic or self-interested) judgments, can be moral agents. It has been suggested that individuals with limited rationality (for example, the mentally disabled) also have basic moral capabilities. Kant argued that whether or not our real self can choose, we are without choice other than believing that we choose unreservedly when we choose. We can also compare the notion of moral agency with the legal principle of *mens rea*, or *guilty mind*, which states that somebody is legally responsible for what he or she does on condition that they know what they are doing and the choices are deliberate. In terms of how this might be viewed using children's rights principles, the notion of 'evolving capabilities' is a possible argument for supporting an argument that children do not inherently posses all qualities to make fully reasoned decisions.

The second approach, *the generational order*, focuses on socio-structural and socio-theoretical questions concerning social equality and social order in a society. That society categorises members by age and segregates them in some respects (rights, deeds, economical participation, ascribed needs, etc.). These issues can be summarised under the overall concept of the *generational order*. Consequently the categorisation of members of society by age is far from being a naive representation of natural distinctions but is rather more a social construction of a 'natural truth'. It is, accordingly, a germane constituent of social order and profoundly connected with other dimensions of social inequality. Social and economic changes and socio-political intervention have thus become central topics in the sociology of childhood.

The analysis of these issues has increased awareness of the generational inequality of societies. For instance, analysis of the socialisation processes means reconstruction of historically and culturally varied concepts, processes and institutions of disciplining and civilising children. Additionally, the approach to formation of *habitus* and the practices of status reproduction need to be taken into account. Children's actions, their resistance, cooperation, and collective action among peers must then be taken into account.

Likewise, common anthropological assumptions concerning a universal human nature based on a view of individual and society as opposed to each other should be excluded from the conceptual inventory of sociological childhood research. Those remain as a vestige of the socialisation approach that justified some forms of childhood and education practices as essential and even a *natural* condition of society whilst others are unvalued. Western middle class childhood appears to be the model of the 'norm' thus concealing social inequality and the interests of social order. This was what Ariès and Benedict appear to have accepted. Ariès (1962) believed that *scholarisation* (i.e.: pp. 308–9) was a major conduit for producing childhood historically, as compulsory and universal schools became the norm. It is a long process of segregation, which isolated and delivered children to reason that has continued up to the present. Ruth Benedict said that:

> From a comparative point of view our culture goes to the extremes in emphasizing contrasts between the child and the adult. The child is sexless, the adult estimates his virility by his sexual activities; the child must be protected from the ugly facts of life, the adult must meet them without psychic catastrophe; the child must obey, the adult must command this obedience: These are all dogmas of our culture, dogmas which, in spite of the facts of nature, other cultures commonly do not share. In spite of the physiological contrasts between child and adult, these are cultural accretions. (Benedict 1955:21–22, originally published in 1938).

Without dismissing generational order arguments, it is noteworthy that recent sociology of childhood studies place greater emphasis on children's agency, that is to say, on their capacity to be actively involved in shaping circumstances in which they live than on generational order. The concept of children's agency has been used in a variety of ways. A thriving body of research on children's everyday lives emphasises their capacity for autonomous action and cultural creation. Researchers working directly with children occasionally struggle with questions about the capacity of children to consent to being studied, how adult defined 'best interests' may be in conflict with children's own perception of the notion and the use of adult authority as a barrier to a real to access and understanding of children as social actors. These latter issues are examined in the final sections of this chapter and where participation is examined in the following chapter. However, agency itself requires closer scrutiny which begins by looking at the work of French sociologist Pierre Bourdieu in the following section where his work on four forms of capital are an important contributory factor to defining agency and how it is used.

Bourdieu

Sociology has been taken to that point where beyond agency the question has turned to children's possession of *capital*. Authors who have gone down this route rely heavily on Pierre Bourdieu. Chapter 9 goes into this topic in greater detail specifically in an examination of the use of the notion of cultural and social capital where it is used in the examination of and attempts to define children's participation in civil society. Bourdieu's work on capital identified and distinguished between four forms of capital which are referred to as economic, cultural, social and symbolic capital. Social and cultural capital are seen as the most valuable in terms of viewing children in the contemporary 'pro-child' sociological context.

Bourdieu defined social capital as: "the aggregate of the actual or potential resources which are linked to possession of a durable network of more or less institutionalised relationships of mutual acquaintance and recognition" (1983:249). His treatment of the concept is generally instrumental and focuses on the advantages of those who possess social capital and the "deliberate construction of sociability for the purpose of creating this resource" (*Ibid.*). The renaissance of interest in social capital as an antidote to contemporary social problems draws on an assumption that problems rest in the decline of the importance of civil society. Inclusion of all social actors, thus children, is seen as a way of drawing society back together. A profusion of social capital is viewed as a necessary condition for modern liberal democracy in which egalitarianism needs to expand to sustain it. Low levels of social capital lead to an excessively inflexible and uncaring political system and high levels of corruption within the political system and oppression of individual freedoms.

Cultural capital is strongly linked to one's *habitus*, which is a person's character and way of thinking (Bourdieu 1986:247). Bourdieu adopted the concept of *habitus* from Marcel Mauss and enlarged the range of the term to include an individual's beliefs and character. It was used relatively systematically in an attempt to resolve the debate between *objectivism* and *subjectivism* in the human sciences. Bourdieu defined *habitus* as a system of robust and compatible 'dispositions' (durable schemes of action, perception and thought).

An individual agent develops dispositions in response to determining structures such as family, class and education and external conditions they encounter. They are, therefore, neither entirely voluntary nor involuntary. Thus the *habitus* offers the practical skills and nature necessary to plot a course within different fields such as sport, profession, art and so on and directs the individual's choices without ever being exactly reduced to set, formal rules. Simultaneously, it is constantly remodelled by those choices including success or failure of previous action. Since it describes neither absolute determination by social factors nor individual autonomy it mediates between *objective* structures of social relations and the individual *subjective* behaviour of actors. Cultural capital consists of three subtypes which he described as *embodied, objectified* and *institutionalised* (Bourdieu 1986:47).

The embodied state is where it is personified in the individual. It is thus both the inherited and acquired properties that make the individual's self. It is not inherited in a genetic sense but time, cultural and tradition bestow elements of the embodied state on the individual, most usually within the family through socialisation, and is thus linked to the *habitus*. The objectified state is that in which objects are owned, such as scientific implements or works of art. Those 'cultural' goods can be traded as an application of *economic capital* and also *symbolically* by using them as cultural capital. In the case of children this is least likely to apply since their legal status seldom gives them either the status of full owner or broker for such transactions. The institutionalised state is formal recognition of cultural capital held by an individual that is most often recognised as academic credentials or qualifications. This mainly occurs in relation to the labour market from which children are generally excluded.

Economic capital is less significant here since children do not usually own capital or means of production. However, if one looks at child workers, especially those who are (street) vendors who must buy stock in order to resell it, it is not irrelevant. In economic terms, capital, goods or real capital refer to readymade durable goods available for use as an aspect of production. Those capital goods may be acquired with money or other capital. It is a question that arises in examination of child street vendors in informal economies, but has tended to be more closely associated with street trading as a deviant rather than respectable occupation. Finally there is linguistic capital which Bourdieu defined as the mastery of and relationship with language (Bourdieu and Passeron 1990:114) in the sense that it signifies manners of speaking and may also be understood as a form of embodied cultural capital. This is like the previous type of capital, perhaps least applied since language acquisition and sophistication are almost always associated with maturation of the individual. It is most frequently assumed that fully nuanced language is exclusive to adults only.

Children's Agency

Thus having examined the importance of capital as contributory to arguments for recognition of full citizenship because the interconnection is inseparable, it now necessary at what children's agency is. Using children's agency and their possession of capital is the route by which they are neither analysed as outsiders to society nor as merely 'emergent' members of society. However, that was not always the case.

As far back as Aristotle's (1987) *De Anima* almost two and a half thousand years ago, the notion of the 'tabula rasa' was used by Ibn Sina (Avicenna) in the eleventh century, arisng again when used by St Thomas Aquinas, (*Summa Theologica*: 1.79.2; see Pojman 1985) in the thirteenth century, John Locke in the seventeenth century and Sigmund Freud in the nineteenth century. Jean Jacques Rousseau, despite his theory of the 'natural man', believed that children 'became' adults. In his view the development of a child was divided into three stages. The first was from birth to the age of about 12 years when calculation and complex thought is not possible and children, he believed, live like animals. The second stage from 12 to about 16 years is when reason begins to develop. Finally from the age of 16 years onwards is when children develop to become adults.

These types of theory have persisted until very recently. David Oldman (1991: 25) used a 'tongue in cheek' chronological table of typical 'privileges' accruing from adolescence to early adulthood including such examples as when a young person can apply for a provisional driving licence or legally consume alcohol in his 'Childhood as a Social Phenomenon' report on Scotland to exemplify accumulation of agency and capital. Some stages appear ludicrously arbitrary or even contradictory in terms of what the Scots 'child' can do, but not the English or Welsh although both are within a single United Kingdom. A critic of this kind of 'evolution' from childhood to adulthood is Danish sociologist Jens Qvortrup who said that:

> Children are reduced to *human becomings*, they are a 'project' to be moulded, whilst shielded from the public issues and major social events… (1991: 7)

Furthermore he saw this as part of a problem in which neither their agency nor the possibility of their having capital was acknowledged:

> The anticipatory point of view reiterates a common sense view of children, as socially and economically, relatively unimportant when compared with adulthood… A corollary of this appears to be that children are not credited with human agency… (*Ibid.*:7–8)
>
> …children belong to society – not in the trivial sense of simply being there, nor as a reduced form of raw material to be moulded, nor as the possession of the society or the state. Childhood is part of society in the sense that children do participate in organised activities, and it constitutes a part of the social structure interacting in many ways with other parts. (*Ibid.*:10)

What Qvortrup is implying is that the agency approach has become intermingled with notions of children learning to be individuals, often through particular activities such as membership of children's movements or organisations. Whilst superficially these organisations are said to be run by children themselves or there is shared responsibility with adults, in point of fact nearly all have been started and overseen by adults. There is to some extent a myth of children's participation within such settings that distracts from the reality of children as participants in everyday life. However, organised participatory activities and events are often viewed as the source of agency and capital, thus the notion of the independent or autonomous child as one who has agency is overlooked.

New Arguments

The sociological development has attracted new support from other quarters. The first has been a feminist critique of the status of children and the second has been from those looking at difference (e.g.: disability, race, gay and lesbian issues) more broadly, often using feminist approaches. These have begun to make a significant contribution to arguments for children's citizenship. Two examples are used here, Lister whose approach is fundamentally feminist but takes account of her feminist background and Moosa-Mitha who uses a difference centred approach that is broadly based on a feminist approach.

Ruth Lister arguing for children's equality says:

> To treat others with respect is seen by the general public as a key responsibility of citizenship and it is a responsibility that children are capable of exercising. However, many would argue that children and young people (and the responsibilities they exercise) do not receive either recognition or respect. In other words, they do not enjoy equality of status.
>
> This is the other side of the current Respect Agenda: asking people (including children and young people) to behave with 'respect' should be met with a renewed respect for the positive contribution many young people make to society and the responsibilities that they take on. This is particularly true of children who are brought up in poverty and may have multiple responsibilities and pressures in the domestic sphere.
>
> The international children's movement, like social movements before it, such as the feminist, civil rights and disability movements can be understood as a struggle for recognition of and respect for children's equal status as citizens. (Lister 2006a:24)

In her article 'A Difference-Centred Alternative to Theorization of Children's Citizenship Rights', Moosa-Mitha (2005) adopts a 'difference' approach that follows a broadly feminist approach, in which she argues that the 'rights revolution' is now central to contemporary political consciousness that has brought with it a profusion of theories about children's rights. She furthermore argues that mainstream liberal theories looking at children's rights seldom take children's rights as citizens seriously. That, she claims, is due to the normative standpoint of liberal theories that continue to perceive children in terms of 'not-yet-citizens' (*Ibid.*:369). Her core argument is for a 'difference-centred theory' (*Ibid.*:382) of children's citizenship rights by repositioning analysis within feminist, anti-racist, gay, lesbian and transgendered theories of citizenship that are difference-centred, thus 'differently equal' (*Ibid.*:386). She proposes an alternative, difference-centred, expression of children's citizenship rights that is achieved through analysis to rights of liberty and equality that aligns notions of childhood with the theories she proposes be used to that end. Thus, she argues, the expansion of existing liberal, normative notions of liberty that are defined by individuals to autonomously make decisions or participate in duties as citizens redefine children's rights to liberty. That operates in terms that address their agency and recognise their presence as participants in the many relationships in which they play a role. In so doing, that also redresses their right to equality from mainstream liberal interpretation of 'equality-as-same' to one that views children as 'differently equal' members of a social environment in which they are full participants.

Moosa-Mitha believes that freedom in difference centred theories is understood in terms of "the right to participate differently in the social institutions and culture of the society" (*Ibid.*:375). Not having freedom, in her point of view, is defined as lacking recognition of participation and the contribution of people who are 'different' that arises because of difference from conventional assumptions of participation and participants. Recognition of difference that comes with changes to these values and also what is practiced within society in order to recognise the agency of citizens who are 'different' is seen in transformative ways that change dominant, established connotations of citizenship into flexible and difference-centred ones. She cites (*Ibid.*:375–76) Lister's summary of this point thus:

> Citizenship as participation represents an expression of human agency in the political arena, broadly defined: citizenship as rights enables people to act as agents. Moreover, citizenship rights are not fixed. They remain the objects of political struggles to defend, reinterpret and extend them. Who is involved in these struggles, where they are placed in the political hierarchy and the political power and influence they can yield will help to determine the outcomes. Citizenship thus emerges as a dynamic concept in which process and outcome stand in a dialectical relationship to each other. (Lister 1997:35)

This, in Moosa-Mitha's view, is a 're-interpretation of freedom' (*Ibid.*:376) that recognises agency and consequently the individual's presence in society through a more comprehensive understanding of participation that can be analysed in relation to expressing children's rights to freedom differently.

Both Lister and Moosa-Mitha are drawing on a lengthy experience of the women's movement and more recent initiatives to end both paternalistic and prejudicial ways of justify exclusion because of difference or 'inferior' qualities as a human being. As the experience of ending difference centred arguments is made inclusive of approaches for allowing children full citizenship grows, the proposition gains far more credence. However, these require further supporting evidence that the often more theoretical sociology of childhood alone does not sustain.

Liberal theory embraces a view that freedom is a fundamental value therefore the just state ensures freedom for citizens. There has, however, always been disagreement among liberals about what freedom means. In their interpretation of freedom, men and women are self-owners who are capable of acquiring and holding property rights over possessions. Adults, therefore, have the right to freedom from forcible interference with their person and property. However, children have been traditionally viewed as the 'chattels' of adult caretakers and have only limited access to ownership and dispossession by their caretakers or other authorised adults which is regarded as normal. Thus, liberal theory has hitherto omitted them because there was not actual need to consider their citizenship rights.

In his 1994 work on covenant theory, O'Neill places great value on what liberal theory does not. That is the continuity of family and community life between generations that is inclusive of the moral norm *reciprocity*. His title, *The Missing Child in Liberal Theory*, suggests it is inclusive of them but in fact it is not exclusively about children. It is an explanation of a covenant alternative to contract liberalism that he believes is an essential part of civic capitalism.

Later O'Neill (2004) directly replaces the notion of welfare state with one of civic capitalism that offers important theoretical means with which to reconsider how social and economic policy making are designed. Without falling into an essentialist perspective, His view is that new social structures are needed to support children and their families. In his view, the civic state and standardisation of opportunity would be a principle necessary to balance intergenerational equity. He believes that a civic state can support family capital rather than individual, thus social and human, capital since families and their relative position in society are the most noteworthy source of inequality for children. His position on civic childhood (see Chap. 4) refers to numerous research studies in social science that show how social environments are contributory to an individual's health and wealth and thereby how investment in early childhood offers the highest socioeconomic returns.

He shows throughout this book how children and young families are disadvantaged in the welfare state and never protected by corporate capitalism. To begin with, private capital obstructs the goal of improving children's opportunities through the course of their life. Then, young people are without a voice in corporate capitalism. Contained inside the moral order of civic capitalism, a state would have no option but to sustain education and health in order to boost human, social and private capital. Thus, in his view, the state would have no other alternative to promotion of civic education as a means of encouraging economic growth. His vision of civic education is a humanistic outlook in which the young learn how to learn instead of being merely being educated to be good workers and consumers.

In each stage of his work, whilst offering the seductive notion of work about childhood itself, his theories are actually about the family in which he is expounding the notion of children as part of the intergenerational continuum rather than individual agents. In so doing he at most implies their membership of society whilst not explicitly describing them as citizens.

Another liberal theorist Freeman (1983, 1992, 1999) adopts an approach that considers childhood a social construct that is historically specific. That construct also emphasises children's vulnerability and dependency on adults because of their physical immaturity. He (1983) uses a Rawlsian liberal framework of analysis with which he interprets liberty as autonomy. Rawls (1971) as a moral and political philosopher is probably the greatest influence on legal philosophy in the twentieth century. His philosophical origins were heavily influenced by the social contract theory that originated during the Enlightenment. Therefore, as a lawyer very much influenced by Rawlsian liberal political theory, Freeman argues that children's rights to autonomy are individuated decision-making about their own lives and should therefore be respected.

However, rather than respecting their rights of real autonomy, their capacity to be autonomous, in his view, should be respected. Freeman elucidates his view by saying that as persons of equal value, children should be shown consideration by protecting them from irrational acts whilst also conceding to them rights of autonomy when they demonstrate a capacity to make independent choices regarding appropriate life choices. According to Freeman children's capacity to make these decisions can be established within a neutral theory of good. That provides a model on which to measure children's capacity on a case-by-case basis. This, in his view, requires decision making by adults on behalf of children using the principle of future-oriented consent. That means that decisions made by adults would find agreement with children, once they are adults. This view of children's rights to liberty as autonomy is also reflected in more recent works by child theorists who place emphasis on children's rights to participation, especially as it is described by Article 12, CRC. It is essentially a narrow view that is to an extent informed rather than influenced by the child sciences but is most easily assimilated by thinkers whose background is law or human rights.

Liberal theory entails a broad range of views, very few of which are directly looking at children, but is collectively an approach that those putting forward the feminist or difference centred point of view (e.g.: Moosa-Mitha 2005) tend to be critical of.

Another significant approach is in the anthropological and social research fields of childhood and medicine. US anthropologist Myra Bluebond-Langner (1980) worked with children aged 18 months to 14 years, with main informants of between 3 and 9 years old, who were dying from cancer. She describes their capacity to deal with their illness and likely death thus:

> ...When first diagnosed, they were concerned about the seriousness of the illness, about the fact they were sicker than they had ever been. When they began to achieve the first remission, they wanted to know about the drugs used in the treatment and their side effects. They were heartened by the fact that although they had been ill, they were now recovering. However, during the first relapse, old doubts returned. They wondered if they would always be sick. They tried to learn everything they could about procedures and treatments they had to endure. After further relapses, they asked about the chronic nature of the illness. They wanted to know if and when the suffering would end. At such a time, the death of a fried provided the needed information. They knew that, like their friends, they too would die.
>
> Often children will decide to conceal their knowledge of the prognosis from adults. (1980:233–4)

In another study in 1989 she examines the place of illness and death in the lives of healthy children and ill siblings at the end stages of the latter's lives. The behaviour displayed by children provided remarkable insights into children's views of their lives as well as of death. Likewise, in her 1996 work children from as young as 2 years old described living in the shadow of illness as siblings of chronically ill children. British sociologist Priscilla Alderson has looked at medical consent and information for children since the early 1990s (Alderson 1993, 1994; Alderson and Montgomery 1996). She has moved toward a position of defence of children's right to integrity, informed consent before surgery and helping share decisions with them, reaching conclusions about the ability of children to comprehend and decide much like Bluebond-Langner.

More recently, she worked with a group of researchers (Alderson et al. 2005a, b) whose work was with premature babies. They are the same gestational age as foetuses, absolutely without rights. Their ethnographic neonatal study illustrated how most of the CRC applies to premature babies. Parents of neonates and staff presented socially and culturally constructed versions of childhood relating to versions of citizenship, duties, responsibilities and rights that, far from denying or trivialising rights, diverted attention to premature babies' rights. They describe how recognition of neonates' citizenship can explain how human rights are embodied, aesthetic, interactive, emotional, political, economic and socially contextualised. The premature babies' "...resistances also demonstrated the relevance of rights to them as sentient, sapient, active meaning makers, within the private family and the public neonatal units" (Alderson et al. 2005a, b: 97) the research took place in. Research findings assess advantages and disadvantages of conceptualising premature babies' needs as rights and acknowledging their status as citizens.

What anthropological and sociological research with children and medicine has attempted successfully is to show that two extremes of human life experienced by children, the absolute end of being and entering the world early, have 'meaning' for individuals experiencing them and qualities displayed provide profound arguments for inclusion. The issue of informed consent, therefore decision sharing on the basis of knowing the consequences of surgery, imply far great competence than an 'adult-in-the-making' type of view of children that has thus far been largely exclusionary. In each of these examples, the rights to dignity, integrity and respect for the person that are described by arguments using either a feminist or difference-centred approach are very easily comparable. However, some of these ideas are not *per se* new, having lineage back to Durkheimian and earlier Kantian theories.

New Social Theory and the Resurgence of Older Ideas

Thus, recent developments in the child sciences have links back to the far distant past of philosophical views of child development, through to contemporary arguments for treating children in the same ways as adults in the paediatric, psychological and other 'medicalised' environments. This is furthermore acknowledgement of what Zelizer (1985) describes as the 'sacralisation' of children's lives and presents a sound argument for a cross-disciplinary review of how children's agency particularly is important.

Taking Qvortrup's critique of the 'human becomings' approach that has dominated hitherto, an argument is perhaps that the collective view of children as lesser than adults has to be abandoned in favour of assessment of the capability of the individual. Adults may also be judged in terms similar to the 'evolving capabilities' method. Turning to an older sociology rather than more recent work on children, Durkheim tells us that:

> If we can say that in a given sense collective representations exist outside of individual consciences, it is because they originate not from individuals taken separately but from their interaction, which is very different. No doubt each one brings its own share in the development of the common result; but private sentiments become social only in combining under the pressure of *sui generis* forces that this association develops. Following combinations and the mutual alterations resulting from them they become something else. A chemical synthesis occurs to concentrate and unite synthesised elements and, by through this process, transforms them. Since this synthesis is the work of the whole, that phase will also be the whole. The resulting outcome thus extends beyond each individual spirit, just as the whole extends beyond the partial. ... It is thus that it is outside of particular individuals. ... To

> really understand what it is we have to take the sum of its entirety into consideration. It is that which thinks, feels and wants although it can only do this through specific principles. That is also how we are able to see that the phenomenon of society is not dependent on the personal nature of individuals. (Durkheim 1963:35–36; *my translation*)

Taking Durkheim further, from his *Rules* (1966:24–25) we may see a more positive view of individuals, here children, in these terms:

> …individual natures (of the members of society) are merely the indeterminate material that the social factor moulds and transforms. Their contribution consists exclusively in very general attitudes, in vague and consequently plastic predispositions …

There is no age or stage of development implied here. It may, for example, describe what might be considered an immediate change of mind by an adult rather than the type of developmental stages Vygotsky or Piaget described within childhood. It may be assumed that having undergone maturation processes and knowing how to access and use information, an adult can change his or her disposition toward something spontaneously. His or her capacity has evolved sufficiently for that to be possible.

In fact, Durkheim's concepts of collective representation and the process of universalisation, correspond to Kantian concepts. Durkheim acknowledged the relevance of Kantian philosophy to his epistemological and moral considerations. Like Kant, the teleological imperative governing human history, was considered by Durkheim to be a progressive liberation of human objectivity through progressive liberation of human thought. Thus, it follows that social facts are studied objectively when they are isolated from their individual manifestations.

If we examine what are highly influential works of the twentieth century, noticeably this form of objectivity is lacking when, for instance, Ariès (1962) and Benedict (1955) are making the most of similarities between children and, needless to say, overlooking innumerable differences. That does not mean they were unaware of differences but had another story to tell which intended to understand the main character of changing childhood. Furthermore, it does not mean that they lost direction, since both more or less compared childhoods historically or cross-culturally without considering the transition of child into adult, but rather more thinking about the transformation of childhood as society and *oikos* (household) changed. It is through the formation of roles within the *oikos* that they pointed to the clear distinction between childhood and adulthood. Their comparative universalities were different social configurations within respective socio-economic parameters.

Ariès generally failed to take into account differences between families and children. Benedict was very much more concerned with cultural conditioning than a more universal view.

During her fieldwork with the Hausa, an Islamic people in Nigeria, Schildkrout (1978) described children's contribution to maintaining *purdah*. Hausa men then earned their income working away from home, whereas women made money by preparing food and embroidery to sell at local markets. They were confined to their family home by purdah, were thus dependent on children to buy their materials and deliver or sell what they made at the markets. Until puberty, both girls and boys had free mobility between households and markets. With puberty, the girls were no longer able to contribute whereas boys continued until they began to be engaged in adult male work. Through this arrangement, children who were spatially mobile actively contributed simultaneously to economic and religious institutions. This is more or less the opposite to contemporary Western hypotheses about children's place in the domestic setting, particularly in the light of recent moves to end all forms of child labour that will have had some impact on this tradition, and diverse constructions of both childhood and adulthood that tend to be Eurocentric and dismissive of what are viewed as 'harmful' traditions. However, Schildkrout's work raises questions about what would happen in the world if there were no children and also how adults are dependent on children?

Whilst rapid change in a modern, dynamic Nigeria may have changed how the Hausa live and child labour prohibition may have reduce overt work practices, Islam has not declined. Therefore the assumption may be that most of what Schildkrout describes continues, albeit more discretely. Instead of thus assuming that children have reduced agency and capital, in fact they indubitably have more since they will be largely responsible for their ability to carry out family duties confronted with recent barriers placed in front of them. With this slightly older fieldwork data, there is nonetheless enough substance to support an argument that this example illustrates adult dependence on children, who themselves function autonomously in a mainly adult world in which their role is accepted. In rather simple terms, although these tasks are carried out by children they are done so in place of adults whereby 'not-yet-adult' may define them, their undertakings are of adult magnitude, thus making them equal partners in decision making and responsibility sharing.

The sociology of childhood in particular is still finding its way and particularly in addressing agency, capital and the critique of the 'human becoming' notion is beginning to offer further clues. If there is anything absolute within examination of the child sciences and social sciences as a whole, it is that from Rhazes to the present children have been set aside as a distinct category. To some extent that creates a strong world tradition that might be used against any argument for a comprehensively inclusive full citizenship for children.

Chapter 9
Children's Human Rights and the Contemporary Interest in Child Participation

This chapter looks at a number of issues beginning with the emergence of the concept of human rights and legal provision in constitutions, basic laws, bills of rights and other legal instruments for the protection of these rights. It eventually moves on to children's rights and the emphasis on children's participation that has occupied a large part of the child rights environment for almost two decades. Some participation specialists have insisted that the solution to the citizenship debate is easily found in this area. Critical examination of some of that work looks at the substance of their arguments for achieving this end.

Children's rights are both an opening and obstacle to resolving the question as to whether children's citizenship is a viable proposition. The present situation, in which the UN Convention on the Rights of the Child (CRC) is a central feature, projects into an unforeseeable future rather than drawing on the past for evidence of an age in which children shared equal status with adult citizens. Previous chapters have hitherto shown that full citizenship for children is a thus far untried hypothesis, but also that it is possible to say that historically children have been 'more equal' and that as modernity shaped approaches to attitudes to children, that it was measurably reduced. Human rights have especially reduced differences between socially separated groups, so that in principle sexism, racism, ageism, homophobia and other prejudices have been identified and attempts are being made to integrate them into civil society. Where they have been identified there are usually socially engaged groups and initiatives actively working on changing the situation of people seen as 'different' to one of acceptance in mainstream society. Extraordinarily, ageism is amongst those groups and tends to be oriented toward actions on behalf of the elderly whereas in actuality it should promote tolerance between age groups, including children. However, it does serve a very useful purpose in illustrating the exclusionary position of childhood.

Whether or not children's rights provides any kind of solution to this open question and more so whether 'participation' rights actually contribute to citizenship is certainly not one of the goals of the CRC. At no point does it at all give reason to believe it is intended to do so. It is nonetheless a human rights instrument that lends credence to

B. Milne, *The History and Theory of Children's Citizenship in Contemporary Societies*,
DOI 10.1007/978-94-007-6521-4_9, © Springer Science+Business Media Dordrecht 2013

arguments for greater inclusion of children in civil society as bearers of an almost universally accepted set of rights.

One of the other key elements in examination of human rights is in the social study of human beings. In common with the notion of human rights, the new discipline *sociology* emerged from Enlightenment philosophy in the late eighteenth century, shortly after the French Revolution, as a positivist science of society (for instance, see Kilminster 1998). Epistemological, ontological and ethical concerns within European philosophy were gradually absorbed into the new discipline and transformed by newly emerging movements in the philosophy of science and philosophy of knowledge, particularly by the French thinker Auguste Comte, often known as the father of sociology, who was heavily influenced by original Enlightenment political philosophers of *social contract*. His intent was to merge all studies of humanity through a *scientific* understanding of the social realm. His sociological scheme was characteristic of nineteenth century humanists in that he believed all human life passed through distinct historical stages. If one could gain control of this process, one could prescribe the solution for all social ills. The discipline developed gradually and contributed to the later development of social and cultural anthropology which take much of their theory from sociology.

Social science is thus contemporaneous to and highly important in any understanding of the translation of philosophical roots into human rights theory and practice. Later in this chapter as we turn to children's participation in civil society where *capital* and *agency* are central to understanding what that participation means. This links the previous chapter to this whilst accommodating human rights as the catalyst for the present interest in children as active participants in their societies.

The Emergence of Human Rights

The advent of the CRC is part of a wider human rights 'consciousness' in the modern world. As previous chapters, especially examination of philosophy, have shown, the notion of human rights has a far longer 'provenance'. In essence, most of the bills, charters, conventions and declarations of rights have grown out of a limited number of precedents such as the French *Déclaration* of 1792 and US Bill of Rights of 1798, both of which owe much of their substance to Enlightenment philosophy. In fact many aspects of what has become 'human rights' derives from the same influence. Thus we find almost direct links with some of the issues examined in the previous chapter such as feminism, where early activists like de Gouges and Wollstonecraft found many ideas they used to advocate the equality of men and women. It is also in part through the growth of intellectual liberalism that gave life to academic disciplines that inform human rights and are the main contribution to the notion of participation that is examined in this chapter.

The starting point, however, is how Enlightenment philosophy developed and out of it a new way of seeing the human being as somebody as a bearer of universal rights came about. Whilst it would be possible, but probably not useful, to start at an earlier point in time, the English Bill of Rights is perhaps the earliest example of the modern period that is chronologically appropriate.

The English Bill of Rights 1689 (*An Act Declaring the Rights and Liberties of the Subject and Settling the Succession of the Crown*) was almost certainly amongst the first to begin to take a route toward the notion of 'human rights' as we know it now. It is a statement of particular positive rights that the people who drew it up considered that citizens of a constitutional monarchy should be entitled to. It asserts the Subject's right to petition the Monarch and that Subject's right to bear arms for defence. It also sets out constitutional requirements, whereby actions of the Crown require the consent of the people it governs who are represented in an elected Parliament. It differs from other 'bills of rights' including the US Bill of Rights although some parts of the first eight amendments to the US Constitution reflect it.[1] It acknowledges the rights of individuals, albeit all of whom were male adults and even there we would find many exceptions.

In France, *La Déclaration des droits de l'Homme et du Citoyen* (The Declaration of the Rights of Man and of the Citizen) of 1789 was the principal document of the French Revolution. It defined individual and collective rights of all estates as one. It was influenced by a doctrine of 'natural rights' in which those rights are considered to be universal. They are legally binding at all times and in all places and relate to 'human nature' itself. Although it laid down fundamental rights for all men rather than only for the French, it neither made any assertion about the status of women nor did it unequivocally address slavery and servitude. Nonetheless, it can be deemed the precursor to international human rights principles. The first article is: '*Men are born and remain free and equal in rights. Social distinctions can be founded only on the common utility*'.

In 1790, Nicolas de Condorcet and Etta Palm d'Aelders appealed to the National Assembly to extend civil and political rights to women. The attempt was unsuccessful. Condorcet declared that "and he who votes against the right of another, whatever the religion, colour, or sex of that other, has henceforth adjured his own". As a consequence, the French Revolution did not lead to recognition of women's rights, which prompted Olympe de Gouges to publish the Declaration of the Rights of Woman and the Female Citizen (*La Déclaration des droits de la femme et de la citoyenne*) in 1791. It is based on the Declaration of the Rights of Man and of the Citizen and attempts to expose the failure of the French Revolution which had originally been committed to sex equality. It is, despite its failure because its predecessor

[1]The English Bill of Rights is one of the fundamental documents of English constitutional law, is substantially different in form and intent from the American Bill of Rights. It was intended to focus on the rights of citizens represented by Parliament against the monarchy. However, some of its basic tenets were adopted in the American Bill of Rights. James Madison, the author of the American Bill, incorporated the ideas of John Locke, whose *Two Treatises of Government* (1698) argued that civil society was created for the protection of property (that which is one's own: 'life, liberty, and estate'). He also put forward the notion that each individual is free and equal in the state of nature and also that natural rights that are inherent to all individuals, a concept Madison mentioned in his speech presenting the Bill of Rights to the 1st Congress.

basically delivered rights literally to 'the Man', an early example of the need to sometimes compartmentalise human rights to achieved certain ends, as indeed the CRC now does for children.

The US Bill of Rights, 1798, consists of the first ten amendments to the Constitution. The amendments define the powers of federal government to protect the rights of all citizens, residents and visitors on the territory of the United States of America. Among the specific rights these amendments guarantee, are those that ensure freedom of speech, press and religion, allow citizens to keep and bear arms, enjoy free assembly, freedom to petition, be free of search and seizure, cruel and unusual punishment and to be compelled to incriminate oneself. It also restricts congressional power by prohibiting the making of any law to establish a (state) religion and by prohibiting the federal government from depriving any person of life, liberty or property without 'due process' of law.

Thomas Paine's (1999) *Rights of Man* has occasionally been cited for its influence on the US Bill and French Declaration. Its two parts were published in 1791 and 1792 respectively as more a response to Edmund Burke's criticism of the French Revolution than in response to either, although he included the latter in the first part. Mary Wollstonecraft's (2004) *A Vindication of the Rights of Women* appeared in 1792, partly in response to Burke, but also following Paine's precedent. One of her causes was the principle that civil and religious liberties were part of one's birthright (Wollstonecraft 2004: xviii) which departs from the narrower extension of rights (to men) espoused in English and American Bills and French Declaration and is probably the closest to a child inclusive proposition.

A new wave of human rights bills and charters began to appear in the twentieth century. In the wake of the First World War, the Geneva Declaration of the Rights of the Child was drafted by Eglantyne Jebb in 1923. It was adopted by the International Save the Children Union in 1923 and endorsed by the League of Nations in September 1924 and is a precursor to the 1959 the United Nations General Assembly adoption of a much expanded version as its own Declaration of the Rights of the Child and eventually the CRC in 1989. However, much of the impetus came as former European colonies gained independence.

Consequently, emergent independent countries pursued a similar route toward extending human rights along lines that share basic principles with the English and American Bills and French Declaration. India is a good example. After independence in 1947, they introduced a Bill of Fundamental Rights enshrined in Part III of the Constitution. It guarantees equality before the law, freedom of speech, association and peaceful assembly, the right to practice religion and the right to constitutional resolutions for protection of civil rights by means of such writs as *habeas corpus*. Violations carry punishments prescribed in the Penal Code. Fundamental Rights are defined as basic 'human freedoms' through which every citizen has the right to enjoy proper and harmonious development of personality. They have their origins in many sources including the English Bill of Rights, US Bill of Rights and French Declaration of the Rights of Man. They apply to all citizens irrespective of race, religion, caste, creed, colour, sex or place of origin. Whenever looking at 'bills of rights' such principles tend to be similar in all nations. There are also more general statements of intent to uphold human rights, particularly as a universal principle.

The Universal Declaration of Human Rights (UDHR) is an 'advisory' declaration adopted by the General Assembly of the United Nations in Paris on 10 December 1948. The 30 articles summarise the position of the General Assembly on the minimum standard of human rights that should be guaranteed to all people. The International Bill of Human Rights consists of the Universal Declaration of Human Rights with the International Covenant on Economic, Social and Cultural Rights and the International Covenant on Civil and Political Rights and its two Optional Protocols. In 1966 the General Assembly adopted both Covenants to complete the International Bill of Human Rights. In 1976, after the Covenants had been ratified by the required number of nations, it entered into force. The UDHR is one of the guiding principles of the CRC as shown in the preamble.

The United Nations Convention on the Rights of the Child

What makes the CRC very different was the process that ultimately lead to it. Eglantyne Jebb's 'Children's Charter' that the International Save the Children Union adopted in 1923, was adopted more or less verbatim by the League of Nations in 1924 as the five point Declaration of the Rights of the Child, often called the Declaration of Geneva. In 1948 it was used as the basis for a seven point Declaration that was adopted by the General Assembly of the then new UN. In 1959 it was further revised as the Declaration of the Rights of the Child that is still valid to the present day. Even at that time there was some lobbying for a more assertive convention. To celebrate 20 years of the Declaration, 1979 was designated International Year of the Child (IYC). At a session of the Commission on Human Rights in early 1978 Poland, who had supported a convention in 1959, proposed that a binding convention mainly based on the 1959 Declaration be drawn up and adopted in 1979. The Polish concern for children was very much influenced by the work of Janusz Korczak at the beginning of the twentieth century.

After consultation with governments and international organisations, it was felt that drafting and adoption of a convention could not be achieved in a year. In 1979 during the IYC an open-ended working group was set up. Any of the 43 member nations of the Commission on Human Rights could join the Working Group and all other UN member states were able to send observers. The first draft submitted by the Polish delegation consisted of 14 articles that were of a mainly economic, social and cultural nature. They omitted a wide range of rights including participation rights and any hint that it might be a means of introducing a notion of full citizenship for children. During 1979 the aim was to complete drafting within 10 years in order to present and adopt the finished convention on the tenth anniversary of the IYC. The core participatory articles (12–16) first appeared as Article 7 that was adopted by the Working Group in 1980. Article 7 expanded to have 7*a* in 1981, further to 7*bis* in 1982, 17*ter* 1987 and 7*quater* in 1988. The five articles were adopted by the Working Group in 1989 and passed on into the official text of the Convention for adoption by the General Assembly on 20 November 1989.

In the passage of drafting (see Detrick 1992) every article had been the subject of debate and dispute. There were controversies over whether childhood begins at conception or birth, freedom of religion and adoption. Given that choice of religion and adoption are both not normally possible under Islam, accommodation had to be made. There were also strong debates on an age limit for children serving in armed forces. It has since been resolved by an optional protocol. Some aspects of civil and human rights have entirely been omitted; there are, for instance, neither full economic nor political franchise rights. All in all, by 1989 what emerged was nonetheless remarkable in its scope and what was to follow. The CRC was opened for signature on 26 January 1990. By 2 September and 30 days after deposit of the 20th ratification, the CRC entered into force. It was the first UN convention that had ever acquired a large number of signatures and ratifications that quickly. At the time of writing this all UN member states except Somalia[2] and the USA[3] have ratified and are in one sense or another in the process of incorporating it into national laws.

It is a convention that most certainly continues the tradition that began with the 'Déclaration des droits de l'Homme et du citoyen' and has some of the aspirations of the 'US Bill of Rights' within the scope of rights it includes. Above all, and as acknowledged in the Preamble, the 'UDHR' and 'International Bill of Human Rights' are reflected in its sentiments. However, it is not a 'perfect' instrument of law, remaining contentious and unpopular in some countries, with both supporters and detractors almost universally. Part of that is because of its content.

Toward the conclusion of drafting, *Defence for Children International*, an NGO which was at the hub of the non-governmental contribution to the process from 1983 onward, was asked to ascertain some kind of classification of the first 41 of the 54 articles (see van Beers et al. 2006:12). They determined that *protection*, *provision* and *participation*, sometimes known as the 3Ps, were the three immediately identifiable groupings and also distinguished each article within its relevant category. This drew attention to participatory articles. Since the CRC entered into force the articles addressing their participation, especially Article 12, the child's right to an opinion, have become an almost self standing focus in the children's rights 'world'.

[2] Somalia has been in a state of civil unrest with no single, internationally accepted government for over 30 years. Consequently there is no single authority or government recognised by the UN that could sign and ratify the CRC.

[3] The USA played an active role in drafting the CRC and signed it on 16 February 1995, but has still to ratify it. Opposition is partly due to 'potential conflicts' with the Constitution and some political and religious conservatives. Two reasons frequently given for not ratifying were that Texas allows capital punishment of children which the CRC does not allow and that it could undermine parents' rights. The Heritage Foundation views the conflict as an issue related to national control over domestic policy. President Obama described the failure to ratify the CRC as "embarrassing" and promised to review this. The USA has however signed and ratified both optional protocols.

Children's Participation and the CRC

One of the most confusing aspects of the way the CRC has been used by 'aficionados' of child participation has been an almost immovable refusal to think beyond Article 12 by many. Their vision has often been constrained by their belief that the 'voice' of children somehow extends a wide range of new liberties to them. Article 13 should complement 12, yet is often almost treated as though it goes a step too far. Freedom of expression is a respected liberal ideal, yet is often censured with an outlook of mild embarrassment for all ages. Whoever speaks out, indeed including many people who make great sense, often shock those who lack the substance to articulate thoughts themselves. There would appear to be an undercurrent of distrust that deepens when children do on occasion speak freely.

As far as many people are concerned young people are, in their minds, not mature and, lacking fluency and vocabulary, often express things badly. Instead of accepting that Article 14 is where the meaningful content and depth of any view held by many children is to be found, the fact that the notion of freedom of religion is found there has led to a virtual disregard of its very strong set of social and civil functions. Therein, the desire to be impeccably politically correct is apparent whereby nobody wishes to upset people of 'other' beliefs. Ironically, much of this comes from a perceptibly secular sector, often NGOs who would appear to be liberal, secular organisations and already have well established policies that describe universal notions of tolerance.

In as much as children are also concerned, it would appear that there are preconceptions about what children should be allowed to talk about. Political activity (and religion) naturally figure highly in this domain (For examples of critique see Alderson 2000, 2001; Cockburn 2002; Davis et al. 2006; Kirby and Bryson 2002; Moss and Petrie 2002; Smith 2007).

A further problem undermining the potential of the CRC is the tendency for participation to be made the focus of a particularistic view of children's rights. In 1992 UNICEF published a 44 page book under the title *Children's Participation: from tokenism to citizenship* by Roger Hart. On page nine there is a 'ladder of participation' Hart 'borrowed' from an essay on adult participation by Sherry Arnstein in 1969 (Hart 1992:8–9). It has eight steps that describe 'levels' of participation in projects. However, Hart says "The Ladder of Participation" is designed to serve as a "beginning typology for thinking about children's participation in projects" (*Ibid.*). The main points to draw attention to here are 'beginning typology' and 'thinking about children's participation'.[4]

Whilst the ladder was never designed as a tool for measurement of participation it has become exactly that. In Johnson et al. (1998) several contributors either used

[4]Participation is well enough defined by any good dictionary, yet there has been considerable competition among 'experts' to redefine what it is because it is 'children's participation' thus held to different to plain 'participation'. The competition to reach a definitive definition has generally confused rather than clarified and offers little if anything toward the notion of the child as a citizen since participation has come to mean quite specific things rather than having all of the all entailing qualities of citizenship.

the ladder itself, something based on it or a variation on a similar theme precisely as a measuring tool. Other authors have continued to do so until the present. To return to Hart, beyond inclusion of the word 'citizenship' in his title, there is nothing one could feasibly consider conclusive or indicative of how children's participation could transform itself or be developed into citizenship. It is in this vein that a steadily growing number of authors have attempted to either say what participation is or measure it without concretely addressing 'citizenship'.

Harry Shier's 'Pathways to Participation' (Shier 2001) was at one time highly influential. It consists of five 'levels' of participation beginning with children being listened to, then supported in expressing their views, thereafter those views are taken into account. Children are then involved in decision making processes and finally 'share power' and responsibility for decisions. It is highly dependent on how workers with children view this process and is also very much linked to Article 12 CRC, whereby:

> 1. States Parties shall assure to the child who is capable of forming his or her own views the right to express those views freely in all matters affecting the child, the views of the child being given due weight in accordance with the age and maturity of the child.

The second part of Article 12 and 'due weight in accordance with the age and maturity' principle is very clearly underscored and overall the intention appears especially mindful of the 'evolving capacities of the child' principle in Article 5. Shier believes that participation, at least the way he understands it, "requires an explicit commitment on the part of adults to share their power; that is, to give some of it away" (*Ibid.*:115). It is by no stretch of the imagination a tool for examination of participation as a gateway to full membership of civil society, especially being so dependent on adult consent rather than a genuine outcome of a negotiated process.

Whereas Hart's (1992) typology sets out eight levels of involvement that children may have in decision making (he only defines five as 'participation'), it has been extremely influential on discussions about the nature of children's participation in decision making. Shier (2001) has suggested that Hart's classification of the activities that should *not* be considered 'participation' is at least as useful for classification of what *is*. The ladder can be criticised for implying a hierarchy with a target at the top to aim for, whereas in reality different degrees of influence over decision making may be apposite in different situations. Shier's (*Ibid.*) typology built on Hart's ladder of participation without intending to replace it and whilst it is not designed with children's participation in decision making concerning their care in mind (see *looked after children* later in this chapter) some issues it raises are relevant.

Social Capital

Thomas (2007:199–218) attempted to draw together a theory of children's participation that relies heavily on typologies. There is some almost superficial examination of 'social and political' participation, including a specifically UK focussed consideration of the lowering of electoral franchise age.[5] This is followed by a very narrow (essentially Anglophone) examination of representative and participatory democracy and democratic inclusion that avoids the issue of exclusion (see Chap. 3).

Therewith he is drawn down a route out of which extrapolation of a single conclusion is almost predestined not to happen. Where he begins to find some ground that remains underexploited, is where he begins to examine the notion of *social capital* and mentions *cultural capital* in passing. He draws heavily on Pierre Bourdieu who defined social capital as "the amalgamation of actual or potential resources linked to possession of a resilient network of more or less institutionalised relationships of reciprocal acquaintance and recognition" (Bourdieu 1983:249 [my translation]). Bourdieu's work on *capital* however identifies and distinguishes between four forms of capital: economic, cultural, social and symbolic capital. Thomas refers only to cultural and social capital, thus missing two entire elements of what is a single but necessarily subdivided concept. *Symbolic capital* is undoubtedly too important to ever exclude from examination of citizenship. It was an 'afterthought' to his first three forms (i.e. Bourdieu 1977) whereby he (1984:238) formulated the notion as an expansion of Max Weber's analysis of *status*. It normally represents resources available to an individual based on honour, status or recognition and acts as a credible representation of cultural value. However, symbolic capital cannot be converted to any of the other three forms of capital.

On the other hand any of the three can also have symbolic value. Thereby, for instance, a child being elected as class representative on a school council may have both social and symbolic value. The value of any object or situation is always the sum of its symbolic plus one or more of the other forms of capital. It is, therefore, always defined by the system within which it is given a value, although different value systems often see the significance of the same thing differently. In examination of the status of *being* a citizen, symbolic capital is perhaps an inexcusable omission.

However, beyond Bourdieu and more popular at present, the current notion of social capital focuses on an imprecise term with roots in the work of American social scientist Robert Putnam (see Putnam 1993, 2000, 2002). He made a distinction between three kinds of social capital he called *bonding*, *bridging* and *linking* capital which have since become omnipresent in examination of contemporary civil society.

---

[5] At present some countries are beginning to lower communal and occasional general electoral rights to age 16. Nicaragua lowered the voting age from 21 to 16 in November 1984. Over recent years in Germany the states of Lower Saxony, Mecklenburg-Western Pomerania, North Rhine-Westphalia, Saxony-Anhalt and Schleswig-Holstein have lowered the age to 16 years for municipal elections. The Isle of Man changed from 18 to 16 in July 2006 with legislation in force in time for the General Election of 23 November 2006. The Austrian Council of Ministers adopted a plan to lower the electoral age to 16 during March 2007. The motion passed into law on 1 July 2007. During May 2007 the Swiss canton of Glarus voted to reduce the voting age from 18 to 16 for cantonal and local elections. In Scotland the SNP's annual conference voted unanimously on 27 October 2007 in favour of a policy of reducing the voting age to 16 as soon as possible.

Social capital examined in this manner is by no means a single thing, whereby people may measurably have *more* or *less* of any of the three forms. To be more precise, it is multifaceted. Bonding social capital broadly speaking refers to connections with people like oneself such as classmates, friends or neighbours, thus places individuals socially. Bridging social capital then refers to links to people who are generally unlike oneself, particularly in a demographic sense. They might, for instance, include people one includes in their phone and e-mail lists that are not contacted regularly but are on the other hand essential in such areas as professional life.

Linking social capital suggests associations with people in positions of power. For children that may be a head teacher or other people in influential positions, particularly those offering financial advantages. An individual's standing, capacity to get things done and such things as future careers often depend on connections to these members of particular influence and interest groups. Essentially, it is the degree to which individuals can bring into play different types of bonding, bridging and linking social capital that has an effect on such conditions as success, progress or welfare. People without bonding, bridging or linking relationships are commonly seen as 'outsiders' who often lack any benefits of strong social capital. Whilst Thomas rightly describes (2007:212) Bourdieu as "analytically more robust that Putnam…" the use of the latter to complement the former offers a reasonably clear insight into a sociological analysis of children as holders and users of each form of capital.

There are, furthermore, a number of constituent parts of social capital that have been described as a 'social glue' between people, organisations and their communities that make it possible for them to work together in pursuit of common objectives. In theory this should be complemented by cultural capital. It is comprised of three taxonomies that Bourdieu describes as *embodied*, *objectified* and *institutionalised* (Bourdieu 1984:47) (see Chap. 8 under the subheading Bourdieu for another examination of this concept). Each of those contributes to thc role of the individual within society and particularly explains the significance of the culture goods human beings carry and acquire that give them uniqueness within a cohesive social order.

Thus, although social and cultural capitals are indisputable parts of what defines membership, Thomas nonetheless omits economic and symbolic capital. Whilst children do on the whole lack direct an immediate access to most forms of *economic capital*, in itself an inhibitor to the nature of full membership citizenship. He overlooks the fact that children are increasingly important contributors to economies as consumers, whether as proxies through adults or through the use of their own resources. In fact, what appears to be exclusion is almost a contradiction in terms since of all three types, economic capital is that which, if only generated and used by adult proxies, in one sense or another comes first. There is an economic cost (thus value) from the moment of birth, if not even a short time after conception, might define it as being the only genuinely lifelong form of participation.

Thomas concludes with a suggestion that a theory of participation should include the following (Thomas 2007:215):

(a) encompass all the sites where children's participation may or may not take place;
(b) be located in a broader context of inter-generational relations;

(c) understand the distinction between ‘participation’ meaning activity that children engage in conjointly with adults, and children and young people’s autonomous activity;
(d) accommodate the new kinds of participatory practice with children and young people that have been developed (particularly in countries of the majority world);
(e) account for the demands for children and young people to have the same political rights as adults.

It is a conspicuously prescriptive proposal that uses a rather abstract language in some places (i.e. ‘sites where… [it] …take place’ or ‘new kinds of participatory practice’) that imply ‘set pieces’ for children in particular places and conditions. They eliminate any real possibility of an inclusive liberal democratic or civic republican notion of undifferentiated participation that may exist within or alongside traditional practices. Part of the overall problem that Thomas is in turn part of is that many people ‘designing’ or operating participatory work do so within particular disciplinary or professional parameters. This suggests the need for critical appraisal of some of these sources since the interrelationship of ‘rights’ and ‘participation’ for children became conjoined under the children’s rights heading.

Lansdown (2005:17) argues that participation not only implies the process through which children contribute to bringing about change but also it presents them with the chance to arrive at a sense of autonomy, independence, enhanced social competence and robustness. She looks at this development in terms of Barker’s (1968) six ‘zones of penetration’ that are levels of children’s participation in different settings:

As an onlooker with no active role.
As part of an audience with a recognisable place but no power.
As members who have potential rather than immediate power.
As an active functionary with power over part of the setting.
As a joint leader with shared immediate authority over the setting; for example, representative of a school council.
As a single leader who has immediate and sole authority.

She goes on to argue that in areas in which children only have the benefit of low levels of participation, the prospect of developing competence is reduced. In her view using Barker’s schematic approach the most valuable preparation for a sense of effectiveness is to achieve a goal for oneself and not just seeing somebody else accomplishing it. In closing this issue, she states that the development of competence continues for the duration of a lifetime. Much of her work, however, focuses on the premise that adults are gatekeepers to participation anyway since children’s capacity is continually evolving. Moreover, Barker’s almost contextually disingenuous use of the six zones simply describes what adults generally experience, let alone children, giving no real guidance to what changes of access to and participation in civil society really means.

A further example is Feinstein and O’Kane’s (2005) *Spider Tool* that proposes a model that is ‘intended to promote reflection, analysis, sharing, dialogue and action planning within organisations’ (*Ibid.*:1). The intent is that participants work together to consider the strength of an organisation in relation to a number of key considerations that they call 'Key Quality Elements'. The outcomes of the evaluation are transferred to a spider web drawing that exemplifies how participants see the organisation they are appraising. The results are intended for use in planning or restructuring the organisation's work. Some participation specialists have interpreted this model as a potential tool for evaluation of a wider range of participatory activities. However, it is again a model that whilst it encourages working together across ages, is both a specialised evaluation tool and is very clearly designed for children to use rather than adults. Thus it is potentially unwelcomed by the latter, who may be unaware of or suspect the original intent.

On the whole it appears that there is confusion about the difference between a typology and a tool. Most of the models appear to be typologies, thus describing standardised or exemplary aspects of participation rather than being tools that can be used to measure it. Of course, there is always a problem in either, since typologies describe norms and there is no provision for how one might account for deviation from that standard and thus measure with a tool that which has no standard described typologically or otherwise.

The History of Child Participation and Its Importance

The history of child participation where it is unambiguously for children rather than part of a wider adult initiated active membership of civil society has a common origin with children's rights in education. In 1917 Maria Montessori (Montessori 1964) was emphatic about the importance of children being free (*Ibid.*:196–97) and bearers of rights (i.e. *Ibid.*:12). Freedom is the starting point for her:

> …honesty ought to make us recognize one day that the fundamental rights of man are those of his own "formation", free from obstacles, free from slavery, and free to draw from his environment the means required for his development. In short, it is in education that we shall find the fundamental solution of the social problems connected with "personality."
>
> Deeply instructive is the revelation made to us by the children; that "the intelligence" is the key which reveals the secrets of their formation, and is the actual means of their internal construction. (Montessori 1964:197)
>
> If Montessori did not believe in "liberty" as Tom Paine knew it, she did believe quite profoundly - for reasons tracing back to St. Francis of Sales more than to Rousseau - that the child left to himself must will what is good for him. In fact, then, Montessori was prepared to let children make the vast majority of decisions for themselves. Though her theory could have led her the other way, Montessori in the classroom was forever urging her in her teachers to leave the children alone, to tolerate disorder and mess and apparently random or even self-punishing behavior, on the grounds that the child probably knew what he was about better than the teacher could know it. (Holmes in Montessori 1912: xxix, cited in van Beers et al. 2007:78–79)

Perhaps Holmes is right to assume that Montessori did not believe in Paine's understanding of liberty. However, there is far more of Kant's idea of the innate liberty of the individual and almost undoubtedly some shades of Hegel's view that children are potentially free and that the life that follows is the epitome of that potential freedom. Thus, in her 'children's rooms' (For example, see Montessori 1965 (1912):44–49 and 62–71) she is not describing a place that is for respite from an adult dominated environment but a school in which a child is able to use 'his liberty' to exploit "the means required for his development". In fact this is a form of 'participation' that still persists in education.

Her contemporary John Dewey (see Chap. 7) tried to amalgamate, reappraise and broaden educational philosophies of Plato and Rousseau. Dewey's pragmatism, focus on human relations, contemplation and appreciation combined with engagement with notions of community and democracy, formed a noteworthy educational typology. For him intellect and its constitution are part of a collective process in which individuals are only a key concept when regarded an indispensable part of his or her society. Schooling has no import other than its fulfilment in the lives of individual members of that society. In 1907 he wrote:

> (From) the standpoint of the child, the great waste in the school comes from his inability to utilize the experiences he gets outside the school in any complete and free way within the school itself; while, on the other hand, he is unable to apply in daily life what he is learning at school. That is the isolation of the school - its isolation from life. (Dewey 1990:75)

It was therefore crucial that education should not be the mere instruction of so-called facts and that the skills and knowledge students garner are entirely integrated into their lives as individuals, human beings and also citizens. He viewed Plato as having placed far too much emphasis on society and Rousseau overstating the importance of the individual. Although finding the medium between the two extremes, his philosophy lacks the test of practice Montessori's work allowed her.

In fact there are shades of both in Alexander Neill's Summerhill School a very few years later. Further on in time, Freire brought Dewey's ideas up to date and positioned them alongside his contemporary (1960s) theories and educational practice. They created the basis for what was to become 'critical pedagogy' which undoubtedly embraces a notion of inclusion that most certainly argues strongly for children's inclusion in civil society. It also provides one of the strongest 'human rights' arguments for children's citizenship.

Education and Children's Participation

Not only are those aspects of participation too little visited by people working with children or having an intellectual input into the question, but there is as yet almost no critique of these oversights. When looking back over the work some of the pioneers in what has since become children's rights we occasionally find a broader vision. Montessori's philosophy (Holmes, in Montessori 1965: xxix) was undoubtedly far more tolerant and courageous than many of the people who form opinion today.

Korczak most emphatically embraced a vision of an extensive range of possibilities in his ideas, Dewey's educational theories trusted children far more than many contemporary child participation devotees and Illich's (1971) critique of education most undoubtedly placed far more trust in the hands and minds of all ages – children included. In fact, when critically examining participation, education offers some positive views on how children might learn to use democracy.

Perhaps most illustrative of all is the work of Alexander Neill (1953, 1962, 1966). In his school, Summerhill, whilst sometimes seen as an anachronism, intellectual and personal freedoms of the kind included in the CRC have been advocated and practised for over 90 years. Children give living example that these principles work. In parts of Africa, South Asia and Latin America they are activists within children's movements.[6] Because those movements exist to organise, defend and represent highly disadvantaged children who work, live on streets or both, they tend not be received as well as more 'respectable' structures. They are a manifestation of the positive use of the principles enshrined in not only the CRC but several of the historically preceding bills of rights and declarations. As a guiding principle in the process toward full citizenship children need to be allowed the right of freely expressed views. Thus all that is incumbent in a principle of free and democratic participation in civil society is also due to them, at least as part of the process to give them political inclusion.

One can compare some aspects of the philosophy of Summerhill with a Peruvian children's organisation. MANTHOC (*Movimiento de Niños, Niñas y Adolescentes Trabajadores Hijos de Obreros Cristianos*) has five philosophical principles:

1. Children and adolescents are not dependent but are autonomous agents. They can and should act on their own behalf.
2. They have an active role in society and they, not adults, should defend children's rights.
3. Advocacy is universal: it does not favour MANTHOC members but all children.
4. MANTHOC views itself as a model for other movements.
5. Children are teachers – not just for peers – but for all people.

MANTHOC initiated a successful experiment in the late 1990s when it opened its own school in Ciudad de Dios in Lima. The school began as a formal after-school programme. Soon children were asking MANTHOC to turn it into a real primary school. Now it has its own curriculum, mainly written by the students. It is licensed by the Department of Education. Instead of grades, it has 'circles'. Children go to the appropriate circle for their educational level, regardless of age. They move to the next circle after achieving certain requirements. This model has turned out to be

[6]Describing 'child led' organisations such as *MANTHOC* in Peru, the *Concerned for Working Children/Bhima Sangha* in India, *ENDA-Jeunesse* throughout West Africa or the *Movimento Nacional de Meninos e Meninas de Rua* in Brazil in detail would be a wasteful indulgence here, however these and numerous other organisations have websites and have produced a sizeable number of publications over the last 30 or so years. At the time of working on this text, the *Concerned for Working Children* are one of the nominees for the 2012 Nobel Peace Prize which of itself endorses the positive nature of this children's organisation.

better for older children who never really attended school. Teachers give individual attention and base lessons on the child workers' strengths. For instance, they use the mathematical skills of street vendors. Children also participate in school administration. They choose the colours and symbols on uniforms and help to improve curricula. In contrast to most Peruvian schools, they do not rule with an 'iron fist' and children generally call their teachers by first names. The results are proven through the development of children and their test results (taken and translated from IFEJANT's website: www.ifejant.org.pe/WWWEnlaces/programas/Educativo.html").

Summerhill School was founded in 1921 as an independent boarding school with the belief that its education and social activities should be made to fit the child, rather than the other way around. It has never had philosophical principles as firmly defined as MANTHOC's. Summerhill has always been run as a democratic community in which pupils have always participated in the self-government of the school. School meetings are held three times a week at which pupils and staff have an equal share in the decision making that affects their day-to-day lives, discussing issues and creating or changing school laws. The rules agreed at meetings are wide ranging, including agreement on acceptable bed times or allowing nudity at the swimming pool. Meetings have also always been used as an opportunity for the community to vote on a course of action to deal with unresolved conflicts and agreeing punishments such as a fine for theft (see Neill 1966, for greater detail).

Today we find education in some countries returning back to what Korczak appears to have done, also underlies Dewey's educational philosophy and would probably see the approval of Neill or Freire. That is the role of 'empowering' children through citizenship education. Howe and Covell examine this topic through the medium of children's rights that advance their knowledge of democratic principles and being citizens. Their chapter on 'catching citizenship' (2007:118–49) looks at what makes a 'children's rights curriculum' that they feel is necessary to promote and sustain democracy by empowering child citizens.

However, when we turn back to the 'pioneers' of the early twentieth century, Janusz Korczak has a highly influential role for a number of reasons. His educational ideas were influenced by Pestalozzi. That is a notion that attempts to reconcile the tension between the education of the individual (seeking freedom) and citizen (for responsibility and function) that was recognised by Rousseau. Thus Korczak looked toward establishing a 'psychological mode of instruction' that conformed with the 'laws of (human) nature'. Thus special emphasis was placed on spontaneity and self-motivation that included responsibilities including decision making and expressing opinions on matters beyond personal spheres.

Children should therewith not only be given convenient answers but should arrive at them themselves. In order to achieve this, their powers of observation, judgement and logic had to be cultivated and self-motivation encouraged. Part of the process was to nurture a sense of social justice combined with his, as also with Pestalozzi, commitment to work with those who were disadvantaged within society. He shared Pestalozzi's notion of education as a key to the improvement of poor social conditions. Thus once he became the director of the Dom Sierot Jewish orphanage in Warsaw in 1912, and also the Catholic orphanage later, his priority was to make a democratic institution. It had a constitution that gave children key roles in the operation of the orphanage (see Korczak 1992: xiv–xv). The constitution allowed them a court, parliament, newsletter and other mechanisms for children to enjoy a wide range of self-government and overviews.

Korczak retained the role of ultimate mediator and overseer in view of the children's need for some adult guidance and probably as a link to the outside world. Later on the children wrote a newsletter *The Little Review* that eventually became a weekly supplement to the main national Jewish daily newspaper *Our Review*. It was to last at least a dozen years until the German occupation of Poland and had a wide adult readership. He was the only adult contributor to the newsletter. Korczak's work was the momentum behind the Polish drive for a children's rights convention after the Second World War that came to fruition after their proposal in 1978. The experience of the orphanages also contributed immensely to the process of incorporating participatory rights into the CRC. In some ways it is perhaps best viewed as an example of child participation in education for citizenship rather than as providing children with any more than pseudo-citizenship. Above all else, not only did it not integrate children into civil society but was also the creation of an adult and very much driven by that same person.

Again contemporary to Korczak and generally held to be far more important, Eglantyne Jebb was trained as a teacher and rather than be imbued in any of the ideological notions Montessori, Dewey or Korczak drew into their work, she was concerned with the condition of children. In what was almost certainly a 'child saving' undertaking in the aftermath of the First World War, she changed the position of children vastly when in 1921 she wrote her 'Children's Charter'. When in 1924 it was adopted by the League of Nations as the *Declaration of the Rights of the Child*, (*Declaration of Geneva*) she set a course that would eventually bring the discourse on children's rights to where it is at present. The *Declaration of Geneva* is neither a charter that would of its own volition put children on a passage toward full citizenship nor was it ever intended to do so.

However what stands out above all among these 'pioneers' of both children's rights and participation is their vision that children are human beings with a place in society that needs be prepared and protected on the basis of their fundamental right to be part of society. Conversely, with the exception of Dewey to some extent, who was the far more theoretical of all four, they also saw themselves as initiators or and perhaps the overseers of something that was distinctly for and about children. That was rather than integrating them into a society without the age discrimination that allowed and maintained separation. Thus, as with a great deal of participation in the contemporary world it was always a notion that was imposed or inculcated from above and consequently 'top down'. That is as opposed to what would be a genuinely democratic process that challenged or dismantled age distinction as a 'bottom up' route that would achieve full societal membership as citizens for children.

Education has frequently been held to be the principal course to some nature of 'liberation through knowledge' for children. That argument is adequate although since education is ultimately adult made and managed it is not reaching that goal. Education is usually defined by curricula that are intended to bring about consistency of 'production' that is measured by those who achieve qualifications. Standards are set and examinations leading to qualification are rarely open to discussion with children and youth who must sit them to acquire qualification and access to higher levels of education. In those areas children's own inputs into education are marginal and rarely reflect children's rights principles.

Participatory rights suggest an inducement for schools councils although they do not usually guarantee members influence on education. Although it reflects on work in the UK only, Mayall (2000:257) remarks that:

> As regards the education service, where children's participation rights are so woefully ignored, there is some pressure to take action, by, for instance, a statutory framework for school councils which give students a say (…)

Thus we see that although education has a 'track record' of at least a full century, in reality little has been achieved since Montessori wrote of her children's houses.

Looked After Children and Those in Need of Protection

We must also consider what are known in the English language as *looked after children* of whom there are many and are very different depending on where one looks worldwide. What is most common is that there is some form of care order whereby a local (occasionally national) authority assumes legal responsibility for a child. The actual parents[7] continue to have parental responsibility. The authority taking responsibility decides where a child should live, which is normally away from home. The responsible authority will seek a court order if a child is not receiving the kind of care it would be reasonable to expect from normal adult caretakers and lack of care is causing that child significant harm. Depending on where this happens, a court or state agency will decide whether or not a child is suffering harm. The responsible authority will usually consult with parents about where a child should live but will make the final decision. A child will often be placed with foster carers[8] or in a home. In the western world particularly, but increasingly as modern methods of child care become more common around the world, children's participation in making decisions about their placement is being encouraged.

There are two ways in which children participate in these processes. Firstly, there is participation in decision making affecting them as individuals. That includes taking their views and wishes into account in both ongoing processes and in measures such as assessment, care or adoption proceedings, family group consultations, care planning and reviews, child protection conferences and complaints. Then there is participation in decision making on issues relating to children as a group, and as part

[7]These can be birth parents, adoptive parents or legal guardians.

[8]This is the first option in countries with fostering schemes although in many of those a placement in an institution will precede that. In countries with no alternative care systems, homes are the usual option although placement with approved relatives is also a possibility.

of development, provision, assessment and evaluation of services and policy. They are occasionally involved in parts of consultation exercises, research and as respondents, advisers or young researchers in studies. They sometime comprise part of a management committee, advisory group or community initiative and sometimes have a pro-active role as peer mentors, counsellors or volunteer workers.

Clearly, adults' assessment and judgement about the appropriateness of children's participation in any given context is informed by adults' own assumptions and understanding of children's capacities and best interests. These also influence, and are themselves influenced by, assumptions within institutions and structures in which decision making happens and the resources allowed for participation. In assessing issues influencing children's opportunities to participate it is necessary to examine influential approaches to thinking about children and childhood. It has been implied that the CRC reflects a shift from a conceptualisation of children as 'objects of concern' to a perception of children as human beings with agency and capacity.

A small-scale study by Hoggan (1991) using Adler's (1985) framework described three contrasting approaches to children's participation adopted by adults as 'protectionist', 'parentalist' and 'liberalist'. That study considered the involvement of children aged 5–12 years and concluded that those children frequently experienced a 'parentalist' stance from professionals. She said that the main factors playing a part in this were:

Lack of resources: Her argument was that there is need to be honest with children about decisions based on available resources rather than on what they feel they might need or want.

Unwillingness to take their views into account: Discussion about what would occur was often in the form of persuasion of children that they should accept adult decisions.

Perceived need to avoid pain on the part of adults: She suggested that adults involved must realise that recovery from traumatic experiences inevitably involves some pain.

Minimising children's perceived competence: Adults regarded challenging behaviour, or what they viewed as developmental delay, in children who have suffered abuse, loss and other traumas as a factor for assessing levels of competence.

In many cases despite policy that either requires or recommends child participation children are excluded. There are always issues around children's ability to comprehend their situation and give articulate, informed views to those who are responsible for their placement. Lack of resources, and probably most frequently shortages of human resources in the form of people with 'hands on' skill, are often close to the reluctance of judges or senior public servants to listen to children. Whilst it is a strongly advocated approach that would contribute to children learning to share and even take control of responsibility for their lives, countervailing forces appear to dilute its potential contribution to imparting the importance of active citizenship to these particular types of children.

As the world becomes increasingly infected by fear of bad things that might happen to children, the notions of freedom of association or peacefully assembly have been very much 'diluted' in the face of angst about 'stranger danger'. Article 14 CRC has received only limited attention because in some respects it confronts notions of protection. Ironically, when considering the notions of privacy, honour and reputation in Article 16, fear of abuse is overshadowed by exactly some of the same facets of attitudes that inhibit freedom of association and peacefully assembly. Both now require presence and allowance for the possibility of intervention in children's 'best interests' in the face of any perceived threat.

More recent inputs into both participation and rights have come from the work of development agencies and UN agencies such as the World Bank. Children's participation in development work has usually been set up and measured using rapid appraisal methods in particular. More recently, validity of young people's roles in structured activities have been 'measured' using one particular 'model'. That is again the ladder scale or variations on the model first used by Hart (1992:9) to serve 'as a beginning typology'. Despite Hart specifying that, few of the 'experts' who tend to staunchly adhere to Hart or one of the modified versions has contributed to development toward any other or more appropriate models. However, it also remains to be seen whether participation needs to be measured since in the first place all social actors are always participant in their society. In the second, civic society varies so much from one place to another that it is probably impossible to set a standard to measure against.

Johnson et al. (1998) nonetheless do precisely this without consequently developing the argument significantly beyond what Hart was saying in 1992. However it is not only the use of models and measurement that attracts critical appraisal, but participatory approaches themselves.

Participatory Approaches in Development – A Critical Appraisal

In a direct critique of NGOs particularly, Cleaver (2002) says:

> Participation has (…) become an act of faith (…) something we believe in and rarely question. This act of faith is based on three main tenets: that participation is intrinsically a 'good thing' (especially for the participants); that a focus on 'getting the techniques right' is the principal way of ensuring the success of such approaches; and that considerations of power and politics on the whole should be avoided as divisive and obstructive. (see, Cooke and Kothari 2002:36)

Bill Cooke and Uma Kothari include a paper by Harry Taylor (Cooke and Kothari 2002:122–138) that challenges the optimistic slant of the 'rapid appraisal' school of thought's line on parallels between participatory development and management. His critique is that participation is part of an attempt to sway power relations between elites and less powerful recipients of programme work.

Rapid appraisal methods seek to gain community perspectives of local needs and to translate findings into action. They nearly are nearly all variations of the Rapid Rural Appraisal (RRA) approach that owes much of its early development to Farming Systems Research and Extension that were promoted by the Consultative

Group on International Agricultural Research Centres in the early 1980s (for instance, see Chambers 1992, and Simmonds 1985).

Those methods have been designed to draw inferences, conclusions, hypotheses or assessments during a very limited period of time. Data are generally collected through interviews with a range of local informants, existing records about the people and place, plus observations made in the neighbourhood or in the homes of the interviewees. The data collected form an information pyramid that can be assembled describing the respondents' problems and priorities. The pyramidal shape is assumed to be a reminder that success depends on building a planning process that rests on a strong community information base. The scientific rigour and validity of the approach depends more than anything else on triangulation. Data collected from one source are validated or rejected by cross-checking with data from at least two other sources or methods of collection.

There are problems. Sometimes it is not even participatory, and is frequently used as a fashionable label for standard techniques. A researcher or team, sometimes critically referred to as a 'hit team', often arrives in a community to 'do a rapid appraisal'. This is an often rushed and exploitative approach that is all too common in project-based evaluations where there is a deadline to meet. Local expectations can also easily be raised too high. If nothing concrete emerges, local people may come to see the process as a fleeting development event. Far too many evaluations claim to be empowering and participatory, but the reality is that for often very pragmatic reasons they are selective rather than inclusive. Unfortunately, despite initial promises neither the respondents nor the wider community are involved in analysis of data. Likewise, people are all too frequently uninformed about the conclusions of the appraisal and there is no follow up or outcome.

The empowerment proposition of rapid appraisal and the influence of the social analysis it generates can create threats to vested interests. Programmes working with children in developing countries have been a particular target for participatory rapid appraisal. Thus Taylor's view (2002) of these participatory methods as a means of influencing power relations between elites and less powerful recipients of programme work is an interesting, if also in some people's view pessimistic, point of view in terms of what has happened in the world of children's participation.[9]

Work with children that is very easily comparable to what Taylor refers to has frequently very deliberately chosen children in 'need' such as street and working children. Those have sometimes been organised into 'children's movements' that are susceptible to criticism and even condemnation for politicisation of child members by adult organisers (Invernizzi and Milne 2002:409–14). This, needless to say, is prevalent among participation programmes working in the South and appears

[9]Much of what is said here is self-critical. A large part of my income over the last two and a half decades was earned as an evaluator. Rapid appraisal has been the only viable choice since such situations as evaluation visits to several communities in a number of geographical dispersed provinces within a few days with *terms of reference* that stipulate a participatory approach demand it. I have always been the first to acknowledge the fact that it is categorically *not* research and is as prone to its failings as it is often useful.

seldom, if ever, to have been tried in the North. Poor, socially and politically weak people are accordingly visited by researchers and sometimes programme planners then later project workers. They appear to be offered something by the very presence of people from the rich North, at the very least the status of being chosen before people elsewhere. In effect they are told what to do, how to do it and results and progress are duly measured before the project comes to an end.

The commissioning 'client' is usually motivated by its campaigning process, political role or even a threat to its financial sustainability rather than being interested in the exact needs and wishes of the people appraised. If they cooperate with the evaluation they may receive benefits. If they do not, they will usually receive nothing, perhaps face some kind of retribution or punishment.

This is a repeated theme Cooke and Kothari's (2002) collection of essays draws attention to and contributes to their choice of *Participation: The New Tyranny?* as the title of their book. That book looks at the topic at community level rather through a specific age group, however one may extrapolate from that that what is said their applies to all people, thus including children. Cleaver (Cooke and Kothari 2002:36–55) states that: "Participatory approaches can be further criticized for their inadequate model of individual action and the links between this and social structure" (*Ibid.*:47). Furthermore, that: "... project approaches that focus strongly on institutions as a development tool often see people as 'inputs', as the 'human resource'. Social difference is recognized through the categorization of people into general occupational or social roles: 'women', (...) and 'the poor'" (*Ibid.*).

The same critique includes children who may well know how to conduct focus groups and role plays after inclusion in 'participatory' development programmes. They may well, for example, have the fact that they should not be working deeply ingrained into them as the objective of the programme. This tends to occur, irrespective of whether that work operates in line with local custom, economic survival strategy and so on, in line with the application of ILO Conventions (138, Minimum Age Convention, 1973 and 182, Worst Forms of Child Labour Convention, 1999) that set out to eliminate child labour.[10]

Despite those limitations, the concentrated power of formalisation of community knowledge through participatory techniques sometimes generates an impressive amount of information. It happens in a relatively short space of time, leaving time for more selective structured formal surveys where and when they are necessary and

[10]Rather than develop this here, I would recommend looking at the International Labour Organisation's *International Programme on Elimination of Child Labour* (IPEC) resources database. Since they began work in the 1980s they have lacked sensitivity toward the children they intend to 'save' as participants in programmes with opinions that sometimes also include explicit arguments for being allowed to work. One notable omission from those resources is: McKechnie, Jim, and Sandy Hobbs (Eds.), 1998, *Working children: Reconsidering the Debates: Report of the International Working Group on Child Labour*. Although the report was published by Defence for Children International Netherlands, IPSCAN and ILO/IPEC were commissioning partners and donors. This report went against the grain of ILO policy and has been notable for the fact that the ILO has always disowned their part in its existence. For other dimensions of the issue see Woodhead (2007).

of value. NGOs working with and for children often depend on periodical evaluation of programmes for prolonged or new funding using rapid appraisal.

What critics have picked up on, is that what is most frequently occurring is participatory approaches are often defined in terms of the design of the project. That will usually be feasible anyway, because after the needs assessment, a recommended approach will have been chosen in advance of the rapid appraisal. Consideration of the impact of the changing social position and value of individuals tends to be less important than the collective action of all participants targeted by the programme. Thus, in many evaluations and research, much of what is 'acted out' by children in (for instance) role plays appears as data on what the needs of the programme beneficiaries are converted into positive outcomes.

They also examine what can be done to change conditions or one or more of several other possibilities, without thorough examination of negative outcomes. In line with views expressed by several contributors to Cooke and Kothari's book (e.g. Mosse, 16–35; Cleaver, 36–55; Francis, 72–87; Cooke, 102–21; Kothari, 139–52 and Mohan, 153–67), what is too often the case, is that after the project goes there is usually no real follow-up or support left behind. People change or revert. Change can bring negative outcomes that are unpredictable and reversion can similarly be 'out of the frying pan into the fire'. However, the northern elite have *done* its participatory development work by showing the people the options and how to *do* them. The management of the 'thereafter' is what nobody in the North sees as a rule.

Despite the notion that development work in 'poor' countries conveys democracy, rights and other 'artefacts' they need before they are emancipated from poverty and other 'negative' aspects of their lives, little is done that suggests extending citizenship to children in even the long term.

However, critique and doubts are beginning to extend to the North. In one example, Tisdall (2008:419–29) asks whether this inclusion is working with her title 'Is the Honeymoon Over? Children and Young People's Participation in Public Decision-Making'. Following the line of her argument, if the enthusiasm for inclusion of young people is in decline then this share in decision making, albeit it a minor role, reduces the political inputs of children. It is thus also removing some of the citizenship-like 'duties' and 'responsibilities' their efforts afford them.

Human Geography, Environmental Planning and Participation

Human geographers and environmental planners have similarly treated participation as an observable situation that serves a particular purpose with specific or intended outcomes. The *Children's Environments Research Group* at the University of Colorado has made participation and rights key issues that have been important components of publications such as *Cities for Children* (Bartlett et al. 1999) and in the journal *Children, Youth and Environments*. British human geographers have made an especially important contribution to children's use of space in which they learn, live and play. We find examples in Holloway and Valentine (2000), whereby

Tracey Skelton's study of teenage girls in two Rhondda valleys places importance on their participation (*Ibid.*:80–88) and Stuart Aitken (*Ibid.*:119–38) looks at parental attitudes to gender and the social construction of children with spaces of identity.

The overall outcome has been to make a very rich and detailed contribution to children's participation. However, on the one hand human geographers focus on very narrow remits within the wider contexts. Where participation is examined in depth an enormous degree of emphasis has been placed on children's roles in sharing decision making with Article 12 CRC as the main identifiable vector of that function. It also has the overall effect of segregating children and adult domains. Many publications convincingly describe children's participation rather than an age neutral, thus all age inclusive, version and those tend to examine schemes where children are by and large the main beneficiaries. They contribute a great deal to an understanding of children in social and physical space.

Consequently, despite the importance of the sector, it is most certainly not directly contributing to the possibility of children attaining a wider decision *sharing* role in civil society that would be part of citizenship on a par with adults.

Indeed, this latter point addresses similar weaknesses that come to the same end in education and development. Arguably, we need to consider the 'evolving capacity' principle and exclude children until the point in time at which they have reached maturity and articulacy that would make the responsibility of sharing possible. On the one hand this opposes a notion of full citizenship for life. It is also fraught with dilemmas such as deciding a particular age at which this is possible despite the reality of individuals all developing differently and reaching the 'standard' at a range of ages that are occasionally very low or high. It hence provides a tenuous but nonetheless real argument for not having set ages.

Participation studies have all been highly influential in the formation of policy among not only such UN agencies as UNICEF and UNESCO and NGOs working with children specifically, but also organisations working with the family, health, development, environment and education. Thus, when using a resource like UNICEF's *Child and Youth Participation Resource Guide* (Upadhyay 2006) many of the several hundred entries tend to come from domains like those examined above. They seldom take a more political and social route to provide resources and sources from which a 'children's rights route' toward an age neutral direction may be extrapolated. Among all disciplines, education started to influence these ideas a full century ago (for instance Montessori, 1965, first published in English in 1912 after some years of practice and an earlier Italian version of that work) but has never bridged the age divide.

If Montessori, Korczak and other 'visionaries' ideas had ever been universally accepted, they should have provided intellectual counsel against the tendency to carry over shadows of a *tabula rasa* notion. That is the view that children begin most (if not all) undertakings without prior knowledge or experience of what they are *learning*. It generally supports the inequity between generations, in which it is frequently assumed adults can *do* 'most' things. In reality, that often proves not to be the case since adults often need to train in new skills until very advanced ages.

Edwards (1996:47–48) gives five reasons why there are problems with children's participation where it is found within projects and programmes and the development of communities and societies generally are touched:

1. Planners use a standard model of childhood which has its roots in nineteenth century Western thinking. This model treats all children as immature and irrational. People are qualified to participate in decisions only when adulthood has been reached, at a predefined age (usually 16 for some things and 18 or even 21 for others). By definition, children's views are considered "childish" and their opinions are not sought.
2. Children are seen as inherently non-productive. Despite the reality that they participate all the time in economic development, family life and culture (especially in non-Western societies), they are routinely excluded from official definitions and measurements of work.
3. Children are treated as by-products of other units of study such as the household, family or parent. The need to collect information which is specific to children's lives is not perceived.
4. Adults may feel that, as they have once been children, they understand the needs of children without having to ask them; children's own views are seen as unnecessary.
5. By treating children as passive and dependent, adults reinforce their monopoly of power in the world over and above that required to nurture children towards adulthood. This is a particularly sensitive area, and one in which adults who are also parents may feel particularly threatened.

Participation as a Contributor to the Citizenship-Like Status of Children

In point of fact, the Edwards line of reasoning extends to more or less all domains and should be seen as a universal analysis of the situation of children within society. The exceptions might be when examining working children's movements in the southern hemisphere. To some degree and that often depends on how one appreciates and appraises their activities, they 'challenge' points except perhaps 4 in his thesis. The examples given in a single collection (Hungerland et al. 2007) by Pedraza-Gómez (23–30), Bourdillon (55–66), Invernizzi (135–44), Coly and Terenzio (179–86) and Reddy (187–96) combined with Liebel (2000), Cussiánovich (1997) and Glauser (1990) show the diversity of situations in which children who work and are occasionally living on streets display qualities that might be compared with the duties and responsibilities of citizenship.

Despite that they tend to be marginalised by the 'mainstream' of society because of the 'deviant' nature of their initiatives. Organised children's movements tend to be adult initiated and rely heavily on adult management. However, child members usually share much of the decision making and political action that give them some of the qualities of their adult trade union equivalents. Regardless of that, trade unions who may not see eye to eye with governments tend to side with those regimes in their opposition to the activities of child workers. In itself that is extraordinary since children throughout Saharan West Africa (see Coly and Terenzio 2007), in India (Reddy 2007) and South and Central America (Liebel 2000; Cussiánovich 1997) rarely directly agitate politically but are more commonly engaged in negotiating fair pay, reasonable hours, equitable working conditions and sometimes even attempting to define what 'exploitation' is themselves. For instance, as Coly and Terenzio say:

> In September 2003 ECOWAS (Economic Community of West African States), ... organised the 'peer review' on child policy. MAEJT and other children participated in the meeting together with ministers and public. It was decided that in each country (...) periodic reviews would bring together government and public organisations including child-led ones.
>
> The children's statement together with the minister's declaration was adopted (...) by the heads of state. The implementation of the 'peer review' is now a decisive matter for the MAEJT, African Global Movement for Children and the African NGO (...) Coalition for children.
>
> In some countries like Guinea Conakry or Senegal the government is even demanding 'more participation' from AMWCY-MAEJT to increase its contribution to the policy, and thus enhance national policies and their definition and implementation. (2007:182)

It is a very active political role that extends citizenship-like qualities, duties and responsibilities to working children in member countries. Whilst they do not have electoral franchise, they enjoy constant dialogue with governments. The children also tend to remain within their families and make a significant contribution to their families' economic survival whilst either continuing to attend school or campaign for provision of schools, teachers, etc. Some of them are significant contributors to familial and community decision making. Yet they are seldom valued for their positive contribution and more for the negative qualities that make 'bad' citizens among adults (see Milne 2005b). They thus belong among those who can be excluded from full membership (see Chap. 3).

Participation in children's activities within these movements tends not to be measured in terms comparable with 'ladder' models or adult focussed schemes like those proposed by Barker or Shier or more sophisticated models such as Feinstein and O'Kane's 'spider'. They are also generally marginal to the children's rights arena since child labour is considered to be both illegal and counterproductive to the aims and intentions of the CRC. The ILO IPEC programme has frequently attempted to end this 'illegal' work by children. However by taking a positive and responsible political course, governments have listened and cooperate with the children rather than simply banning their work.

Thus it becomes apparent that there is no 'even playing' field in either child participation or rights, or indeed where the two conjoin. Despite the inclusion of the word 'citizenship' (e.g.: Hart 1992) in titles the tendency is to not actually touch on the topic. This runs counter the objective of defining citizenship and perhaps more particularly in contemporary views of a 'global citizenship' in which human rights are integral. The use of separable adult and child versions of measurements of delivery of and participation in membership of all nature of situations from projects through to civil society and understanding of a separation of human rights (for adults) and children's rights has made these entirely separate domains to the citizenship topic this research examines.

There are an almost excessive number of models. Each of them suits a specific discipline or practice area and normally addresses a narrow remit, for identifying participation particularly. That has obscured the possibility of identifying a generic participation that is or could become synonymous with citizenship.

Child participation and children's rights was never one and the same thing when they 'emerged' in the early twentieth century, although since the 1989 adoption of the CRC they have been closely associated with each other. In the early stages, participation was clearly definable as an educative process in which children were being prepared for citizenship and their active role in civil society more generally. Children's rights were conceived out of a wish to improve child protection. Neither is an entirely natural part of the other and similarly neither was ever intended as a 'portal' into children's full citizenship. This is to the point that the association of the two and the limitations they singularly and jointly place on the topic tend toward creation of an obstacle to the resolution of the question this research poses.

One of the most difficult questions to resolve is almost always that regarding the legal status of children. Almost universally there are only two statuses: under and above the age of majority. To be below majority, or of minority age, means that children are under the authority and care of adults and all forms of autonomous activity or decision making depend on the approval of at least one adult. The following chapters examine issues that explain rather than offer a resolution to this question.

Chapter 10
Issues Concerning the Legal Status, Welfare, Policy Making and Inclusion of Children in Governance and Full Citizenship

In Chaps. 10 and 11 questions regarding the legal status, welfare, policy making and inclusion of children in governance and full citizenship take the lead from the two preceding chapters toward the eventual conclusions. The latter chapter looks at a number of issues that give views of children's status from different legal, welfare and policy positions. These either hinder or aid the route to which full citizenship might eventually be achieved. Both chapters also give insights into the way social research that should be more influential in some cases is disregarded and is clearly very significant in others.

Children are an important stakeholder group; according to recent UN statistics they constitute roughly 34 % of the world's population and their actions play an important role in the future. The CRC created a notion that children's views must be taken seriously, albeit that with caveats, in Article 12. Despite the energy and enthusiasm of children's participation champions, including those examined in both Chaps. 8 and 9, their views have failed to inform the provision of resources for the improvement of their lives. Despite significant insights on the operation of public institutions children's views have seldom contributed to scrutiny of governance. This chapter goes beyond children's participation and the fact that there is little dialogue across the statutory and complementary areas where law and policy are formed.

The history of children's participation in the South has recently begun to inform a new wave of consideration of children in the North as active citizens. Essentially this is an additional question about why the theoretical framework for analysis of the children's rights generation is still failing children and is not the sole focus in this work. It might be that the 'citizenship question' contributes to analysis of the participation question rather than the other way round. Nonetheless, whilst questions of the nature of why the number of street children worldwide appears to be growing, displacement, refugeeism and trafficking are increasing (see United Nations General Assembly 2002) and other rights issues are important, the contribution of detailed examination of these specific issues here would be a distraction.

B. Milne, *The History and Theory of Children's Citizenship in Contemporary Societies*, DOI 10.1007/978-94-007-6521-4_10,

In the preceding chapter, it was shown that the impact of the process of inclusion or 'participation' still passes by children who lack networks, agency and social capital in both North and South despite governments' commitment through ratification of the CRC. One of the objectives of this and the following chapter is to examine why this is the case. Thus, this chapter sets out to look briefly at the topic areas, legal status, welfare, policy making and inclusion of children in governance around the world. To some extent it also shows the disparity between social research with children examined in Chap. 8 and the role of human rights instruments, despite many of them being foundations of law making, and the participation of children in civil society as partners, if even not equals. Chapter 11 then takes outstanding 'loose ends' to briefly include them before drawing toward analysis and conclusions.

This brief examination focuses on parts of each area that are as proximate as possible to the question of citizenship and also, to some extent at least, draw on the notion of 'human becoming' that was addressed in previous chapters. The 'human becoming' notion is given more substance when separation by classifiable age groups that is not entirely a reflection of capabilities, maturity or any other aspect of an individual's nature is taken into account. It is also a very brief examination of a very extensive set of fields that take in only very few aspects of many varied legal systems, forms of government, policy and law making for very obvious practical reasons.

Children as Legal Persons

One of the main issues for examination is the status of children as legal persons. Although there are caveats (see Chap. 2) achieving the age of majority is the normal threshold for adulthood[1] as it is described by national and some international laws. In this chapter there are ages or timelines that one might call 'litmus tests' or 'signposts' where the time in an individual's life is achieved when it may be considered that actions they take show a development of their assumed capabilities or mark a stage *en route* to full competence. This includes even incidences when the latter does not allow them all privileges an adult will normally enjoy although it may entail the same degree of responsibility as those of majority age. Reaching the age at which majority begins is the chronological juncture at which children legally assume at least the greater part of majority control over their persons, actions and decisions. The legal control and responsibilities of parents or other caretakers over and for them terminate at that moment. However, this does not mean 'full control' over one's life.

There is, on the other hand, a drawback in looking at the law as it is presented in secular codified forms since it is complemented by or even contradicted by cultural

[1] This is and may always be a contentious notion since adulthood is a subjective cultural notion where assumptions are often made on the basis of Northern values. It is also a legal standard that is usually incorporated into constitutions, basic laws and other laws. In contrast there are numerous examples of traditions in which age is classified not by chronological age but by generation or age related status. Thus here we are guided by the children's rights standard that describes *childhood* as 0–18 years of age as the norm.

and religious practices that assume the role of laws within groups who practice them. There is no single standard against which the precise end of childhood is definable. Thus, using the typical civil legal age 18 years (see also the definition of childhood in Chap. 1) it is very unlikely that legislation alone can be used to resolve what this research has set out to examine. The starting point here is secular civil legislation.

In simple terms there are certain things which a person who attains the age of majority is permitted to do which they could not do before. The slow accrual of 'privileges' Oldman (1991:25) described in Scotland lists examples such as when a young person can apply for a provisional driving licence or legally consume alcohol. These do not exactly mark the transition from childhood as an event but as a process. In Scotland, for instance, one can marry at age 16 years but electoral franchise and age at which an individual can own his or her own house is 18 years. Elsewhere in the world there are differences in legal timelines at which an individual may enter into a binding contract, vote, buy or consume alcohol or tobacco, have a driving licence or marry without obtaining consent of legally responsible adults. The ages at which such rights or powers may be exercised vary between different national jurisdictions. Those ages may also vary considerably between and within jurisdictions including by gender (or sexuality) as in the example of ages of sexual consent.

The basic principle begins with the notion that there are some things in life (illness, death, etc.) over which nobody has lawful control. Thus individuals assume majority control over their life at a particular age instead of 'full' control which is oxymoronic by its nature. Thus, of interest for this work it is the period prior to the age of majority, or minority, during which the child has minority control over his or her person and actions. Then adult caretakers have majority control and power to overrule most of a child's decisions and desires and occasionally reverse actions. Age of majority is frequently confused with the similar concept, the age of license, which also relates to the onset of adulthood in a much broader and abstract manner. The criterion is that one neither needs nor can one obtain legal permission to grow up because that happens naturally.

Thus in the USA the legal notion of 'licence', meaning 'permission', can allude to a legally enforceable right or privilege to do something such as leaving school without parental permission. The age of majority is legal recognition that one has grown into an adult and that therewith (generally) no permission is required. Many ages of licence are correlated to the age of majority, but they are nonetheless legally distinct concepts. One need not have attained the age of majority to have permission to exercise certain rights and responsibilities. In fact, some ages of licence are higher than the age of majority such as the age of licence to purchase alcohol is 21 in all states in the USA although most states' age of majority is 18 (except: Nebraska and Alabama, 19; Mississippi, 21; and American Samoa and Puerto Rico where it is 14).[2] Other variants include examples like the age of majority in the Republic of Ireland at 18 although one must be over 21 years of age to stand for election. Almost

[2] 'Minimum Age Limits Worldwide', International Centre for Alcohol Policies: http://icap.org/

all nations automatically bestow the status of majority on minors who are married and a few do so for minors in their armed forces, except as electors in both cases. Whilst people may decide to form a family or to defend or even die for their country, it would appear almost anachronistic that one of the most fundamental components of democratic decision making is denied to individuals who have made, in either instance, a far more life changing choice.

Decision Making

When somebody is still a legal minor, decision making for oneself would usually be measured in terms of the pros and cons of different choices. Some choices are profoundly influenced by attitudes, values and beliefs. Similarly, they may be influenced by an individual's emotional state or the position of other people who are important in one's lives. Thus, some decisions will be or appear to be unwise or unusual and individuals may or may not acknowledge that they have made mistakes. Likewise, people are reluctant to give up autonomy and the right to make their own decisions. The law in many countries states that it is acknowledged that some people are not able to make decisions themselves.

Decision making for them has traditionally included *parens patriae*, whereby a state has the authority to act on behalf of children or incompetent adults (For instance, see Mnookin 1975:226–293). In most legal systems this appears in the principle that makes the protection of the *best interests* of a child the first and single most important concern of courts. For instance, in proceedings affecting the validity of a marriage, children will not usually be parties in their own right, nor will they be parties to any agreement spouses may make.

In such proceedings courts are often asked to accept and implement any agreement between the couple regarding responsibility for their children. Jon Elster (1989) sees this as a 'randomised' process in which there are probably three 'solomonic judgments'. In a custody case, leaving aside cases in which one parent is demonstrably unfit and assuming that a drawn-out dispute is against the immediate interests of the child, a court will, firstly, presume strongly in favour of the mother or, secondly, presume in favour of the primary carer, who is highly likely to be the mother or, thirdly, toss a coin (see Elster 1989:123–74). He considers these decisions paradigmatically indeterminate since, whilst the first two options may be preferable in the short to medium term, he argues that there is a case for randomisation in the longer term.

When there are random decisions usually it is done when the agreement is seen to be in the best interests and welfare of a child. However it would appear that many jurisdictions do not define exactly how or why such decisions should be made. What is lacking is a clear and agreed framework for making decisions on their behalf following an appropriate assessment of individual capacity to make precise decisions.

The assumption is that they are not competent to make it for themselves, despite a trend toward 'inclusive' laws, so there is often a legal argument based on a 'best interests' principle. This principle is a primary consideration in the CRC (Article 3, 1) that is supported by the evolving capacities principle (Article 5). Although Article 12 essentially advocates inclusion, particularly Part 2 in such cases, the assumption is often that the age and maturity of the child is not yet well enough developed to include him or her. It thus appears that broadly speaking use of the *parens patriae* principle is unhelpful in searching for a precise answer in law. When seen in terms of the CRC, or within a human rights framework, the state itself has not taken steps to either make or enforce laws which align with the participatory principles, let alone move toward a more responsible role with some of the qualities of self-determination of citizenship.

Majority

There are several other ages one could turn to examine when majority might be considered to have begun.[3] Marriage is the first example chosen as a possible litmus test for full citizenship rights since marriageable age usually allows consenting partners entering that relationship to assume a life like any other family. The 'normal' age range for marriage without parental consent is between 18 and 21 years, although a few countries allow it as young as 16 although China is 22 for males (and 20 for females). However in Ethiopia the legal age is 18 years for both males and females. In Mali, Mozambique and Niger over 50 % of girls are married prior to reaching 18, in Yemen around 64 % of girls are married before 18 or in Bangladesh 81 % of girls marry before 18. In practice though, children in rural areas are married young and it is not uncommon to see girls as young as 6 years of age being married and it is still unusual for a girl to be 16 and unmarried. In Brunei no minimum marriage age has been as yet specified.

Numerous countries allow marriage at age 16 with consent and a few allow girls particularly to be married as young as 12 or 13 years. Of course, a conceptual problem arises here since the age of sexual consent does not always correspond with marriage ages. Thus in Ethiopia it is 15 years for both sexes and in Brunei age 14 for males and age 16 for females, in Mali and Yemen both must be married before sex occurs. Marriage age in Yemen is 9 years, whereby in 1999 the minimum marriage age of 15 for girls, although rarely enforced, was abolished.[4] The onset of puberty, which was interpreted to be age 9, was set as the requirement for the consummation of a marriage. In some countries the age of consent is higher for those, particularly girls, engaged in commercial sex. In some countries the age of consent

[3]The following ages are mainly taken from United Nations and NGO websites but have been cross-checked through comparison of the given ages between two or more sites. One, however, comes from a single site – in this case ages of consent are taken from the AIDS charity AVERT on http://www.avert.org/aofconsent.htm.

[4]See also the UN Convention on Consent to Marriage, Minimum Age for Marriage and Registration of Marriages. There are at present 16 signatories and 55 state parties.

is higher when one partner is in a position of trust with regard to the other, usually the male partner, or when one partner takes advantage of the other's immaturity. In some cases girls marry just after menarche and others prior to puberty. A married person is then, for most intents and purposes, considered an adult.

Age of consent laws tend not to not apply when the partners are married, thus young traditional marriages occasionally appear to challenge established legal standards. Some countries cover this by having regional laws that may overrule the national law. Likewise, in some cases the age of consent is lower when partners are of a similar age, although no matter how young. In those cases the traditional marriage age also determines the earliest actual transition to adulthood in their society.

Markers for the Beginning of Adulthood

The age at which a person becomes an adult thus varies significantly in different countries in the world. It often depends upon what constitutes being an adult. Most countries look at that in terms of an age at which children can legally work as well as marry, vote, buy alcohol, be conscripted or be charged with a crime. Child labour is an interesting measure. Great variations exist as to the age when one may work in different countries. Wherever this is a factor for considering who is an adult, the age can range from no laws at all in countries like Papua New Guinea, Yemen and Liberia through to countries that set minimum age requirements for child labour. The lowest set ages are in countries like Bangladesh, Paraguay or Syria where the minimum age is 12 years. However, many children working in developing countries begin work before reaching the minimum legal age. Most countries set minimum ages at 15–16 years old and in a few cases the minimum age may be 14.

In many countries legal voting ages at 18 define who is an adult. A few countries are promoting earlier and some even lowering voting ages. Austria and Germany, for instance, now allow 16 year olds to vote in municipal elections. In Italy, however, one cannot vote for a senator until age 25. In Liechtenstein voters must still wait until they are 30 to vote at all. Electoral franchise is a much favoured argument for lowering the age at which full citizenship begins amongst children's rights activists. However, it assumes that a universal and accessible electoral system is available to all and tends to overlook the variations in who actually has franchise; for instance consideration of the inclusion or exclusion of women, people in prisons or mental hospitals, persons subject to the German *Berufsverbot* and comparable examples.

Another common litmus test for determining when one is an adult is the age at which one can purchase alcohol. The USA generally has 21 years, which is actually quite high, however in some countries alcohol can be purchased by either anyone or nobody of any age. In the former it is not generally treated with the same *rite de passage* veneration as in many countries with a minimum drinking age. In the majority of northern nations the consumption age is 18 although a few countries, including Spain, France, Austria, and Germany, have set drinking age at 16 years and some countries allow children under the drinking age to consume alcohol but not buy it themselves. However, consumption of alcohol is usually taken into account when young people transgress laws and is usually seen as a negative when it is proven that it has been used in full knowledge of possible outcomes. Where a person is unambiguously proven to have been forced or deceived into consuming alcohol, as with any other intoxicants, then whoever has responsibility for giving it, irrespective of age, is liable to prosecution. This then becomes a question of responsibility before the law rather than simply a process of prosecution and punishment, since both instigator and the legal minor who has been deceived or forced to break the law may both be subject of protection orders of one kind or another.

Responsibility Before the Law

Legislation stipulates when children are considered criminally responsible or an adult in the eyes of criminal law. Countries with low marriage, drinking or child labour ages tend to also assess criminal responsibility earlier. For instance, the USA considers 7 year olds criminally responsible and under some very exceptional circumstances eligible to be charged as an adult.

> In the US, the age of criminal responsibility is established by state law. Only 13 states have set minimum ages, which range from 6 to 12 years old. Most states rely on common law, which holds that from age 7 to age 14, children cannot be presumed to bear responsibility but can be held responsible (UNICEF 1997).

The defence of childhood is a form of legal argument that excludes defendants falling within that definition from criminal liability for their deeds if, at that time, they had not reached age of criminal responsibility. After reaching a particular age there may be levels of responsibility determined by age and nature of offence allegedly committed. Behaviour of an antisocial nature may well be reproved in a more positive way that discourages society's use of the word *criminal*. Thus one finds the age of criminal responsibility treated in two different ways. The first is as a definition of the process for dealing with young offenders whereby a range of ages beginning with a minimum specifies exclusion of juveniles from the adult system of trial and penalty. The majority of countries have separate juvenile justice systems independent of adult criminal justice:

> In Japan, offenders below age 20 are tried in a family court, rather than in the criminal court system. In all Scandinavian countries, the age of criminal responsibility is 15, and adolescents under 18 are subject to a system of justice that is geared mostly towards social services, with incarceration as the last resort (UNICEF 1997).

Hearings are basically welfare based and usually deal with children as 'clients' in need of obligatory measures of management, treatment or care. The second considers the physical capability of a child to commit a crime. Thus children are considered normally incapable of committing some acts such as sexual crimes or other offences that require abilities of a more mature nature.

Some countries link childhood with diminished responsibility on the ground of what is normally considered mental illness. Differences between children below criminal responsibility who are prosecuted and young offenders are classified according to assessed levels of capability. The children's rights lobby does not consider this constructive since it implies that children are somehow defective rather than simply lacking the acumen that comes with age and experience. This is an aspect of the *parens patriae* principle, whereby each nation will consider the nature of its own society and substantiation of the age at which antisocial behaviour begins to manifest itself. Some societies are indulgent toward the young and inexperienced and prefer not to expose them to the criminal justice process, instead pursuing other means of dealing with them. Thus there is a policy of *doli incapax* (incapable of wrong) that rules out liability for all acts that would otherwise have been criminal up to a particular age. Thereby no matter what a young person has done there cannot be criminal prosecution.

In 1998 the principle of *doli incapax* that presumed that children aged under 14 were incapable of telling right from wrong that had been enshrined in English common law since the seventeenth century was abolished (Bandalli 1998). In Nordic countries an offence committed by somebody less than age 15 years is usually considered an outcome of phenomena in the child's development. The authorities will usually take administrative processes to assure the normal development of that child through methods ranging from therapy to placement in a special unit. Since they are not administered by the criminal justice system they are not dependent on the gravity of the offence but based on the normal circumstances of the child. However, this kind of policy of treating minors as incapable of committing crimes does not necessarily reflect public opinion. If the underlying principle of the rationale is that children below a certain age lack the capacity to form the *mens rea* of an offence it is questionable as to whether or not this is a sustainable argument. The counter argument is that given different speeds at which individuals develop both physically and intellectually an age limit may be arbitrary and irrational. Nonetheless the perception that children should not be exposed to criminal justice the same as adults endures. They have neither had experience of life nor do many people consider that they have the same mental and intellectual capacities as adults, thus it may be considered disproportionate to treat young children in the same way as adults.

In 1993, 2 year old James Bulger was shopping with his mother in Liverpool. He wandered off, was found and led away by two 10-year-old boys, Jon Venables and Robert Thompson. They later assaulted and killed him and left his body on a railway line. The case shocked people in Britain for a number of reasons. The age of the killers and the fact that they were caught on closed-circuit television so that images of them making off with James were broadcast on national television caused widespread disbelief. Moreover, the indifference of passers-by who saw James being led away by his killers in obvious distress did little to help. The two boys were tried in an adult court with virtually full media coverage. Their identities were not protected. In the public domain they were treated as though they were adults.

The Bulger case opened up public debate about the nature of children and childhood. It brought with it contrasting representations of children, whereby James and similar children represented pure innocence and the killers represented pure evil. However, I would argue that this was initially a particularly British phenomenon. About 1 year after the Bulger case, the small Norwegian city Trondheim was affected by an analogous tragedy. Five year old Silje Marie Raedergard was playing with two 6 year old boys. The game turned violent; they stripped her, beat her unconscious and then ran away. She froze to death in the snow.

Similarities with the Bulger case were remarkable. What was surprising were the differences in the perception of children and how the Norwegian authorities and Silje's mother reacted. Trondheim is a close, cohesive community. Many people in the city knew who the killers were, yet their names were never published. They were protected from media exposure. The boys lived in the same neighbourhood as Silje and her family. Immediately news of her death was made public. The police and the local schoolmaster opened up the school that both Silje and the boys attended and talked to both children and parents. Stress was placed on how safe children were. There was a call for calm and no retribution. After 2 days, the boys went back to school accompanied by psychologists. There were no protests and no parents withdrew their own children. The *Guardian* reported the local paper's position: "…the culprits were just 6 years old; how did they know what they were doing? In Norway, where the age of criminality is 15 – as opposed to 10 in Britain – they were treated as victims not killers…" (Hattenstone 2000).

It is difficult to assemble a comprehensive single international overview of the history of juvenile justice. Junger-Tas and Decker (2008) have compiled a collection of in-depth analyses of the juvenile justice systems in 19 different countries in the EU, Canada and USA. Much of what is available looks at European countries or USA with a great deal of emphasis on differences between the Anglo-Saxon countries and Europe. Others, especially looking at the UK, concentrate on the nineteenth century (e.g.: Hawes 1971). Goldson and Muncie (2009) include a number of authors who look at the history, except that the overview is limited to mainly Europe and North America. The rest of the world largely requires country by country examination. Thus this research relies on that which is most accessible and relevant.

Books like Dickens' *Oliver Twist* and Henry Mayhew's *London Labour* and the parliamentary 'blue books' helped to generate the overstated notion of a Victorian 'criminal class' in England. There are two dominant popular views of that period. The first is of a 'golden age' of law and order in which behaviour was generally better than over the period since roughly the early Industrial Revolution, when the treatment of juvenile criminals was less enlightened than today. The other sees the world as a place of chaos in which the administration of law was simultaneously benevolent and harsh. It was benevolent in that it acknowledged the state's duty to provide welfare for the poor, but also harsh since it regarded the poor as highly untrustworthy and treated them accordingly. Dishonesty by child or adult alike was treated ruthlessly. Very few societies had criminal legal systems that can be compared with those of the present day or indeed a notion of separation by ages.

The earliest significant theories of childhood criminality developed out of a notion of biological determinism in Christian European societies. Pamela Cox and Heather Shore (2002) edited a collection of essays examining the development of a notion of juvenile delinquency in Britain and mainland Europe between 1650 and 1950. One sees that the Christian ethic made it difficult to think of children as being other than tainted by 'original sin' although not completely devoid of moral reserve. They were thus not thought of as inhuman or inherently evil. Although the view of the young offender was seriously prejudiced by established theories that saw things in terms of biological determinism, they were the first to benefit from the 'new penology' of redemption. They were the first simply because they were young and could not be held morally accountable for their actions. Moreover, that was because they were considered more impressionable than older criminals.

Mary Carpenter (see Manton 1976) wrote her *Reformatory Schools: For the Children of the Perishing and Dangerous* in 1851 with which she coined the term 'dangerous classes' in reference to the lower or poor classes being prone to crime. That work was influential, having some effect on the drafting of the Youthful Offenders Act 1854 which recognised reformatory schools. She started a reformatory school in Bristol herself but also advocated good quality free day-schools and feeding children in industrial schools as a means of reducing the propensity for wrong doing.

In the USA (see Platt 1977) a child-saving 'movement' emerged during the nineteenth century and influenced the development of juvenile justice systems. The child-savers particularly stressed the value of redemption and prevention through early detection of deviance and intervention through education and training. The child savers' intention was to mitigate the roots of child delinquency and furthermore change the treatment of juveniles.

The first US juvenile court was convened in Chicago in 1899, founded on two principles advocated by child savers. These two principles were founded on the basis of juveniles not being ready to be held accountable for their actions and because they were not yet fully developed and it would be easier to rehabilitate them than adults.

The quintessence of the juvenile court was recognition of the obligation of the state for its neglected and failing children. The intent was not simply to classify them criminals and steer them further into a milieu of vice and crime in reaction to severe measures and the lessons learned amongst experienced adult criminals. Previously 'delinquent' children had been those who had committed a crime, were tried in adult courts and sentenced to adult prisons.

Other children such as street sellers and orphans were generally ignored by courts unless they were accused of criminal deeds. Under those circumstances they were often treated more harshly than children from poor but 'respectable' families. The rationale had been that young people who came before courts or other agencies appointed to deal with them were being helped instead of punished. They were being helped so there was no need for procedural safeguards. The behaviour of young people was labelled and categorised and they were stripped of their few rights. However, the outcome of reforms in Europe and the USA was that children and youth, with the exception of those for whom *doli incapax* applied, would actually be helped. They were therewith acknowledged to be children and any similarity of treatment to that of adults very quickly ended. Thus, if anything, juvenile justice enforces the separable notions of childhood and innocence, adolescence and youth as the end of innocence at the threshold of development into adulthood.

Cultural Definitions of Childhood and Becoming an Adult

Beyond the administration of justice there are also cultural definitions of child and adult. Marriage ages have already been examined. There are also various forms of initiation that are cultural, religious or a combination of the two. In different cultures they may determine that someone is an adult before legal ages for adulthood apply. For example, coming of age ceremonies for Jewish children, *bat* or *bar mitzvahs* occur when a child is 12 or 13 years old (See Chap. 5). Children have a firmly fixed place in Jewish society in which childhood is rather short although clearly defined and ending with the *b'nai mitzvah*. Their law says that every Jewish girl becomes a *bat mitzvah* automatically at age 12 years and a boy becomes a *bar mitzvah* at age 13 years because boys mature later than girls. As a *bat* or *bar mitzvah* a child becomes duty-bound by God's commandments as specified in the Torah. Until *b'nai mitzvah* parents are liable for their children but subsequently participate in all areas of Jewish belief and practice as an adult.

Many local traditions consider a child an adult long before a child is legally considered an adult. Latin American families have coming of age parties for their 15 year old daughters, called *quince años*[5] and some others including Mexicans celebrate the same calling it *quinceañeras*. The *quince años* or *quinceañera* is celebrated in a unique and different way from other birthdays. Besides referring to the actual festivities it is also used to refer to the young woman whose 15th birthday is being celebrated in manner analogous to the *bat mitzvah*. The closest equivalent to it in the English-speaking world is perhaps the debutante ball for those turning 18 years.

Celebration of a Hispanic 15th birthday is highly ritualised and traditionally begins with a religious ceremony. Then a party or reception is held at home or in a hall. Festivities include food and music and commonly a dance is performed by the *quinceanera* and her 'court'. Her court is usually comprised of young girls (*Damas*) and young men (depending where it is they are called *Chambelán*, *Escorte* or *Galán*) or a combination of both. There are traditionally 14 persons in the court, which with the celebrant totals 15. It is the point at which there is recognition of her journey from childhood to maturity and therewith a girl is considered a woman and ready for all the responsibilities of adulthood. A 'last doll' is used as part of the ceremony, often in the form of a decoration and token of the event.

In some versions of the custom the doll represents the last thing of childhood now that the celebrant will focus on other things such as having her own children. In some places *cápias* (printed ribbons with the celebrant's name and date of birth) are pinned to the doll whilst the girl mingles with her guests. She thanks them for their attendance and gives them a keepsake of the event. There is a considerable number of extant and lost traditions that mark such transitions (see Chap. 7 for anthropological examination

[5] I had a number of *aijados* (godchildren) in Lima, Peru. As their *compadre* (co-parent, equivalent to godparent) I was expected to contribute generously to the celebration and give the young woman my blessing. I never attended an *aijada*'s *quince años* celebration but went to others and, being a stranger, took the time to find out about the event which I attempt to recall here.

of related issues). Some are formal *rites de passage* that mark events such as menarche, betrothal or 'first marriage' (e.g. Fuller 1976), first hunt or acceptance as a form of apprentice. All of them occur before the civil legal definition of majority.

A more contentious signpost is that a person may also almost be considered an adult if he or she is drafted or volunteers for military service. In most countries this age is 18, though a few countries set the age at 16 or 17. The Optional Protocol to the CRC on the involvement of children in armed conflict (Article 1 and Article 4, 1) stipulates that 'States Parties shall take all feasible measures to ensure that members of their armed forces who have not attained the age of 18 years do not take a direct part in hostilities.' However, some countries where there has been civil war or continual internal conflict have recruited children as combatants and for other military services (there have been, for instance, stories about girls taken as prostitutes by the Lord's Liberation Army in Uganda).

Many nations have historical accounts of child heroes, for instance the British example of Jack Cornwell VC (see Unknown 1918). However, apart from Nicaragua making all former child *guerrillas* full citizens at the end of their revolution in 1979 very few child soldiers were ever viewed as adults but rather more as children who had lost their innocence. It is the bridge between innocence and being or becoming knowing and part of the adult world that in this situation defines perception of the young fighters as child or adult heroes. In many respects the involvement of children in any form of armed conflict as either directly affect civilians or fighters goes against the grain of principles and practice in most societies. In the contemporary world it is considered a situation of especially difficult circumstances. The approach to dealing with children affected generally follows welfare standards using the 'best interests' principle that we find, for instance, in the CRC, Article 3, 2. 'States Parties undertake to ensure the child such protection and care as is necessary for his or her well-being, taking into account the rights and duties of his or her parents, legal guardians, or other individuals legally responsible for him or her, and, to this end, shall take all appropriate legislative and administrative measures.' Where there are no adult caretakers and reunification is not possible, the means to achieving this end will often be through welfare provisions such as institutions, fostering and adoption.

Welfare

It has, if anything, been for a large part the outcome of children as they are perceived by those who make and administer laws that led to the form of child welfare operational today. Welfare itself is not absolutely the same as child welfare although both have the same origins. Welfare was originally delivered collectively and free of the state. In mediaeval times in Europe hospitals were commonly church run and the word *hospital* should not be understood in today's terms. Then they were communities where the elderly and feeble particularly were cared for (Williams 2007). Until the Reformation, it was a religious duty for all Christians to undertake seven corporal works of mercy. These were acts aimed at relieving physical suffering.

In accordance with the teaching of Christ in the New Testament, *Matthew* 25, 32–46 (see also Unknown 1971:62–3), people were required to feed the hungry, give drink to the thirsty, welcome the stranger, clothe the naked, visit the sick, visit prisoners and bury the dead. Christian parishes were the earliest basic administrative units in Europe and also had responsibility for their poor (Williams 2007). The nearby Islamic countries had *zakat*, or the giving of alms, which is a legal concept and the third of the *Five Pillars of Islam*. There are rules attached to *zakat*, although generally it is obligatory to give away 2.5 % of one's income and savings and 5–10 % of the harvest to the poor. Beneficiaries include the impoverished, low paid, people unable to pay debts, stranded travellers and anybody else needing assistance. The principle of *zakaah* charges that the rich should look after the poor. In Judaism charity is similarly embodied in *tzedakah*, justice, whereby the poor are entitled to charity as a right rather than benevolence. *Tzedakah* is regarded an extension of the ancient *maser ani*, poor-tithe, as well as practices including allowing the poor to glean a field, gather harvest during *shmita* (sabbatical year) and other benevolent practices. Voluntary charity, alongside prayer and atonement, is regarded as penance for the outcome of bad deeds.

With the introduction of 'poor laws' as the medieval age ended, the responsibility in Europe passed on to secular parishes (see Slack 1990). In England, for example, Elizabethan Poor Laws enshrined this right. In 1572 an Act made provision for the punishment of sturdy beggars who were then sent back to their parish of origin, ostensibly for help, and the relief of the impotent poor. The 1574 Act in Scotland duplicated the English Act although it remained in force in Scotland until 1845. In England it was superseded in 1598 and 1601 with an Act that provided for a compulsory poor rate, creation of 'overseers' of relief and provision for 'setting the poor on work'. There was no general apparatus for enforcement and Poor Law operation was inconsistent between places.

This system, with modifications, remained largely intact until a campaign initiated by Utilitarian reformers. They considered fiddling with the facts beyond the pale. The new poor law of 1834 was the result of their campaign, and where a principle of 'less eligibility' was enforced support in the new system would only be offered if a person went into a 'Poor House' or 'Work House'.[6] There the standard of living awaiting them was below that on which the poorest labourer could survive. There was no distinction between adult and child recipients of this form of assistance.

As the nineteenth century drew to a close, a new notion of welfare began to develop. One aspect of that was unemployment insurance whereby contributions and benefit levels were laid down by parliaments. The insurance principle was preferred for the finance of this new welfare, since some governments were anxious about raising income tax. In Germany, for instance, Bismarck faced enormous resistance to a tax-based welfare, complicated because he did not have the power to levy taxes on income. Until they became national institutions friendly societies and mutually-owned bodies operated health schemes that complimented unemployment benefits.

[6]Often referred to as the 'House'.

In 1889 the first Act of Parliament for the prevention of cruelty to children, the *Children's Charter*, was passed in the UK. It enabled the state to intervene in relations between parents and children for the first time ever. The police were given powers to arrest anyone found ill-treating a child and enter a home if a child was thought to be in danger. The Act included additional guidelines on the employment of children[7] and outlawed begging. In 1894 it was amended and extended and allowed children to give evidence in court, recognition of mental cruelty and it became an offence to refuse an ill child medical attention. Thus, in the UK as was also happening elsewhere, regulation of employment, education and new protective measures were separating the domains of adulthood and childhood. It was also happening at a time when campaigns for equal contract and property rights for women, opposition to 'chattel' marriage and virtual ownership of married women and children by husbands and crusade for political franchise was at its height. Thus the nature of separatism by age that still persists in most places became entrenched.

Child welfare essentially emerged as a set of government and private services designed to protect them and promote family stability. The notion of a state approved child welfare system dates back to Plato's *Republic* (1998:65). His account of a discussion between Socrates, Adeimantus, Glaucon and Thrasymachus surmised that the interests of the child could be best served by removing children from the custody of parents and placing them under state care. To prevent an uprising from dispossessed parents:

> We shall have to invent some ingenious kind of lots which the less worthy may draw on each occasion of our bringing them together, and then they will accuse their own ill-luck and not the rulers.

Furthermore:

> The proper officers will take the offspring of the good parents to the pen or fold, and there they will deposit them with certain nurses who dwell in a separate quarter; but the offspring of the inferior, or of the better when they chance to be deformed, will be put away in some mysterious, unknown place, as they should be.

However, since the advent of modern child welfare those who come to the attention of welfare workers most frequently do so because of situations that are generally collectively termed child *abuse* or *neglect*. The former is more or less made up of

[7] In 1833 the Government passed the first Factory Act to improve conditions for children working in factories for very long hours in places where conditions were often appalling. It set out that no child under 9 years of age could work, employers required a medical or age certificate for child workers, children between the ages of 9 and 13 could work no longer than 9 h and those aged 13–18 worked no more than 12 h a day, they could no longer work at night, at least 2 h schooling had to be given each day and four factory inspectors appointed to enforce the law throughout England and Wales. Further Acts in 1844, 1847, 1850, 1853, 1867, 1874 and 1901 eventually brought the working age to a minimum of 12 years. The Education Act of 1870 effectively created the modern system of education in England. It gave rise to a national system of compulsory state education that assured the existence of a dual system of voluntary denominational schools and non-denominational state schools. Elementary education became to all intents and purposes free with the 1891 Education Act. Both processes limited children's availability for employment.

physical, emotional and sexual abuse and anything that can be classified as one or more of those. Thus, child employment may be physical abuse as well as economic exploitation but will probably be comprised of all three if a child is working in any part of the 'sex industry'. The latter, neglect, includes failure to take adequate measures to protect a child from harm as well as all forms of oversight in their care.

The CRC, Article 3 (see Appendix I for full text) sees child welfare as part of the 'best interests' principle:

1. In all actions concerning children…
2. States Parties undertake to ensure the child such protection and care as is necessary for his or her well-being…
3. States Parties shall ensure that the institutions, services and facilities responsible for the care or protection of children shall conform with the standards established by competent authorities…

The most detailed expression of the vision the CRC includes is given in Article 19 (see Appendix I), where who is responsible and what that entails are described.

Given that all nation states member of the UN have ratified the CRC without reservation or declaration to the contrary, the assumption projected is that welfare is provided on a comparatively equitable basis. In point of fact, the comments on many of the initial and subsequent reports to the Committee on the Rights of the Child show enormous variance in availability, delivery and, above all else, understanding of the concept of welfare. However, the common standard is that the distinguishing characteristics of social work practice in child welfare are derived from the nature of children. In particular, they recognise the characteristics of dependency and development and also special concern and responsibility for children that all social groups demonstrate. Moreover, it appears to be universally recognised that the years of childhood are of particular significance for future development. Whatever occurs during the developmental process is of concern because it may discourage, interfere with or adversely influence the kind of development considered desirable. Furthermore, community, society or state have a stake in this, by producing the kind of person it needs or wants and who maintains its traditions, values and ideals the provision of welfare shapes the social order. As its basic unit, the family has, through parents particularly, assured the child of the close and continuing individual relationships, attention, concern, special interest and love which are promoted as the most important stimulants of healthy development.

Child welfare assumes that the primary and unique need of the child is parental care but provides alternatives where this fails in most countries. This is encapsulated in CRC Article 20 (alternative care)[8] and Article 21 (adoption). However, these distinctions within welfare reinforce the division into adulthood and

[8] Article 20, part 3 states: Such care could include, *inter alia*, foster placement, *Kafala* of Islamic law, adoption, or if necessary placement in suitable institutions for the care of children. When considering solutions, due regard shall be paid to the desirability of continuity in a child's upbringing and to the child's ethnic, religious, cultural and linguistic background.

childhood because they assume and underpin the notion of dependency that is further reinforced by the CRC principle of 'evolving capabilities' (Article 5).

The impact of global economy and national social policies on welfare and changes in the established social order and care as such are in need of introspective, pragmatic appreciation from the point of view of children's welfare. That is especially so in the context of particular new forms of social control targeted at young people's norm-violations in which some of the typical features of the modern welfare state model have been questioned. As such, there is much discussion about present contradictions and challenges in the field of social work related with young people. It bears in mind that as part of the process of modernisation, the regulation of the family and childrearing has acquired an important place in the production of social order.

One of the results of this has been the creation of a system of control and care (penal-welfare complex, Garland 1985, 2001) that has been gradually built around the theme of childrearing. This system comprises of an interesting, ongoing dynamic of endeavour to achieve a balance between punishments and support (see Skehill 2004).

There is a gradual transformation of the social context of social work with children and youth, which is an essential for the production and maintenance of social order and cohesion between adults and the young. Early intervention, risk-assessment and multi-professional collaboration have dominated service sectors such as maternity and neonatal clinics, day care facilities, schools and the fields of child welfare, youth work and social work. That is in accordance with international, particularly Anglo-American, models that are being used to modernise welfare delivery (for instance see Lister 2006a; Such and Walker 2005; Schütter 2006). Social work thus operates as a function of governance that has the explicit role of transferring *objective* legislation and policy to the *subjective* sphere of individuals and families through mediation in the 'social space' between the two domains (Donzelot 1980). Traditionally, social work had a strong ethical commitment to the accrual of social capital and the maintenance of social solidarity and the *status quo* generally.

In turn, social policy on children reflects how welfare is designed and delivered alongside education, health, housing, poverty and social security. Social policies for children have risen high on the agenda for governments across the world in recent years as they seek to promote successful outcomes for children as 'beings' and 'becomings'. It also, one should add, for less well off nations periodically attracts generous funding from international organisations such as the World Bank.

Recently, links between children's rights, poverty and development have led to renewed examination of international policies, particularly globalisation, and also looking at causes and not only consequences of programmes to eliminate child labour and poverty. The structural problems of market globalisation and social polarisation in the twenty-first century and human rights theories are being used as a basis for international and social policies with international agencies and NGOs. They are also being analysed in relation to children. The needs of disabled and institutionalised children and the right to social security in line with CRC Article 26 are also being given particular attention.

The Future for Children

Lorenz (2006:138) has argued that the impact of neo-liberal policies, individualisation of risks, the privatisation of social solidarity and the emphasis on economy are being felt in every European welfare state. Consequently, he claims, the basic instruments used to produce social order and social solidarity have all undergone varying degrees of reorientation. This is, in fact, disseminating worldwide.

As global vision gradually displaces localised development of social policy 'worldwide' efforts are being made. In May 2002 the United Nations General Assembly Special Session (UNGASS) on Children was held to follow-up the 1991 Summit for Children. It brought together all signatory governments to reaffirm commitment to the CRC and also focus on emerging issues essential for securing the human rights of children. The outcome of this meeting was *A World Fit for Children* which outlines commitments for achieving the aims of the CRC promises made in 1991 and also a set of 'Millennium Development Goals'. Under the heading 'Partnerships and participation', Item 32 (UNICEF 2006b:23–24) states:

> In order to implement the present Plan of Action, we will strengthen our partnership with the following actors, who have unique contributions to make, and encourage the use of all avenues for participation to advance our common cause - the well-being of children and the promotion and protection of their rights:
>
> (1) Children, including adolescents, must be enabled to exercise their right to express their views freely, according to their evolving capacity, and build self-esteem, acquire knowledge and skills, such as those for conflict resolution, decision-making and communication, to meet the challenges of life. The right of children, including adolescents, to express themselves freely must be respected and promoted and their views taken into account in all matters affecting them, the views of the child being given due weight in accordance with the age and maturity of the child. The energy and creativity of children and young people must be nurtured so that they can actively take part in shaping their environment, their societies and the world they will inherit. Disadvantaged and marginalized children, including adolescents in particular, need special attention and support to access basic services, build self-esteem and to prepare them to take responsibility for their own lives. We will strive to develop and implement programmes to promote meaningful participation by children, including adolescents, in decision-making processes, including in families and schools and at the local and national levels.
>
> (2) Parents, families, legal guardians and other caregivers have the primary role and responsibility for the well-being of children, and must be supported in the performance of their child-rearing responsibilities. All our policies and programmes should promote the shared responsibility of parents, families, legal guardians and other caregivers, and society as a whole in this regard.
>
> (3) Local governments and authorities, through, *inter alia*, strengthened partnerships at all levels, can ensure that children are at the centre of agendas for development. By building on ongoing initiatives, such as child-friendly communities and cities without slums, mayors and local leaders can significantly improve the lives of children.
>
> (4) Parliamentarians or members of legislatures are key to the implementation of this plan of action, the success of which will require that they promote awareness raising; adopt necessary legislation; facilitate and appropriate the financial resources needed for this purpose; and monitor their effective utilization.

The Inclusion of Children

This is, of course a highly idealised document that aims to direct policy toward a more child inclusive environment and in some respects runs counter to social controls aimed at young people's norm-violations. Children's civic engagement is held to be essential for achieving the Millennium Development Goals and other development commitments including universal education and eradication of poverty. In the view of the UN, children's contributions are said to improve services and policies and their involvement in social organisations and political decisions improves the quality, efficiency and integrity of services. Community participation in public decisions may help improve public services, hold public officials accountable, ensure justice and reinforce the rule of law.

The achievement of the Millennium Development Goals requires the participation of all groups in society. However, there is a trade off that demands high standards from children and penalties for those who do not conform. Those might, for instance, include the kind of 'anti-social behaviour orders' (see Squires 2008) recently introduced in Britain that occasionally restrain the ability of children to exercise their right to express their views freely because their manner of doing so does not conform with adult standards of what is acceptable and responsible.

The Crick Report (DfEE 1998) stipulates that children and young people should be made aware of their responsibilities toward themselves and others in regard to duties and obligations to family, friends, school, community, state and society. The concept of responsibility itself is defined in broad terms as:

> (a) care for others; (b) premeditation and calculation about what effect actions are likely to have on others; and (c) understanding and care for the consequences. (*Ibid*.:13)

It also states that social and moral responsibility is promoted by:

> ...children learning from the very beginning self-confidence and socially and morally responsible behaviour both in and beyond the classroom, both towards those in authority and towards each other... ...guidance on moral values and personal development are essential preconditions of citizenship. (*Ibid*.:11)

Morality embraces values we maintain about what is right or wrong and good or bad. In *Good Thinking: Education for Citizenship and Moral Responsibility* (The Citizenship Foundation, 2001:3) moral responsibility is described as involving values such as:

> Social justice; political equality; respect for difference; human rights; co-operation; civility; respect for the rule of law; and a commitment to negotiation and debate as the proper way to resolve disagreements over public policy.

This, the Crick Report says, occurs even at primary school age when:

> ...children are already forming through learning and discussion, concepts of fairness, and attitudes to law, to rules, to decision-making, to authority, to their local environment and social responsibility etc. (*Ibid*.:11)

In the European Union, policy is that children should be considered citizens and treated accordingly (Schuurman and Sutton 2004). In a democratic Europe the vision is for guaranteed participation of all citizens including children. Within the EU the guiding principle is that children's rights should be ensured and that it should be possible for them to participate in all decisions that affect them. In order to achieve this goal, some attempts to involve children as active citizens in policy and planning have been made at local and national levels.

A programme and policy guide '*Children as Active Citizens*' was the outcome of a meeting held in Bangkok in January 2007. The topic under discussion by experts and organisations working in that part of the world was that more than one third of the world's children live in East Asia, South Asia and the Pacific. Whereas in the West it is normal to place stress on individual rights, in most of Asia societies place greater emphasis on the responsibility of each individual towards family, community and society. Their starting point was that by definition civil rights are protections and privileges given to citizens. Citizenship itself means a collection of rights and duties that define membership of a community and within that community civil rights essentially describe individual rights. However, in societies where individuals exist as part of the whole and individual rights are not a priority, ensuring civil rights for those children is a considerable challenge. Thus their starting point is (IAWGCP 2008:8):

> Just like any other set of rights, there is a long distance between ratifying an international convention and reforming national legislation to fulfil, implement and monitor the rights of all citizens. Children's civil rights are among the least-understood and least-realized rights. Implementing children's civil rights is the most challenging aspect of the CRC, a challenge that applies equally to resource-rich countries… Starting positions are extremely low for most children. This should not, however, discourage decisive actions. The progressive realization of children's civil rights requires a long-term vision and a plan with concrete benchmarks for achieving this vision – even if it takes a generation to transform relations between children and adults.

The IAWGCP wrote the guide bearing in mind that civil rights and citizenship are closely linked to country specific political, social and cultural contexts. Consequently, two key chapters in Part Three of the guide (7.) 'Citizenship competencies and civic engagement' (*Ibid.*:49–58) and (9.) 'Children influencing public decisions' (*Ibid.*:65–74) look at incorporating the contexts into how this might be done. Perhaps more importantly, it allows for the fact that it may take an entire generation to transform the relations between children and adults.

There is no claim that having waited, only that generation will see the goals achieved. However, it projects a minimum realistic value in seeing children contribute to governance in that region of the world. Therefore the approach is to look at children's civil rights in the broader governance context rather than to look at children in isolation. It ensures that children and young people will be represented in local and national governance bodies albeit allowing for the fact that children are not normally considered part of public decision making and the public arena tends to be hostile to their inclusion. They feel that participation by itself is insufficient for improvement of the performance of government services.

Constraints on the availability of resources, socio-political context and political and decentralised structures affect government performance and without accountability and resources, participation can deliver little (Crook and Manor 1998:8–10). Children's opportunity to influence public decisions (IAWGCP 2008:66) is governed extensively by a country's political system and degree of democratisation, the level of devolution of political authority, influence and character of civil society and the independence of the media and justice.

Davila-Ortega and Freeburg (2006:11) say:

> "Training young people for democracy and governance is a growing area of interest for NGOs and governments. Young people often lack information about electoral reforms and parliamentary development, which impacts their capacity to be effectively engaged in democratic governance."

One assumption is that devolution may open up opportunities for children's involvement in governance. However, at the same time local authorities are frequently more uninformed about international obligations than devolved agencies and may consequently feel less bound by the CRC than national authorities do.

It must be borne in mind that vertical relationships between patrons (the 'political class') and clients are the foundation of both an authoritarian social order and horizontal networks based on trust between equals are the source democratic social order (Putnam 1993). However, as societies change and the primacy of the individual increases, for child and youth inclusive policies to work the decline in social trust that is associated with increasing self-interest over the past few decades (for instance, see Rahn and Transue 1998). Thus, a key question will be how to design policies that are aimed at bottom up strategies that will circumvent the barriers such as the 'distance' between local and national governance and allow for the self-interest that is undermining young people's agency (*Ibid.*).

Children's Inclusion in Governance

One of the models one might suggest is children's involvement in governance. In France children's municipal councils have existed since the 1980s. In 1990 when France ratified the CRC there were at least 200, 2 years later the number had doubled.[9] At present there is something in the region of 1600. The possibility of young people aged 9–16 years (although there are councils with participants up to age 25 years) and contributing to local affairs has been made possible by the councils. At the congress of the French association of children's councils *anacej* (association

[9]In 1993 I had a contract to write a working paper 'Children's Participation in Education for Democracy and Peace in Europe', for UNICEF ICDC, Florence, Italy, published by UNICEF Chile in 1994. It came in the wake of Roger Hart's *Children's Participation: From tokenism to citizenship* in 1992 that had oriented a great deal of interest in children's participation. As a result the French children's councils were a major item in this paper. At that time there were just over 300 of them.

nationale des conseils d'enfants et de jeunes) in October 1998 a constitution was formulated in which one of the fundamental principles was that:

> *La participation à la vie publique locale et régionale des enfants et des jeunes, citoyens d'Europe et du monde, est une exigence car elle est source de socialisation, d'échanges, de paix et de solidarité.*
>
> (The participation of children and youth in local and region public life, (as) citizens of Europe and the world, is a condition because it is a foundation of socialisation, communications, peace and solidarity. [My translation])

This sets a far more universal aim than most (adult) grassroots public representation and may, thus, impose a notion of a rather superficial activity for young people entirely separated from adult governance. However, in 2000 *anacej* and DIV (Délégation Interministérielle à la Ville) carried out an exploratory study of the participation of children and youth councils in three communes: Achères, Clichy sous Bois and Evry. In conclusion they found:

> *En cela, et nous retrouvons là un propos récurrent dans tout ce document, les conseils pourraient alors vraiment, dans le cadre de cette collaboration à la politique de la ville, être un élément réel et moteur d'une démarche participative sur la commune.*
>
> (Given that we find a recurrent observation throughout this document, councils could really seriously consider this a driving force for participatory initiative within the framework of collaboration in communal politics. [My translation])

Their argument is often anchored in the European Union's argument that every individual, irrespective of age, is formally a citizen according to Article 17 of the EC Treaty (European Union 2002):

1. ...Every person holding the nationality of a Member State shall be a citizen of the Union. Citizenship of the Union shall complement and not replace national citizenship.
2. Citizens of the Union shall enjoy the rights conferred by this Treaty and shall be subject to the duties imposed thereby.

It is also supported by the Charter of Fundamental Rights of the European Union (2000) in which:

> Article 20
> *Equality before the law*
> Everyone is equal before the law.
>
> Article 21
> *Non-discrimination*
> 1. Any discrimination based on any ground such as sex, race, colour, ethnic or social origin, genetic features, language, religion or belief, political or any other opinion, membership of a national minority, property, birth, disability, age or sexual orientation shall be prohibited.

EU policy has moved in the direction of child and youth inclusion whereby the active participation of young people in decisions and actions at local and regional level is considered essential if the EU is ever to be able are foster more democratic, inclusive and successful societies. The general view is that participation in the democratic life of any community is about far more than voting or standing for election to any kind of (political) office albeit they are recognised as important elements in this sphere. It is not only in Europe though, Eliana Guerra (2005:151–68) described children's participation in governance and setting the municipal budget in Barra Mansa, Brazil.

Every year since 1998 large numbers of children took part in discussions to elect child councillors and discuss children's priorities. Those elected learn how to represent peers within democratic structures, prioritise use of available resources and develop projects within the complex and frequently slow and very bureaucratic political process of city governance. The initiative came in 1997 when the municipality instigated activities entitled *Citizenship Knows No Age* for local children aged between 9 and 15 years. An evaluation found that children's councils were 'emerging as important mechanisms for the expansion of citizen participation in public policy and management' (*Ibid.*:166). It was felt that their role could be strengthened if the children could be persuaded to take a more active role within the project management committee. It is part of a progressive view of children's political roles in Brazil where the communal franchise is already 16 although mandatory suffrage from is age 18 (although military conscripts do not have a vote).

The EU similarly views participation and active citizenship as having the right, means, space and opportunity and, when and where necessary, the support to participate in and influence decisions and become engaged in activities that should contribute towards creating a better society. To that effect some countries are beginning to lower communal and even general electoral rights down to age 16 (see also Chap. 8). The German federal states of Lower Saxony, Mecklenburg-Western Pomerania, North Rhine-Westphalia, Saxony-Anhalt and Schleswig-Holstein have already lowered the age to 16 years for municipal elections. Austria has already voted to do so and in Scotland the SNP adopted a policy of reducing the voting age for all elections to 16 as soon as possible. Other countries and parts of countries have also done the same or are in the process of changing voting ages. However, there is neither noticeable enthusiasm for lowering the minimum age at which individuals are eligible to stand for political office or the idea of lifelong electoral franchise.

Whether we are looking at existing laws, the process of law making, policy that directs law making, welfare provision or any form of governance in which all or any of those occur, the general impression is of some moves to lower ages in some domains that appear to be almost diametrically opposite to each other such as communal voting ages and criminal responsibility.[10] Alongside those extremes there is an apparent growing tendency to invest less trust in the capabilities of an increasingly educated and informed young population. Protection seems to be increasing because of fears for their wellbeing. If this all taken to be part of what one understands to be

[10]In some federal states in Mexico the minimum ages at which children are subject to penal law it is 6 years although in most states 11 or 12 years and age 11 for federal crimes. In Bangladesh, India, Myanmar, Nigeria, Pakistan, South Africa, Sudan and Tanzania it is age 7. In Belgium, Brazil, Colombia, Democratic Republic of the Congo, Peru and the International Criminal Court the official age of criminal responsibility is age 18, although in Brazil, Colombia and Peru there are separate juvenile laws from age 12 that do not 'criminalise' young offenders. In the UK the ages are 8 years in Scotland (it is possible for children even younger than eight, in rare cases, to appear in court, although the Lord Advocate must intervene before anyone under 16 years can be charged before an adult court) and age 10 in England and Wales and Northern Ireland. However, there is a campaign for raising criminal responsibility to 18 in all parts of the UK.

'social justice' then a theoretical route to understanding this can be extrapolated out of John Rawls (1971) *A Theory of Justice*.

All of those aspects of the control of state authority over children is consistent with Rawls' proposition[11] in that at least a set of procedural principles of justice on which society should be founded. They should be extended to children as well as adults. Taking Rawls' position as describing 'social justice' in a very broad sense, his theory corroborates a view that the application of children's rights may not always be left to children themselves. They should though, be supposed to be able to exercise their rights unless society as a whole agrees that someone else should make decisions for them. His system of justice calls for people understanding the necessity and preparedness to support a distinctive set of principles for conveying basic rights and duties and the determination of what is understood to be appropriate distribution of benefits and complexities of social cooperation. The objective is to allow the individual to act in keeping with a personal conception of his or her best interests although that must not be to the detriment of others.

Thus, individuals participate in a common development of evolving principles that consists of fair treatment for everyone in the present and future. This concurs with use of Kohlberg's ideas (see Chap. 7), which allow for lowering the threshold at which an evolving capacities argument is valid.

The central notion is all of society must contribute to deciding on these principles and that they are selected in a hypothetical state in which individuals are unaware of specific interests and circumstances in real life. The assumption is that all of members of society are self-interested in decision making. However, unawareness of their situation and the specific configuration of their society guarantee the Rawlsian notion that individuals decide on principles of justice open-mindedly, with equality in mind. Thus no individual has to act as an instrument of the interests of other individuals. Everybody would be a human being rather than a 'human becoming' who would need to evolve his or her capabilities and pass through the liminal phase of increasing 'privileges' accumulated through adolescence to early adulthood. These are what David Oldman (1991:25) illustrates as a drawn out *rite de passage*.

Of course, it would naturally require a global 'level playing field' for the distinctions adult individuals and child individuals to be merged. Only then would the principles of justice deliver all aspects of citizenship including duties, responsibilities, complexities and shortcomings equally. Unfortunately the proposition itself is highly unlikely on account of the degree to which the proverbial 'playing field' is uneven.

Therefore, for instance, there is disparity where welfare is well established and at the heart of one nation's social structures. Another nation may have achieved no more than adopting a notion of welfare that it can neither afford to operate nor has

---

[11] On page 460 of *A Theory of Justice* he acknowledges both Piaget and Kohlberg (see Chap. 8) as the intellectual source of his view that by and large shuns a long, drawn out process of becoming a full human being.

had prior experience of. Despite a shared set of principles, the differences will arise anyway. Shared principles such as almost universal ratification of the CRC are assumed to create a set of common standards worldwide. Yet practice of governance from base to the highest level of political office and the cultures and traditions that influence law, policy and moreover the perception of the role of children itself is seldom likely to reach the ideal Rawls' theory expounds.

Attempts to precipitate global actions such as the Millennium Development Goals and *A World Fit for Children*'s plans for partnerships and participation, previously detailed in examination of Item 32, to deliver children's rights are doubtless overambitious. On the other extreme, the attempt by ventures such as the large numbers of children's councils in France, and similar initiatives in other countries, to be influential in communal political life is encouraging. Whilst they do not specifically name citizenship as their specific goal for children, there is good reason to believe those efforts contribute positively toward that end.

Chapter 11
Complementary Areas That Contribute to Notions of Children's Citizenship

This chapter looks at some 'loose ends'. That notion often implies what has been overlooked erroneously (or deliberately). In fact nothing substantial has been forgotten intentionally. Nonetheless, in an attempt to balance other chapters without taking diversionary routes to explain the relevance of some issues, these have been kept back as examples of matters that are very germane. They do not deal categorically with citizenship but have great bearing on how we think of it. Children's, thus human, rights are at the core of this entire work. The first issue looked at here is how there is both a global view and a regional or continental view that are human rights instruments but that are designed to fit more appropriately, albeit it not perfectly, into their own setting.

The African Children's Charter and European Convention on the Exercise of Children's Rights

The *African Charter on the Rights and Welfare of the Child* (ACRWC), sometimes known as the African Children's Charter (ACC) was adopted by the Organisation for African Unity in 1990. It entered into force on November 29, 1999. By February 2009, only 3 of the 53 countries in Africa had not signed the ACRWC (see Appendix II) and it had been ratified by 45, whereby some countries which ratified did not sign and others have signed but not ratified. It was the first regional treaty on children's rights. How it differs from the CRC is in that member states of the African Union believed the CRC missed important socio-cultural and economic issues particular to Africa. Some states which are still non-signatories are also gross violators of human rights generally. These include the Democratic Republic of the Congo (DRC), Sahrawi Arab Democratic Republic, Somalia and Sudan. Violations include the recruitment of child labour, child soldiers, child trafficking, drug abuse, early childhood marriage, harmful cultural practices like female genital mutilation and male child preference and sexual exploitation.

B. Milne, *The History and Theory of Children's Citizenship in Contemporary Societies*, DOI 10.1007/978-94-007-6521-4_11, © Springer Science+Business Media Dordrecht 2013

Emphasis in the ACRWC is on African cultural values and experience when dealing with the rights of the child in instances that challenge traditional African views. Those often conflict with the CRC in areas such as early child marriage, parental rights and obligations towards children and those born out of wedlock. Many African campaigners felt that specifically saying that the CRC is higher than customs, traditions, culture or religious practice did not correspond with rights, duties and obligations in the ACRWC. It also has a clearer definition of the child as *every human being* aged less than 18 years. Article 1 CRC allows for exceptions, Article 2 ACRWC does not. It also tackled particular African issues affecting children such as the abolition of *apartheid* and similar systems. Now that *apartheid* is over, the same provision applies for children living under regimes practicing ethnic, religious or other forms of discrimination. It protects expectant mothers and those with infants and young children in prisons, allows girls the right of return to school after childbirth, prohibits marriage or betrothal of children, promotes constructive action for girls' education and makes special reference to care of the child by extended families. It also prohibits the use of children as beggars, recruitment of children into the armed forces or armed conflict, protects internally displaced and refugee children, disabled children and encourages state parties to provide support for parents in 'times of need'.

Unlike the CRC there is a means by which children can petition the ACRWC's Committee of Experts regarding infringements of their rights (Articles 44 and 45). Thus its nature is both very complementary to and contrasts with the CRC. Moreover, it illustrates a quite different concept of personhood that suggests a very different approach to citizenship to that which emerges out of most other human rights documents. Those are usually very distinctly European conceptually. Articles 12, 13, 14 and 16 express some views such as freedom of expression and religion or a view of privacy that is essentially alien to societies that do not understand a concept of personalised private spheres (see also ENDA editions 2001:21–89).

However, Europe also has a vision that projects a European notion of childhood and children's rights through the *European Convention on the Exercise of Children's Rights* (ECECR) (see Appendix III) that was adopted by the Council of Europe in 1995 and entered into force on 1 July 2000. Thus far 28 have signed the convention and 17 have ratified out of 48 countries.

Each ratifying country is required to specify at least three types of family proceedings before judicial authorities to which the Convention will apply which include care procedures and removal and restriction of parental responsibilities. It is, thus, very different to the ACRWC and more concerned with collecting and offering information on the exercise of children's rights, obtaining the views of children and raising awareness about their rights. Everything relates to their guardianship and representation in all cases or legal acts concerning them or their property. In essence it is more about families than the rights of individual children as per the CRC. It also goes a long way toward advocating a uniformity of European approaches to *looked after children* without giving them the degree of participation the CRC describes. It places a very different emphasis on children's needs rather than on their active role as citizens within society more broadly. It does not go as far as the CRC in any respect and also fails to thoroughly address children themselves as those who bear rights that are safeguarded by adults. Surprisingly, a number of countries where children's rights are well established such as Denmark, the Netherlands, Switzerland and the United Kingdom have neither signed nor ratified the ECECR.

The Influence of Religion

It is not only continental and regional notions of what children are. Their status and such issues as protection and provision for them can also define them. In states that are theocratic or very much influenced by religion there are other questions arising that influence any move toward a universal notion of the child citizen. Savitri Goonesekere (Ali et al. 2007:16) has the following to say about the influence of Islam:

> Legislative reform takes the form of reviewing old laws or enacting new ones. Participation rights are addressed incidentally in this context, as when laws of evidence and procedure are modified so as to facilitate children's access to justice and protect child witnesses and victims. (…)The age of majority is often addressed as a topic for reform because 'protection' requires identification of children by an appropriate age cohort. Law reforms do not in general adopt a holistic approach to definition of childhood in terms of the CRC's overarching concept of child rights. Inconsistencies in the definition of childhood for varying purposes remain untouched, even when legislation clarifies an age of majority.
>
> Family law and personal status is also an area that has been addressed in law reform. (…) There is in general a reluctance to address (…) citizenship (…) for law reform. A few countries in Islamic jurisdictions and mixed legal systems have reviewed the approach to passport laws, citizenship and visas from the perspective of women's and children's rights. The plural legal systems and Islamic law studies show how women's rights and issues of discrimination on the basis of gender have been addressed to only a limited extent in law reform. We have noted that both women and children were denied legal rights in all four legal traditions. Despite the changes in the law that have occurred over time, some reform on women's rights continues to interface with reforms on child law. This is seen in the area of criminal laws on sexual exploitation and trafficking, domestic violence, harmful customary practices, citizenship and immigration, HIV/AIDS, guardianship and custody and forced marriage.
>
> The reform initiatives on women's rights and children's rights have been pursued invariably as parallel projects and not on the basis of connected approaches to realizing the standards of both CEDAW and the CRC. (…) The plural mixed legal system study shows that law reform has not touched a range of discriminatory colonial and customary laws.

Whilst this looks specifically at Islam, the same can be said to an extent for other religions. The family is more often than not the locus of their vision of the child, protected by their adult caretakers rather than as bearers of rights as individuals, thus 'guardianship and custody' take centre stage. Also, where Goonesekere refers to citizenship it is in the context of nationality. It is a concept that is sometimes at odds with the notion of a global religious community (for instance, the idea of a 'Nation of Islam') that places individual rights behind the collective ones of the belief group, thus often relegating the principle of the individual civil and human rights of each person when referring to adults let alone children. Whilst most states operate secular legal systems, some are more influenced by others than one or more religions within their boundaries.

The USA and Children's Rights

In the USA a number of conservative religious organisations including the Christian Coalition, Concerned Women for America, Eagle Forum, Family Research Council, Focus on the Family, John Birch Society, National Center for Home Education and Rutherford Institute have been at the forefront of opposition to the CRC. These and other organisations made a considerable effort to represent the CRC as a threat, with the greater part of opposition claims arising from unsubstantiated concerns about national sovereignty, states' rights and the parent-child relationship. Some opponents believed the CRC arrogates national and state sovereignty, would undermine parental authority and inevitably allow and encourage children to sue parents, join gangs, have abortions and dictate how people raise and teach their children.

Those claims and assessments were a result of misconceptions, incorrect information and lack of understanding about the implementation of international human rights treaties in the USA. Extraordinarily, opponents of the CRC criticised provisions added by the Reagan and Bush Senior administrations during the drafting process that attempted to reflect rights American children have under their Constitution and were those that effectively prompted the need to have explicitly participatory rights. Right wing, fundamentalist Christian, Republican Senator Jesse Helms expressed an opinion that: "…the Convention on the Rights of the Child is incompatible with the God-given right and responsibility of parents to raise their children" and that "the Convention has the potential to severely restrict States and the Federal Government in their efforts to protect children and to enhance family life". Thus, in a doctrine that essentially teaches tolerance and respect for each other, US fundamentalists have used Christianity to underline the moral duties of the family above the possibility of protected personal rights ensured constitutionally. In fact the US Constitution never specifically mentions children as bearers of the rights it protects. In their recent book comparing children's rights in the USA with countries where it is widely accepted that children should have more rights, Albertson Fineman and Worthington (2009) call the tension between religion and human rights 'competing paradigms'.

It seems quite extraordinary that when one turns to the *travaux préparatoires* for the CRC, during the early 1980s the USA was profoundly involved in drafting what were to become participation articles 12, 13, 14 and 15 (Detrick 1992:224–96). Those are the wholly human rights based notions, mostly based on the International Bill of Human Rights. It is those the religious right finds most threatening. In roughly a decade and a half the USA went from being at the very heart of driving the drafting process to full adoption to becoming the most notorious objector to the CRC. They signed in 1995 but as yet have not signalled when they might ratify. Worldwide they are only matched by Somalia who signed in 2002 but have no internationally recognised government who would be able to ratify. In the USA the competing paradigms continue to dominate the lobby for unconditional ratification. During his presidential campaign in October 2008, President Obama was asked about the CRC and answered thus: "It's important that the United States return to its position as a global leader and promoter of human rights. It is embarrassing to find ourselves in the company of Somalia, a lawless land. I will review this and other treaties and ensure that the United States resumes its global leadership in human rights." At the time of writing this there has still been no review.

In other countries, including the UK, there has been protest, attempts to derogate or be exempted from legislation prohibiting corporal punishment by Christian groups. They often justify their stance by citing Old Testament passages in 2 *Samuel* and *Proverbs*. The key New Testament text cited in support of harsh physical punishment of children is usually *Hebrews* 12:6–7.[1] The argument essentially supports a notion of the need for hard discipline as an important part of learning to be a 'decent' and 'virtuous' adult. That line of reasoning most certainly keeps children subservient to the will of parents and elders.

The Influence of the CRC

Despite religious barriers, in fact most countries have ratified the CRC and children's rights have improved somewhat as reports to the Committee on the Rights of the Child tend to indicate. The exception is no notably great steps forward in civil and human rights terms that would give good measure of children being integrated into their societies as equal members. If anything, they are now somewhat more protected in the name of children's rights than previously and are more easily identifiable as a 'group' with needs for special provisions and protection than before.

This separation of people into identity groups is one of the issues that appear to inhibit the integration of people into a more consistent identity as equal citizens irrespective of age, gender or other status within nation states. More recently, the *Convention on the Rights of Persons with Disabilities* (CRPD) (see Appendix III) was adopted on 13 December 2006 by the United Nations in New York and opened for signature on 30 March 2007. It received its twentieth ratification on 3 April and entered into force on 3 May 2008. At the time of writing this, there have been 129 ratifications and 154 signatories out of a possible 192 countries. Those include the European Union which 'concluded' the treaty (thus, ratified it to the extent responsibilities of member states could be transferred to the EU) on 23 December 2010. The Optional Protocol to the Convention on the Rights of Persons with Disabilities has 65 ratifications and 90 signatories.

States parties must guarantee that persons with disabilities enjoy inherent rights to life on an equal basis with others (Article 10), ensure equal rights and the advancement of women and girls with disabilities (Article 6) and protect children with disabilities (Article 7). They shall have equal rights and not be separated from parents against their will, except when authorities determine that this is in their best interests.

[1] For more details look at the *Global Initiative to End All Corporal Punishment of Children*'s website on www.endcorporalpunishment.org for more details on religious groups in this context.

They should never be separated from parents on the basis of the disability of either child or parents (Article 23). Countries must also recognise that all persons are equal before the law, prohibit discrimination on the basis of disability and guarantee equal legal protection (Article 5). In short, it goes somewhat further than the CRC towards equality that begins to address issues similar to citizenship as an expression of full membership of society since the CRPD attempts to secure *full* membership of society for those it represents. Despite the guiding principle that all human rights are indivisible as with other treaties such as the CRC or those dealing with women's or ethnic rights, it does have an element of what critics of human rights treaties consider to be separation into particular human typologies and interest groups working a little counter the indivisibility principle.

On the other hand, repeating and reinforcing principles through specialised treaties reinforces standalone ones like the CRC by placing principles in more than one context to make indivisibility make sense within diversity. Whether or not that contributes toward delivering full membership of any society depends on how many of the treaties are signed and ratified by a particular state. With regard to citizenship this probably contributes very little at all. The examples in this chapter are in fact clear illustration of the dichotomies that probably work against universal principles ever being entirely possible. Indeed, one might go further and look the kind of view of citizenship propounded by Ruth Lister (1997, 1998, 2006a, b, 2008) and other feminist scholars. Those, however, are predicated on the provenance of the progress of women in Western society. Whilst they advocate for women worldwide, they tend to be more uncompromising than conciliatory and do not work well for the kind of continental regional identity the ACRWC promotes and where religion is a *force majeur* in resisting societal change in the first place.

This chapter has taken these examples of 'loose ends' in order to fill in some gaps in preceding chapters. They have been consciously separated into this chapter with a very clear objective. That is to exemplify the difficulty in applying any kind of universal principle to begin with and more so when a more abstract concept such as children's citizenship is the question to be resolved. It also rounds off foregoing chapters and moves data toward analysis and conclusion.

Children's Views on Citizenship

Whilst citizenship education is becoming more widely available to mostly secondary age but also some primary age children little is known about children's own views on their position before attaining majority. Ruth Lister and a group of colleagues have examined this question in the UK (e.g.: Lister et al. 2003; Smith et al. 2005) by talking to young people. In the first article they take young people's views from a series of interviews and in the second examined their inclusionary understanding of what citizenship is. It was based on a major qualitative study that examined young people's status as citizens. The hypothesis is that UK social policy presumes that young people do not have citizenship therefore it requires intervention to develop it. That supposition is not based on concepts of citizenship but how youth is conceived to be. Their research found that youths interviewed expressed a number of different versions of citizenship, frequently concurrently. There were particular narrow conceptions described, like the employment-oriented model that can also exclude young people. Alternatively, there were views that related to "a constructive stance towards the community" (2003: 238) that better emphasised young people's citizenship. The article concluded by recommending a more conceptually all-inclusive view of citizenship in order that young people's citizenship status as citizens becomes more acceptable.

What that research ultimately reveals without making that point overtly, is that citizenship education is informing 'citizens to be' but see that there are difference points of view depending on whether the interviewed youth see it as a social, economic or political role in their society.

The second study began with the proposition that citizenship literature includes surprisingly few empirical studies. They looked at how young people in one city perceived citizenship and their own transition into citizens. Five distinct models predominated of which the foremost was a 'universal status' which was followed by 'respectable economic independence' then 'constructive social participation' and finally, but less often, both a 'social-contractual model' and the 'right to a voice'. The degree to which the youth interview recognised themselves as citizens reflected those models and their own life experience. Clear distinctions were described between what it meant to be a 'good' and 'first class' citizens, in which respect they had greater difficulty expressing their rights rather than responsibilities. On the whole, their views drew on an assured understanding of the concept of citizenship that went more in the direction of a communitarian than either a liberal or civic-republican paradigm. One of the authors' concluding points was how comprehension of the notion of citizenship can be either inclusionary or exclusionary.

Very few studies have examined young people's views to the extent of either of these studies which are both examples of UK youth rather than offering a wider perspective. Howe and Covell (2007) in Canada, Holden and Clough's (1998) contributors looked at Australia and Europe, as well as the UK. However both books look primarily at citizenship education. Guerra (2005) examines young people's participation in governance and allocation of a municipal budget in Barra Mansa near Rio de Janeiro in Brazil. She describes a limited view of participation in civil society that, despite the title 'Citizenship Knows No Age' and including children's views on what they are doing, is not actually describing citizenship. Carbajal and Ljuslin (2012) examining the situation of illegal immigrant youth in Switzerland through their words, ask the question whether citizenship is possible but are largely confusing it with nationality and participation in civil society. These studies typically exemplify the majority of the relatively few child and youth inclusive studies that that introduce the word citizen or citizenship but then do not actually go beyond child participation. It is, therefore, very difficult to draw any real conclusions about children's views or what their expectations may be.

Chapter 12
Conclusion

History, philosophy and theology give us clear enough pictures of childhood in a few but significant sample places over the last two and a half thousand years to see that it is not entirely different at any point in that time to the present. Children have almost without exception gone through a period between birth and adulthood that whilst different in form and range of ages has always been the time in which the skills of adulthood are learned. Within those different childhoods there have been some shared responsibilities for many of them. Often those came in the form of economic roles ranging from minor domestic duties to full engagement in the labour force. Even where the latter occurred, there are only a few early industrialised countries where children worked fulltime in factories, mills and mines with little apparent time for leisure. Historically, many of those were children with no alternative care at home who accompanied parents to their workplaces. Child labour itself is as laden with assumptions and insinuations that make exceptions appear to be rules[1] as the view of the child of equal status to adult is full of romantic notions.

The three descriptive representations of childhood that emerged toward the end of the eighteenth century (for instance, see Cunningham 1991) persisted into the twentieth century. The concept of '*the changing social value of children*' expressed by Viviana Zelizer (1985) applies to children who are not 'abandoned and reared by animals', 'prodigies' and 'heroes' particularly. In other, it applied to the vast majority

[1]Recent child labour studies have moved away from the historical notion of the fully employed child without a childhood. Even where they worked they were less well paid, were not represented by unions as they emerged, had no workplace tenure as assured employment appeared and far more. Likewise, when one examines data from the period between the Factories Acts and the beginning of compulsory education in nineteenth century England one sees that one of the reasons for having compulsory school attendance was the *increased* numbers of idle children and youth who politicians felt threatened by, which tells us they were already there (For instance, see Corrigan 1979).

B. Milne, *The History and Theory of Children's Citizenship in Contemporary Societies*, DOI 10.1007/978-94-007-6521-4_12,

of children (in the Western world)[2] as the twentieth century began. That was when what had been more or less 'chattels' for centuries were capitalised, given a financial value and were being increasingly 'sacralised'. It was the period when there was unprecedented change for children. The child 'sciences' that now include developmental psychology, paediatrics and child psychiatry came into their own. As children ceased to merely be the property of parents and were gradually becoming individual bearers of rights, 'childhood' as we now know it appeared. It was often driven by new knowledge coming out of those child sciences. Some of the most significant steps toward creating child protection and welfare happened then, including contradictions between protection and participation that often stop them being full citizens.

In part these contradictions drove the incentive to give children a comprehensive set of rights that were both 'guaranteed' by being in the form of a convention that makes states parties duty bound to incorporate it into nation laws and allowed them guided participation in civil society alongside ensured protection and provision. However, no amount of examination reveals any attempt to embed full citizenship in the CRC (see Detrick 1992).[3] Thus, despite contrary views from some aficionados of children's participation, those rights are an end in themselves that have been achieved, which whilst fuelling moves in that direction are not the driving force.

Analytic induction of texts examined for this work does not draw toward a conclusion that there are historic indicators that may lead us to a view that children have ever enjoyed what we today consider full citizenship. Philosophy has occasionally alluded to the notion but never pursued it conclusively. When looking at the contribution of the child sciences and social sciences there are few indicators that point to *child citizens* in any place or at any time throughout history. Anthropology offers examples of what we would regard to be children fulfilling adult roles in their society. These are very frequently determined by the kind of economy and survival strategies they include. Similarly, there are issues relating to life cycle that include longevity, child bearing age, marriage age, symbolic adulthood and initiation ages that make those definitions unlike those we regard typical. Whilst citizenship describes membership, it is often difficult to apply that principle in a society that is idealised as egalitarian but on close inspection will almost certainly be far more layered and structured than first imagined.

When looking at governance, law and policy making and 'politics of childhood', although there are changes such as the lowering of electoral franchise in a growing number of countries, there are also countervailing forces that are reinforcing separateness. In the first instance, ages are being lowered by usually 2 years without other aspects of citizenship bestowed on youth. Furthermore, a range of measures for the protection of children against abuse and neglect, raising the age at which military

[2]Zelizer was mainly writing about the USA but her work can be extended to advanced industrial societies at comparable stages.

[3]This requires examination of the entire book, which is a Sisyphean task given its length is 712 pages.

service may begin and so on are more clearly defining the line between childhood and adulthood. Bringing together notions of *children* and *citizenship* is very recent and limited mainly to the children's rights world.

Morphological analysis of motif and event types revealed that there appeared to be no more than 12 generic narratemes. Whereas some were frequently present, many texts did not present functions necessary to construct an account of *children's citizenship* in either varying or unvarying sequence. The functions can be reproduced as:

1. Child as helpless infant (including *tabula rasa* and similar concepts).
2. Child needing nurturance and guidance.
3. Child needing good order and discipline (for instance, see conduct books or Hobbes).
4. Child should be educated (both meaning schooling and social and economic training for their future).
5. Adults (parents and others) bear responsibility for the child's life including their protection, actions, events and general demeanour (this includes 'ownership' of children; filial hierarchies such as the Confucian view, etc.).
6. Adults guide a child in choice of direction (education, career, choice of life partner and so on).
7. A child carries over traditions, family 'duties' and allegiances or loyalty (to church, partisan alignment with a political group or party, friendships, business, etc.).
8. A child grows up, gains privileges (or rewards), often in return for increased responsibilities, as he or she becomes more skilled (Locke and Rousseau).
9. A child learns the value and demands of their role described in 7 and begins to display loyalty to other adults such as community leaders, those ruling or governing them (aristocracy, monarchy, parliament, etc.) and their god or gods (except in 'atheist' states and the most secular societies).
10. The child learns the value of material and financial things ('children's businesses').
11. He or she assumes increasing responsibility to both family and society (for instance, AIDS orphans in parts of Africa).
12. He or she begins to prepare and plan for their own adulthood (initiation events and *rites de passage*, conscription into military as the 'gateway' to adulthood and citizenship; pre-university examinations, etc.).

Thereafter adulthood and citizenship are an assumed state with exceptional reasons for exclusion of the kind described in Chap. 3.

The 12 functions that are the outcome of morphological analysis describe the commonalties between different childhoods from all sources of data over the entire period this research considers and all cultural variants included over that time. They also describe most childhoods today. That is an age of children's rights and increasing awareness of the vulnerability of children that is seeing layer upon layer of protection build up. The consequence is that childhood, rather than becoming part of the lifelong continuum between birth and death, is now becoming increasingly sacralised.[4] As childhood becomes *globalised,*[5] values often instituted in the West are being disseminated globally. Thus reasons for child protection vary from universal birth registration (see Plan International 2005, 2006), all forms of child abuse and injury (see Peden et al. 2008; United Nations General Assembly 2002; United Nations 2006; Howe 2005, etc.) to increasing anxieties about issues predominating in the West[6] such as overprotection and 'demonization' (for instance, see Goldson 2000). The demonization of children seems to be very present throughout British society and increasing elsewhere. The murder of James Bulger (see Chap. 10) was good example of a key event in the British context.

In the UK and increasingly around the world, children are becoming either more protected or demonised as phenomena such as child murders, drug use, vandalism and other events attract increasingly accessible media events. The very British notion of the *anti-social behaviour order* or ASBO (see Squires 2008) as a 'criminalisation of nuisance' has exacerbated the negative representation of children and youth who are not controlled and contained. This allows such notions as 'good' and 'bad' citizens (see Chap. 3; also Milne 2005a, b: 277–83) that justify restriction or withdrawal of rights from adults. It also attempts to contain young people who are a nuisance. Strikingly, a report commissioned by the security firm ADT (ADT 2006: 26) shows that of the six European countries surveyed, Great Britain came behind Spain and France in respect of the public's feeling that anti-social behaviour was growing. Around 90 % of Spanish and 77 % of French respondents against 65 % of British people felt that was the case. There was a 'universal' attribution of the anti-social behaviour *problem* to young people (*Ibid.*:27).

Working in countries dispersed across the world over roughly the last decade has brought with it the experience of seeing increased concern about anti-social behaviour. There have been comparable views to those held in the UK expressed in Baku, Hanoi and Tbilisi. Children and youth are rejecting older values. Alcohol and drug abuse alongside increased violence including gang 'wars' and muggings are attracting media and governmental attention. Not only do the views of informants compare with, but also reproduce the British experience of the 1990s.

---

[4]The world *sacralisation* originated in the province of religion and is used when an object, idea or person is basically regarded as vulnerable or untouchable. Depending on how it is used its antonym can be either *secularisation* or *diabolisation* which both seem very far removed from the position of the child, although the latter may well describe the 'threats' to children in the world around them. It is perhaps notable that *demonization* of young people has become an issue on the contemporary agenda.

[5]There are several organisations including *Global Children's Movement, Global Movement for Children* and *Global Children's Foundation* already using the expression and *Childhood: A journal of global child research* published by Sage which is one of the most influential journals of its kind.

[6]During work in Viet Nam it has come to my notice that increasing drug use, violence and vandalism in public places, materialism (children 'must have' MP3 players, computers, etc.) and things we are already well acquainted with in the West are becoming major issues, not yet documented but encroaching on domains I have worked in such as with street child and the physical and emotional punishment of children.

Child protection is a far more complicated matter. The range of issues it entails takes in all aspects of child abuse, neglect and exploitation. Thus every issue from localised child care within families to global issues such as child labour and trafficking is included. Recently, in order to separate domains dealt with under the broad heading 'child protection', the expression *well-being* has become part of the language of protection. Thus, those children who are either potential victims of the violence and disorder or who need to be secluded from these threats require increased protection.

A 2007 report on well-being by UNICEF placed the UK bottom in a list of 21 countries. The report's authors said that they used the most up-to-date information to assess whether children felt loved, special, valued and supported within the family and community. They also looked at whether the family and community were being supported in this task by public policy and resources. British society appeared very unequal with high levels of poverty leading to children having low esteem of themselves and their lives. It portrayed a generation of young people who are unhappy, unhealthy and who engage in risky behaviour. They also have poor relationships with their family and their peers, low expectation of life and do not feel safe much of the time.

Whilst this report looked at 20 European nations and the USA, the picture of a number of other European countries is only marginally more encouraging. Much of the developing world still looks to the West as a model for their development. Children and youth are also influenced by the West to some degree. Some of the negative aspects of young lives are also giving rise to demonization of young people. As a countervailing force, protection against both allowing children to become like counterparts in the West, and against those who are already demonised, is adopting Western methods of dealing with so-called 'problems'.

To some extent these protecting, overprotecting and demonising measures are disenfranchising young people. Thus, as the 'global child' becomes more protected, the contradictory nature of the intent to extend greater participation in civil society to them becomes more complicated. It is also here that the emphasis sometimes placed on rights and participation in particular lacks persuasive qualities.

There is a second morphology that works only for more recent perceptions of the development of the individual that includes 'experiments' (one might, for instance, include Korczak's orphanages or *Bhima Sangha* in Bangalore as examples here). It applies to projects and programmes employing recent trends in children's rights and *participation* particularly. The morphemes one can bring together to assemble a taxonomy consisting of functions reproduce as follows:

1. The controlled or manipulated child who is an onlooker in an adult led project with no active role or share in decision making (many countries' family courts where the presence of children is required).
2. Present but inactive, thus as a spectator with a definable place and role but no influence of activities and decisions (typically adult sports events as a 'supporter', attending political events such as rallies or demonstrations).
3. As a member of an informed group taking part in an activity but with a latent or partial input rather than direct influence in decisions and steering actions (for

instance, a typical school trip to see a municipal council or national parliament at which children meet and are allowed to questions politicians).
4. As an active participant in an adult designed event, consulted and informed (possibly trained) and having influence over part of the situation (children's rights conferences and meetings in which adults and children co-organise, both are committee members and speakers; environmental activities such as designing 'eco-gardens' in public places).
5. As an initiator and organiser with responsibility shared with other children and one or more adult participants and direct influence and input into the event ('children's conferences' where adults participate and there are usually adult observers).
6. As a sole organiser who has direct and sole authority for the event which may also be shared with other children and in which child-initiated decisions will be shared with one or a number of adults (exclusively 'children's conferences' with adult attendance or participation but no observers, etc.).

In Korczak's orphanages one would recognise both 4 and 5 depending entirely on what the activity and degree of adult involvement was. *Bhima Sangha*'s child members' activities extend over a range of 4, 5 and 6 according to the particular event and whether it is an own event or one they are attending organised by others. Beyond this there are child only events which are excluded since they reproduce adult only actions that are not all-age-inclusive.

The latter taxonomy is based on what is almost certainly a small literature about the exception rather than the rule because most participation 'measurement' has been done in projects that do not tend to reproduce real life situations. As a consequence, it is very difficult to either combine the two taxonomies, if indeed any purpose might be served by attempting to do so. What does not emerge from either is an indicator *en route* to establishing what either tells us about the state of children being full citizens.

It is strikingly similar to Hart's eight rung ladder (1992:9). His essay attempts to address citizenship as the second part of his title, '*From tokenism to citizenship*' makes very clear. However, he does not achieve that. In his concluding pages he locates "the family as the primary setting for development of children's sense of social responsibility" (*Ibid.*:44) and sees schools as the potential domain for "the venue for fostering young people's understanding and experience of democratic participation" (*Ibid.*:43). However, schools do not yet achieve that. All in all, his analysis does not draw toward a notion of children's citizenship as his title promises.

The problem with many attempts to move beyond this kind of taxonomy is that, in common with Hart, they examine the Western world and generally look at projects and programmes in operation. Studies in 'other cultures' of the kind that have been carried out in India, Peru and throughout West Africa and looked at in this study tend to be set apart. There is perhaps a stigmatic view that assumes that democratic processes in developing nations, some of which have a less than perfect record of maintaining democracy, cannot contribute. Nonetheless, where they are included here the morphemes generated are actually very similar, thus are incorporated in the taxonomy above.

Content analysis of material used for this work also fails to reveal significant clues or indeed evidence for an argument for the existence of children having the benefit of anything at all similar to modern citizenship. Early in this work, Chaps. 4 and 6 examined antiquity and particularly looked at what has been said about childhood in two places approximately 2,500 years ago. In point of fact, much of what is *known* is little more than a 'snapshot' of a small part of all childhoods in those places. Plato recounting Socrates' thoughts only tells us a significant amount about a particular class and group but not about the entire population. The texts used for this work that describe childhood also do not achieve this end, thus what is written rather than being evidence based seems to be derived from the known conditions of adults at that time from which a certain amount of knowledge about children has been extrapolated.

Likewise, what we take from the Confucian tradition is as much reconstructed as the Socratic/Platonic world. Much of the social history of the time of K'ung Fu Tzu appears to be drawn from an equally narrow spectrum of the many different cultures, classes and social statuses and then packed out with his philosophy and interpretation and reproduction thereafter. Consequently, we know mainly about the social environment in which either philosopher lived and from which both drew their ideas. The majority of both populations consisted of people of lower class or caste who were also free but without the privileges of the elite and are almost entirely absent from history. Outsiders such as 'foreigners', servant and slave classes and outcasts are mentioned almost in passing but never adequately described in a manner that allows us to substantively *know* about them. In fact we know far more about free, privileged men than anybody else.

Historians have largely deconstructed and reconstructed what little detail there is to describe those populations. Thus children play a relatively minor role in history. However, there is enough said about them that we know they were not full citizens and in their respective ways acquired that status in a manner that has generally not changed in its essence. Children still grow up and become citizens through very clear processes. In the larger masses of the population in the Confucian world the same standard applied even where cultural practice differed and in the Hellenic world what a Socrates, Plato or Aristotle saw was the measure of how people should be. No amount of examination of texts suggests that even Spartan children had anything like equivalence to contemporary citizenship status since boys particularly and girls only slightly less were taken from parents soon after birth. For those who would gain full membership of Spartan society life became effectively a lengthy *rite de passage* until membership began. The others were left to die or became slaves.

Later in history, there is the story of St Anselm, Archbishop of Canterbury from 1093 to 1109. It tells how an abbot told Anselm about difficulties bringing up boys under his charge. He was severe, beating boys for every misdemeanour. Anselm could not contain dislike for that treatment and reprimanded the abbot for unreasonable and cruel treatment of the boys. He believed that compassion and reason would succeed instead and thus came to be regarded a 'pioneer' of child protection. The entire story is handed down rather than an actual record, first written by his biographer Eadmer (Southern 1972) in about 1,124.

It is a very brief, basically anecdotal, account that time has embellished and contributed to the 'spare the rod and spoil the child' debate that persists to the present. The *conduct books* that appeared around two centuries later show that little had changed and made the incongruous character of the 'little adult' view transparent. Although children were expected to behave *like* adults and doubtless played a key role in the economic survival of families with specific responsibilities, they were nonetheless being 'brought up'. The regime was severe and Anselm's recommended compassion and reason was going to have to wait until the second half of the twentieth century before it became an 'expected' standard.

Between the Anselm story and the extensive data that can be taken from conduct books we have the contrast of an anecdote upon which little reconstruction and elucidation of another side of history is virtually impossible. The conduct books explicitly describe and warn of the weak nature and bad behaviour of children without rigid control and often severe regime. It does not at all suggest objectivity but is consistent, replicable and its contribution to testing the hypothesis is toward disproving rather than proving children had a citizen-like status in any sense in European societies. Elsewhere so many cultural traits are constant that, when there are eventually exceptions such as different notions of childhood in pre-modern societies such as hunter gatherers, pastoralists, itinerant and nomadic groups or isolated island communities, they are more exceptional that normative. Nevertheless, whenever closely scrutinised they contain sufficient breaks, diversions and omissions to suggest missing causes and formative structures in ethnographies that do not set out to look at children. That makes it possible to reconstruct and expound another dimension in which enough data has usually been found. It proves often that whilst generally shorter than contemporary western equivalents, there is nonetheless a very distinct childhood.

It is only when we draw near the contemporary world and an embryonic notion of children's rights that appears in the work of visionaries such as Montessori, Korczak or Dewey that there are indicators toward a concept of the child as citizen. As the twentieth century progressed it becomes particularly strongly reinforced by those looking at moral development such as Kohlberg. Children's liberationists attempted to deliver an egalitarian notion that children should have the right to decide for themselves in matters that directly concern them. It was a radical proposition advanced by children's liberationists in the 1970s (for instance: Firestone 1970; Farson 1974; Holt 1975) that did not enter the thoughts of lawmakers until the mid-1980s by when drafting of the CRC was well advanced. In due course, Articles 13–16 were to be taken in as a modified form of the same principles in the International Covenant on Civil and Political Rights and International Covenant on Economic, Social and Cultural Rights that deliver children the same basic human rights as everybody else. At this point in time analysis takes one in the other direction and where there are omissions particularly, but also breaks and diversions in children's rights literature, we are drawn toward 'participation' texts particularly.

Whilst on the surface promoting age-free values and apparent egalitarianism within those texts, there is much indicative of separatism in the way projects are clearly set up *for* children. There is a new set of values that describe participation in a manner that, quintessentially, mirrors variables that could apply equally as well to adults. Following the example of Hart's eight rungs on his 'ladder' one can very easily transpose participation from 'token participation' to 'full inclusion and participation' in most western democracies. Bearing in mind that Hart (1992:8) tells us "the ladder metaphor is borrowed from an article on adult participation…", we already know that the situation of children is compared to that of adults. In the original version (Arnstein 1969:216–24) the article looks at what was then a controversy that had been disputed mainly in terms of aggravated rhetoric and disingenuous euphemisms.

The debate was chiefly over 'citizen participation', 'citizen control' and the 'maximum feasible involvement of the poor'. Arnstein's article was written to stimulate an enlightened discourse in which typologies of citizen participation were proposed using examples from three federal social programmes in the USA. Those were urban renewal, anti-poverty and model cities. Her typology was designed to be provocative and set out as a ladder pattern. Each rung corresponded to the extent of citizens' power in determining their part in particular plan or programme elements.

Hart's version is a modification in which most possible degrees between exclusion and inclusion are found. Whilst this suggests that the situation of children is comparable with adults, the separate nature of projects and models demonstrating how that operates makes it exactly that: comparable but not equal.

Thus, when we draw together conclusions drawn from three analytical methods we find only scant evidence for there ever having been an equal status for adults and children in the past or present and only very few experiments and projects at present moving toward that goal.

There are however domains in which children are increasingly gaining a foothold and sharing decision making. In medicine, informed consent and the kind of study carried out with premature neonates and siblings of ill and dying children (Alderson 1993; Alderson et al. 2005a, b; Bluebond-Langner 1980, 1989, 1996) is drawing children into responsibility for their own lives. They are treated as *the* patient and even at age 5 if they have the wish are drawn into the process. As with adults, the choice is with them. The last word is with adult caretakers, but as Bluebond-Langner so eloquently describes them, they are capable of expressing their desire to die[7] rather than undergo prolonged and sometimes painful treatment that may only buy a little time rather than give them the chance to grow into adulthood. She also uses the concept of the 'shadow' of illness on families, especially siblings and shows how they too share in decision making, taking responsibility and attempting, also like adults, to understand impending bereavement.

Education now has school councils active in many countries in which varying degrees of responsibility (see Edwards 2001; The Citizenship Foundation 1998) are

[7]Myra Bluebond-Langner has not only worked with dying children (1978) but the reason she uses the expression 'private worlds' in her title becomes patently clear when one reads the interviews and how wise those sick children appear to be.

shared with teachers and governors.[8] Many are probably more of an 'alibi function' than a *bona fide* partnership between adults and children, although there are discussions, shared decisions and some schools now put candidates for teaching posts to the test by having them interviewed by children.[9] Despite the increased share in decision making, the role of children in governance and operation of schools remains generally limited.

Thus medicine and education are giving children *some* duties for themselves and others that also carry great responsibilities. Children sometimes do things some, if not many, adults find difficult or even impossible to do. They have the attributes that theoretically qualify them whilst many adults might be disqualified from citizenship if such criteria were the measure of who is or is not fully accepted as a citizen.

Where there is an enormous barrier to overcome is where social theory, law and policy making and political ideology have the greatest potential for driving change. The *tabula rasa* notion that persists almost unchallenged despite the work of such people as Kohlberg (1984) or Alderson et al. (2005a, b) justifies a preference for a perception of the *human* or *citizen becoming* as a means of permitting only minor and slow change. Indeed little seems to have changed since Jean-Jacques Rousseau wrote in Book Two of *Émile* that:

> Nature wants children to be children before they are men. If we try to pervert this order we shall produce a forced fruit that will have neither ripeness nor flavour and that will soon spoil. We will have young doctors and old children. Childhood has its ways of seeing, thinking, and feeling that are proper to it. Nothing is less sensible than to try and substitute our ways. I would like no more to require a young child be five feet tall than that he have judgement at the age of ten. Indeed, what use would reason be to him at that age? It is the curb of strength, and the child does not need this curb. (1979: 258)

Some objections to an idea of a child as an equal to an adult were also expressed in his Preface, whereby he says:

> We know nothing of childhood, and with our mistaken notions the further we advance the further we go astray. The wisest writers devote themselves to what a man ought to know without asking what a child is capable of learning. They are always looking for the man in the child without considering what he is before he becomes a man. (*Ibid.*:3)

Examination of two and a half millennia of history, philosophy, theology and the more recent contribution of literature, child sciences, the social sciences and other sources show how close Rousseau still is to the truth. We know *little* of childhood.

---

[8]I am using the British term *governor*, in fact school boards take a large variety of forms that include teachers, administrators, parents, local politicians and officials, etc., and increasingly have either a link to the school council or (as in Welsh secondary schools for example) that council has representation on the board of governors, directors or whatever form it takes who share varying degrees of decision making with at least full share in the Netherlands and parts of Germany at the pinnacle of that role.

[9]The Swansea school where I had two children and formerly served as parent governor and link governor to the school council, children from Year 1 (age 6) upward had interviewed all permanent post candidates for at least 3 years.

One of the main reasons for this is that there is no single childhood, as too there is no single standard by which to measure or define what it is.

In some ways children's rights are the 'red herring' here since the framework they exist within gives an impression of a standard. This too contributes to the weakness of the child participation approach. It takes 'samples' of children in very few places, thus contributes little to developing a notion of the young citizen. One of the greatest flaws is the lack of a definitive statement. There is an open question: what are children participating in? Since most work on participation is related to 'projects' it does not tend to look at civil society broadly. Citizenship, on the other hand, means full membership of civil society with its attendant privileges, rights along with duties and responsibilities. The CRC draws on the International Bill of Human Rights[10] for civil and human rights for children, with only the exception of Article 12 (see Appendix I) that assures children who are capable of forming views the right to express them. It does not seek to extend economic and political rights to them. Furthermore, it is very restrained in how far it proposes a share of duties and responsibilities that are part of citizenship to children. An 'evolving capacities' principle in Article 5 also makes that a conditional matter that belief, custom, law and the maturity of each individual regulate. Children's rights and the proposition of most participation projects, including those in the CRC, fall short of describing or leading to full citizenship.

During the early to mid 1970s a number of authors (e.g. Adams et al. 1971; Farson 1974; Holt 1975) were writing about children's rights well before the drafting of the CRC began in 1979. One of their key themes was 'liberation' and closer examination of what they were expressing takes us further in the direction of citizenship for children that children's rights came out in the CRC in 1989. It is as if the experts who drafted the CRC steered clear of these predominantly US authors cum activists for the human rights of children.

In 1973 Hillary Rodham (now Clinton) was then a practicing lawyer who sometimes worked in the area of children's rights. She wrote an article in which she said children's rights was a 'slogan in need of a definition' (Rodham 1973). Some experts still claim that children's rights are still not well defined, indeed that there is no conventionally accepted definition or theory of the rights given to children. Extraordinarily, Rodham did not enter into arguments about liberation and citizenship despite her contemporaries being engaged on those topics. Equally extraordinary is that 20 years after her article was published, her husband became President of the USA. He did not appear to have advice from her on what action to take. Whilst the USA had an active role in drafting the Convention and signed it in 1995, they did not ratify it during his time in office nor have they since. It may be that the spirit of the work of predominantly US authors who wanted far more than the CRC offers hangs over the USA like 'the sword of Damocles' with constitutional implications.

[10]This is made up of the International Covenant on Economic, Social and Cultural Rights, International Covenant on Civil and Political Rights and Optional Protocol to the latter (see also Chap. 7).

It is perhaps ironic that ratification of this convention could put children closer to becoming citizens in the USA than in nations who were early signatories and ratified soon thereafter. There are precedents that point in that direction.

In 1865 the Thirteenth Amendment to the Constitution formally outlawed slavery and involuntary servitude, except where it was punishment for convicted criminals. This was followed by the Fourteenth Amendment of 1868 that granted full citizenship to African Americans. The Fifteenth Amendment of 1870 prohibited denial of the right to vote based on a citizen's race, colour or having been a slave. It was ratified on February 3, 1870. The Nineteenth Amendment prohibits any United States citizen to be denied the right to vote based on sex. It was first introduced it in 1878 but it was 41 in 1919 that Congress submitted the amendment to the states for ratification and it came into effect in 1920. The Constitution previously allowed states to determine qualifications for voting, and until the amendment went through Congress most states disenfranchised women. Effectively all US nationals except minors in law are full citizens. The precedents, along with opposition to the CRC from political and religious conservatives and organisations such as the Heritage Foundation which sees it as a threat to national control over domestic policy, appear to stand in the way (see also: Chap. 11, subheading 'The USA and children's rights').

Another approach to citizenship is that pursued by Manfred Liebel (see Liebel 2000, 2004, 2007a, b; Liebel et al. 2001, 2008). On the one hand, he looks at a range of premises such as liberal and republican theories, whereby he comes to the conclusion that only the latter offers the possibility of citizenship to children.

On the other hand he examines the question from his own experience in the field in Peru. Amongst the indigenous people of the Andes he found child members of community councils. His view is that this is a possible doorway to full membership of civil society. My own view, using my own experience of Peru and the Andean indigenous people particularly, is that it mostly certainly is *participation* in civil society but with very limited scope for expansion into full citizenship. The indigenous people have been marginalised by dominant groups who control political life in their country. These are predominantly European or *mestizo* (of mixed heritage or descent) and practice something similar to *apartheid* that more or less reduces the political participation of indigenous people to local civil politics only. It does not, therefore, open any manner of door to full membership, thus citizenship.

Eliana Guerra (2005) describes how children in the municipality of Barra Mansa in Brazil are actively involved in governance and use of the municipal budget. However, their participation is rather more limited to issues and expenditure in child related areas than to the overall business of their municipal council. Under other circumstances, both Liebel and Guerra's researches may be very good models on which to base a hypothesis that children have the skills required to contribute to society as full citizens. However, such examples are very few, thus by and large remain to be tried, tested and proven more widely.

Liebel also shares the view of a number of people who believe children's movements, particularly working children's movements that exist in several parts of the world, as another doorway to participation in civil society. To some extent they do, they are actively engaged in political activities in defence of their rights and also to extend them to acknowledge their role in society. Most children's movements are adult initiated and led, but children do make or at least vote on all actions and decisions. They also educate their members on their rights, citizenship and a number of other qualities and values that are part of citizenship whether they are held by adults or not. The problem is that most of the working children's movements are in countries where there is a contradiction between the policy of governments who aim to eliminate all child labour and the reality at ground level. Other children's movements still only have a small minority of children in their country in their membership; therefore do not have a great deal of political influence. Both are again examples of active participation in some aspects of civil society, particularly on the political periphery, but tend not to open doors to children achieving full citizenship. What they do achieve is preparation of children for citizenship by introducing them to democratic processes such a choosing candidates, voting, taking part in public actions, discussion and debate and other skills that even some adults do not possess (see also: Chap. 9, subheading 'Education and children's participation').

Thus said, it is most certain that a large part of the answer to the question here is within the different childhoods and social environments in which they exist. Whilst childhood, like citizenship, is not homogeneous there is little likelihood that despite the encroaching use of 'global citizenship' as a term to describe the adoption of some universal values, particularly in areas of child protection such as prevention of various forms of exploitation of children, in fact any single nation state will extend the full rights of citizen to its children in the foreseeable future. It remains, in that sense, far more a romantic notion. However, what is imaginable is that, as with medicine and education, children will slowly gain greater access to citizen-like qualities and privileges. Therewith, as one nation observes change in others it will diffuse with time. Beyond that there also needs to be radical change worldwide so that adults who are excluded from citizenship, meaning both nationality and full participation in civil society as bearers of all rights, are given full membership so that their children may inherit the same.

In order to fully explain, and perhaps even to justify, the *exclusion* of children from full citizenship one is confronted with a teleological rationalisation of what *inclusion* might mean. When looking at an essentially western, democratic version of what citizenship is in a modern secular world, the development of civil, social and political rights in liberal democracies that have a relatively short history beginning with the French and American Revolutions provide answers in both directions. Arguably children already share virtually all cultural rights and many social rights with adults. It is in the areas of economic and political rights, thus their agency in those domains, that inclusion becomes a 'loaded' issue. In the economic sphere children are heavily protected against the inexorable burden of fiscal duties and responsibilities that would fall on them if they had full economic rights. They are also protected against exploitation on the basis of their immaturity and inexperience. However one might argue that in both cases even adults do not always appear to be adequately able to deal with either. However deeply one looks into the question of children as economic actors it is unlikely that the answers deviate very far from a protection motif.

However politics are not actually much better. Here children are not comparably protected from the political domain, but are generally seen as lacking in the necessary skills to understand it. Thus it remains easy to exclude them from political franchise with small concessions to lower voting ages but not as often the ages at which children can assume political office. Simultaneously we have the paradox of the growing global trend toward schools councils, children's municipalities and so on that expose children to the type of political process that is the limit of most citizens' experience. Ironically children tend to be closer to the people they elect in their schools and communities than most adults are to people they elect. Therefore children have greater opportunities for learning about the consequences of bad choices than adult counterparts. Thus it is difficult to see where *inclusion* is not justifiable. However, the weight of history tends to come down on the side of inexperience as the final word. Furthermore, as the morphological analysis of history describes, it shows the necessity for a continuation of a view of childhood as a period of 'becoming' in which the evolving capacities of the child *prove* the need for prudence rather than impetuous change. Of course, to the discerning historian this may be familiar since it bears many of the properties of resistance to the emancipation of women.

How far does the romantic view of a past in which there was little or no difference between children and adults contribute to these conclusions? Firstly, history as presented by authors such as Ariès is too selective to warrant much more examination than has been afforded in this work. Secondly, Golden Age and utopian views appear to contribute even less. They either describe imagined pasts when a search for eternal youth blurs the distinctions between children and adults or generally fail to include children at all. They also tell of 'egalitarian' societies that are often anything but that, as indeed *Utopia* very specifically does.

Particularly useful elements of Golden Age and utopian ideas have been used as principles by political extremes such as the German and Italian fascist movements from the 1920s to 1940s and socialist societies like the Soviet Union or People's Republic of China. Hannah Arendt (1962: for instance: 348, 366 [footnote 6 in Chap. 9]) analysed the origins of totalitarian regimes. She observed that children's and youth movements were used to underpin social control, reaching into family and community. Those movements and organisations set them aside by their ages in order to groom them for the adulthood the state desired them to reach. In such societies youth is highly valued but inclusion controlled. Citizen's rights are usually not among the principles on which those societies were founded to begin with. In them children are usually very far from being full citizens. There are numerous exclusions from citizenship for all ages anyway. Otherwise, apart from small groups of 'hippies', 'New Agers' and their ilk, there is little application of those notions.

It is perhaps then not extraordinary that a work of literature, *Les Misérables*, gives an appropriate closing note. It is set at the time of the French Revolution when all people were considered equal by revolutionaries who gave France the motto *Liberté, Égalité, Fraternité* (Liberty, Equality, Fraternity). Petit Gavroche is an exemplar of a child, albeit a fictional character never referred to or addressed as citizen (*citoyen*) although it was the form of address between adult revolutionaries of both sexes. When he is shot dead (Hugo 1994:822), he is simply a "little great soul". That death is heroic but his final actions are shown as defiant and playful. He epitomises Dominique Julia's (Becchi and Julia 2004:85) hero typology, in many respects it describes all of the positive and courageous qualities the exemplary child should bear. However, he was different, an outsider and street child, frivolous and childish. He was never the citizen and whilst the hero, never acknowledged for that quality. *Égalité* and *Fraternité* were not for children, only for citizens – adults. As it was then, so it is today and will almost certainly remain so for the immediate future.

There is a repeated theme of the child in a state of change or becoming. This reflects the Aristotelian 'becoming' process (see Chap. 2). It is given special critical attention by Qvortrup (see Chap. 8) and arises elsewhere in differently expressed but amounting to much the same thing, Moosa-Mitha (see Chap. 8) is critical of 'citizen becomings' or 'potential citizens' in liberal theory and 'not-yet-citizens' (see Chap. 4). It is a notion that is arises too often to be excluded as the dominant view, thus a very difficult hurdle to overcome.

Is children's citizenship thus consigned to being a romantic notion rather than a future reality? Two centuries ago the best informed people would have said women would never have gained full citizenship rights. It may have been their opinion that women should be 'liberated'. They certainly had access to knowledge of parts of the world and history that evidenced the need for change. Children have neither. However, we live in a world where a basic principle of human rights is that *all people* are equal. Since that includes age, the principle must be that we work toward that end. The question is resolved by assuming that if we arrive at a stage when egalitarian human rights principles are all operational, that it is a natural outcome. If human rights in general follow the course of women's rights then we may conclude that with time it should be an inevitable outcome.

In Chap. 2, Gorgias' *On Non-Existence* which examines the notion that '*nothing exists*' was used as part of my basis for raising the initial question. The session in which it was debated concluded that since *nothing* could be the subject of debate it must exist. In that sense, the fact that *children's citizenship* is receiving attention would signify that it likewise exists. A lively debate is required in order to put substance to it, make it an incontrovertible right and in time to amend such instruments as the CRC to fully acknowledge that reality. It is clearly not something that will happen universally in the short term and that does not excuse any discouragement of progress toward that goal in the longer term. It requires at least one country to take the courage and initiative to grant their children full citizenship, thereafter make it work and provide incontrovertible evidence for other states to take the same steps. At that point in time it ceases to be a romance and become a reality.

Appendices

Appendix I

Convention on the Rights of the Child
Adopted by the General Assembly of the United Nations on 20 November 1989

Preamble
The States Parties to the present Convention,

Considering that, in accordance with the principles proclaimed in the Charter of the United Nations, recognition of the inherent dignity and of the equal and inalienable rights of all members of the human family is the foundation of freedom, justice and peace in the world,

Bearing in mind that the peoples of the United Nations have, in the Charter, reaffirmed their faith in fundamental human rights and in the dignity and worth of the human person, and have determined to promote social progress and better standards of life in larger freedom,

Recognizing that the United Nations has, in the Universal Declaration of Human Rights and in the International Covenants on Human Rights, proclaimed and agreed that everyone is entitled to all the rights and freedoms set forth therein, without distinction of any kind, such as race, colour, sex, language, religion, political or other opinion, national or social origin, property, birth or other status,

Recalling that, in the Universal Declaration of Human Rights, the United Nations has proclaimed that childhood is entitled to special care and assistance,

Convinced that the family, as the fundamental group of society and the natural environment for the growth and well-being of all its members and particularly children, should be afforded the necessary protection and assistance so that it can fully assume its responsibilities within the community,

Recognizing that the child, for the full and harmonious development of his or her personality, should grow up in a family environment, in an atmosphere of happiness, love and understanding,

B. Milne, *The History and Theory of Children's Citizenship in Contemporary Societies*,
DOI 10.1007/978-94-007-6521-4,

Considering that the child should be fully prepared to live an individual life in society, and brought up in the spirit of the ideals proclaimed in the Charter of the United Nations, and in particular in the spirit of peace, dignity, tolerance, freedom, equality and solidarity,

Bearing in mind that the need to extend particular care to the child has been stated in the Geneva Declaration of the Rights of the Child of 1924 and in the Declaration of the Rights of the Child adopted by the United Nations on 20 November 1959 and recognized in the Universal Declaration of Human Rights, in the International Covenant on Civil and Political Rights (in particular in articles 23 and 24), in the International Covenant on Economic, Social and Cultural Rights (in particular in article 10) and in the statutes and relevant instruments of specialized agencies and international organizations concerned with the welfare of children,

Bearing in mind that, as indicated in the Declaration of the Rights of the Child, "the child, by reason of his physical and mental immaturity, needs special safeguards and care, including appropriate legal protection, before as well as after birth",

Recalling the provisions of the Declaration on Social and Legal Principles relating to the Protection and Welfare of Children, with Special Reference to Foster Placement and Adoption Nationally and Internationally; the United Nations Standard Minimum Rules for the Administration of Juvenile Justice ("The Beijing Rules"); and the Declaration on the Protection of Women and Children in Emergency and Armed Conflict,

Recognizing that, in all countries in the world, there are children living in exceptionally difficult conditions, and that such children need special consideration,

Taking due account of the importance of the traditions and cultural values of each people for the protection and harmonious development of the child, Recognizing the importance of international co-operation for improving the living conditions of children in every country, in particular in the developing countries,

Have agreed as follows:

Part I

Article 1

For the purposes of the present Convention, a child means every human being below the age of 18 years unless, under the law applicable to the child, majority is attained earlier.

Article 2

1. States Parties shall respect and ensure the rights set forth in the present Convention to each child within their jurisdiction without discrimination of any kind, irrespective of the child's or his or her parent's or legal guardian's race, colour, sex, language, religion, political or other opinion, national, ethnic or social origin, property, disability, birth or other status.
2. States Parties shall take all appropriate measures to ensure that the child is protected against all forms of discrimination or punishment on the basis of the status, activities, expressed opinions, or beliefs of the child's parents, legal guardians, or family members.

Article 3

1. In all actions concerning children, whether undertaken by public or private social welfare institutions, courts of law, administrative authorities or legislative bodies, the best interests of the child shall be a primary consideration.
2. States Parties undertake to ensure the child such protection and care as is necessary for his or her well-being, taking into account the rights and duties of his or her parents, legal guardians, or other individuals legally responsible for him or her, and, to this end, shall take all appropriate legislative and administrative measures.
3. States Parties shall ensure that the institutions, services and facilities responsible for the care or protection of children shall conform with the standards established by competent authorities, particularly in the areas of safety, health, in the number and suitability of their staff, as well as competent supervision.

Article 4

States Parties shall undertake all appropriate legislative, administrative, and other measures for the implementation of the rights recognized in the present Convention. With regard to economic, social and cultural rights, States Parties shall undertake such measures to the maximum extent of their available resources and, where needed, within the framework of international co-operation.

Article 5

States Parties shall respect the responsibilities, rights and duties of parents or, where applicable, the members of the extended family or community as provided for by local custom, legal guardians or other persons legally responsible for the child, to provide, in a manner consistent with the evolving capacities of the child, appropriate direction and guidance in the exercise by the child of the rights recognized in the present Convention.

Article 6

1. States Parties recognize that every child has the inherent right to life.
2. States Parties shall ensure to the maximum extent possible the survival and development of the child.

Article 7

1. The child shall be registered immediately after birth and shall have the right from birth to a name, the right to acquire a nationality and, as far as possible, the right to know and be cared for by his or her parents.
2. States Parties shall ensure the implementation of these rights in accordance with their national law and their obligations under the relevant international instruments in this field, in particular where the child would otherwise be stateless.

Article 8

1. States Parties undertake to respect the right of the child to preserve his or her identity, including nationality, name and family relations as recognized by law without unlawful interference.

2. Where a child is illegally deprived of some or all of the elements of his or her identity, States Parties shall provide appropriate assistance and protection, with a view to speedily re-establishing his or her identity.

Article 9

1. States Parties shall ensure that a child shall not be separated from his or her parents against their will, except when competent authorities subject to judicial review determine, in accordance with applicable law and procedures, that such separation is necessary for the best interests of the child. Such determination may be necessary in a particular case such as one involving abuse or neglect of the child by the parents, or one where the parents are living separately and a decision must be made as to the child's place of residence.
2. In any proceedings pursuant to paragraph 1 of the present article, all interested parties shall be given an opportunity to participate in the proceedings and make their views known.
3. States Parties shall respect the right of the child who is separated from one or both parents to maintain personal relations and direct contact with both parents on a regular basis, except if it is contrary to the child's best interests.
4. Where such separation results from any action initiated by a State Party, such as the detention, imprisonment, exile, deportation or death (including death arising from any cause while the person is in the custody of the State) of one or both parents or of the child, that State Party shall, upon request, provide the parents, the child or, if appropriate, another member of the family with the essential information concerning the whereabouts of the absent member(s) of the family unless the provision of the information would be detrimental to the well-being of the child. States Parties shall further ensure that the submission of such a request shall of itself entail no adverse consequences for the person(s) concerned.

Article 10

1. In accordance with the obligation of States Parties under article 9, paragraph 1, applications by a child or his or her parents to enter or leave a State Party for the purpose of family reunification shall be dealt with by States Parties in a positive, humane and expeditious manner. States Parties shall further ensure that the submission of such a request shall entail no adverse consequences for the applicants and for the members of their family.
2. A child whose parents reside in different States shall have the right to maintain on a regular basis, save in exceptional circumstances personal relations and direct contacts with both parents. Towards that end and in accordance with the obligation of States Parties under article 9, paragraph 1, States Parties shall respect the right of the child and his or her parents to leave any country, including their own, and to enter their own country. The right to leave any country shall be subject only to such restrictions as are prescribed by law and which are necessary to protect the national security, public order (*ordre public*), public health or morals or the rights and freedoms of others and are consistent with the other rights recognized in the present Convention.

Article 11

1. States Parties shall take measures to combat the illicit transfer and non-return of children abroad.
2. To this end, States Parties shall promote the conclusion of bilateral or multilateral agreements or accession to existing agreements.

Article 12

1. States Parties shall assure to the child who is capable of forming his or her own views the right to express those views freely in all matters affecting the child, the views of the child being given due weight in accordance with the age and maturity of the child.
2. For this purpose, the child shall in particular be provided the opportunity to be heard in any judicial and administrative proceedings affecting the child, either directly, or through a representative or an appropriate body, in a manner consistent with the procedural rules of national law.

Article 13

1. The child shall have the right to freedom of expression; this right shall include freedom to seek, receive and impart information and ideas of all kinds, regardless of frontiers, either orally, in writing or in print, in the form of art, or through any other media of the child's choice.
2. The exercise of this right may be subject to certain restrictions, but these shall only be such as are provided by law and are necessary:

   (a) For respect of the rights or reputations of others; or
   (b) For the protection of national security or of public order (*ordre public*), or of public health or morals.

Article 14

1. States Parties shall respect the right of the child to freedom of thought, conscience and religion.
2. States Parties shall respect the rights and duties of the parents and, when applicable, legal guardians, to provide direction to the child in the exercise of his or her right in a manner consistent with the evolving capacities of the child.
3. Freedom to manifest one's religion or beliefs may be subject only to such limitations as are prescribed by law and are necessary to protect public safety, order, health or morals, or the fundamental rights and freedoms of others.

Article 15

1. States Parties recognize the rights of the child to freedom of association and to freedom of peaceful assembly.
2. No restrictions may be placed on the exercise of these rights other than those imposed in conformity with the law and which are necessary in a democratic society in the interests of national security or public safety, public order (ordre public), the protection of public health or morals or the protection of the rights and freedoms of others.

Article 16

1. No child shall be subjected to arbitrary or unlawful interference with his or her privacy, family, home or correspondence, nor to unlawful attacks on his or her honour and reputation.
2. The child has the right to the protection of the law against such interference or attacks.

Article 17

States Parties recognize the important function performed by the mass media and shall ensure that the child has access to information and material from a diversity of national and international sources, especially those aimed at the promotion of his or her social, spiritual and moral well-being and physical and mental health. To this end, States Parties shall:

(a) Encourage the mass media to disseminate information and material of social and cultural benefit to the child and in accordance with the spirit of article 29;
(b) Encourage international co-operation in the production, exchange and dissemination of such information and material from a diversity of cultural, national and international sources;
(c) Encourage the production and dissemination of children's books;
(d) Encourage the mass media to have particular regard to the linguistic needs of the child who belongs to a minority group or who is indigenous;
(e) Encourage the development of appropriate guidelines for the protection of the child from information and material injurious to his or her well-being, bearing in mind the provisions of articles 13 and 18.

Article 18

1. States Parties shall use their best efforts to ensure recognition of the principle that both parents have common responsibilities for the upbringing and development of the child. Parents or, as the case may be, legal guardians, have the primary responsibility for the upbringing and development of the child. The best interests of the child will be their basic concern.
2. For the purpose of guaranteeing and promoting the rights set forth in the present Convention, States Parties shall render appropriate assistance to parents and legal guardians in the performance of their child-rearing responsibilities and shall ensure the development of institutions, facilities and services for the care of children.
3. States Parties shall take all appropriate measures to ensure that children of working parents have the right to benefit from child-care services and facilities for which they are eligible.

Article 19

1. States Parties shall take all appropriate legislative, administrative, social and educational measures to protect the child from all forms of physical or mental violence, injury or abuse, neglect or negligent treatment, maltreatment or exploitation, including sexual abuse, while in the care of parent(s), legal guardian(s) or any other person who has the care of the child.

2. Such protective measures should, as appropriate, include effective procedures for the establishment of social programmes to provide necessary support for the child and for those who have the care of the child, as well as for other forms of prevention and for identification, reporting, referral, investigation, treatment and follow-up of instances of child maltreatment described heretofore, and, as appropriate, for judicial involvement.

Article 20

1. A child temporarily or permanently deprived of his or her family environment, or in whose own best interests cannot be allowed to remain in that environment, shall be entitled to special protection and assistance provided by the State.
2. States Parties shall in accordance with their national laws ensure alternative care for such a child.
3. Such care could include, *inter alia*, foster placement, Kafala of Islamic law, adoption, or if necessary placement in suitable institutions for the care of children. When considering solutions, due regard shall be paid to the desirability of continuity in a child's upbringing and to thc child's ethnic, religious, cultural and linguistic background.

Article 21
States Parties that recognize and/or permit the system of adoption shall ensure that the best interests of the child shall be the paramount consideration and they shall:

(a) Ensure that the adoption of a child is authorized only by competent authorities who determine, in accordance with applicable law and procedures and on the basis of all pertinent and reliable information, that the adoption is permissible in view of the child's status concerning parents, relatives and legal guardians and that, if required, the persons concerned have given their informed consent to the adoption on the basis of such counselling as may be necessary;
(b) Recognize that inter-country adoption may be considered as an alternative means of child's care, if the child cannot be placed in a foster or an adoptive family or cannot in any suitable manner be cared for in the child's country of origin;
(c) Ensure that the child concerned by intercountry adoption enjoys safeguards and standards equivalent to those existing in the case of national adoption;
(d) Take all appropriate measures to ensure that, in intercountry adoption, the placement does not result in improper financial gain for those involved in it;
(e) Promote, where appropriate, the objectives of the present article by concluding bilateral or multilateral arrangements or agreements, and endeavour, within this framework, to ensure that the placement of the child in another country is carried out by competent authorities or organs.

Article 22

1. States Parties shall take appropriate measures to ensure that a child who is seeking refugee status or who is considered a refugee in accordance with applicable international or domestic law and procedures shall, whether unaccompanied or

accompanied by his or her parents or by any other person, receive appropriate protection and humanitarian assistance in the enjoyment of applicable rights set forth in the present Convention and in other international human rights or humanitarian instruments to which the said States are Parties.

2. For this purpose, States Parties shall provide, as they consider appropriate, co-operation in any efforts by the United Nations and other competent intergovernmental organizations or non-governmental organizations co-operating with the United Nations to protect and assist such a child and to trace the parents or other members of the family of any refugee child in order to obtain information necessary for reunification with his or her family. In cases where no parents or other members of the family can be found, the child shall be accorded the same protection as any other child permanently or temporarily deprived of his or her family environment for any reason, as set forth in the present Convention.

Article 23

1. States Parties recognize that a mentally or physically disabled child should enjoy a full and decent life, in conditions which ensure dignity, promote self-reliance, and facilitate the child's active participation in the community.
2. States Parties recognize the right of the disabled child to special care and shall encourage and ensure the extension, subject to available resources, to the eligible child and those responsible for his or her care, of assistance for which application is made and which is appropriate to the child's condition and to the circumstances of the parents or others caring for the child.
3. Recognizing the special needs of a disabled child, assistance extended in accordance with paragraph 2 of the present article shall be provided free of charge, whenever possible, taking into account the financial resources of the parents or others caring for the child, and shall be designed to ensure that the disabled child has effective access to and receives education, training, health care services, rehabilitation services, preparation for employment and recreation opportunities in a manner conducive to the child's achieving the fullest possible social integration and individual development, including his or her cultural and spiritual development.
4. States Parties shall promote, in the spirit of international co-operation, the exchange of appropriate information in the field of preventive health care and of medical, psychological and functional treatment of disabled children, including dissemination of and access to information concerning methods of rehabilitation, education and vocational services, with the aim of enabling States Parties to improve their capabilities and skills and to widen their experience in these areas. In this regard, particular account shall be taken of the needs of developing countries.

Article 24

1. States Parties recognize the right of the child to the enjoyment of the highest attainable standard of health and to facilities for the treatment of illness and rehabilitation of health. States Parties shall strive to ensure that no child is deprived of his or her right of access to such health care services.

2. States Parties shall pursue full implementation of this right and, in particular, shall take appropriate measures:

    (a) To diminish infant and child mortality;
    (b) To ensure the provision of necessary medical assistance and health care to all children with emphasis on the development of primary health care;
    (c) To combat disease and malnutrition including within the framework of primary health care, through inter alia the application of readily available technology and through the provision of adequate nutritious foods and clean drinking water, taking into consideration the dangers and risks of environmental pollution;
    (d) To ensure appropriate pre-natal and post-natal health care for mothers;
    (e) To ensure that all segments of society, in particular parents and children, are informed, have access to education and are supported in the use of basic knowledge of child health and nutrition, the advantages of breast-feeding, hygiene and environmental sanitation and the prevention of accidents;
    (f) To develop preventive health care, guidance for parents and family planning education and services.

3. States Parties shall take all effective and appropriate measures with a view to abolishing traditional practices prejudicial to the health of children.
4. States Parties undertake to promote and encourage international co-operation with a view to achieving progressively the full realization of the right recognized in the present article. In this regard, particular account shall be taken of the needs of developing countries.

Article 25
States Parties recognize the right of a child who has been placed by the competent authorities for the purposes of care, protection or treatment of his or her physical or mental health, to a periodic review of the treatment provided to the child and all other circumstances relevant to his or her placement.

Article 26

1. States Parties shall recognize for every child the right to benefit from social security, including social insurance, and shall take the necessary measures to achieve the full realization of this right in accordance with their national law.
2. The benefits should, where appropriate, be granted, taking into account the resources and the circumstances of the child and persons having responsibility for the maintenance of the child, as well as any other consideration relevant to an application for benefits made by or on behalf of the child.

Article 27

1. States Parties recognize the right of every child to a standard of living adequate for the child's physical, mental, spiritual, moral and social development.
2. The parent(s) or others responsible for the child have the primary responsibility to secure, within their abilities and financial capacities, the conditions of living necessary for the child's development.

3. States Parties, in accordance with national conditions and within their means, shall take appropriate measures to assist parents and others responsible for the child to implement this right and shall in case of need provide material assistance and support programmes, particularly with regard to nutrition, clothing and housing.
4. States Parties shall take all appropriate measures to secure the recovery of maintenance for the child from the parents or other persons having financial responsibility for the child, both within the State Party and from abroad. In particular, where the person having financial responsibility for the child lives in a State different from that of the child, States Parties shall promote the accession to international agreements or the conclusion of such agreements, as well as the making of other appropriate arrangements.

Article 28

1. States Parties recognize the right of the child to education, and with a view to achieving this right progressively and on the basis of equal opportunity, they shall, in particular:

   (a) Make primary education compulsory and available free to all;
   (b) Encourage the development of different forms of secondary education, including general and vocational education, make them available and accessible to every child, and take appropriate measures such as the introduction of free education and offering financial assistance in case of need;
   (c) Make higher education accessible to all on the basis of capacity by every appropriate means;
   (d) Make educational and vocational information and guidance available and accessible to all children;
   (e) Take measures to encourage regular attendance at schools and the reduction of drop-out rates.

2. States Parties shall take all appropriate measures to ensure that school discipline is administered in a manner consistent with the child's human dignity and in conformity with the present Convention.
3. States Parties shall promote and encourage international co-operation in matters relating to education, in particular with a view to contributing to the elimination of ignorance and illiteracy throughout the world and facilitating access to scientific and technical knowledge and modern teaching methods. In this regard, particular account shall be taken of the needs of developing countries.

Article 29

1. States Parties agree that the education of the child shall be directed to:

   (a) The development of the child's personality, talents and mental and physical abilities to their fullest potential;
   (b) The development of respect for human rights and fundamental freedoms, and for the principles enshrined in the Charter of the United Nations;

(c) The development of respect for the child's parents, his or her own cultural identity, language and values, for the national values of the country in which the child is living, the country from which he or she may originate, and for civilizations different from his or her own;
(d) The preparation of the child for responsible life in a free society, in the spirit of understanding, peace, tolerance, equality of sexes, and friendship among all peoples, ethnic, national and religious groups and persons of indigenous origin;
(e) The development of respect for the natural environment.

2. No part of the present article or article 28 shall be construed so as to interfere with the liberty of individuals and bodies to establish and direct educational institutions, subject always to the observance of the principles set forth in paragraph 1 of the present article and to the requirements that the education given in such institutions shall conform to such minimum standards as may be laid down by the State.

Article 30

In those States in which ethnic, religious or linguistic minorities or persons of indigenous origin exist, a child belonging to such a minority or who is indigenous shall not be denied the right, in community with other members of his or her group, to enjoy his or her own culture, to profess and practise his or her own religion, or to use his or her own language.

Article 31

1. States Parties recognize the right of the child to rest and leisure, to engage in play and recreational activities appropriate to the age of the child and to participate freely in cultural life and the arts.
2. States Parties shall respect and promote the right of the child to participate fully in cultural and artistic life and shall encourage the provision of appropriate and equal opportunities for cultural, artistic, recreational and leisure activity.

Article 32

1. States Parties recognize the right of the child to be protected from economic exploitation and from performing any work that is likely to be hazardous or to interfere with the child's education, or to be harmful to the child's health or physical, mental, spiritual, moral or social development.
2. States Parties shall take legislative, administrative, social and educational measures to ensure the implementation of the present article. To this end, and having regard to the relevant provisions of other international instruments, States Parties shall in particular:

   (a) Provide for a minimum age or minimum ages for admissions to employment;
   (b) Provide for appropriate regulation of the hours and conditions of employment;
   (c) Provide for appropriate penalties or other sanctions to ensure the effective enforcement of the present article.

Article 33
States Parties shall take all appropriate measures, including legislative, administrative, social and educational measures, to protect children from the illicit use of narcotic drugs and psychotropic substances as defined in the relevant international treaties, and to prevent the use of children in the illicit production and trafficking of such substances.

Article 34
States Parties undertake to protect the child from all forms of sexual exploitation and sexual abuse. For these purposes, States Parties shall in particular take all appropriate national, bilateral and multilateral measures to prevent:

(a) The inducement or coercion of a child to engage in any unlawful sexual activity;
(b) The exploitative use of children in prostitution or other unlawful sexual practices;
(c) The exploitative use of children in pornographic performances and materials.

Article 35
States Parties shall take all appropriate national, bilateral and multilateral measures to prevent the abduction of, the sale of or traffic in children for any purpose or in any form.

Article 36
States Parties shall protect the child against all other forms of exploitation prejudicial to any aspects of the child's welfare.

Article 37
States Parties shall ensure that:

(a) No child shall be subjected to torture or other cruel, inhuman or degrading treatment or punishment. Neither capital punishment nor life imprisonment without possibility of release shall be imposed for offences committed by persons below 18 years of age;
(b) No child shall be deprived of his or her liberty unlawfully or arbitrarily. The arrest, detention or imprisonment of a child shall be in conformity with the law and shall be used only as a measure of last resort and for the shortest appropriate period of time;
(c) Every child deprived of liberty shall be treated with humanity and respect for the inherent dignity of the human person, and in a manner which takes into account the needs of persons of his or her age. In particular every child deprived of liberty shall be separated from adults unless it is considered in the child's best interest not to do so and shall have the right to maintain contact with his or her family through correspondence and visits, save in exceptional circumstances;
(d) Every child deprived of his or her liberty shall have the right to prompt access to legal and other appropriate assistance, as well as the right to challenge the legality of the deprivation of his or her liberty before a court or other competent, independent and impartial authority, and to a prompt decision on any such action.

Article 38

1. States Parties undertake to respect and to ensure respect for rules of international humanitarian law applicable to them in armed conflicts which are relevant to the child.
2. States Parties shall take all feasible measures to ensure that persons who have not attained the age of 15 years do not take a direct part in hostilities.
3. States Parties shall refrain from recruiting any person who has not attained the age of 15 years into their armed forces. In recruiting among those persons who have attained the age of 15 years but who have not attained the age of 18 years, States Parties shall endeavour to give priority to those who are oldest.
4. In accordance with their obligations under international humanitarian law to protect the civilian population in armed conflicts, States Parties shall take all feasible measures to ensure protection and care of children who are affected by an armed conflict.

Article 39
States Parties shall take all appropriate measures to promote physical and psychological recovery and social reintegration of a child victim of: any form of neglect, exploitation, or abuse; torture or any other form of cruel, inhuman or degrading treatment or punishment; or armed conflicts. Such recovery and reintegration shall take place in an environment which fosters the health, self-respect and dignity of the child.

Article 40

1. States Parties recognize the right of every child alleged as, accused of, or recognized as having infringed the penal law to be treated in a manner consistent with the promotion of the child's sense of dignity and worth, which reinforces the child's respect for the human rights and fundamental freedoms of others and which takes into account the child's age and the desirability of promoting the child's reintegration and the child's assuming a constructive role in society.
2. To this end, and having regard to the relevant provisions of international instruments, States Parties shall, in particular, ensure that:

   (a) No child shall be alleged as, be accused of, or recognized as having infringed the penal law by reason of acts or omissions that were not prohibited by national or international law at the time they were committed;
   (b) Every child alleged as or accused of having infringed the penal law has at least the following guarantees:

      (i) To be presumed innocent until proven guilty according to law;
      (ii) To be informed promptly and directly of the charges against him or her, and, if appropriate, through his or her parents or legal guardians, and to have legal or other appropriate assistance in the preparation and presentation of his or her defence;
      (iii) To have the matter determined without delay by a competent, independent and impartial authority or judicial body in a fair hearing according to law, in the presence of legal or other appropriate assistance and,

unless it is considered not to be in the best interest of the child, in particular, taking into account his or her age or situation, his or her parents or legal guardians;

(iv) Not to be compelled to give testimony or to confess guilt; to examine or have examined adverse witnesses and to obtain the participation and examination of witnesses on his or her behalf under conditions of equality;

(v) If considered to have infringed the penal law, to have this decision and any measures imposed in consequence thereof reviewed by a higher competent, independent and impartial authority or judicial body according to law;

(vi) To have the free assistance of an interpreter if the child cannot understand or speak the language used;

(vii) To have his or her privacy fully respected at all stages of the proceedings.

3. States Parties shall seek to promote the establishment of laws, procedures, authorities and institutions specifically applicable to children alleged as, accused of, or recognized as having infringed the penal law, and, in particular:

   (a) the establishment of a minimum age below which children shall be presumed not to have the capacity to infringe the penal law;
   (b) whenever appropriate and desirable, measures for dealing with such children without resorting to judicial proceedings, providing that human rights and legal safeguards are fully respected.

4. A variety of dispositions, such as care, guidance and supervision orders; counselling; probation; foster care; education and vocational training programmes and other alternatives to institutional care shall be available to ensure that children are dealt with in a manner appropriate to their well-being and proportionate both to their circumstances and the offence.

Article 41

Nothing in the present Convention shall affect any provisions which are more conducive to the realization of the rights of the child and which may be contained in:

(a) The law of a State Party; or
(b) International law in force for that State.

Part II

Article 42

States Parties undertake to make the principles and provisions of the Convention widely known, by appropriate and active means, to adults and children alike.

Article 43

1. For the purpose of examining the progress made by States Parties in achieving the realization of the obligations undertaken in the present Convention, there shall be established a Committee on the Rights of the Child, which shall carry out the functions hereinafter provided.

2. The Committee shall consist of eighteen experts of high moral standing and recognized competence in the field covered by this Convention.[1]

   The members of the Committee shall be elected by States Parties from among their nationals and shall serve in their personal capacity, consideration being given to equitable geographical distribution, as well as to the principal legal systems.
3. The members of the Committee shall be elected by secret ballot from a list of persons nominated by States Parties. Each State Party may nominate one person from among its own nationals.
4. The initial election to the Committee shall be held no later than six months after the date of the entry into force of the present Convention and thereafter every second year. At least four months before the date of each election, the Secretary-General of the United Nations shall address a letter to States Parties inviting them to submit their nominations within two months. The Secretary-General shall subsequently prepare a list in alphabetical order of all persons thus nominated, indicating States Parties which have nominated them, and shall submit it to the States Parties to the present Convention.
5. The elections shall be held at meetings of States Parties convened by the Secretary-General at United Nations Headquarters. At those meetings, for which two thirds of States Parties shall constitute a quorum, the persons elected to the Committee shall be those who obtain the largest number of votes and an absolute majority of the votes of the representatives of States Parties present and voting.
6. The members of the Committee shall be elected for a term of four years. They shall be eligible for re-election if renominated. The term of five of the members elected at the first election shall expire at the end of two years; immediately after the first election, the names of these five members shall be chosen by lot by the Chairman of the meeting.
7. If a member of the Committee dies or resigns or declares that for any other cause he or she can no longer perform the duties of the Committee, the State Party which nominated the member shall appoint another expert from among its nationals to serve for the remainder of the term, subject to the approval of the Committee.
8. The Committee shall establish its own rules of procedure.
9. The Committee shall elect its officers for a period of two years.
10. The meetings of the Committee shall normally be held at United Nations Headquarters or at any other convenient place as determined by the Committee. The Committee shall normally meet annually. The duration of the meetings of the Committee shall be determined, and reviewed, if necessary, by a meeting of the States Parties to the present Convention, subject to the approval of the General Assembly.

---

[1] The General Assembly, in its resolution 50/155 of 21 December 1995, approved the amendment to article 43, paragraph 2, of the Convention on the Rights of the Child, replacing the word "ten" with the word "eighteen". The amendment entered into force on 18 November 2002 when it had been accepted by a two-thirds majority of the States parties (128 out of 191).

11. The Secretary-General of the United Nations shall provide the necessary staff and facilities for the effective performance of the functions of the Committee under the present Convention.
12. With the approval of the General Assembly, the members of the Committee established under the present Convention shall receive emoluments from the United Nations resources on such terms and conditions as the Assembly may decide.

Article 44

1. States Parties undertake to submit to the Committee, through the Secretary-General of the United Nations, reports on the measures they have adopted which give effect to the rights recognized herein and on the progress made on the enjoyment of those rights:

   (a) Within two years of the entry into force of the Convention for the State Party concerned,
   (b) Thereafter every five years.

2. Reports made under the present article shall indicate factors and difficulties, if any, affecting the degree of fulfilment of the obligations under the present Convention. Reports shall also contain sufficient information to provide the Committee with a comprehensive understanding of the implementation of the Convention in the country concerned.
3. A State Party which has submitted a comprehensive initial report to the Committee need not in its subsequent reports submitted in accordance with paragraph 1(b) of the present article repeat basic information previously provided.
4. The Committee may request from States Parties further information relevant to the implementation of the Convention.
5. The Committee shall submit to the General Assembly, through the Economic and Social Council, every two years, reports on its activities.
6. States Parties shall make their reports widely available to the public in their own countries.

Article 45

In order to foster the effective implementation of the Convention and to encourage international co-operation in the field covered by the Convention:

(a) The specialized agencies, the United Nations Children's Fund and other United Nations organs shall be entitled to be represented at the consideration of the implementation of such provisions of the present Convention as fall within the scope of their mandate. The Committee may invite the specialized agencies, the United Nations Children's Fund and other competent bodies as it may consider appropriate to provide expert advice on the implementation of the Convention in areas falling within the scope of their respective mandates. The Committee may invite the specialized agencies, the United Nations Children's Fund and other United Nations organs to submit reports on the implementation of the Convention in areas falling within the scope of their activities;

(b) The Committee shall transmit, as it may consider appropriate, to the specialized agencies, the United Nations Children's Fund and other competent bodies, any reports from States Parties that contain a request, or indicate a need, for technical advice or assistance, along with the Committee's observations and suggestions, if any, on these requests or indications;
(c) The Committee may recommend to the General Assembly to request the Secretary-General to undertake on its behalf studies on specific issues relating to the rights of the child;
(d) The Committee may make suggestions and general recommendations based on information received pursuant to articles 44 and 45 of the present Convention. Such suggestions and general recommendations shall be transmitted to any State Party concerned and reported to the General Assembly, together with comments, if any, from States Parties.

Part III

Article 46
The present Convention shall be open for signature by all States.

Article 47
The present Convention is subject to ratification. Instruments of ratification shall be deposited with the Secretary-General of the United Nations.

Article 48
The present Convention shall remain open for accession by any State. The instruments of accession shall be deposited with the Secretary-General of the United Nations.

Article 49

1. The present Convention shall enter into force on the thirtieth day following the date of deposit with the Secretary-General of the United Nations of the twentieth instrument of ratification or accession.
2. For each State ratifying or acceding to the Convention after the deposit of the twentieth instrument of ratification or accession, the Convention shall enter into force on the thirtieth day after the deposit by such State of its instrument of ratification or accession.

Article 50

1. Any State Party may propose an amendment and file it with the Secretary-General of the United Nations. The Secretary-General shall thereupon communicate the proposed amendment to States Parties, with a request that they indicate whether they favour a conference of States Parties for the purpose of considering and voting upon the proposals. In the event that, within four months from the date of such communication, at least one third of the States Parties favour such a conference, the Secretary-General shall convene the conference under the auspices of the United Nations. Any amendment adopted by a majority of States Parties present and voting at the conference shall be submitted to the General Assembly for approval.

2. An amendment adopted in accordance with paragraph 1 of the present article shall enter into force when it has been approved by the General Assembly of the United Nations and accepted by a two-thirds majority of States Parties.
3. When an amendment enters into force, it shall be binding on those States Parties which have accepted it, other States Parties still being bound by the provisions of the present Convention and any earlier amendments which they have accepted.

Article 51

1. The Secretary-General of the United Nations shall receive and circulate to all States the text of reservations made by States at the time of ratification or accession.
2. A reservation incompatible with the object and purpose of the present Convention shall not be permitted.
3. Reservations may be withdrawn at any time by notification to that effect addressed to the Secretary-General of the United Nations, who shall then inform all States. Such notification shall take effect on the date on which it is received by the Secretary-General.

Article 52
A State Party may denounce the present Convention by written notification to the Secretary-General of the United Nations. Denunciation becomes effective one year after the date of receipt of the notification by the Secretary-General.

Article 53
The Secretary-General of the United Nations is designated as the depositary of the present Convention.

Article 54
The original of the present Convention, of which the Arabic, Chinese, English, French, Russian and Spanish texts are equally authentic, shall be deposited with the Secretary-General of the United Nations.

In witness thereof the undersigned plenipotentiaries, being duly authorized thereto by their respective Governments, have signed the present Convention.

There are also two options protocols:

Optional Protocol on the involvement of children in armed conflict

Optional Protocol on the sale of children, child prostitution and child pornography

Appendix II

African Charter on the Rights and Welfare of the Child, OAU Doc. CAB/LEG/24.9/49 (1990), entered into force Nov. 29, 1999. (Extracts)

PREAMBLE

The African Member States of the Organization of African Unity, Parties to the present Charter entitled 'African Charter on the Rights and Welfare of the Child',

CONSIDERING that the Charter of the Organization of African Unity recognizes the paramountcy of Human Rights and the African Charter on Human and People's Rights proclaimed and agreed that everyone is entitled to all the rights and freedoms recognized and guaranteed therein, without distinction of any kind such as race, ethnic group, colour. sex, language, religion, political or any other opinion, national and social origin, fortune, birth or other status,

RECALLING the Declaration on the Rights and WeLfare of the African Child (AHG/ST.4 Rev.l) adopted by the Assembly of Heads of State and Government of the Organization of African Unity, at its Sixteenth Ordinary Session in Monrovia, Liberia. From 17 to 20 July 1979, recognized the need to take appropriate measures to promote and protect the rights and welfare of the African Child,

NOTING WITH CONCERN that the situation of most African children, remains critical due to the unique factors of their socio-economic, cultural, traditional and developmental circumstances, natural disasters, armed conflicts, exploitation and hunger, and on account of the child's physical and mental immaturity he/she needs special safeguards and care,

RECOGNIZING that the child occupies a unique and privileged position in the African society and that for the full and harmonious development of his personality. the child should grow up in a family environment in an atmosphere of happiness, love and understanding,

RECOGNIZING that the child, due to the needs of his physical and mental development requires particular care with regard to health, physical, mental, moral and social development. and requires legal protection in conditions of freedom, dignity and security,

TAKING INTO CONSIDERATION the virtues of their cultural heritage, historical background and the values of the African civilization which should inspire and characterize their reflection on the concept of the rights and welfare of the child,

CONSIDERING that the promotion and protection of the rights and welfare of the child also implies the performance of duties on the part of everyone,

REAFFIRMING ADHERENCE Lo the principles of the rights and welfare of the child contained in the declaration, conventions and other instruments of the Organization of African Unity and in the United Nations and in particular the United Nations Convention on the Rights of the Child; and the OAU Heads of State and Government's Declaration on the Rights and Welfare of the African Child.

HAVE AGREED AS FOLLOWS:

PART 1: RIGHTS AND DUTIES

CHAPTER ONE: RIGHTS AND WELFARE OF THE CHILD

Article 1: Obligation of States Parties

1. Member States of the Organization of African Unity Parties to the present Charter shall recognize the rights, freedoms and duties enshrined in this Charter and shall undertake to the necessary steps, in accordance with their Constitutional processes and with the provisions of the present Charter, to adopt such legislative or other measures as may be necessary to give effect to the provisions of this Charter.
2. Nothing in this Charter shall affect any provisions that are more conductive to the realization of the rights and welfare of the child contained in the law of a State Party or in any other international Convention or agreement in force in that State.
3. Any custom, tradition, cultural or religious practice that is inconsistent with the rights, duties and obligations contained in the present Charter shall to the extent of such inconsistency be discouraged.

Article 2: Definition of a Child

For the purposes of this Charter, a child means every human being below the age of 18 years.

Article 3: Non-Discrimination

Every child shall be entitled to the enjoyment of the rights and freedoms recognized and guaranteed in this Charter irrespective of the child's or his/her parents' or legal guardians' race, ethnic group, colour, sex, language, religion, political or other opinion, national and social origin, fortune, birth or other status.

Article 4: Best Interests of the Child

1. In all actions concerning the child undertaken by any person or authority the best interests of the child shall be the primary consideration.
2. In all judicial or administrative proceedings affecting a child who is capable of communicating his/her own views, and opportunity shall be provided for the views of the child to be heard either directly or through an impartial representative as a party to the proceedings. and those views shall be taken into consideration by the relevant authority in accordance with the provisions of appropriate law.

Article 5: Survival and Development

1. Every child has an inherent right to life. This right shall be protected by law.
2. States Parties to the present Charter shall ensure, to the maximum extent possible, the survival, protection and development of the child.
3. Death sentence shall not be pronounced for crimes committed by children.

Article 6: Name and Nationality

1. Every child shall have the right from his birth to a name.
2. Every child shall be registered immediately after birth.
3. Every child has the right to acquire a nationality.
4. States Parties to the present Charter shall undertake to ensure that their Constitutional legislation recognize the principles according to which a child shall acquire the nationality of the State in the territory of which he has been born if, at the time of the child's birth, he is not granted nationality by any other State in accordance with its laws.

Article 7: Freedom of Expression
Every child who is capable of communicating his or her own views shall be assured the rights to express his opinions freely in all matters and to disseminate his opinions subject to such restrictions as are prescribed by laws.

Article 8: Freedom of Association
Every child shall have the right to free association and freedom of peaceful assembly in conformity with the law.

Article 9: Freedom of Thought, Conscience and Religion

1. Every child shall have the right to freedom of thought conscience and religion.
2. Parents. and where applicable, legal guardians shall have a duty to provide guidance and direction in the exercise of these rights having regard to the evolving capacities, and best interests of the child.
3. States Parties shall respect the duty of parents and where applicable, legal guardians to provide guidance and direction in the enjoyment of these rights subject to the national laws and policies.

Article 10: Protection of Privacy
No child shall be subject to arbitrary or unlawful interference with his privacy, family home or correspondence, or to the attacks upon his honour or reputation, provided that parents or legal guardians shall have the right to exercise reasonable supervision over the conduct of their children. The child has the right to the protection of the law against such interference or attacks.

Article 31: Responsibility of the Child
Every child shall have responsibilities towards his family and society, the State and other legally recognized communities and the international community. The child, subject to his age and ability, and such limitations as may be contained in the present Charter, shall have the duty;

(a) to work for the cohesion of the family, to respect his parents, superiors and elders at all times and to assist them in case of need;
(b) to serve his national community by placing his physical and intellectual abilities at its service;
(c) to preserve and strengthen social and national solidarity;

(d) to preserve and strengthen African cultural values in his relations with other members of the society, in the spirit of tolerance, dialogue and consultation and to contribute to the moral well-being of society;
(e) to preserve and strengthen the independence and the integrity of his country;
(f) to contribute to the best of his abilities, at all times and at all levels, to the promotion and achievement of Afncan Unity.

CHAPTER THREE: MANDATE AND PROCEDURE OF THE COMMITTEE

Article 42: Mandate

The functions of the Committee shall be:

(a) To promote and protect the rights enshrined in this Charter and in particular to:

  (i) collect and document information, commission inter-disciplinary assessment of situations on African problems in the fields of the rights and welfare of the child, organize meetings, encourage national and local institutions concerned with the rights and welfare of the child, and where necessary give its views and make recommendations to Governments;
  (ii) formulate and lay down principles and rules aimed at protecting the rights and welfare of children in Africa;
  (iii) cooperate with other African, international and regional Institutions and organizations concerned with the promotion and protection of the rights and welfare of the child.

(b) To monitor the implementation and ensure protection of the rights enshrined in this Charter.
(c) To interpret the provisions of the present Charter at the request of a State Party, an Institution of the Organization of African Unity or any other person or Institution recognized by the Organization of African Unity, or any State Party.
(d) Perform such other task as may be entrusted to it by the Assembly of Heads of State and Government, Secretary-General of the OAU and any other organs of the OAU or the United Nations.

Article 43: Reporting Procedure

1. Every State Party to the present Charter shall undertake to submit to the Committee through the Secretary-General of the Organization of African Unity, reports on the measures they have adopted which give effect to the provisions of this Charter and on the progress made in the enjoyment of these rights:

   (a) within two years of the entry into force of the Charter for the State Party concerned: and
   (b) and thereafter, *every three years.*

2. Every report made under this Article shall:

   (a) contain sufficient information on the implementation of the present Charter to provide the Committee with comprehensive understanding of the implementation of the Charter in the relevant country; and

(b) shall indicate factors and difficulties, if any, affecting the fullfilment of the obligations contained in the Charter.

3. A State Party which has submitted a comprehensive first report to the Committee need not, in its subsequent reports submitted in accordance with paragraph I (a) of this Article, repeat the basic information previously provided.

Article 44: Communications

1. The Committee may receive communication, from any person, group or non-governmental organization recognized by the Organization of African Unity, by a Member State, or the United Nations relating to any matter covered by this Charter.
2. Every communication to the Committee shall contain the name and address of the author and shall be treated in confidence.

Article 45: Investigations by the Committee

1. The Committee may, resort to any appropriate method of investigating any matter falling within the ambit of the present Charter, request from the States Parties any information relevant to the implementation of the Charter and may also resort to any appropriate method of investigating the measures the State Party has adopted to implement the Charter.
2. The Committee shall submit to each Ordinary Session of the Assembly of Heads of State and Government every two years, a report on its activities and on any communication made under Article [44] of this Charter.
3. The Committee shall publish its report after it has been considered by the Assembly of Heads of State and Government.
4. States Parties shall make the Committee's reports widely available to the public in their own countries.

CHAPTER FOUR: MISCELLANEOUS PROVISIONS

Article 46: Sources of Inspiration

The Committee shall draw inspiration from International Law on Human Rights, particularly from the provisions of the African Charter on Human and Peoples' Rights, the Charter of the Organization of African Unity, the Universal Declaration on Human Rights, the International Convention on the Rights of the Child, and other instruments adopted by the United Nations and by African countries in the field of human rights. and from African values and traditions

Appendix III

European Convention on the Exercise of Children's Rights (Extracts)

Strasbourg, 25.I.1996

PREAMBLE

The member States of the Council of Europe and the other States signatory hereto,

Considering that the aim of the Council of Europe is to achieve greater unity between its members;

Having regard to the United Nations Convention on the rights of the child and in particular Article 4 which requires States Parties to undertake all appropriate legislative, administrative and other measures for the implementation of the rights recognised in the said Convention;

Noting the contents of Recommendation 1121 (1990) of the Parliamentary Assembly on the rights of the child;

Convinced that the rights and best interests of children should be promoted and to that end children should have the opportunity to exercise their rights, in particular in family proceedings affecting them;

Recognising that children should be provided with relevant information to enable such rights and best interests to be promoted and that due weight should be given to the views of children;

Recognising the importance of the parental role in protecting and promoting the rights and best interests of children and considering that, where necessary, States should also engage in such protection and promotion;

Considering, however, that in the event of conflict it is desirable for families to try to reach agreement before bringing the matter before a judicial authority,

Have agreed as follows:

CHAPTER I – SCOPE AND OBJECT OF THE CONVENTION AND DEFINITIONS

Article 1 – Scope and object of the Convention

This Convention shall apply to children who have not reached the age of 18 years.

The object of the present Convention is, in the best interests of children, to promote their rights, to grant them procedural rights and to facilitate the exercise of these rights by ensuring that children are, themselves or through other persons or bodies, informed and allowed to participate in proceedings affecting them before a judicial authority.

For the purposes of this Convention proceedings before a judicial authority affecting children are family proceedings, in particular those involving the exercise of parental responsibilities such as residence and access to children.

Every State shall, at the time of signature or when depositing its instrument of ratification, acceptance, approval or accession, by a declaration addressed to the Secretary

General of the Council of Europe, specify at least three categories of family cases before a judicial authority to which this Convention is to apply.

Any Party may, by further declaration, specify additional categories of family cases to which this Convention is to apply or provide information concerning the application of Article 5, paragraph 2 of Article 9, paragraph 2 of Article 10 and Article 11.

Nothing in this Convention shall prevent Parties from applying rules more favourable to the promotion and the exercise of children's rights.

Article 2 – Definitions

For the purposes of this Convention:

the term "judicial authority" means a court or an administrative authority having equivalent powers;

the term "holders of parental responsibilities" means parents and other persons or bodies entitled to exercise some or all parental responsibilities;

the term "representative" means a person, such as a lawyer, or a body appointed to act before a judicial authority on behalf of a child;

the term "relevant information" means information which is appropriate to the age and understanding of the child, and which will be given to enable the child to exercise his or her rights fully unless the provision of such information were contrary to the welfare of the child.

CHAPTER II – PROCEDURAL MEASURES TO PROMOTE THE EXERCISE OF CHILDREN'S

RIGHTS

A. PROCEDURAL RIGHTS OF A CHILD

Article 3 – Right to be informed and to express his or her views in proceedings

A child considered by internal law as having sufficient understanding, in the case of proceedings before a judicial authority affecting him or her, shall be granted, and shall be entitled to request, the following rights:

to receive all relevant information;

to be consulted and express his or her views;

to be informed of the possible consequences of compliance with these views and the possible consequences of any decision.

Appendix IV

Convention on the Rights of Persons with Disabilities (Extracts)

Preamble

The States Parties to the present Convention,

(a) *Recalling* the principles proclaimed in the Charter of the United Nations which recognize the inherent dignity and worth and the equal and inalienable rights of all members of the human family as the foundation of freedom, justice and peace in the world,
(b) *Recognizing* that the United Nations, in the Universal Declaration of Human Rights and in the International Covenants on Human Rights, has proclaimed and agreed that everyone is entitled to all the rights and freedoms set forth therein, without distinction of any kind,
(c) *Reaffirming* the universality, indivisibility, interdependence and interrelatedness of all human rights and fundamental freedoms and the need for persons with disabilities to be guaranteed their full enjoyment without discrimination,
(d) *Recalling* the International Covenant on Economic, Social and Cultural Rights, the International Covenant on Civil and Political Rights, the International Convention on the Elimination of All Forms of Racial Discrimination, the Convention on the Elimination of All Forms of Discrimination against Women, the Convention against Torture and Other Cruel, Inhuman or Degrading Treatment or Punishment, the Convention on the Rights of the Child, and the International Convention on the Protection of the Rights of All Migrant Workers and Members of Their Families,
(e) *Recognizing* that disability is an evolving concept and that disability results from the interaction between persons with impairments and attitudinal and environmental barriers that hinders their full and effective participation in society on an equal basis with others,
(f) *Recognizing* the importance of the principles and policy guidelines contained in the World Programme of Action concerning Disabled Persons and in the Standard Rules on the Equalization of Opportunities for Persons with Disabilities in influencing the promotion, formulation and evaluation of the policies, plans, programmes and actions at the national, regional and international levels to further equalize opportunities for persons with disabilities,
(g) *Emphasizing* the importance of mainstreaming disability issues as an integral part of relevant strategies of sustainable development,
(h) *Recognizing also* that discrimination against any person on the basis of disability is a violation of the inherent dignity and worth of the human person,
(i) *Recognizing further* the diversity of persons with disabilities,
(j) *Recognizing* the need to promote and protect the human rights of all persons with disabilities, including those who require more intensive support,

(k) *Concerned* that, despite these various instruments and undertakings, persons with disabilities continue to face barriers in their participation as equal members of society and violations of their human rights in all parts of the world,

(l) *Recognizing* the importance of international cooperation for improving the living conditions of persons with disabilities in every country, particularly in developing countries,

(m) *Recognizing* the valued existing and potential contributions made by persons with disabilities to the overall well-being and diversity of their communities, and that the promotion of the full enjoyment by persons with disabilities of their human rights and fundamental freedoms and of full participation by persons with disabilities will result in their enhanced sense of belonging and in significant advances in the human, social and economic development of society and the eradication of poverty,

(n) *Recognizing* the importance for persons with disabilities of their individual autonomy and independence, including the freedom to make their own choices,

(o) *Considering* that persons with disabilities should have the opportunity to be actively involved in decision-making processes about policies and programmes, including those directly concerning them,

(p) *Concerned* about the difficult conditions faced by persons with disabilities who are subject to multiple or aggravated forms of discrimination on the basis of race, colour, sex, language, religion, political or other opinion, national, ethnic, indigenous or social origin, property, birth, age or other status,

(q) *Recognizing* that women and girls with disabilities are often at greater risk, both within and outside the home, of violence, injury or abuse, neglect or negligent treatment, maltreatment or exploitation,

(r) *Recognizing* that children with disabilities should have full enjoyment of all human rights and fundamental freedoms on an equal basis with other children, and recalling obligations to that end undertaken by States Parties to the Convention on the Rights of the Child,

(s) *Emphasizing* the need to incorporate a gender perspective in all efforts to promote the full enjoyment of human rights and fundamental freedoms by persons with disabilities,

(t) *Highlighting* the fact that the majority of persons with disabilities live in conditions of poverty, and in this regard recognizing the critical need to address the negative impact of poverty on persons with disabilities,

(u) *Bearing in mind* that conditions of peace and security based on full respect for the purposes and principles contained in the Charter of the United Nations and observance of applicable human rights instruments are indispensable for the full protection of persons with disabilities, in particular during armed conflicts and foreign occupation,

(v) *Recognizing* the importance of accessibility to the physical, social, economic and cultural environment, to health and education and to information and communication, in enabling persons with disabilities to fully enjoy all human rights and fundamental freedoms,

(w) *Realizing* that the individual, having duties to other individuals and to the community to which he or she belongs, is under a responsibility to strive for the promotion and observance of the rights recognized in the International Bill of Human Rights,
(x) *Convinced* that the family is the natural and fundamental group unit of society and is entitled to protection by society and the State, and that persons with disabilities and their family members should receive the necessary protection and assistance to enable families to contribute towards the full and equal enjoyment of the rights of persons with disabilities,
(y) *Convinced* that a comprehensive and integral international convention to promote and protect the rights and dignity of persons with disabilities will make a significant contribution to redressing the profound social disadvantage of persons with disabilities and promote their participation in the civil, political, economic, social and cultural spheres with equal opportunities, in both developing and developed countries,

Have agreed as follows:

Article 1

Purpose
The purpose of the present Convention is to promote, protect and ensure the full and equal enjoyment of all human rights and fundamental freedoms by all persons with disabilities, and to promote respect for their inherent dignity. Persons with disabilities include those who have long-term physical, mental, intellectual or sensory impairments which in interaction with various barriers may hinder their full and effective participation in society on an equal basis with others.

Article 2

Definitions
For the purposes of the present Convention:

"Communication" includes languages, display of text, Braille, tactile communication, large print, accessible multimedia as well as written, audio, plain-language, human-reader and augmentative and alternative modes, means and formats of communication, including accessible information and communication technology;

"Language" includes spoken and signed languages and other forms of non spoken languages;

"Discrimination on the basis of disability" means any distinction, exclusion or restriction on the basis of disability which has the purpose or effect of impairing or nullifying the recognition, enjoyment or exercise, on an equal basis with others, of all human rights and fundamental freedoms in the political, economic, social, cultural, civil or any other field. It includes all forms of discrimination, including denial of reasonable accommodation;

"Reasonable accommodation" means necessary and appropriate modification and adjustments not imposing a disproportionate or undue burden, where needed in a particular case, to ensure to persons with disabilities the enjoyment or exercise on an equal basis with others of all human rights and fundamental freedoms;

"Universal design" means the design of products, environments, programmes and services to be usable by all people, to the greatest extent possible, without the need for adaptation or specialized design.

"Universal design" shall not exclude assistive devices for particular groups of persons with disabilities where this is needed.

Article 3

General principles

The principles of the present Convention shall be:

(a) Respect for inherent dignity, individual autonomy including the freedom to make one's own choices, and independence of persons;
(b) Non-discrimination;
(c) Full and effective participation and inclusion in society;
(d) Respect for difference and acceptance of persons with disabilities as part of human diversity and humanity;
(e) Equality of opportunity;
(f) Accessibility;
(g) Equality between men and women;
(h) Respect for the evolving capacities of children with disabilities and respect for the right of children with disabilities to preserve their identities.

Article 4

General obligations

1. States Parties undertake to ensure and promote the full realization of all human rights and fundamental freedoms for all persons with disabilities without discrimination of any kind on the basis of disability. To this end, States Parties undertake:

   (a) To adopt all appropriate legislative, administrative and other measures for the implementation of the rights recognized in the present Convention;
   (b) To take all appropriate measures, including legislation, to modify or abolish existing laws, regulations, customs and practices that constitute discrimination against persons with disabilities;
   (c) To take into account the protection and promotion of the human rights of persons with disabilities in all policies and programmes;
   (d) To refrain from engaging in any act or practice that is inconsistent with the present Convention and to ensure that public authorities and institutions act in conformity with the present Convention;
   (e) To take all appropriate measures to eliminate discrimination on the basis of disability by any person, organization or private enterprise;
   (f) To undertake or promote research and development of universally designed goods, services, equipment and facilities, as defined in article 2 of the pres-

ent Convention, which should require the minimum possible adaptation and the least cost to meet the specific needs of a person with disabilities, to promote their availability and use, and to promote universal design in the development of standards and guidelines;

(g) To undertake or promote research and development of, and to promote the availability and use of new technologies, including information and communications technologies, mobility aids, devices and assistive technologies, suitable for persons with disabilities, giving priority to technologies at an affordable cost;

(h) To provide accessible information to persons with disabilities about mobility aids, devices and assistive technologies, including new technologies, as well as other forms of assistance, support services and facilities;

(i) To promote the training of professionals and staff working with persons with disabilities in the rights recognized in the present Convention so as to better provide the assistance and services guaranteed by those rights.

2. With regard to economic, social and cultural rights, each State Party undertakes to take measures to the maximum of its available resources and, where needed, within the framework of international cooperation, with a view to achieving progressively the full realization of these rights, without prejudice to those obligations contained in the present Convention that are immediately applicable according to international law.
3. In the development and implementation of legislation and policies to implement the present Convention, and in other decision-making processes concerning issues relating to persons with disabilities, States Parties shall closely consult with and actively involve persons with disabilities, including children with disabilities, through their representative organizations.
4. Nothing in the present Convention shall affect any provisions which are more conducive to the realization of the rights of persons with disabilities and which may be contained in the law of a State Party or international law in force for that State. There shall be no restriction upon or derogation from any of the human rights and fundamental freedoms recognized or existing in any State Party to the present Convention pursuant to law, conventions, regulation or custom on the pretext that the present Convention does not recognize such rights or freedoms or that it recognizes them to a lesser extent.
5. The provisions of the present Convention shall extend to all parts of federal States without any limitations or exceptions.

Article 5

Equality and non-discrimination

1. States Parties recognize that all persons are equal before and under the law and are entitled without any discrimination to the equal protection and equal benefit of the law.
2. States Parties shall prohibit all discrimination on the basis of disability and guarantee to persons with disabilities equal and effective legal protection against discrimination on all grounds.

3. In order to promote equality and eliminate discrimination, States Parties shall take all appropriate steps to ensure that reasonable accommodation is provided.
4. Specific measures which are necessary to accelerate or achieve de facto equality of persons with disabilities shall not be considered discrimination under the terms of the present Convention.

Article 7

Children with disabilities

1. States Parties shall take all necessary measures to ensure the full enjoyment by children with disabilities of all human rights and fundamental freedoms on an equal basis with other children.
2. In all actions concerning children with disabilities, the best interests of the child shall be a primary consideration.
3. States Parties shall ensure that children with disabilities have the right to express their views freely on all matters affecting them, their views being given due weight in accordance with their age and maturity, on an equal basis with other children, and to be provided with disability and age-appropriate assistance to realize that right.

Bibliography

Abella, Rosalie S. 1984. *Discrimination in employment; Law and legislation; Canada*. Ottawa: Minister of Supply and Services Canada.
Ackers, Louise, and Helen Stalford. 2004. *A community for children?: Children, citizenship, and internal migration in the EU*. Aldershot: Ashgate.
Adams, Paul, Nan Berger, Michael Duane, Leila Berg, Alexander S. Neill, and Robert Ollendorff. 1971. *Children's rights: Toward the liberation of the child*. New York: Praeger.
Adler, Ruth. 1985. *Taking juvenile justice seriously*. Edinburgh: Scottish Academic Press.
ADT. 2006. *Anti-social behaviour across Europe: An overview of research commissioned by ADT Europe*. Sunbury-on-Thames: ADT Fire and Security plc.
Agamben, Giorgio, Davide Giuriato, and Clemens-Carl Härle. 2004. *Kindheit und Geschichte: Zerstörung der Erfahrung und Ursprung der Geschichte*. Frankfurt am Main: Suhrkamp.
Agarwal, Bina. 1994. *A field of one's own: Gender and land rights in South Asia*. Cambridge: Cambridge University Press.
Alanen, Leena. 1988. Rethinking childhood. *Acta Sociologica* 31(1): 53–67.
Albasi, Tiziana. 1991. *Gli affanni del vivere e del morire: schiavi, soldati, donne, bambini nella Roma imperiale*. Brescia: Grafo.
Albertson Fineman, Martha, and Karen Worthington. 2009. *What is right for children? The competing paradigms of religion and human rights*. Abingdon: Ashgate Publishing.
Alderson, Priscilla. 1993. *Children's consent to surgery*. Buckingham: Open University Press.
Alderson, Priscilla. 1994. Researching children's right to integrity. In *Children's childhoods: Observed and experienced*, ed. Berry Mayall. London: Routledge.
Alderson, Priscilla. 2000. *Young children's rights: Exploring beliefs, principle and practice*. London: Jessica Kingsley.
Alderson, Priscilla. 2001. Students' rights in British schools: Trust, autonomy, connection and regulation. In *Children, home and school: Autonomy, connection or regulation?* ed. Rosalind Edwards, 24–40. London: Routledge.
Alderson, Priscilla, and Jonathan Montgomery. 1996. *Health care choices: Making decisions with children*. London: Institute for Public Policy Research.
Alderson, Priscilla, Joanna Hawthorne, and Margaret Killen. 2005a. The participation rights of premature babies. *The International Journal of Children's Rights* 13(1/2): 31–50.
Alderson, Priscilla, Joanna Hawthorne, and Margaret Killen. 2005b. Are premature babies citizens with rights? The edges of citizenship. In *Children's citizenship: An emergent discourse on the rights of the child*, Special Edition 9 of the *Journal of Social Sciences*, ed. Antonella Invernizzi and Brian Milne, 83–99. Delhi: Kamla-Raj Enterprises.
Alexandre-Bidon, Danièle, and Didier Lett. 2004. *Les enfants au Moyen Age*. Paris: Hachette.

DOI 10.1007/978-94-007-6521-4,

Ali, Shahreen Sardar, Savitri Goonesekere, Emilio Garcia Mendez, and Rebeca Rois-Kohn. 2007. *Protecting the world's children: Impact of the convention on the rights of the child in diverse legal systems*. Cambridge: UNICEF with Cambridge University Press.

Andersen, Hans Christian. 1994. *Fairy tales*. Harmondsworth: Penguin Popular Classics.

Aquinas, Thomas. 1981. *Summa theologica*, vol. 1. Notre Dame/Indianapolis: Christian Classics.

Archard, David. 1993. *Children: Rights and childhood*. London: Routledge.

Archard, David. 2003. *Children, family and the state*. Aldershot: Ashgate.

Archard, David, and Colin Macleod (eds.). 2002. *The moral and political status of children: New essays*. Oxford: Oxford University Press.

Arendt, Hannah. 1962. *The origins of totalitarianism*. Cleveland/New York: The World Publishing Company.

Ariès, Philippe. 1962. *Centuries of childhood*. New York: Random House.

Aristotle. 1908. *The politics & economics of Aristotle*. Trans. Edward English Walford and John Gillies. London: G. Bell & Sons.

Aristotle. 1969. *Metaphysics*, Books 10 to 14. Trans. G. Cyril Armstrong. London/Cambridge, MA: Heinemann/Harvard University Press.

Aristotle. 1987. *De Anima*. Trans. Hugh Lawson-Tancred. London: Penguin Classics.

Aristotle. 1999a. *Nicomachean ethics*. Trans. William D. Ross. Kitchener: Batoche Books.

Aristotle. 1999b. *Politics*. Trans. Benjamin Jowett. Kitchener: Batoche Books.

Arnstein, Sherry R. 1969. A ladder of citizen participation. *Journal of the American Institute of Planners* 35(4): 216–224.

Baldwin, James M. 1895. *Mental development in the child and the race: Methods and processes*. New York: Macmillan & Co.

Balme, David M. 1991. *Aristotle, history of animals, books VII-X*. Cambridge, MA: Harvard University Press.

Bandalli, Sue. 1998. Abolition of the presumption of Doli Incapax and the criminalisation of children. *The Howard Journal of Criminal Justice* 37(2): 114–123.

Barker, Roger. 1968. *Ecological psychology*. Stanford: Stanford University Press.

Barry, Stéphane, and Norbert Gualde. 2006. La plus grande épidémie de l'histoire. *L'Histoire* 310: 45–46.

Bartlett, Sheridan, Roger Hart, David Satterthwaite, Ximena de la Barra, and Alfredo Missair. 1999. *Cities for children: Children's rights, poverty and urban management*. London: Routledge.

Beaumont, Laura. 2006. *Childhood in ancient Athens*. London: Routledge.

Becchi, Egle, and Dominique Julia. 2004. *Histoire de l'enfance en Occident*. Paris: Editions du Seuil.

Benedict, Ruth. 1955. Continuities and discontinuities in cultural conditioning. In *Childhood in contemporary cultures*, ed. Margaret Mead and Martha Wolfenstein. Chicago: University of Chicago Press.

Benjamin, Walter. 2006. *Berliner Kindheit um neuenzehnhundert*. Frankfurt am Main: Suhrkamp.

Bennett, Jonathan. 1974. The conscience of Huckleberry Finn. *Philosophy* 49:123–134.

Berlin, Isaiah. 1969. *Four essays on liberty*. Oxford: Oxford University Press.

Berthrong, John. 1998. *Transformations of the Confucian way*. Boulder: Westview Press.

Bibby, Reginald W. 1990. *Mosaic madness: The poverty and potential of life in Canada*. Toronto: Stoddart.

Bluebond-Langner, Myra. 1980. *The private worlds of dying children*. Princeton: Princeton University Press.

Bluebond-Langner, Myra. 1989. Worlds of dying children and their well siblings. *Death Studies* 13(1): 1–16.

Bluebond-Langner, Myra. 1996. *In the shadow of illness: Parents and siblings of the chronically ill*. Princeton: Princeton University Press.

Blustein, Jeffrey. 1982. *Parents and children: The ethics of the family*. New York: Oxford University Press.

Bogin, Barry. 1990. The evolution of human childhood. *BioScience* 40(1): 16–25.

Bolte, Johannes, and Georg (Jiri) Polívka. 1913. *Anmerkungen zu den Kinder- und Hausmärchen der Brüder Grimm*. Leipzig: Dieterich'sche Verlagsbuchhandlung Theodor Weicher (Erster Band).
Bös, Mathias. 2002. *The legal construction of membership: Nationality law in Germany and the United States*, Program for the study of Germany and Europe, working paper series no. 00.5. Heidelberg: Institute of Sociology, University of Heidelberg.
Boswell, John. 1988. *The kindness of strangers: The abandonment of children in Western Europe from late antiquity to the renaissance*. Harmondsworth: Penguin.
Boulding, Elise. 1980. *Children's rights and the wheel of life*. Edison: Transaction Publishers.
Bourdieu, Pierre. 1977. *Outline of a theory of practice*. Cambridge: Cambridge University Press.
Bourdieu, Pierre. 1983. Ökonomisches Kapital, kulturelles Kapital, soziales Kapital. In *Soziale welt*, Sonderheft 2: Soziale Ungleichheiten, ed. Reinhard Kreckel. Goettingen: Otto Schartz & Co.
Bourdieu, Pierre. 1984. *Distinction: A social critique of the judgement of taste*. London: Routledge & Kegan Paul.
Bourdieu, Pierre. 1986. The (three) forms of capital. In *Handbook of theory and research in the sociology of education*, ed. John G. Richardson, 241–258. New York/London: Greenwood Press.
Bourdieu, Pierre, and Jean-Claude Passeron. 1990. *Reproduction in education, society and culture*. London: Sage.
Boyer, Pascal. 2001. *Religion explained: The evolutionary origins of religious thought*. London: Random House.
Braudel, Fernand. 1973. *Capitalism and material life, 1400–1800*. New York: HarperCollins.
Brennan, Samantha, and Noggle Robert. 1998. John Rawls's Children. In *The philosopher's child*, ed. Susan Turner and Gareth B. Matthews, 203–232. Rochester: University of Rochester Press.
Bronfenbrenner, Urie, Frank Kessel, William Kessen, and Sheldon White. 1986. Toward a critical social history of developmental psychology: A propaedeutic discussion. *American Psychologist* 41: 1218–1230.
Browne, Edward Granville. 2001. *Islamic medicine*. New Delhi: Goodword Books.
Buckingham, David. 2000. *After the death of childhood: Growing up in the age of electronic media*. Cambridge: Polity Press.
Buehler-Niederberger, Doris. 1998. The separative view. Is there any scientific approach to children. In *Children and childhood in our contemporary societies*, ed. Deepak Kumar Behera, 51–66. Delhi: Kamla-Raj Enterprises.
Cantwell, Nigel. 1992. The origins, development and significance of the United Nations convention on the rights of the child. In *The United Nations convention on the rights of the child: A guide to the 'Travaux Préparatoires'*, ed. Sharon Detrick, 19–30. Dordrecht: Martinus Nijhoff Publishers.
Caplow, Theodore, Howard M. Bahr, Bruce A. Chadwick, and Margaret Holmes Williamson. 1982. *Middletown families: Fifty years of change and continuity*. Minneapolis: University of Minneapolis Press.
Caplow, Theodore, Howard M. Bahr, Bruce A. Chadwick, Dwight W. Hoover, Laurence A. Martin, Joseph B. Tamney, and Margaret Holmes Williamson. 1983. *All faithful people: Change & continuity in Middletown's religion*. Minneapolis: University of Minneapolis Press.
Carbajal, Myriam, and Nathalie Ljuslin. 2012. Être jeune, privée-e de statut légal et citoyen-ne, est-ce possible? *Tsantsa* 17: 106–115.
Cardona, George. 1998. *Panini: A Survey of Research*. Delhi: Motilal Banarsidass.
Cardwell, Sarah. 2006. Patterns, layers and values: Poliakoff's the lost prince. *Journal of British Cinema and Television* 3(1): 134–141, Edinburgh: Edinburgh University Press.
Carey, Susan. 1985. *Conceptual change in childhood*. Cambridge: MIT Press.
Carpenter, Mary. 1851. *Reformatory schools: For the children of the perishing and dangerous*. London: C. Gilpin.
Cartledge, Paul. 2001. *Spartan reflections*. London: Duckworth.
Cartledge, Paul. 2002. *The Spartans*. London: Pan Books.
Chambers, Robert. 1992. *Rural: Rapid, relaxed and participatory*, Discussion paper 331. Brighton: University of Sussex, Institute of Development Studies.

Chrysostom, John. 1986. *On marriage and family life*. Trans. Catharine P. Roth and David Anderson. Crestwood: St. Vladimir's Seminary Press.
Cleaver, Frances. 2002. Institutions, agency and limitations of participatory approaches to development. In *Participation: The new tyranny?* ed. Bill Cooke and Uma Kothari. London: Zed Books.
Coburn, Thomas. 1984. Scripture in India: Towards a typology of the word in Hindu life. *Journal of the American Academy of Religion* 52(3): 435–459.
Cockburn, Tom. 1998. Children and citizenship in Britain. *Childhood* 5(1): 99–118.
Cockburn, Tom. 2002. *Concepts of social inclusion/exclusion and childhoods*. Paper presented at the ESRC Children and Social Inclusion Seminar University of Edinburgh. Edinburgh: Edinburgh University Press. December 2002.
Cohen, Howard. 1980. *Equal rights for children*. Totowa: Littlefield/Adams.
Cohen, Elizabeth F. 2005. Neither seen nor heard: Children's citizenship in contemporary democracies. *Citizenship Studies* 9(2): 221–240.
Cohn, Norman. 1993. *The pursuit of the millennium: Revolutionary millenarians and mystical anarchists of the middle ages*. London: Pimlico.
Colby, Anne, and Lawrence Kohlberg. 1987. *The measurement of moral judgment, volume 1: Theoretical foundations and research validation*. Cambridge: Cambridge University Press.
Coles, Robert. 1986a. *The moral life of children*. Boston: Houghton Mifflin.
Coles, Robert. 1986b. *The political life of children*. Boston: Houghton Mifflin.
Coles, Robert. 1997. *The moral intelligence of children*. New York: Random House.
Coly, Hamidou, and Fabrizio Terenzio. 2007. The stakes of children's participation in Africa: The African movement of working children and youth. In *Working to be someone: Child focussed research and practice with working children*, ed. Beatrice Hungerland, Manfred Liebel, Brian Milne, and Anne Wihstutz. London: Jessica Kingsley.
Committee on the Elimination of Discrimination against Women (CEDAW). 2003. Press Release WOM/1373 – *Experts in women's anti-discrimination committee raise questions concerning reports of Switzerland on compliance with convention*. New York: CEDAW/UNIFEM.
Coogan, Michael D. (ed.). 2005. *Eastern religions*. London: Duncan Baird Publishers.
Cooke, Bill, and Uma Kothari (eds.). 2002. *Participation: The new tyranny?* London: Zed Books.
Cornille, Catherine (ed.). 2006. *Song divine: Christian commentaries on the Bhagavad Gita*. Leuven: Peeters.
Corrigan, Paul. 1979. *Schooling the smash street kids*. London: Macmillan.
Corsaro, William. 2005. *The sociology of childhood*. Thousand Oaks: Pine Forge Press.
Cox, Pamela, and Heather Shore (eds.). 2002. *Becoming delinquent: British and European youth, 1650–1950*. Aldershot: Ashgate.
Crawford, Sally. 1999. *Childhood in Anglo-Saxon England*. Stroud: Alan Sutton.
Crook, Richard C., and James Manor. 1998. *Democracy and decentralisation in South Asia and West Africa: Participation, accountability and performance*. Cambridge: Cambridge University Press.
Cunningham, Hugh. 1991. *The children of the poor: Representations of childhood since the seventeenth century*. Oxford: Blackwell.
Cunningham, Hugh. 2005. *Children and childhood in Western society since 1500*. London: Pearson/Longman.
Cunningham, Hugh. 2006. *The invention of childhood*. London: BBC Books.
Curtis Report. 1946. *Report of the care of children committee*, Cmnd 6922. London: HMSO.
Cussiánovich, Alejandro. 1997. Protagonismo: ¿Qué es? In *Jóvenes y Niños Trabajadores: Sujetos Sociales. Ser Protagonistas*, 11–28. Lima: ediciónes ifejant.
Dagens, Bruno. 1995. *Angkor: Heart of an Asian empire*. London: Thames and Hudson.
Dagens, Bruno. 2003. *Les Khmers*. Paris: Les Belles Lettres.
Davies, Andrew, and Geoffrey Pearson (eds.). 1999. Histories of crime and modernity, Introduction. *The British Journal of Criminology* 39(1): 1–9.
Davila-Ortega, Luis, and Emily Freeburg. 2006. *Youth, democratic governance and the MDGs report in Asia and the Pacific*. Presented to the UNDP Regional Centre, Bangkok: Global Youth Action Network.

Davin, Anna. 1996. *Growing up poor: Home, school and street in London, 1870–1914*. London: Rivers Oram Press.
Davis, John M., Stephen Farrier, and Claire Whiting. 2006. *Literature review participation* (unpublished draft version only).
de Mause, Lloyd (ed.). 1974. *The history of childhood*. New York: Psychohistory Press.
Deferrari, Roy J. 1955. St. Augustine. *The Good of Marriage* from *Saint Augustine: Treatises on marriage and other subjects*. Eds. and Trans. Charles T. Wilcox, et al. Washington, DC: Catholic University of America.
Delanty, Gerard. 2006. Nationalism and cosmopolitanism. In *Handbook of nations and nationalism*, ed. Gerard Delanty and Krishnan Kumar. London: Sage.
Dench, Geoff, Kate Gavron, and Michael Young. 2006. *The new East End: Kinship, race and conflict*. London: Profile Books.
Department for Education and Employment. 1998. *Education for citizenship and the teaching of democracy in schools: Final report of the advisory group on citizenship* (The Crick Report). London: DfEE.
Department for Education and Skills. 2003. *Every child matters: Change for children*. Annesley: DfES Publications.
Department for Education and Skills. 2004. *Every child matters: Change for children in social care*. Annesley: DfES Publications.
Descartes, René. 1985. *The philosophical writings of Descartes*, vol. 1. Trans. J. Cottingham, R. Stoothoff, and D. Murdoch. Cambridge: Cambridge University Press.
Detrick, Sharon (ed.). 1992. *The United Nations convention on the rights of the child: A guide to the 'Travaux Préparatoires'*. Dordrecht: Martinus Nijhoff Publishers.
Devine, Thomas. 2006. *The Scottish Nation, 1700–2007*. London: Penguin.
Dewey, John. 1966 (1916). *Democracy and education: An introduction to the philosophy of education*. London: Free Press.
Dewey, John. 1990 (1907). *The school and society*. Chicago: University of Chicago Press.
Dickens, Charles. 1993 (1853). *Bleak house*. Ware Hertford: Wordsworth Editions.
Dickens, Charles. 1994a. *The personal history of David Copperfield*. Harmondsworth: Penguin Classics.
Dickens, Charles. 1994b. *Great expectations*. Harmondsworth: Penguin Classics.
Dickens, Charles. 2003 (1838). *Oliver twist or the Parish boy's progress*. Harmondsworth: Penguin Books.
Dixon, Suzanne (ed.). 2001. *Childhood, class and kin in the Roman world*. London: Routledge.
Dobbs, Darrell. 1996. Family matters: Aristotle's appreciation of women and the plural structure of society. *American Political Science Review* 90(1): 74–89.
Donaldson, Margaret. 1978. *Children's minds*. Glasgow: Fontana.
Donohue Jr., Charles. 1983. The canon law on the formation of marriage and social practice in the later middle ages. *Journal of Family History* 8: 144–158.
Donzelot, Jacques. 1980. *The policing of families: Welfare versus the state*. London: Hutchinson.
Downes, David. 1966. *The delinquent solution*. London: Routledge & Kegan Paul.
Draper, Patricia. 1976. Social and economic constraints on child life among the !Kung. In *Kalahari hunter-gatherers: Studies of the ¡Kung San and their neighbours*, ed. Richard B. Lee and Irven DeVore, 199–271. Cambridge, MA: Harvard University Press.
Duggan, Christopher. 1994. *A concise history of Italy*, Cambridge concise histories. Cambridge: Cambridge University Press.
Durkheim, Émile. 1963. *Sociologie et Philosophie*. Paris: Presses Universitaires de France.
Durkheim, Émile. 1966. *The rules of sociological method*. New York: Free Press.
Durkheim, Émile. 1986. The forms of capital. In *Handbook for theory and research for the sociology of education*, ed. John G. Richardson, 241–258. Westport: Greenwood Press.
Eadmer (Richard W. Southern, ed.). 1972. *The life of St Anselm, Archbishop of Canterbury*. Oxford: Clarendon Press.
Eckel, Malcolm. 2000. Buddhism. In *Eastern religions*, ed. Michael D. Coogan, 110–209. London: Duncan Baird Publishers.

Edwards, Michael. 1996. Institutionalising children's participation in development. *PLA Notes* 1996(25): 47–48.

Edwards, Rosalind (ed.). 2001. *Children, home and school: Autonomy, connection or regulation?* London: Routledge.

Elster, Jon. 1989. *Solomonic judgements: Studies in the limitation of rationality*. New York: Cambridge University Press.

Emlyn-Jones, Chris. 1999. *Plato: Crito*. London: Bristol Classical.

ENDA editions. 2001. *Voice of African children: Work, strength and organisation of working children and youth*. Dakar: ENDA.

ENDA TM. 2004–09. *Calao express* (Online newsletter, quarterly (irregular) publication). Dakar: ENDA TM, équipe jeunesse action.

Engels, Friedrich. 1999 (1845). *The condition of the working class in England*. Oxford: Oxford World's Classics.

Eppel, Emanuel Montague. 1966. *Adolescence and morality*. London: Routledge & Kegan Paul.

Erikson, Erik H. 1950. *Childhood and society*. New York: Norton.

Erikson, Erik H. 1968. *Identity: Youth and crisis*. New York: W.W. Norton.

European Union. 2000. *Charter of fundamental rights of the European Union*. Brussels: European Union.

European Union. 2002. *Consolidated version of the treaty establishing the European community*. Brussels: European Union.

Evans, John K. 1991. *War, women and children in ancient Rome*. London: Routledge.

Fairbank, John King. 1992. *China: A new history*. Cambridge, MA: Belknap Press of Harvard University Press.

Fanon, Frantz. 2001. *The wretched of the earth*. Harmondsworth: Penguin Books.

Farson, Richard. 1974. *Birthrights*. London: Collier Macmillan.

Fass, Paula (ed.). 2003. *The encyclopedia of the history of childhood*. New York: Thomson/Gale.

Faulks, Keith. 2000. *Citizenship*. London: Routledge.

Feigl, Herbert. 1967. *The 'Mental' and the 'Physical': The essay and a postscript*. Minneapolis: University of Minnesota Press.

Feinstein, Clare, and Claire O'Kane. 2005. *The Spider Tool: A self assessment and planning tool for child led initiatives and organisations*. Kathmandu: Save the Children Sweden.

Ferguson, Harry (Thomas H.). 1993. *Protecting children in time: A historical sociological study of the abused child and child protection in Cleveland from 1880 to the 'Cleveland Affair' of 1987*. Ph.D. Dissertation, University of Cambridge, February 1993: BLDSC number: D062112.

Finer, Samuel. 1999. *The history of government from the earliest times*. Oxford: Oxford University Press.

Firestone, Shulamith. 1970. *The dialectic of sex: The case for feminist revolution*. London: Jonathon Cape.

Fox, Marvin. 1990. *Interpreting Maimonides*. Chicago: University of Chicago Press.

Franklin, Bob. 1986. 'Introduction' and 'Children's Political Rights'. In *The rights of children*, ed. Bob Franklin, 1–23 and 24–53. London: Basil Blackwell.

Freeman, Michael. 1983. *The rights and wrongs of children*. London: Frances Pinter.

Freeman, Michael. 1992. The limits of children's rights. In *The ideologies of children's rights*, ed. Michael Freeman and Philip Veerman. The Hague: Martin Nijhoff.

Freeman, Michael. 1999. *The moral status of children: Essays on the rights of the child*. The Hague: Martinus Nijhoff.

Freire, Paulo. 1972. *The pedagogy of the oppressed*. Harmondsworth: Penguin Books.

Freud, Sigmund. 1996. *Drei Abhandlungen zur Sexualtheorie*. Frankfurt am Main: Fischer. (Originally published 1905.)

Fuller, Christopher. 1976. *The Nayars today*. Cambridge: Cambridge University Press.

Garland, David. 1985. *Punishment and welfare*. Aldershot: Gower.

Garland, David. 2001. *The culture of control crime and social order in contemporary society*. Oxford: Oxford University Press.

Gelman, Susan. 2003. *The essential child*. New York: Oxford University Press.

Gibson, Barbara, and Ted Schwarz. 1995. *Rose Kennedy and her family: The best and worst of their lives and times*. New York: Birch Lane Press.
Gies, Frances, and Joseph Gies. 1987. *Marriage and the family in the middle ages*. New York: Harper & Row.
Gilligan, Carol. 1982. *In a different voice*. Cambridge: Harvard University Press.
Glauser, Benno. 1990. Street children: Deconstructing a construct. In *Constructing and reconstructing childhood: Contemporary issues in the sociological study of childhood*, ed. Allison James and James Prout. London: Falmer.
Goffman, Erving. 1959. *The presentation of self in everyday life*. Garden City: Doubleday.
Goffman, Erving. 1967. *Interaction ritual*. New York: Pantheon.
Golden, Mark. 1990. *Children and childhood in classical Athens*. Baltimore/London: Johns Hopkins University Press.
Golding, William. 2002. *Lord of the flies*. London: Faber and Faber.
Goldson, Barry. 2000. The demonization of children: From the symbolic to the institutional. In *Children in society: Contemporary theory, policy and practice*, ed. Pam Foley, Jeremy Roche, and Stan Tucker. London: Palgrave Macmillan.
Goldson, Barry and John Muncie (eds.). 2009. *Youth crime and juvenile justice*, 3 vols. London: Sage.
Goodman, Paul. 1971. *Compulsory miseducation*. Harmondsworth: Penguin Education.
Goody, Jack. 1983. *The development of the family and marriage in Europe*. Cambridge: Cambridge University Press.
Gordon Jr., Raymond G. (ed.). 2005. *Ethnologue: Languages of the world*, 15th ed. Dallas: SIL International.
Gottfried, Robert S. 1983. *The Black Death*. New York: The Free Press.
Graham, Mark. 2006. *How Islam created the modern world*. Beltsville: Amana Publications.
Green, Andy. 1990. *Education and state formation: The rise of education systems in England, France and the USA*. London: Macmillan.
Gregory, Richard. 1987. *Oxford companion to the mind*. Oxford: Oxford University Press.
Grimm, Jacob and Grimm Wilhelm. 1984. *Kinder- und Hausmärchen gesammelt durch die Brüder Grimm*, Erster Band. Frankfurt am Main: Insel Verlag.
Gross, Beatrice, and Ronald Gross (eds.). 1977. *The children's rights movement*. New York: Anchor.
Gruber, Howard E., and J. Jacques Vonèche. 1977. *The essential Piaget*. Northvale: J. Aronson.
Guerra, Eliana. 2005. Citizenship knows no age: Children's participation in the governance and municipal budget of Barra Mansa, Brazil. *Children Youth and Environments* 15(2): 151–168.
Gutek, Gerald L. 1972. *A history of the Western educational experience*. New York: Random House.
Hall, Julian (ed.). 1971. *Children's rights: Towards the liberation of the child*. London: Elek Books.
Hansen, Mogens Herman. 2006. *Polis: An introduction to the ancient Greek city-state*. Oxford: Oxford University Press.
Hardman, Charlotte. 2001. Can there be an anthropology of children? *Childhood* 8(4): 501–517.
Hart, Roger. 1992. *Children's participation: From tokenism to citizenship*, Innocenti essays, no. 4. Florence: UNICEF.
Hart, Mary H., and John Llewelyn Davies. 1880. *The children of the street: Mary Carpenter's work in relation to our own*. London: W. Swan Sonnenschein & Allen Co.
Hattenstone, Simon. 2000. They were punished enough by what they did. *The Guardian*, G2, 30 October: 1.
Hawes, Joseph. 1971. *Children in urban society: Juvenile delinquency in nineteenth century America*. Oxford: Oxford University Press.
Heater, Derek. 1990. *Citizenship: The civic ideal in world history, politics and education*. London: Longman.
Heater, Derek. 1999. *What is citizenship?* Cambridge: Polity Press.

Heater, Derek. 2004. *A brief history of citizenship*. Edinburgh: Edinburgh University Press.
Hegel, Georg W.F. 2001 (1820). *Philosophy of right (Grundlinien der Philosophie des Rechts)*. Trans. Samuel W. Dyde, 1896. Kitchener: Batoche Books.
Hewlett, Barry S., and Michael E. Lamb. 2005. *Hunter gatherer childhoods: Evolutionary developments and cultural perspectives*. Edison: Aldine Transaction.
Heywood, Colin. 2006. *A history of childhood: Children and childhood in the West from medieval to modern times*. Cambridge: Polity Press.
Higonnet, Anne. 1998. *Pictures of innocence: The history and crisis of ideal childhood*. New York: Thames and Hudson.
Hinton, Rachel. 2008. Children's participation and good governance: Limitations of the theoretical literature. *The International Journal of Children's Rights* 16(3): 285–300.
Hobbes, Thomas. 1642. *De Cive* (Howard Warrender (Ed.), 1983). Oxford: Oxford University Press.
Hobbes, Thomas. 1650. *The elements of law, natural and politic*, Parts I and II (John Gaskin (Ed.), 1994). Oxford: Oxford University Press.
Hobbes, Thomas. 1651. *Leviathan* (John Plamenatz (Ed.), 1976). Glasgow: Collins/Fontana.
Hoggan, Pauline. 1991. The role of children in permanency planning. *Adoption and Fostering* 15(4): 31–34.
Holden, Cathie, and Nick Clough (eds.). 1998. *Children as citizens: Education for participation*. London/Philadelphia: Jessica Kingsley Publishers.
Holloway, Sarah, and Gill Valentine. 2000. *Children's geographies: Playing, living, learning*. London: Routledge.
Holt, John. 1975. *Escape from childhood*. Harmondsworth: Penguin.
Hösle, Johannes. 2002. *Vor aller Zeit: Geschichte einer Kindheit*. München: dtv.
Houlgate, Laurence D. 1980. *The child and the state*. Baltimore: Johns Hopkins University Press.
Howe, David. 2005. *Child abuse and neglect: Attachment, development and intervention*. Basingstoke: Palgrave Macmillan.
Howe, Robert Brian, and Katherine Covell. 2007. *Empowering children: Children's rights education as a pathway to citizenship*. Toronto: Toronto University Press.
Hugo, John J. 1969. *St. Augustine on nature, sex, and marriage*. Chicago: Scepter.
Hugo, Victor. 1994 (1862). *Les Misérables*, vols. 1 and 2. Ware: Wordsworth Editions.
Hume, David. 1739–40. *A treatise of human nature: Being an attempt to introduce the experimental method of reasoning into moral subjects* (1995). Edinburgh: Akros Publications.
Hungerland, Beatrice, Manfred Liebel, Brian Milne, and Anne Wihstutz (eds.). 2007. *Working to be someone: Child focussed research and practice with working children*. London: Jessica Kingsley.
Icher, François. 2002. *Apprentis et Compagnons au Moyen Âge*. Paris: Editions du Sorbier.
Illich, Ivan. 1971. *Deschooling society*. Harmondsworth: Penguin Education.
Inter-Agency Working Group on Children's Participation (IAWGCP). 2008. *Children as active citizens*. Bangkok: Inter-Agency Working Group on Children's Participation.
Invernizzi, Antonella, and Brian Milne. 2002. Are children entitled to contribute to international policy making? A critical view of children's participation in the international campaign for the elimination of child labour. *The International Journal of Children's Rights* 10(4): 403–431.
Invernizzi, Antonella and Brian Milne (eds.). 2005. 'Children's citizenship: An emergent discourse on the rights of the child, Special Edition 9, *Journal of Social Sciences*. Delhi: Kamla-Raj Enterprises.
Invernizzi, Antonella, and Jane Williams (eds.). 2007. *Children and citizenship*. London: Sage.
Isin, Engin, and Bryan S. Turner. 2002. *Handbook of citizenship studies*. London: Sage.
Ivanhoe, Philip. 2000. *Confucian moral self cultivation*. Indianapolis: Hackett Publishing.
Jablonka, Ivan. 2006. *Ni père ni mère. Histoire des enfants de l'Assistance publique (1874–1939)*. Paris: Editions du Seuil.
Jackson, Brian, and Dennis Marsden. 1962. *Education and the working class*. Harmondsworth: Penguin.

James, Allison, and James Prout (eds.). 1990. *Constructing and reconstructing childhood: Contemporary issues in the sociological study of childhood*. London: Falmer.
James, Allison, Chris Jenks, and Alan Prout. 1998. *Theorizing childhood*. Cambridge: Polity Press.
Jenks, Chris. 2005. *Childhood*. London: Routledge.
Jephcott, Pearl (.A.P). 1942. *Girls growing up*. London: Faber and Faber.
Jephcott, Pearl (.A.P). 1943. *Clubs for girls. Notes for new helpers at clubs*. London: Faber and Faber.
Jephcott, Pearl (.A.P). 1948. *Rising twenty*. London: Faber and Faber.
Jephcott, Pearl (.A.P). 1954. *Some young people. A study of adolescent boys and girls*. London: George Allen & Unwin.
Jephcott, Pearl (.A.P). 1967. *A time of one's own. Leisure and young people*. Edinburgh: Oliver and Boyd.
Johnson, Victoria, Edda Ivan-Smith, Gill Gordon, Pat Pridmore, and Patta Scott (eds.). 1998. *Stepping forward*. London: Save the Children, IDS/Institute of Education.
Joseph, Sandra (ed.). 1999. *A voice for the child: The inspirational words of Janusz Korczak*. London: Thorsons.
Jowett, Benjamin (ed. and trans.). 1870. *Charmides, or temperance*. APSUE Electronic Classics Series Publication (E-book).
Jowett, Benjamin (ed. and trans.). 1901. *The republic of Plato*. New York: P. F. Collier & Son.
Junger-Tas, Josine, and Scott H. Decker (eds.). 2008. *The international handbook of juvenile justice*. New York: Springer.
Kagan, Jerome, and Sharon Lamb (eds.). 1987. *The emergence of morality in young children*. Chicago: University of Chicago Press.
Kamp, Kathryn A. 2001. Where have all the children gone?: The archaeology of childhood. *Journal of Archaeological Method and Theory* 8(1): 1–34.
Kant, Immanuel. 1781 (1963). *Critique of pure reason*. Trans. Norman Kemp Smith. London: Macmillan/St Martin's Press.
Kant, Immanuel. 1795 (2007). *Perpetual peace: A philosophical sketch*. Minneapolis: Filiquarian Publishing.
Kant, Immanuel. 1996. *The metaphysics of morals*, ed. Mary Gregor. Cambridge: Cambridge University Press.
Kaplan, Justin D. 1950. *The dialogues of Plato*. New York: Pocket Books.
Keane, John. 2003. *Global civil society?* Cambridge: Cambridge University Press.
Keane, John. 2009. *The life and death of democracy*. London: Simon & Schuster.
Kelly, John. 2005. *The great mortality, an intimate history of the Black Death, the most devastating plague of all time*. New York: Harper Collins Publisher Inc.
Kempe, C.Henry, and Ray E. Helfer (eds.). 1974. *The battered child*. Chicago: Chicago University Press.
Kempe, C. Henry, Frederic N. Silverman, Brandt F. Steele, William Droegemuller, and Henry K. Silver. 1962. The battered child syndrome. *Journal of the American Medical Association* 181: 17–24.
Kilminster, Richard. 1998. *The sociological revolution: From the enlightenment to the global age*. London: Routledge.
King, Michael. 2004. The child, childhood and children's rights within sociology. *King's Law Journal* 15(2): 273–300.
Kingsley, Charles. 1995. *The water babies*. Harmondsworth: Penguin Popular Classics.
Kirby, Perpetua, and Sara Bryson. 2002. *Measuring the magic – Evaluating and researching young people's participation in public decision making*. London: Carnegie Young People Initiative.
Kivisto, Peter, and Thomas Faist. 2007. *Citizenship: Discourse, theory and transnational prospects*. Oxford: Blackwell Publishing.
Kohlberg, Lawrence. 1981a. *The philosophy of moral development: Moral stages and the idea of justice: Essays on moral development*, vol. I. San Francisco: Harper & Row.

Kohlberg, Lawrence. 1981b. From is to ought: How to commit the naturalistic fallacy and get away with it in the study of moral development. In *Essays on moral development: The philosophy of moral development*, vol. I, ed. Lawrence Kohlberg. San Francisco: Harper & Row.

Kohlberg, Lawrence. 1981c. *Essays on moral development: The philosophy of moral development*, vol. I. San Francisco: Harper & Row.

Kohlberg, Lawrence. 1984. *The philosophy of moral development: Moral stages and the idea of justice: Essays on moral development*, vol. II. San Francisco: Harper & Row.

Kohlberg, Lawrence, Charles Levine, and Alexandra Hewer. 1983. *Moral stages: A current formulation and a response to critics*. Basel: Karger.

Konner, Melvin. 2005. Hunter-gatherer infancy and childhood: The !Kung and others. In *Hunter-gatherer childhoods evolutionary, developmental, and cultural perspectives*, ed. Barry Hewlett and Michael Lamb, 19–64. Edison: Aldine Transaction.

Korczak, Janusz. 1992. *When I am little again and the child's right to respect*. Trans. E.P. Kulawiec. New York: University Press of America.

Kozulin, Alex. 1990. *Vygotsky's psychology: A biography of ideas*. Cambridge, MA: Harvard University Press.

Kramers, Johannes H., Hamilton A.R. Gibb, and Evariste Lévi-Provençal (eds.). 1954. *The encyclopaedia of Islam*. Leiden: Brill.

Kroll, Jerome. 1977. The concept of childhood in the middle ages. *Journal of the History of Behavioural Sciences* 13(4): 384–393.

Kymlicka, Will, and Wayne Norman. 2000. Citizenship in culturally diverse societies: Issues, contexts, concepts. In *Citizenship in diverse societies*, ed. Will Kymlicka and Wayne Norman. Oxford: Oxford University Press.

Ladd, Rosalind Ekman. 1996. *Children's rights re-visioned*. Belmont: Wadsworth.

Lane, Harlan. 1979. *Wild boy of Aveyron*. London: Paladin.

Lansdown, Gerison. 2005. *The evolving capacities of the child*. Florence: UNICEF.

Lassman, Peter, and Ronald Speirs. 1994. *Weber: Political writings*. Cambridge: Cambridge University Press.

Lee, Nick. 2005. *Childhood and human value: Development, separation and separability*. Maidenhead: Open University Press.

Lee, Richard B., and Irven DeVore (eds.). 1976. *Kalahari hunter-gatherers: Studies of the ¡Kung San and their neighbours*. Cambridge, MA: Harvard University Press.

Lett, Didier. 2000. *Famille et parenté au Moyen Âge*. Paris: Hachette Education.

Levy, Reuben. 1969. *The social structure of Islam*. Cambridge: Cambridge University Press.

Liebel, Manfred. 2000. *La Otra Infancia: Niñez trabajadora y acción social*. Lima: ediciónes ifejant.

Liebel, Manfred. 2004. *A will of their own. Cross-cultural perspectives on working children*. London/New York: Zed Books.

Liebel, Manfred. 2007a. *Wozu Kinderrechte. Grundlagen und Perspektiven*. Weinheim/München: Juventa.

Liebel, Manfred. 2007b. Citizenship from below: Children's rights and social movements. In *Children and citizenship*, ed. Antonella Invernizzi and Jane Williams, 32–43. London: Sage.

Liebel, Manfred, Bernd Overwien, and Albert Recknagel (eds.). 2001. *Working children's protagonism: Social movements and empowerment in Latin America, Africa and India*. Frankfurt/London: IKO.

Liebel, Manfred, Ina Nnaji, and Anne Wihstutz (eds.). 2008. *Kinder. Arbeit. Menschenwürde*. Frankfurt/London: IKO.

Linsel, Susanne. 2002. *Kindheit im Mittelalter*. München: GRIN Verlag.

Lipman, Matthew. 1980. *Philosophy in the classroom*, 2nd ed. Philadelphia: Temple University Press.

Lister, Ruth. 1997. *Citizenship: Feminist perspectives*. Basingstoke: Macmillan.

Lister, Ruth. 1998. From equality to social inclusion: New labour and the welfare state. *Critical Social Policy* 18(2): 215–226.

Lister, Ruth. 2006a. Children and citizenship. *childRight* 223: 22–25.

Lister, Ruth. 2006b. Children (but not women) first: New labour, child welfare and gender. *Critical Social Policy* 26(2): 315–335.

Lister, Ruth. 2008. Unpacking children's citizenship. In *Children and citizenship* (Antonella Invernizzi and Jane Williams (Eds.), 2007), 9–19. London: Sage.

Lister, Ruth, Noel Smith, Sue Middleton, and Lynne Cox. 2003. Young people talk about citizenship: Empirical perspectives on theoretical and political debates. *Citizenship Studies* 7(2): 235–253.

Livi-Bacci, Massimo. 2000. *The population of Europe*. London: Blackwell.

Locke, John. 1959. *An essay concerning human understanding*, vol. I. New York: Dover Publications.

Locke, John. 1965. *Two treatises of government*. New York: American Library.

Locke, John. 1971. *John Locke on education*. New York: Teachers College Press.

Lorenz, Walter. 2006. *Perspectives on European social work – From the birth of nation state to the impact of globalisation*. Opladen/Farmington Hills: Barbara Budrich Publishers.

Loudon, Irvine. 1997. *Western medicine: An illustrated history*. Oxford: Oxford University Press.

Luhmann, Niklas. 1990. The cognitive program of constructivism and a reality that remains unknown. In *Selforganization: Portrait of a scientific revolution*, ed. Wolfgang Krohn, Günter Küpper, and Helga Nowotny, 64–85. Boston: Kluwer Academic Publishers.

Lynd, Robert Staughton, and Helen Merrell Lynd. 1929. *Middletown: A study in modern American culture*. New York: Harcourt Publishers Ltd. College Publishers.

Lynd, Robert Staughton, and Helen Merrell Lynd. 1937. *Middletown in transition: A study in cultural conflicts*. New York: Harcourt, Brace and Company.

Machiavelli, Niccolò. 1532. *The prince* (Peter Bondanella (Ed. and Trans.), 2005). Oxford: Oxford University Press/Oxford World's Classics.

Malthus, Thomas. 1798. *An essay on the principle of population* (Geoffrey Gilbert (Ed.), 2008). Oxford: Oxford Paperbacks.

Manheimer-Gommès, Marcel. 1899. Les troubles mentaux de l'enfant. *Précis de psychiatrie de l'enfant*. Paris.

Manton, Jo. 1976. *Mary Carpenter and the children of the streets*. London: Heinemann Educational.

Manville, Philip. 1994. Towards a new paradigm of Athenian citizenship. In *Athenian identity and civic ideology*, ed. Alan Boegehold and Adele Scafuro, 21–33. Baltimore: Johns Hopkins University Press.

Marshall, Thomas. 1950. *Citizenship and social class, and other essays*. Cambridge: Cambridge University Press.

Marshall, Thomas. 1964. *Class, citizenship and social development*. Garden City: Doubleday.

Marshall, Sherrin. 1991. Childhood in early modern Europe. In *Children in historical and comparative perspective: An international handbook and research guide*, ed. Joseph M. Hawes and N. Ray Hiner. Westport: Greenwood Press.

Marshall, Robert. 1993. *Storm from the East: From Genghis Khan to Khubilai Khan*. London: BBC Books.

Marx, Karl. 1844. On the Jewish question. *Deutsch-Französische Jahrbücher.* Paris: Karl Marx and Arnold Ruge.

Marx, Karl. 1993. *Grundrisse*. Harmondsworth: Penguin.

Marx, Karl, and Friedrich Engels. 2005. *The communist manifesto*. London: Longman.

Matthews, Gareth B. 1980. *Philosophy and the young child*. Cambridge, MA: Harvard University Press.

Matthews, Gareth B. 1994. *The philosophy of childhood*. Cambridge, MA: Harvard University Press.

Mayall, Berry (ed.). 1994. *Children's childhoods: Observed and experienced*. London: Routledge.

Mayall, Berry. 2000. *Towards a sociology for childhood. Thinking from children's lives*. Buckingham: Open University Press.

Mayhew, Henry. 1851a. *London labour and the London poor*. Ware: Wordsworth Classics of World Literature.

Mayhew, Henry. 1851b. *London characters and crooks*. London: The Folio Society.
Mays, John Barron. 1954. *Growing up in the city: A study of juvenile delinquency in an urban neighbourhood*. Liverpool: Liverpool University Press.
Mays, John Barron. 1962. *Education and the urban child*. Liverpool: Liverpool University Press.
Mays, John Barron. 1965. *The young pretenders: A study of teenage culture in contemporary society*. London: M. Joseph.
McAuliffe, Jane D. (ed.). 2006. *The encyclopaedia of the Qur'an*, 1st Edition in five volumes plus index. Leiden: Brill Publishers.
McComiskey, Bruce. 2002. *Gorgias and the new sophistic rhetoric*. Carbondale: Southern Illinois University Press.
McFarlane, Alan. 1986. *Marriage and love in England: Modes of reproduction 1300–1840*. Oxford: Basil Blackwell.
McKechnie, Jim, and Sandy Hobbs (eds.). 1998. *Working children: Reconsidering the debates: Report of the international working group on child labour*. Amsterdam: Defence for Children International.
McLaughlin, Corinne, and Gordon Davidson. 1990. *Builders of the dawn: Community lifestyles in a changing world*. Summertown: Book Publishing Company.
McLaughlin, Mary Martin. 1974. Survivors and surrogates: Children and parents from the ninth to the thirteen centuries. In *The history of childhood*, ed. Lloyd Mause, 101–182. New York: Psychohistory Press.
McNeill, William. 1963. *The rise of the West: A history of the human community*. Chicago: University of Chicago Press.
Mead, Margaret. 1967. An investigation of the thought of primitive children, with special reference to animism. In *Personalities and cultures*, ed. Robert C. Hunt, 213–237. Garden City: Natural History Press.
Mead, Margaret, and Martha Wolfenstein (eds.). 1955. *Childhood in contemporary cultures*. Chicago: University of Chicago Press.
Mehler, Jacques, and Thomas G. Bever. 1967. Cognitive capacity of very young children. *Science* 158(3797): 141–142.
Mencher, Joan P. 1965. The Nayars of South Malabar. In *Comparative family systems*, ed. Meyer F. Nimkoff, 163–191. Boston: Houghton Mifflin.
Mill, John Stuart. 1859. *On liberty* (Edward Alexander (Ed.), 1999). Peterborough: Broadview Press.
Mill, John Stuart. 1869. The subjection of women. In *J. S. Mill: 'On Liberty' and other writings* (Stefan Collini (Ed.), 2000). Cambridge texts in the history of political thought. Cambridge: Cambridge University Press.
Miller, Patricia. 1993. *Theories of developmental psychology*. New York: W. H. Freeman & Co.
Mills, Jean, and Richard Mills (eds.). 2002. *Childhood studies: A reader in perspectives of childhood*. London: Routledge.
Milne, Brian. 1993. Family disintegration: The family as fading focal point. *Childhood* 1(3): 156–164.
Milne, Brian. 1994a. '*Children's participation in education for democracy and peace in Europe*, for UNICEF ICDC. Florence: UNICEF Chile.
Milne, Brian. 1994b. Children's participation in democratic processes: Do children need to learn about citizenship or do adults need to learn about childhood? *Molake*, May.
Milne, Brian. 1996a. Children's participation: How far can children be involved? In *Monitoring children's rights*, ed. Eugeen Verhellen. Dordrecht: Martinus Nijhoff.
Milne, Brian. 1996b. Children's rights and the changing face of work in the field. *PLA Notes* (25). London: IIED.
Milne, Brian. 1996c. Family and community studies and the missing children: Finding children a place in contemporary society. In *Contemporary society: Childhood and complex order*, ed. Georg Pfeffer and Deepak Kumar Behera. New Delhi: Manak Publications.
Milne, Brian. 1997a. La Participación de los Niños: una visión general de su contribución en los procesos democráticos. *NATs* III(3–4): 27–40, Verona. English edition: Children's participation: A global overview of children's share in democratic processes. NATs III(3–4): 25–38.

Milne, Brian. 1997b. Who's kidding whom? Can we really talk about an anthropology of children? *Journal of Social Sciences*, Inaugural edition 1(1): 21–27.
Milne, Brian. 1998. Our children are missing: On the recent appearance of childhood as a research topic. In *Children and childhood in our contemporary societies*, ed. Deepak Kumar Behera. New Delhi: Manak Publications.
Milne, Brian. 2005a. Kinder als "gute" oder "schlechte" Bürger. Ist die UN-Kinderechtskonvention der Schlüssel zu Bürgerschaft (citizenship) von Kindern? In *Von sozialen Subjekten: Kinder und Jugendliche in verschiedenen Welten*, ed. Bernd Overwien. Frankfurt am Main: IKO.
Milne, Brian. 2005b. Is 'Participation' as it is described by the United Nations Convention on the Rights of the Child (UNCRC) the key to children's citizenship. In *Children's citizenship: An emergent discourse on the rights of the child*, Special Edition 9, *Journal of Social Sciences*, ed. Antonella Invernizzi and Brian Milne. Delhi: Kamla-Raj Enterprises.
Milne, Brian. 2006. Responsible citizenship or delinquency: The case of working children in India. In *Childhoods in South Asia*, ed. Deepak Kumar Behera. New Delhi/Singapore: Pearson Education.
Milne, Brian. 2007. Do the participation articles in the convention on the rights of the child present us with a recipe for children's citizenship? In *Working to be someone: Child focussed research and practice with working children*, ed. Beatrice Hungerland, Manfred Liebel, Brian Milne, and Anne Wihstutz. London/Philadelphia: Jessica Kingsley Publishers.
Milne, Brian. 2008. From chattels to citizens? Eighty years of Eglantyne Jebb's legacy to children and beyond. In *Children and citizenship*, ed. Antonella Invernizzi and Jane Williams. London: Sage Publications.
Mnookin, Robert. 1975. Child custody adjudication: Judicial functions in the face of indeterminacy. *Law and Contemporary Problems* 39: 226–293.
Montessori, Maria. 1964 (1917). *Spontaneous activity in education*. Cambridge, MA: Robert Bentley.
Montessori, Maria. 1965 (1912). *Montessori method: Scientific pedagogy as applied to child education in 'The Children's Houses'*. Cambridge, MA: Robert Bentley.
Montgomery, Heather, and Mary Kellett (eds.). 2009. *Children and young people's worlds: Developing frameworks for integrated practice*. Bristol: The Policy Press with Open University.
Moosa-Mitha, Mehmoona. 2005. A difference-centred alternative to theorization of children's citizenship rights. *Citizenship Studies* 9(4): 369–388.
More, Sir Thomas. 1516 (2004). *Utopia*. Harmondsworth: Penguin Classics.
Moss, Peter, and Pat Petrie. 2002. *From children's services to children's spaces: Public policy, children and childhood*. London: Falmer.
Munro, Dana C. 1914. The children's crusade. *The American Historical Review* 19: 516–524.
Musgrove, Frank. 1968. *Youth and social order*. London: Routledge & Kegan Paul.
Narayanan, Vasuda. 2005. Hinduism. In *Eastern religions*, ed. Michael D. Coogan, 8–109. London: Duncan Baird Publishers.
Nasr, Seyyed Hossein. 2003. *Islam: Religion, history and civilization*. New York: Harper Collins.
Neill, Alexander S. 1953. *The free child*. London: Herbert Jenkins.
Neill, Alexander S. 1962. *Summerhill: A radical approach to education*. London: Victor Gollancz.
Neill, Alexander S. 1966. *Freedom not licence!* Oxford: Hart.
Nimkoff, Meyer F. (ed.). 1965. *Comparative family systems*. Boston: Houghton Mifflin Company.
Nish, Ian (ed.). 1998. *The Iwakura mission to America and Europe: A new assessment*. London: Routledge/Curzon.
NSPCC. 2005. *A pocket history of the NSPCC*. London: NSPCC.
O'Neill, Onora. 1988. Children's rights and children's lives. *Ethics* 98(3): 445–463.
O'Neill, John. 1994. *The missing child in liberal theory*. Toronto: Toronto University Press.
O'Neill, John. 2004. *Civic capitalism: The state of childhood*. Toronto: Toronto University Press.
O'Neill, John. 2006. Citizenship, well-being and sustainability: Epicurus or Aristotle? *Analyse & Kritik: Zeitschrift für Sozialtheorie* 28(2): 158–172, Stuttgart: Lucius & Lucius.
Ogg, Frederic, and Walter Sharp. 1926. *Economic development of modern Europe*. New York: Macmillan.

Ojha, Phanindra Nath, and Jagdish Chandra Jha. 1987. *Studies in Indian history and culture*. Patna: Kashi Prasad Jayaswal Research Institute.

Oldman, David. 1991. *Childhood as a social phenomenon: National report for Scotland*, Eurosocial report 36/9. Vienna: European Centre.

Oldstone-Moore, Jennifer. 2005. Confucianism. In *Eastern religions*, ed. Michael D. Coogan, 314–415. London: Duncan Baird Publishers.

Opie, Iona, and Peter Opie. 1959. *The lore and language of school children*. Oxford: Clarendon Press.

Orme, Nicholas. 2001. *Medieval children*. London: Yale University Press.

Owen, Robert. 1816. *Address to the inhabitants of New Lanark, 1 January 1816*. New Lanark: New Lanark World Heritage Site. http://www.newlanark.org/robertowen.shtml.

Owen, Robert. 1841. *A development of the principles & plans on which to establish self-supporting home colonies, 1841*. http://www.newlanark.org/robertowen.shtml.

Ozment, Steven. 1983. *When fathers ruled: Family life in reformation Europe*. Cambridge, MA: Harvard University Press.

Packman, Jean. 1981. *The child's generation: Child care policy in Britain*. Oxford: Blackwell.

Paine, Thomas. 1999. *Rights of man*. Minneola: Dover Publications.

Parsons, Talcott, and Robert F. Bales. 1955. *Family, socialization, and interaction process*. New York: The Free Press.

Partridge, George E. 1912. *Genetic philosophy of education: An epitome of the published writings of G. Stanley Hall*. New York: Sturgis and Walton Co.

Peden, Margie, Kayode Oyegbite, Joan Ozanne-Smith, Adnan A. Hyder, Christine Branche, A.K.M. Fazlur Rahman, Frederick Rivara, and Kidist Bartolomeos (eds.). 2008. *World report on child injury prevention*. Geneva: UNICEF and World Health Organisation.

Pelagius. 417. *Pelagius' letter and statement of belief to Pope Innocent I*. http://www.reference.com/browse/pelagius.

Pettit, Philip. 1997. *Republicanism. A theory of freedom and government*. Oxford: Clarendon Press.

Phaire, Thomas. 1545. *The Boke of Chyldren* (Rick Bowers (Ed.), 1999). Tempe: Arizona Center for Medieval and Renaissance Studies.

Piaget, Jean. 1929. *The child's conception of the world*. London: Routledge & Kegan Paul.

Piaget, Jean. 1936. *La naissance de l'intelligence chez l'enfant*. Geneva: Delachaux et Niestlé.

Piaget, Jean. 1965. *The moral judgment of the child*. New York: Free Press.

Piaget, Jean. 1977. Foreword. In *The essential Piaget*, ed. Howard E. Gruber and J. Jacques Vonéche. London: Routledge & Kegan Paul.

Piaget, Jean. 2001a. *The psychology of intelligence*. London: Routledge.

Piaget, Jean. 2001b. *Studies in reflecting abstraction* (Recherches sur l'abstraction réfléchissante). Ed. and Trans. Robert L. Campbell. Hove: Psychology Press.

Plan International. 2005. *Universal birth registration: Permanent proof of identity in a turbulent world*. Woking: Plan International.

Plan International. 2006. *Global guidelines for universal birth registration: An analysis of the concluding observations and general comments of the UN Committee on the Rights of the Child*. Woking: Plan International.

Plato. 1970. *Laws*. Trans. Trevor Saunders. Harmondsworth: Penguin.

Plato. 1998. *Republic*. Ed. and Trans. Robin Waterfield. Oxford: Oxford World's Classics/Oxford Paperbacks.

Plato. 2005. *Meno and other dialogues*. Trans. Robin Waterfield. Oxford: Oxford World's Classics/ Oxford University Press.

Platt, Anthony M. 1977. *The child savers: The invention of delinquency*. Chicago: Chicago University Press.

Pojman, Louis. 1985. *Ethics*. Belmont: Wadsworth Publishing Company.

Pollock, Linda. 1983. *Forgotten children: Parent–child relations from 1500 to 1900*. Cambridge: Cambridge University Press.

Pollock, Linda. 2001. Parent–child relations. In *Family life in early modern times*, ed. Marzio Barbagli and David I. Kertzer, 1500–1789. New Haven: Yale University Press.

Pollock, Linda, and Marilyn Brown. 2002. *Constructions of childhood between Rousseau and Freud*. Burlington: Ashgate.
Porter, Roy. 1997. *The greatest benefit to mankind: A medical history of humanity from antiquity to the present*. London: Harper Collins.
Postman, Neil. 1982. *The disappearance of childhood*. New York: Delacorte Press.
Propp, Vladímir. 1968. *Morphology of the folktale*. Austin: University of Texas Press (First edition: Leningrad, 1928).
Purdy, Laura M. 1992. *In their best interest? The case against equal rights for children*. Ithaca: Cornell University Press.
Putnam, Robert D. 1993. *Making democracy work*. Princeton: Princeton Press.
Putnam, Robert D. 2000. *Bowling alone: The collapse and revival of American Community*. New York: Simon & Schuster.
Putnam, Robert D. (ed.). 2002. *Democracies in flux: The evolution of social capital in contemporary society*. Oxford: Oxford University Press.
Qvortrup, Jens. 1991. *Childhood as a social phenomenon: An introduction to a series of national reports*, Eurosocial report 36/0, 2nd ed. Vienna: European Centre for Social Welfare, Policy and Research.
Qvortrup, Jens. 1993. Societal position of childhood: The international project childhood as a social phenomenon. *Childhood* 1(2): 119–124.
Qvortrup, Jens. 1994. Childhood matters: An introduction. In *Childhood matters: Social theory, practice and politics*, ed. J. Qvortrup, M. Bardy, G. Sgritta, and H. Wintersberger. Aldershot: Avebury.
Raedts, Peter. 1977. The children's crusade of 1212. *Journal of Medieval History* 3(4): 279–323.
Rahn and Transue. 1998. Social trust and value change: The decline of social capital in American youth, 1976–1995. *Political Psychology* 19(3): 545–565.
Ralph Lewis, Brenda. 1996. Prince John. *Britannia Biography, Britannia Internet Magazine*. http://www.britannia.com/history/biographies/princejohn.html.
Rawls, John. 1971. *A theory of justice*. Cambridge: Harvard University Press.
Rawson, Beryl (ed.). 1991. *Marriage, divorce and children in ancient Rome*. Oxford: Clarendon Press.
Rawson, Beryl. 2005. *Children and childhood in Roman Italy*. Oxford: Oxford University Press.
Reddy, Nandana. 2007. Working with working children in India. In *Working to be someone: Child focussed research and practice with working children*, ed. Beatrice Hungerland, Manfred Liebel, Brian Milne, and Anne Wihstutz. London: Jessica Kingsley.
Rees, Brinley. 1988. *Pelagius: A reluctant heretic*. Woodbridge/Suffolk: The Boydell Press.
Renaut, Alain. 2002. *La libération des enfants: Contribution philosophique à une histoire de l'enfance*. Paris: Bayard et Calmann-Lévy.
Rice Jr., Eugene F. 1970. *The foundations of early modern Europe: 1460–1559*. New York: W.W. Norton & Co.
Riesenberg, Peter. 1956. *Inalienability of sovereignty in medieval political thought*. New York: Columbia University Press.
Riesenberg, Peter. 1992. *Citizenship in the Western tradition: Plato to Rousseau*. Chapel Hill/ London: University of North Carolina Press.
Riley-Smith, Jonathan (ed.). 2001. *The Oxford illustrated history of the crusades*. Oxford: Oxford University Press.
Rodgers, Gerry, and Guy Standing (eds.). 1981. *Child work, poverty and underdevelopment*, 81–112. Geneva: ILO.
Rodham, Hillary. 1973. Children under the law. *Harvard Educational Review* 43: 487–514.
Rosenwein, Barbara H. 2001. *A short history of the middle ages*. Peterborough: Broadview Press.
Rousseau, Jean-Jacques. 1979. *Émile or on education*. New York: Basic Books.
Rousseau, Jean-Jacques. 1998. *The social contract*. London: Wordsworth Editions.
Rousseau, Jean-Jacques. 2004. *Discourse on the origin of inequality*. Minneola: Dover Publications.
Runciman, Steven. 1951. *A history of the Crusades, Volume III: The kingdom of acre and the later Crusades*. Cambridge: Cambridge University Press.
Runciman, Steven. 1966. *Byzantine civilisation*. London: Edward Arnold.

Saint Augustine. 1998. *The confessions*. Trans. Henry Chadwick. Oxford: Oxford World's Classics.

Salisbury, Eve. 2002. *The trials and joys of marriage*. Kalamazoo: Medieval Institute Publications.

Sawyer, Caroline. 2008. Children and citizenship. *The International Journal of Children's Rights* 16(4): 565–567.

Schildkrout, Enid. 1978. Age and gender in Hausa Society: Socio-economic roles of children in urban Kano. In *Age and sex as principles of social differentiation*, ed. Jean La Fontaine. London: Academic Press.

Schildkrout, Enid. 1981. The employment of children in Kano (Nigeria). In *Child work, poverty and underdevelopment*, ed. Gerry Rodgers and Guy Standing, 81–112. Geneva: ILO.

Schleicher, August. 1859. *Zur Morphologie der Sprache*. St Peterburg: Kaiserlichen Akademie der Wissenschaften.

Schulz, Fritz. 1943. Roman registers of births and birth certificates. Part II. *The Journal of Roman Studies* 33, Parts 1 and 2: 55–64.

Schütter, Silke. 2006. Die Regulierung von Kindheit im Sozialstaat. Kinder und Kindheit in New Labours Gesellschaftsentwurf. *Neue Praxis* 36(5): 467–482.

Schuurman, Mieke, and Diana Sutton. 2004. *Children are European citizens too: Children in the EU treaty*. Brussels: Euronet.

Seifert, Karl-Heinz. 1976. *Bundeswahlrecht. Wahlrechtsartikel des Grundgesetzes, Bundeswahlgesetz, Bundeswahlordnung und wahlrechtliche Nebengesetze*. München: Vahlen.

Selassie, Alemante G. 2003. Ethnic federalism: Its promise and pitfalls for Africa. *Yale Journal of International Law* 28(1): 51–108.

Selleck, Richard. 1985. Mary Carpenter: A confident and contradictory reformer. *History of Education* 14(2): 101–115.

Setton, Kenneth M., Robert Lee Wolff, and Harry W. Hazard (eds.). 2005. *A history of the crusades: The later crusades, 1189–1311*. Madison: The University of Wisconsin Press.

Shahar, Shulamith. 1990. *Childhood in the middle ages*. London: Routledge.

Shakespeare, William. (1599) 1952. *As you like it*. London: J. M. Dent.

Sharma, Jagdish Prasad. 1968. *Republics in ancient India, C. 1500 BC–500 BC*. Leiden: Brill.

Shier, Harry. 2001. Pathways to participation: Openings, opportunities and obligations. *Children and Society* 15: 107–117.

Shinwell, Emanuel. 1963. *The labour story*. London: Macdonald.

Shore, Heather. 1999. *Artful dodgers: Youth and crime in early nineteenth century London*. London: Boydell Press.

Simmel, Georg. 1949. The sociology of sociability. *The American Journal of Sociology* 55(3): 254–261.

Simmel, Georg. 1966. *Über sociale Differenzierung: Sociologische und psychologische Untersuchungen*. Amsterdam: Liberac N.V. Publishers.

Simmonds, Norman. 1985. *Farming systems research: A review*, World Bank technical paper 43. Washington, DC: The World Bank.

Skehill, Caroline. 2004. *History of the present of child protection and social work in Ireland*. Lewinstone: The Mellen Press.

Slack, Paul. 1990. *The English poor law, 1531–1782*. Cambridge: Cambridge University Press.

Smith, Adam. 1973. *The wealth of nations*. Harmondsworth: Pelican Classics.

Smith, Anne-Marie. 2007. The children of Loxicha, Mexico: Exploring ideas of childhood and the rules of participation. *Children, Youth and Environments* 17(2): 33–55.

Smith, Noel, Ruth Lister, Sue Middleton, and Lynne Cox. 2005. Young people as real citizens: Towards an inclusionary understanding of citizenship. *Journal of Youth Studies* 8(4): 425–443.

Smout, Thomas C. 1972. *History of the Scottish people, 1560–1830*. London: Fontana.

Sofaer Derevenski, Joanna (ed.). 2000. *Children and material culture*. London: Routledge.

Sommerville, Charles J. 1982. *The rise and fall of childhood*. Beverley Hills: Sage Publications.

Southern, Richard. 1990. *Western society and the church in the middle ages*, The Penguin history of the church volume 2. Harmondsworth: Penguin.

Southern, Richard. 1993. *The making of the middle ages*. London: Pimlico.
Spence, Thomas. 1793. *The real rights of man* (later republished under the title *The Nationalization of the Land* in 1882), facsimile pamphlet.
Spengler, Joseph. 1966a. Values and fertility analysis. *Demography* 3(1): 109–130.
Spengler, Joseph. 1966b. The economist and the population question. *American Economic Review* 56(1 and 2): 1–24.
Squires, Peter (ed.). 2008. *ASBO nation: The criminalisation of nuisance*. Bristol: The Policy Press.
Stafford, Charles. 1995. *The roads of Chinese childhood: Learning and identification in Angang*. Cambridge: Cambridge University Press.
Stanford, Charles S. 1834. *Plato's apology of Socrates, Crito and Phaedo* (from the text by Bekker, with the Latin version of Ficinus and notes by Charles Stuart Stanford). Dublin: University Press for William Curry Junior and Company.
Steiner, Rudolf. 2006. *Education of the child*. London: Rudolf Steiner Press. (Originally published in 1911.)
Still, Sir George Frederic. 1931. *A history of paediatrics. The progress of the study of diseases of children up to the end of the XVIIIth century*. London: Oxford University Press.
Stokes, Michael. 2005. *Dialectic in action: An examination of Plato's Crito*. Swansea: The Classical Press of Wales.
Such, Elizabeth, and Robert Walker. 2005. Young citizens or policy objects? Children in the 'Rights and Responsibilities' debate. *Journal of Social Policy* 34(1): 38–57.
Summerskill, Ben. 2000. Princess the palace hides away. *The Observer*, July 23.
Tames, Richard. 2002. *Ancient Greek children* (People in the Past Series-Greece). London: Heinemann.
Taylor, Harry. 2002. Insights into participation from critical management and labour process perspectives. In *Participation: The new tyranny?* ed. Bill Cooke and Uma Kothari. London: Zed Books.
The Citizenship Foundation. 1998. *Citizenship for all: A wide ability teacher's resource guide*. Cheltenham: Stanley Thornes Ltd.
Thomas, Nigel. 2007. Towards a theory of children's participation. *The International Journal of Children's Rights* 15: 199–218.
Thoreau, Henry D. 2007. *Walden; or, life in the woods*. Edison: Castle Books. (First published 1854.)
Timimi, Sami. 2002. *Pathological child psychiatry and the medicalization of childhood*. New York: Brunner/Routledge.
Timimi, Sami. 2006. *Critical voices in child and adolescent mental health*. New York: Free Association Books.
Tisdall, Kay. 2008. Is the honeymoon over? Children and young people's participation in public decision-making. *The International Journal of Children's Rights* 16(3): 419–429.
Tisdall, Kay, John Davis, Malcolm Hill, and Alan Prout (eds.). 2006. *Children, young people and social inclusion: Participation for what?* Bristol: The Policy Press.
Tönnies, Ferdinand. 1896. *Hobbes Leben und Lehre*. Stuttgart: Frommann.
Tönnies, Ferdinand. 2005. *Gemeinschaft und Gesellschaft*. Darmstadt: Wissenschaftliche Buchgesellschaft.
Treadgold, Warren. 1997. *A history of the Byzantine state and society*. Stanford: Stanford University Press.
Turner, Victor. 1969. *The ritual process: Structure and anti-structure*. Chicago: Aldine Publishing Co.
Turner, Susan, and Gareth B. Matthews (eds.). 1998. *The philosopher's child*. Rochester: University of Rochester Press.
Twain, Mark. 1994a. *The adventures of Tom Sawyer*. Harmondsworth: Penguin Popular Classics.
Twain, Mark. 1994b. *The adventures of Huckleberry Finn*. Harmondsworth: Penguin Popular Classics.
UNICEF. 1997. *Progress of nations*. New York: The United Nations Children's Fund.

UNICEF. 2000. *The state of the world's children 2001*. New York: The United Nations Children's Fund.

UNICEF. 2001. *The state of the world's children 2002*. New York: The United Nations Children's Fund.

UNICEF. 2002. *The state of the world's children 2003*. New York: The United Nations Children's Fund.

UNICEF. 2003. *The state of the world's children 2004*. New York: The United Nations Children's Fund.

UNICEF. 2004. *The state of the world's children 2005*. New York: The United Nations Children's Fund.

UNICEF. 2005. *The state of the world's children 2006*. New York: The United Nations Children's Fund.

UNICEF. 2006a. *The state of the world's children 2007*. New York: The United Nations Children's Fund.

UNICEF. 2006b. *A world fit for children*. New York: The United Nations Children's Fund. (Reprint.)

UNICEF. 2007a. *The state of the world's children 2008*. New York: The United Nations Children's Fund.

UNICEF. 2007b. *Child poverty in perspective: An overview of child well-being in rich countries*. New York: The United Nations Children's Fund.

UNICEF. 2008. *The state of the world's children 2009*. New York: The United Nations Children's Fund.

United Nations. 2006. United Nations General Assembly, 61st Session, *Report of the independent expert for the United Nations study on violence against children*, A/61/299, 29 August 2006.

United Nations Committee on the Rights of the Child. 2001. *Concluding observations of the committee on the rights of the child: Egypt. 21/02/2001*, CRC/C/15/Add.145 (Concluding Observations/Comments). Geneva: UNHCHR.

United Nations General Assembly. 2002. *A world fit for children*. New York: United Nations General Assembly.

United States Office of Personnel Management Investigations Service. 2001. *Citizenship laws of the world*. Washington, DC: Office of Personnel Management.

Unknown. 1918. *Jack Cornwell: The story of John Travers Cornwell, VC*. Toronto: Hodder and Stoughton. (Sourced on the University of Toronto website.)

Unknown. 1971. *The living Bible*. London: Coverdale House Publishers.

Upadhyay, Junita (Compiler). 2006. *Child and youth participation resource guide*. Bangkok: UNICEF.

van Beers, Henk, Vo Phi Chau, Judith Ennew, Pham Quoc Khan, Tran Thap Long, Brian Milne, Trieu Thi Anh Nguyet, and Vu Thi Son. 2006. *Creating an enabling environment: Capacity building in children's participation, Viet Nam, 2000–2004*. Bangkok: Save the Children Sweden.

van Beers, Henk, Antonella Invernizzi, and Brian Milne. 2007. *Beyond article 12: Essential readings in children's participation*. Bangkok: Black on White.

Van der Veer, Réne, and Jan Valsiner (eds.). 1994. *The Vygotsky reader*. Oxford: Blackwell.

van Gennep, Arnold. 1960. *The rites of passage*. Trans. Monika B. Vizedom and Gabrielle L. Caffee. Chicago: University of Chicago Press. (Originally published 1909.)

Vygotsky, Lev. 1978. In *Mind in society: The development of higher psychological processes*, ed. Michael Cole. Cambridge, MA/London: Harvard University Press.

Vygotsky, Lev. 1987. *The collected works of L. S. Vygotsky*. New York/London: Kluwer Academic/Plenum Publishers.

Walker, Lawrence J. 1989. A longitudinal study of moral reasoning. *Child Development* 60(1): 157–166.

Walker-Smith, J.A. 1997. Children in hospital. In *Western medicine: An illustrated history*, ed. Irvine Loudon, 221–231. Oxford: Oxford University Press.

Wall, John. 2008. Human rights in light of childhood. *The International Journal of Children's Rights* 16(4): 523–543.

Walzer, Michael. 1989. *The company of critics: Social criticism and political commitment in the twentieth century*. London: Halban.

Warner, Marina. 1983. *Joan of Arc: The image of female heroism*. Harmondsworth: Penguin.

Weatherford, Jack. 2004. *Genghis Khan and the making of the modern world*. New York: Three Rivers Press.

Weber, Max. 1951. *The religion of China: Confucianism and Taoism*. New York: Free Press.

Weber, Max. 1958. *The city*. New York: Free Press.

Weber, Max. 1992. *Economy and society*. Berkeley: University of California Press.

Weinfeld, Morton. 1981. The development of affirmative action in Canada. *Canadian Ethnic Studies* 13(2): 23–39.

Wertsch, James V. 1985. *Vygotsky and the social formation of mind*. Cambridge, MA/London: Harvard University Press.

Whyte, William F. 1943. *Street corner society: The social structure of an Italian slum*. Chicago: University of Chicago Press.

Wiedemann, Thomas. 1989. *Adults and children in the Roman empire*. London: Routledge.

Williams, Ian. 2007. *The alms trade: Charities, past, present and future*. New York: Cosimo Books.

Willmott, Peter. 1969. *Adolescent boys of East London*. Harmondsworth: Penguin.

Willmott, Peter, and Michael Young. 1968. *Family and class in a London suburb*. London: Routledge & Kegan Paul.

Winstanley, Gerrard. 1649a. *A declaration from the poor oppressed people of England*, facsimile pamphlet.

Winstanley, Gerrard. 1649b. *The true levellers standard ADVANCED: Or, the state of community opened, and presented to the sons of men*, facsimile pamphlet.

Winstanley, Gerrard. 1652. *The law of freedom in a platform*, facsimile pamphlet.

Wolfenstein, Martha. 1954. *Children's humor: A psychological analysis*. Glencoe: Free Press.

Wolfenstein, Martha. 1955. French parents take their children to the park. In *Childhood in contemporary cultures*, ed. Margaret Mead and Martha Wolfenstein. Chicago: University of Chicago Press.

Wollstonecraft, Mary. 2004. *A vindication of the rights of women*. London: Penguin Books.

Woodhead, Martin. 2007. Harmed by work or developing through work? Issues in the study of psychosocial impacts. In *Working to be someone: Child focussed research and practice with working children*, ed. Beatrice Hungerland, Manfred Liebel, Brian Milne, and Anne Wihstutz. London: Jessica Kingsley.

Wordsworth, William. 1807 (1981). *Poems, in two volumes*. New Haven: Yale University Press.

Wringe, C.A. 1981. *Children's rights: A philosophical study*. London: Routledge & Kegan Paul.

Yao, Xinzhong. 2000. *An introduction to Confucianism*. Cambridge: Cambridge University Press.

Young, Agnes F., and Elwyn T. Ashton. 1956. *British social work in the nineteenth century*. London: Routledge & Kegan Paul.

Young, Michael, and Peter Willmott. 1957. *Family and kinship in East London*. London: Routledge & Kegan Paul.

Zacour, Norman. 2005. The children's crusade. In *A history of the crusades: The later crusades, 1189–1311*, ed. Kenneth M. Setton, Robert Lee Wolff, and Harry W. Hazard, 325–342. Madison: The University of Wisconsin Press.

Zelizer, Viviana. 1985. *Pricing the priceless child: The changing social value of children*. New York: Basic Books.

Zuckerman, Michael. 1993. History and developmental psychology, a dangerous liaison: A historian's perspective. In *Children in time and place: Developmental and historical insights*, ed. Glen H. Elder, John Modell, and Ross D. Parke, 230–240. Cambridge: Cambridge University Press.

Index

B. Milne, *The History and Theory of Children's Citizenship in Contemporary Societies*,
DOI 10.1007/978-94-007-6521-4, © Springer Science+Business Media Dordrecht 2013

MIX
Papier aus verantwortungsvollen Quellen
Paper from responsible sources
FSC® C105338

If you have any concerns about our products,
you can contact us on
ProductSafety@springernature.com

In case Publisher is established outside the EU,
the EU authorized representative is:
Springer Nature Customer Service Center GmbH
Europaplatz 3, 69115 Heidelberg, Germany

Printed by Libri Plureos GmbH
in Hamburg, Germany